PENGUIN

THE LETTERS OF JOHN AND ABIGAIL ADAMS

JOHN ADAMS, lawyer, writer, diplomat, was born in 1735 in Braintree, Massachusetts. He was a delegate from Massachusetts to the First and Second Continental Congresses, where he played a key role in creating a constituency for American independence from Great Britain. He served on the committee that drafted the Declaration of Independence and other important Congressional committees, including the Board of War and Ordnance, where his labors were crucial for supporting the military struggle. Between 1778 and the signing of a peace treaty with Great Britain in 1783, he was a diplomat in Europe, where his greatest success was in gaining from the Netherlands both recognition of the new United States and much-needed loans. Subsequently he served as George Washington's vice-president and as the second president of the United States. He died on July 4th, 1826.

ABIGAIL SMITH ADAMS was born in 1744 in Weymouth, Massachusetts. She was educated at home but read widely and deeply both as a young woman and throughout her life. During her husband's nearly eleven-year absence from home, she cared for an extended family, managed the family farms, and carried on an extensive correspondence with her husband and her friends. She was also an important supporter and advisor to her husband during his years in the national government. She died in 1818.

FRANK SHUFFELTON is a professor of English and American literature at the University of Rochester. His other publications include *Thomas Hooker, 1586–1647* (1977); *Thomas Jefferson: A Comprehensive Annotated Bibliography of Writings About Him, 1826–1980* (1983); *Thomas Jefferson, 1981–1990: An Annotated Bibliography* (1992); ed., *A Mixed Race: Ethnicity in Early America* (1993); ed., *The American Enlightenment* (1993); and the Penguin Classics edition of *Thomas Jefferson's Notes On the State of Virginia* (1998).

The Letters of
John and Abigail Adams

Edited with an Introduction and Notes by
FRANK SHUFFELTON

PENGUIN BOOKS

PENGUIN BOOKS
Published by the Penguin Group
Penguin Group (USA) Inc., 375 Hudson Street, New York, New York 10014, U.S.A.
Penguin Group (Canada), 90 Eglinton Avenue East, Suite 700, Toronto,
Ontario, Canada M4P 2Y3 (a division of Pearson Penguin Canada Inc.)
Penguin Books Ltd, 80 Strand, London WC2R 0RL, England
Penguin Ireland, 25 St Stephen's Green, Dublin 2, Ireland (a division of Penguin Books Ltd)
Penguin Group (Australia), 250 Camberwell Road, Camberwell, Victoria 3124,
Australia (a division of Pearson Australia Group Pty Ltd)
Penguin Books India Pvt Ltd, 11 Community Centre, Panchsheel Park, New Delhi – 110 017, India
Penguin Group (NZ), 67 Apollo Drive, Rosedale, North Shore 0632, New Zealand
(a division of Pearson New Zealand Ltd)
Penguin Books (South Africa) (Pty) Ltd, 24 Sturdee Avenue, Rosebank,
Johannesburg 2196, South Africa

Penguin Books Ltd, Registered Offices: 80 Strand, London WC2R 0RL, England

This edition first published in Penguin Books 2004

10

Introduction and notes copyright © Frank Shuffelton, 2004
All rights reserved

Grateful acknowledgment is made for permission to reprint selections from the following copyrighted works:
The Adams Papers: Adams Family Correspondence, Volumes I-IV, Cambridge, Mass.: The Belknap Press of
Harvard University Press. Volume I: December 1761–May 1776, edited by L. H. Butterfield. Copyright ©
1963 by the Massachusetts Historical Society. Volume II: June 1776–March 1778, edited by L. H. Butterfield.
Copyright © 1963 by the Massachusetts Historical Society. Volume III: April 1778–September 1780, edited by
L. H. Butterfield and Marc Friedlaender. Copyright © 1973 by the Massachusetts Historical Society. Volume
IV: October 1780–September 1782, edited by L. H. Butterfield and Marc Friedlaender. Copyright © 1973 by
the Massachusetts Historical Society. Reprinted by permission of the publisher.

LIBRARY OF CONGRESS CATALOGING-IN-PUBLICATION DATA
Adams, John, 1735–1826.
[Familiar letters of John Adams and his wife Abigail Adams, during the Revolution]
The letters of John and Abigail Adams / edited with an introduction by Frank Shuffelton.
p. cm.
Originally published: Familiar letters of John and Abigail Adams, during the Revolution.
New York : Hurd and Houghton, 1876.
Includes bibliographical references (p.   ).
ISBN 978-0-14-243711-7
1. Adams, John, 1735–1826—Correspondence.   2. Adams, Abigail, 1744–1818—Correspondence.
3. Presidents—United States—Correspondence.   4. Presidents' spouses—United States—Correspondence.
5. United States—History—Revolution, 1775–1783—Sources.   I. Adams, Abigail, 1744–1818.   II. Title.
E322.A4 2003
973.4'4'0922—dc21   2003051174
[B]

Printed in the United States of America
Set in Adobe Sabon

Contents

Introduction

I

Among the celebrations in 1876 of the centennial of American independence, Charles Francis Adams offered under the title of *Familiar Letters of John Adams and His Wife Abigail Adams, During the Revolution* this collection of letters exchanged between his grandparents from 1774 to 1783. Charles Francis Adams had behind him a distinguished career as a politician and diplomat, but he had also become in effect the self-designated historian of the Adams family. In 1840 he had published a collection of Abigail Adams's letters that was sufficiently popular to get a fourth edition before the decade was out. He then edited and published between 1851 and 1856 a ten-volume collection of the writings of John Adams that continues to be an authoritative source for material not yet reedited in the ongoing Adams Papers project. When in 1876 he brought together in a single volume letters written by both Abigail and John, he claimed they would supplement "the materials for a history of action [with] those for one of feeling."

As Charles Francis Adams saw it, the American Revolution had typically been portrayed in terms of the great men like Patrick Henry, James Otis, George Washington, Thomas Jefferson, and Samuel Adams who were thought to have made it. But such accounts overlooked the "moral principle in the field, to the power of which a great majority of the whole population of the colonies, whether male or female, old or young, had been long and habitually trained to do homage."[1] The failure of American historians in the one hundred years since independence to recognize the "moral principle" behind the Revolution was connected, in Adams's view, to the failure to recognize the contributions of the Adams family to the continuing project of American liberty. The centennial year of independence offered an apt occasion for once again trying to set the record straight by recentering the historiography of the Revolution on character, both private and public.

Charles Francis was carrying on a campaign for recognition that his grandfather had begun in the years after he returned home to Braintree, Massachusetts, in 1801, defeated in his candidacy for a second term as president. John Adams began writing an autobiography in 1802, although he gave up work on it in 1807 and never published it, and in 1809 he began a series of combative newspaper essays in the *Boston Patriot* that were intended to defend his actions in public office. John Adams was always sensitive to criticism, perhaps because he thought that only his sense of his own honor could uphold him in a world where advantages of birth and wealth seemed to count most.

Difficult to bear were the partisan attacks during his presidency, but he was particularly embittered by Alexander Hamilton's 1800 *Letter . . . concerning the Public Character and Conduct of John Adams, Esq.* that claimed to show "great and intrinsic defects in his character, which unfit him for the Office of Chief Magistrate."[2] Adams's ire was further raised in 1805 when his old friend Mercy Otis Warren published her three-volume history of the American Revolution. Warren was a Jeffersonian in politics, and her critical portrayal of Adams led him into a heated, angry series of letters upbraiding her and her history. Attacked from one side for not being sufficiently Federalist and from the other for being a supposed defender of monarchy, Adams's sense of being misunderstood led him into continued defenses of his character and actions, but it also caused him to take particular care in organizing and preserving his papers.

John Quincy Adams used these resources when he began to write a biography of his father, but he was diverted from this project by his own concerns in the United States Congress. After failing, like his father, to be reelected to a second term as president, John Quincy returned to Washington as a representative from Massachusetts. Speaking out against slavery and the efforts of both Southern and Northern representatives in Congress to prevent any discussion of the issue placed him in a position similar to the one his father had sometimes claimed for himself, the lonely upholder of virtue and right. It remained for John Quincy's son, Charles Francis Adams, to establish the grounds for regarding his grandparents as being at the moral center of the American Revolution if not its ideological center.[3] Charles Francis Adams claimed in the introduction to his 1876 edition of *Familiar Letters* that the moral principle of liberty energizing patriots in the field and in "the senate" was grounded in "the sentiment that pervaded the dwellings of the entire population." The tendency to see the history of the American Revolution in terms of mythicized heroes underestimated the extent to which they articulated the sentiments of ordinary people, and at the same time it privileged the workings of the head over the "workings of the heart," which motivated revolutionary action and national unity.

In the letters of Abigail and John Adams, their grandson sought to find the secret spirit behind the Revolution, the real motivating force that energized a people to desire a new national order. By linking the correspondence of John, who was at the center of the debates in the Continental Congress leading up to declaring independence, and Abigail, who was at home managing the family farm in Braintree while caring for four young children, Charles Francis found a ready-made link between the "home sentiment" of many American households and the larger scenes of debate and discourse in the public sphere. John, the revolutionary leader and eventual president, could reveal himself as a caring husband and father at heart, and Abigail, an archetypal republican mother, could demonstrate her mastery of business affairs, political observation, and cultural breadth. The private person in the home could correspond to the public person in "the senate," and their complementary qualities and voices could reaffirm a supposed American consensus between private citizens and their elected leaders.

This was an appropriately celebratory, patriotic gesture for someone writing in 1876, and it was perhaps an even more necessary one at the moment when Reconstruction was ending amid efforts to paper over the recent episode of violent dissent, the Civil War. Furthermore, by recognizing that the genuine "home sentiment" of the Revolution so much depended "upon the female portion of the people" and by giving Abigail Adams an equal voice with that of her more famous husband, Charles Francis Adams made available his grandmother's progressive attitudes about women's rights to a generation struggling with this issue.[4] The Adams family's understanding of the American Revolution was not merely an exercise in genealogical vanity but a serious contribution to the ongoing discussion of the Revolution's meaning that is still relevant for us today.

A number of paradoxes, however, complicate Charles Francis Adams's attempt to represent his grandparents as American Everypersons, beginning perhaps with the sense that it is difficult to think of Abigail and John Adams as merely ordinary people. They played unusual roles in the public life of the nation, and even as a so-called founding father John Adams stood out as a person who was as likely to differ with his friends and political allies as with his opponents. Only persons with the rich personalities and considerable abilities such as both John and Abigail possessed could, after all, perform the complex signification Charles Francis Adams required of them. But that was also just the point. The Adams family story of John and Abigail's distinguished contributions to the nation was in Charles Francis's hands also a story about the triumph of democracy in America, as talent and virtue lifted his grandparents, particularly his grandfather, above relatively humble beginnings.

II

John Adams's origins were respectable enough but not above the middling sort in the Massachusetts of 1735, when he was born. However, his father, another John Adams, a shoemaker and farmer in Braintree, and his mother, Susanna Boylston Adams, had ambitions for themselves and for their eldest son. The elder John Adams served fourteen terms as a deacon in his church and was elected as a Braintree selectman nine times, in addition to serving at various times as a militia officer, tax collector, and tithingman. Susanna Adams, a strong-minded person, managed the household with an eye toward enhancing the family's reputation and standing in their community.

John and Susanna Adams were determined to give the young John a good education, even though he at first was a reluctant student and insisted he wanted only to be a farmer. His father refused to entertain that possibility—he was determined that young John would become a minister—and under the guidance of Joseph Marsh, his second schoolmaster, young John discovered a taste for books and learning. In eighteen months he was ready to be tested for admission to Harvard, where he was admitted in the middle rank of the class of 1755. (The standing of a pupil's family determined class rank at the time of admission; thus Adams's position in his class reflected his father's middling position in the community.) In college Adams pursued his love for books and study but also discovered the pleasures of social life, leading to a realization that he had no desire for the ministry. After graduation, he taught school in Worcester, Massachusetts, while he considered his career options, and in 1756 he began to read for the law under the direction of James Putnam, Worcester's leading attorney. Although Adams had begun to find a place in Worcester society, such as it was, it was too much of a backwater to be the scene of fame that he thirsted for, and he returned to Braintree to begin his law practice there and in Boston.

Adams was admitted to the Boston bar in 1758, sponsored by Jeremiah Gridley, the most respected of Boston's lawyers, and by James Otis. Gridley became Adams's mentor, offering the use of his legal library and welcoming him into his "Sodalitas club" of young lawyers, but it was Otis who soon became a hero to the young Adams. His fiery address to the Massachusetts Superior Court in 1761 in protest of British customs officers' use of writs of assistance as nearly unlimited search warrants was the first of the protests against an expansive imperial power that would lead to the Revolution of 1775.

Adams's immediate concerns upon his return to Braintree and Boston were not political but directed toward establishing a law practice that could support him and bring him the "distinction" he craved. Matters went slowly, and Adams felt, as he also frequently did in later life, that he was on his own against an uncaring world. "But it is my Destiny to dig Treasures with my own fingers. No Body will rent or sell me a Pick axe."[5] When he lost his first case because he had prepared a defective writ, he was chagrined, blamed his problems on an inadequate preparation for the law by his teacher Putnam, and set himself to a rigorous course of study to overcome his deficiencies.

Adams did find time during the early years of his law practice to fall in love twice, first and briefly with an unknown young woman, the second time with Hannah Quincy, the daughter of Colonel Josiah Quincy, Braintree's leading citizen. He wrote a friend that he was "over head and ears" in love with her, but when she responded coquettishly to his hints about marriage, he hesitated, and she accepted another's proposal instead.[6] Adams may have remembered Jeremiah Gridley's advice to him, offered at the time of their first meeting, not to marry early. "For an early Marriage will obstruct your Improvement, and in the next Place, twill involve you in Expence," said Gridley.[7] Depressed at the failure of his romantic fantasies, Adams committed himself as passionately to his public life as he had, however briefly, to the prospects of love and marriage. "Let Love and Vanity be extinguished," he vowed, "and the Great Passions of Ambition, Patriotism, break out and burn."[8]

He continued to study, developed his law practice, and began to throw his energies into working for the public good of Braintree. When he began to court Abigail Smith, the daughter of the Reverend William Smith of Weymouth, he was ready to assume the role of husband, and the passion that marked his earlier romantic forays was repeated with Abigail. He wrote to her that Weymouth had become as dear to him as Braintree and that she had appeared to him in his dreams "with her fair Complexion, her Crimson Blushes and her million Charms and Graces." More important, perhaps, he told her, "I begin to find that an increasing Affection for a certain Lady, (you know my Dear) quickens my Affections for every Body Else, that does not deserve my hatred. A Wonder if the Fires of Patriotism, do not soon begin to burn!"[9] Abigail returned his affections; they were married in the fall of 1764, and almost as predicted the fires of patriotism leapt up in earnest with the Stamp Act crisis of 1765, which began to draw him more actively into politics.

Adams had begun to contribute political essays to the press even before his marriage; in 1763 he satirized Massachusetts politicians' scrambles for office and power in a series of essays purportedly by a rustic named Humphrey Ploughjogger, and he wrote more serious essays, also published anonymously under the signature "U." In 1765 he wrote a more extensive essay, "A Dissertation on the Canon and Feudal Law," in which he described the complicity of "the Romish clergy" and power-hungry nobles and monarchs in keeping the common people "in a state of servile dependence." However, said Adams, "it was a love of universal liberty and a hatred, a dread, a horror, of the infernal confederacy before described, that projected, conducted, and accomplished the settlement of America."

He had begun writing this essay as a member of Jeremiah Gridley's "Sodalitas," but the inspiration was clearly the growing concern for assertions of British power that had been assailed by James Otis and others. The first of four installments of the "Dissertation" appeared just before Boston mobs took to the street in protest of the Stamp Act, and Adams wrote into the final lines of his text a condemnation of the act as the first step "toward the subversion of the whole system of our fathers."[10] The "Dissertation" attracted notice, being reprinted by Thomas Hollis in the *London Chronicle,* and marked Adams as an intellectual leader in the growing American resistance to imperial authority.

For all of Adams's patriotic fervor, he was committed to the rule of law. He and his cousin Samuel Adams agreed on the necessity to stand up for American liberty, but while Sam Adams was organizing political protests in the streets, John was concerned with establishing the legal underpinnings of resistance based upon the English constitution and the colonists' "Rights derived from the great Legislator of the universe." When he drew up instructions from the town of Braintree to its representatives in the legislature, he argued that the Stamp Act was "directly repugnant to the Great Charter itself."[11] His respect for the law, however, led him to abhor the mob violence and disturbances that broke out in response to the Stamp Act and the subsequent quartering of British troops in Boston. In the years immediately after the temporary resolution of the Stamp Act crisis, Adams attended to his law practice, which had become quite successful, and resisted appeals to take a more active role in continuing protests organized by more radical Whig leaders like James Otis and Samuel Adams. His law practice required him to follow the judicial circuit from Taunton and Worcester south and west of Boston to Falmouth (now Portland) in Maine. Many of the lawyers and judges he worked with on the circuit supported Governor Thomas Hutchinson against the popular party, and many of them would become loyalists when the Revolution broke out. Adams privately made clear his support for the Sons of Liberty, the radical patriots in Boston, in spite of occasionally deploring their methods, but he kept a low profile politically. His sentiments at this time are best reflected in a diary entry he made for Christmas day 1765.

> At Home. Thinking, reading, searching, concerning Taxation without Consent, concerning the great Pause and Rest in Business. By the Laws of England Justice Flows, with an uninterrupted Stream: In that Musick, the Law knows of neither Rests nor Pauses. Nothing but Violence, Invasion or Rebellion can obstruct the River or untune the Instrument.[12]

Adams's deepest instincts were to preserve the instrument of the law as a measure of justice and order, but he would soon enough reimagine the laws of England as the laws of Massachusetts and America.

On March 5, 1770, violence threatened to untune the instrument for sure when a squad of British soldiers under the command of Captain Thomas Preston fired on a threatening Boston mob, killing five people—the Boston Massacre. When Preston and the soldiers were charged with murder, it seemed as if they would be unable to secure legal representation, but Adams agreed to lead the defense. This clearly reflected his basic belief in the rule of law and the right of everyone to a fair trial, but it also seems likely that he was encouraged in this regard by Samuel Adams and other patriot leaders who wanted to avoid the appearance of mob law. Adams secured the acquittal of Preston and six of the eight soldiers charged with murder; the other two were found guilty of the lesser charge of manslaughter. Adams's judicial victory marked him as a man of principle and confirmed his position as a leading member of the Boston bar, but it did not hurt his standing with the patriot party. After the Boston Massacre, Adams became increasingly involved in politics and in the cause of liberty. He was elected in 1770 as a Boston representative to the legislature, and his disapproval of mob protests was tempered by increasingly harsh British measures. When the Boston Tea Party occurred in 1773, he went so far as to call it the "grandest Event" yet in the protests against arbitrary imperial power.[13]

In 1774 he was chosen, along with Samuel Adams, James Bowdoin, and Robert Treat Paine, to the Massachusetts delegation to the First Continental Congress, but before leaving for Philadelphia, he made one final trip to the circuit court held in Maine (still a part of Massachusetts). Charles Francis Adams begins his selection of letters between John and Abigail at this point, when his grandfather was acutely aware of the political sympathies of the other lawyers and the judges on the circuit. Because many of them were either loyalists or lukewarm at best to the patriot cause, Adams shows in his letters to Abigail a canny political sense of how to deal with men of differing opinions. When he arrived in Philadelphia at the end of the summer, he and Samuel Adams were the radical members of the Massachusetts delegation, but he muted his opinions about the necessity of American independence in order to bring along more reluctant delegates from other colonies to a similar position. During the two-month session of Congress, however, delegates sharing Adams's sentiments managed to call for a boycott of British goods, the creation of a Continental Association to enforce the boycott, and the drafting of a declaration of rights and grievances to present to the king. Adams enhanced his reputation as a patriot leader by working effectively behind the scenes in Congress, but when he returned home late in 1774, he began publishing a series of twelve letters in the *Boston Gazette* in defense of the independence of colonial legislatures from the rule of the English Parliament. He called for a republican "government of laws and not of men." These letters, published under the pseudonym Novanglus, responded to an able defense of the Tory point of view that was appearing in the Boston press from a writer calling himself Massachuttensis, who was in reality Daniel Leonard, an old legal acquaintance of Adams's.

The paper war between Novanglus and Massachuttensis ended after April 19, 1775, with the beginning of hostilities at Lexington and Concord, by which time Adams was preparing to return to Philadelphia and the Second Continental Congress. In the coming years he would spend increasingly longer stretches of time away from Braintree and his family, and he would at the same time play an increasingly important role in the creation of the new nation. He was a major force in Congress for the cause of independence during the spring of 1776, ultimately serving on the committee to draft the Declaration of Independence. His political skills and the effect of his speeches on the floor led Richard Stockton of New Jersey to call him "the Atlas of American Independence," and he subsequently played a key role in charting the development of governments on both the state and national levels.[14] George Wythe of Virginia, after a discussion about forms of government, asked him to write out his ideas, and when Adams showed the letter of reply to Richard Henry Lee, the Virginians urged its publication.

Adams's *Thoughts on Government* was published anonymously in April 1776, much to the pleasure of Adams and also of Abigail, as she notes in her letter to him dated May 9, 1776 (letter 103). Adams's brief essay made clear what he meant by a government of laws and not of men by calling for a representative democratic government with power so distributed through the legislative and executive branches that they served to check and balance each other. It also made clear that he had become a presence in national politics, and in the months following the declaration of independence, he performed heroic service as chair of the Board of War, becoming in effect the nation's first secretary of defense.

Adams's involvement in public life at the national level led to further appointments that took him farther from Braintree than he had ever imagined possible. In 1778 he was sent by Congress to join Benjamin Franklin as an envoy to France, and with only a few intervals at home, he spent most of the next eleven years abroad on diplomatic service. These were years of trial for Adams—he had at the outset to deal with difficult colleagues in France in the persons of Silas Deane, Arthur Lee, and Benjamin Franklin, whose quarrels inevitably involved him; he had to deal with the culture shock of new manners and new languages, and he often had to deal with his own ill health—but the years brought victories as well. He negotiated a treaty with the Dutch, established credit for the new nation with Dutch bankers, and participated in the final negotiations for the peace treaty with Britain signed in Paris in 1783. Temporary separations from wife and family had been a regular part of his work as a lawyer attending the circuit courts, but those separations had been for relatively brief periods and not overshadowed by the threats of war as were the later separations. Beginning in August 1774, Adams made five trips to attend Congress. His shortest stay was in his term in the First Continental Congress, slightly more than two months, but in 1776 and 1777 he was away for ten months at a time, and when he returned briefly in 1779 from his diplomatic errand in Paris, he spent much of his time attending the Massachusetts state constitutional convention. Once again, his public service was significant—his draft of a constitution was the basis for the document approved in 1780 after he had returned to Europe, and it became a model for later American constitution makers— but it came at a cost to his domestic happiness. When the Treaty of Paris concluded hostilities with Britain, Abigail and John were determined to be separated no longer, and in June 1784, she and their only daughter sailed to Europe to join him. Except for relatively brief times during his presidency, the two Adamses would never be separated for such lengthy periods again. The letters in this collection, then, span what is arguably the most important period of John Adams's public service, but they also let us see the strength of John and Abigail's relationship during its most stressful years.

III

Although Charles Francis Adams gave his grandfather top billing in the title of his 1876 collection, *Familiar Letters of John Adams and His Wife Abigail Adams, During the Revolution,* his grandmother's letters occupy the moral center of his volume. John Adams was clearly of greater political and historical importance, but the moral principle behind the Revolution, "the sentiment that pervaded the dwellings of the entire people," appeared most sharply in Abigail's letters. Her letters reveal, directly and indirectly, the difficulties faced by men and women in ordinary walks of life as they tried to maintain farms, businesses, and families amid the anxieties of wartime. Abigail's letters also show the formation of a revolutionary spirit as she comments on issues of the day, national and local, bringing to bear her own vigorous moral sense. Charles Francis Adams surely recognized the appeal of his grandmother's epistolary voice when his 1840 edition of her letters was a minor best-seller. He had defined that volume as a "history of feeling" that importantly contributed to the many histories of action that already had appeared. If readers in the centenary year of 1876 needed to be reminded of the spirit of the revolutionary generation, Abigail Adams's letters had proven their ability to speak to modern audiences.

But Charles Francis did not see his grandmother as a proto-feminist as some later writers have been inclined to do. In spite of his sympathy for feminine points of view such as his grandmother's, Charles Francis Adams's view of the role of women in society was considerably more traditional than his youthful political radicalism on behalf of abolition had been. Women were most effective, he thought, in passing on the lessons of religion and virtue in their home life and as teachers of children because their teaching was less a matter of reason and logic than of feelings and "high and pure motives" uncontaminated by private interest, ambition, or the love of fame. A woman's lot in times of trouble, he claimed, was to be "a passive spectator of events."[15] The Abigail Adams who emerges out of her letters, however, is articulate and reasoned about her opinions, a shrewd manager of the family's economic interests, and an effective supporter of her husband's political career. No shrinking violet of the hearthside, she is someone who deservedly has become an icon for American feminists and champions of women's rights.

Her request to her husband, in her letter of March 31, 1776 (letter 91), that he "remember the ladies" as he and his colleagues worked for American independence and freedom has become a watchword. Her quiet radicalism might seem to complicate Charles Francis's effort to portray his grandmother as an American Everywoman, but in fact Abigail Adams understood her role as wife and mother in terms not so different from those of her grandson. She understood the meaning of her own life in terms of traditional roles in which a wife was her husband's partner and support but never quite his equal. Her position in the world, as she saw it, reflected primarily the accomplishments of her husband. Late in her life when a friend of the family proposed to edit her letters, she demurred, telling a female friend, "A pretty figure I should make. No. No. I have not any ambition to appear in print. Heedless and inaccurate as I am, I have too much vanity to risk my reputation before the public."[16]

For all that, Abigail Adams was by no means a mere figure in the background of the Adams family history. If the social standing of John Adams's family gave plausibility to him as a representative of the "middling sort" in Massachusetts, Abigail Adams had a more distinguished ancestry. Born in 1744 as the second of three daughters of the Reverend William Smith and his wife, Elizabeth Quincy Smith, of Weymouth, she was the descendant of some of the leading Puritan ministers of early New England as well as of its lay leaders. Her father was the son and grandson of wealthy merchants, and her grandfather Colonel John Quincy was the leading citizen of Braintree in his generation. John Adams was the first of his family to graduate from college, but the Quincys had generations of Harvard graduates. The elder John Adams became a selectman after proving himself in a number of minor town offices, but Quincys became selectmen soon after they returned from college. When John and Abigail married in 1764, there was apparently some invidious comment in the neighborhood that he was marrying above himself. Local legend has it that after her older sister Mary's wedding, their father preached a sermon from Luke 10:42, "Mary hath chosen that good part, which shall not be taken away from her." Speaking to the local gossipers, William Smith supposedly preached after Abigail's wedding on Luke 7:33, "For John . . . came neither eating bread nor drinking wine, and ye say, He hath a devil."

The marriage was one between spiritual and intellectual equals. Abigail was educated at home by her mother and grandmother Quincy, partly because her delicate health kept her there, partly because as she later explained, "Female education in the best families, went no further than writing and arithmetic; in some few and rare instances, music and dancing."[17] Her letters in this volume, with their frequent quotations from her favorite poets and other authors, show that she learned much more than mere "writing." She clearly knew Shakespeare, Dryden, Pope, James Thomson, and Edward Young well and had read widely in history, in addition to having the familiarity with the Bible one might expect of a minister's daughter. Her letters frequently show her mastery of style as well as of content and the wit and playfulness that enchanted John Adams (not a notably playful sort himself). She typically signed letters to her young women friends "Diana," playing out the pastoral literary games of the era, and she used the same name on her letters to John Adams during their courtship. By the time of the letters in this collection, however, she had changed her fanciful pen name to Portia, the name of the wife of the Roman republican patriot Lucius Junius Brutus. But if her wit and intelligence were a match for her husband's, she also had learned how to manage a New England household. The Smiths and Quincys had slaves among their servants, but she learned how to do things herself as well as to direct hired servants in the many requirements of keeping a house and farm. After her marriage, she and John took up residence on his small farm in Braintree, where all her skills of management and economy were put to good use.

In the decade between John and Abigail's marriage in 1764 and his departure for the First Continental Congress, Abigail was busy managing an increasingly complicated household. John's legal practice made a residence in Boston desirable, and in the spring of 1768 they moved there but returned to Braintree three years later. After little more than a year in the rural community of his birth, however, Adams decided to purchase a house in Queen Street in Boston and moved the family back there in August 1772, where they stayed until the spring of 1774. Abigail oversaw these frequent moves and the setting up of a second house in Boston, and in the meantime she bore five children, whom her husband fondly remembers at the end of many of his letters. Her daughter Abigail, always referred to by the family and in these letters as "Nabby," was born in 1765, and she was followed by three brothers: John Quincy born in 1767, Charles in 1770, and Thomas Boylston in 1772. A daughter, Susannah, was born in 1768, but, a sickly child, she died fourteen months later while Abigail was pregnant with Charles. A sixth child, Elizabeth, was stillborn in 1777 while John was attending Congress in Philadelphia; his concern and Abigail's state of mind can be discerned in letters of this period.

The moves between Braintree and Boston, the frequent pregnancies, and concern for the children played out against the background of increasing political tensions in Massachusetts, including the violence of the Boston Massacre. Yet Abigail Adams managed to deal with domestic affairs, to find time to read, and to correspond with a small circle of family and friends. These latter included particularly her older sister, Mary, who had married John Adams's friend Richard Cranch, and friends from her youth like Hannah Storer. In a letter of 1771 to her cousin Isaac Smith she noted the conflict between housewifely concerns and her own intellectual inclinations: "Women you know Sir are considerd as Domestick Beings, and altho they inherit an Eaquel Share of curiosity with the other Sex, yet but few are hardy eno' to venture abroad, and explore the amazing variety of distant Lands." She confessed that "had nature formed me of the other Sex, I should certainly have been a rover." Nevertheless, she went on to opine, "Tis natural I believe for every person to have a partiality for their own Country. Dont you think this little Spot of ours better calculated for happiness than any other you have yet seen or read of. Would you exchange it for England, France, Spain or Ittaly?"[18] Before she went abroad in 1784 to join her husband in Paris, her ambitions to be a "rover" were limited either to local travels in Massachusetts or to the realms of her reading and imagination.

Abigail Adams was particularly close during these years to Mercy Otis Warren, the sister of James Otis and wife of patriot leader James Warren. She visited the Warrens at their home in Plymouth when John was away, and the Warrens visited her when they were passing through Braintree. The two women shared both political and intellectual interests, although Mercy Warren, who had begun to publish political satires of Governor Hutchinson and other Tory leaders, was always more eager than Abigail for a place in the public eye. As John Adams became more involved in the patriot cause, Abigail began to read more deeply into the political theory and propaganda that supported American arguments against parliamentary and royal authority. She read James Burgh's three-volume *Political Disquisitions* with its warnings against political abuse of power, Charles Rollin's *Ancient History* with its accounts of ancient republics that fell because of corruption and private ambition, and Catherine Macaulay's *History of England*, which applied the same lessons to present-day Britain. In letters to Mercy Warren and others she quoted John Dickinson's *Letters from a Farmer in Pennsylvania*, calling him "the admired Farmer," and she followed closely her husband's Novanglus letters. Macaulay was of particular interest to both Adams and Warren because she was both an ardent Whig and an example of feminine intellectual achievement.

Warren corresponded with Macaulay, the two women discussed her work, and in her letter to Isaac Smith expressing her suppressed ambitions to be a "rover," Abigail asked for information about Macaulay's life. "I have a curiosity to know her Education, and what first prompted her to engage in a Study never before Exhibited to the publick by one of her own Sex and Country, tho now to the honour of both so admirably performed by her."[19] When Thomas Paine's *Common Sense* appeared in January 1776, it is scarcely any wonder that Abigail Adams appreciated its effective political rhetoric and embraced its arguments with enthusiasm in a letter to her husband (letter 86). She had for some time believed in the necessity of independence from the mother country, and in spite of her apparent agreement that women are "Domestick Beings," she was not afraid to express her political opinions to her husband. If she commanded John to "remember the ladies," her knowledge of politics and history, as well as that of her friend Mrs. Warren, gave authority to the notion that women had something to say about the political world beyond their thresholds.

Unlike her friend from Plymouth, Abigail Adams expressed her political opinions only to a small circle of friends in her private correspondence, and her letters to her husband contain direct political advice mostly during the months before declaring independence. The stirring call to remember the ladies is replaced by more general patriotic sentiments that supported John but did not challenge him. If she somewhat muted her political opinions in her letters to her husband, her domestic concerns during his absence nonetheless often demanded that she act independently to care for the family, the household, and the farm.

Unusual challenges presented themselves to her during the period covered by these letters. She was accustomed to overseeing household affairs as a traditional wifely domain, but taking on responsibility for the farm was a considerable extension of her role. She had to find help in a tight labor market caused by the departure of many local men for military service, deal with difficult tenants, and worry about planting and harvesting crops.

Looking beyond the household door enabled her to become a useful informant to John about local conditions and sentiments. Her letters are full of news about the conduct of the war in the Boston and New England area, about political affairs in Braintree and in Massachusetts in general, and about the stresses and difficulties in the local economy. On May 27, 1776, he tendered his praise, writing, "I think you shine as a stateswoman of late, as well as a farmeress" (letter 107). In the years ahead Abigail helped keep the family fortunes afloat by becoming a merchant on a small scale, sending requests to John for items she might sell in the neighborhood, and she bought property on his behalf. Maintaining the family economy was only one of her concerns, however, because she had to deal with two serious epidemics, the first of dysentery in 1775 (see her letter of September 8, letter 59) and the second of smallpox in the following year. In August 1776, she took the family into Boston to be inoculated, and since this involved infecting herself and the children with live smallpox virus, it was a dangerous procedure.

Letters from John were frequently slow in coming because of disruptions in the mails or his preoccupation with other business, and she was often thrown back on her own resources to pay the accounts and the taxes and to care for the health and education of the family, as for example in deciding to take the children to Boston for inoculation. At times her letters contain glimpses of a desire for more room to act and think apart from her responsibilities to husband and family. While staying with the family in Boston at her aunt's house in 1776, she is pleased to have a room with "a very convenient, pretty closet, with a window which looks into her flower garden. . . . I do not covet my neighbor's goods, but I should like to be the owner of such conveniences. I always had a fancy for a closet with a window, which I could more particularly call my own" (letter 135). Abigail's desire for a room of one's own—"closet" in eighteenth-century terminology referred to a small private room—would not be satisfied during the years of the Revolution, when the needs of small children, the farm and household, and her distant husband constrained her time and attention. Her desire for her own space was always second to her desire for the success and well-being of John and the children; the views she entertained in her own "closet" were always subordinated to his on important issues. He recognized her independence of mind ironically by commending its support of *his* thinking, as when he wrote on May 22, 1776: "Your sentiments of the duties we owe to our country are such as become the best of women and the best of men. Among all the disappointments and perplexities which have fallen to my share in life, nothing has contributed so much to support my mind as the choice blessing of a wife whose capacity enabled her to comprehend, and whose pure virtue obliged her to approve, the views of her husband" (letter 106). In later years when John and Abigail were together in Europe and in America, when he was a diplomat, vice president, and then president of the United States, she became a trusted political confidante, but the groundwork for playing this role was laid during the years covered in this volume, when she was both "farmeress" on her own and "stateswoman" in private in her correspondence with her husband.

IV

These letters assembled by Charles Francis Adams for the nation's centennial celebrations cover the period from mid-1774 until 1783, when the Revolution concludes with the Treaty of Paris. If the Adamses are not exactly the Everypersons their grandson tried to suggest, their letters do present an interesting sort of inside history of the Revolution in which reports from the home front appear in context with accounts of events on the national level, the war in Braintree superimposed on a war of international dimension. A different sort of inside view of the Revolution might be obtained by looking at the lives of men like George Robert Twelves Hewes or Joseph Plumb Martin, a shoemaker and a farmer who were on the front lines of the Revolution, but where their lives show us the impact of the Revolution on individuals, the letters of John and Abigail Adams reveal the formation of Revolutionary political and social networks.[20] The archives of the Revolution are full of documents and texts that inform us about the Revolutionary leaders in Congress and in the field, and there are many, but not as many, reports from the people whose more immediate concerns were the day-to-day survival of themselves and their families. John's letters open a window onto the formation of the legal and administrative structures that advanced the Revolutionary cause, and Abigail's connect us to the world of family and neighborhood that supported the vision of republican government. As such they present a nearly unique view of the formation and maintenance of Revolutionary sentiment, much as Charles Francis Adams claimed for them in 1876.

In the dozen years or so after the Stamp Act, John Adams's Whiggish sentiments in favor of the rights of English America seemed at times to be constrained by his dismay about unruly mobs and other forms of revolutionary social upheaval. By the time of these letters, however, his determination to pursue American independence outweighs, but does not totally displace, his concern about popular disorder. The letters show a political leader straining against the frustration of working with colleagues whose opinions are not so advanced as his, particularly with John Dickinson, "the Farmer," as he was known. In 1774 Dickinson was, at the national level, the most prominent champion of American political rights, but by June 1776 different sentiments from his prevailed. The drive toward independence was powered by events, by popular support, and by numerous voices at the national level, including Adams's own. Abigail's enthusiastic response to Thomas Paine's *Common Sense* points to the strength of popular sentiment, but on the floor of the Continental Congress itself John Adams was a significant and canny presence who put that voice on the political stage. His letters to her detailing his frustration at dealing with those hoping for a rapprochement with England suggest a good sense of political timing and strategy. He was aware of the need to create support for independence and to have leaders from colonies other than Massachusetts take leadership roles.

If his letters home display his frustrations and his occasional testiness toward his colleagues, they also show something about the strains of building a revolutionary coalition. Ironically, one of his more important services was unintentionally occasioned by his correspondence with Abigail. He was clearly chagrined when the letters he wrote to her and to James Warren on July 24, 1775, fell into British hands and were published, because he had criticized the "fidgets, the whims, the caprice, the vanity, the superstition, the irritability of some of us" (letter 54). The letter to Warren went further in referring to Dickinson as "a certain great fortune and piddling genius." If the British publication succeeded in provoking a quarrel between Adams and Dickinson, it also made it clear to a public outside of Congress that Dickinson was not above criticism, that his reluctance for independence might be out of date.

The incident of the intercepted letters casts a shadow on this correspondence, because it reminds us of the difficulty and uncertainty of passing letters back and forth in these years, a difficulty made even greater by John's diplomatic assignment to Europe, where he had to find means to get his letters back to Braintree. At the same time the possibility of interception reminds the Adamses of the risk of disclosing gossip or confidential information. Abigail's use of the pen name Portia reflects this as does John's care not to reveal names or important details of public business. Nevertheless, in the years after the declaration of independence the letters of the Adamses reveal a great deal about their activities during the Revolution and the range of their interests. They reflect both Abigail's concerns for the progress of the war—Braintree was open to British naval depredations, particularly early in the war—and John's role as chair of the Board of War. Military news of various sorts appears in the letters of each of them, and John Adams's outspokenness engenders comments on the character and appearance of his associates both in America and abroad. Later he expresses his trials and frustrations in his early years abroad on diplomatic service as he found himself caught between squabbling members of the American delegation and also at odds with Franklin's style of personal diplomacy. The emotional history of the Revolution as revealed in John Adams's letters occurs in statements of revolutionary purpose, in noble sentiments about independence and the public good, and also in a good deal of heartburning and irritation.

Abigail Adams's letters to her husband in turn connect him to the people of Braintree and Massachusetts whom he represented and whose political and moral support he depended on. She relays news from local friends and relatives such as his brother-in-law Richard Cranch, her uncle Dr. Cotton Tufts, the Braintree minister Anthony Wibird, James and Mercy Warren, and assorted Quincy cousins, aunts, and uncles. She writes as well about the problems of finding help on the farm and about the welfare and doings of John's law students, the house servants, and farm laborers. They exchange news about Joseph Bass, a young Braintree man who travels to Philadelphia as John's manservant, and pass on news to Joseph's family. She reports the latest news about state politics, the local economy, and the morale of her fellow citizens. If she is less inclined than he is to complain of the venality or shallowness of those around her, she does offer glimpses of the changing social understandings of Revolutionary America.

Some neighbors were less inclined to defer to the Quincys or to the wife of the Massachusetts congressional delegate. Others had their eye on the opportunities afforded by the Revolution to make their fortunes, by shipping as privateers or taking advantage of the law of supply and demand. When Bostonians thought Burgoyne's invasion in 1775 might threaten their city, Abigail was appalled at the teamsters' charges for moving goods to safer locations (letter 194). "To their shame be it told, not a small trunk would they carry under eight dollars, and many of them, I am told, asked a hundred dollars a load; for carting a hogshead of molasses eight miles, thirty dollars. O human nature! or rather, O inhuman nature!"

Her letters are not least interesting for the rumors and fears they report. People in Braintree and in Boston were always exposed to British attack, and information was slow in coming on troop and fleet movements, on the outcome of battles, and on the truthfulness of reports such as the one about the supposed assassination of Franklin. Above all, her letters pass on news of the immediate family, the children, who are never far from their minds in these letters. Abigail reports on the children's health, their doings, their educational progress, and John in turn always sends on his love to his "young prattlers" as they are called on at least one occasion.

The letters of John and Abigail Adams during the Revolution thus provide an intimate view of the feelings, mostly hopeful but occasionally anxious or irritated, of two people who were in their own ways in touch with the heartbeat of the young nation. Their letters to each other often reveal them at their best. John Adams's published treatises and pamphlets are not models of literary style or elegance, weighted down as they frequently are with displays of his massive legal knowledge, but in his familiar letters his lively, thoughtful, sometimes testy personality comes through. The energy of his best letters is matched by the sprightliness and wit of Abigail's. These qualities in her attracted him during their courtship, and they enlivened their marriage and the correspondence printed here.

As we can see by some of the letters, John Adams often worried about how he would be remembered by history, about whether his services to the nation would be always overlooked. At various points he is annoyed, even slightly envious, of the attention given to John Dickinson or Benjamin Franklin, and even when in his old age he had restored his old friendship with Thomas Jefferson, he was restive in the face of the acclaim his younger colleague was receiving as the author of the Declaration of Independence. But in the campaign for a place in historical memory he had a secret weapon. None of the other major Revolutionary leaders had a spouse who combined such a fierce loyalty to her husband's interests and a lively pen as did Abigail Adams. The collection of their letters to each other as edited by their grandson in 1876 has deservedly become a minor American literary classic.

Notes to the Introduction

1. Charles Francis Adams, "Memoir," in *Familiar Letters of John Adams and His Wife Abigail Adams, During the Revolution* (New York: Hurd and Houghton, 1876), v–vi.
2. Alexander Hamilton, *Writings* (New York: Library of America, 2001), 935.

3. This claim was furthered by Charles Francis Adams Jr. in his *Three Episodes of Massachusetts History* (Boston: Houghton Mifflin, 1892). Jeffersonians had already made a strong claim for their hero in that regard, and the Adams response to the Jeffersonians was written by Charles Francis's son Henry Adams in his *History of the United States of America During the Administrations of Thomas Jefferson and James Madison* (New York: Scribner's, 1889–91).

4. Charles Francis Adams, "Memoir," v–vii.

5. *Diary and Autobiography of John Adams,* ed. L. H. Butterfield, et al. (Cambridge: Harvard University Press, 1962), 1:63.

6. John Ferling, *John Adams: A Life* (Knoxville: University of Tennessee Press, 1992), 26–27.

7. *Diary,* 1:55.

8. Ibid., 1:87.

9. *Adams Family Correspondence,* ed. L. H. Butterfield, et al. (Cambridge: Harvard University Press, 1963), 1:8, 5.

10. *The Political Writings of John Adams,* ed. George A. Peek Jr. (New York: Liberal Arts Press, 1954), 5–7, 20.

11. *Political Writings,* 5, 24. On the relations between John and Samuel Adams, see Ferling, 43–46.

12. *Diary,* 1:273.

13. Ferling, 93.

14. Ferling, 150.

15. Charles Francis Adams, "Memoir," vii.

16. Ibid., xxxi.

17. Ibid., xi.

18. *Adams Family Correspondence,* 1:76.

19. Ibid., 1:77.

20. For Hewes, see Alfred F. Young, *The Shoemaker and the Tea Party* (Boston: Beacon Press, 1999); for Martin, see Joseph Plumb Martin, *A Narrative of a Revolutionary Soldier* (New York: Signet, 2001).

A Brief Adams Calendar,
1774–83

June 18, 1774. John Adams elected as delegate from Massachusetts to the First Continental Congress.

June–July 1774. Travels for the last time on the eastern circuit of the Massachusetts Superior Court, in present-day Maine.

August 10, 1774. Leaves Braintree to attend the First Continental Congress in Philadelphia.

October 29, 1774. Leaves Philadelphia to return home, arriving thirteen days later.

Winter 1774–75. Serves as Braintree's delegate to the Massachusetts Provincial Congress; writes the Novanglus letters.

Late April 1775. Returns to Philadelphia for the Second Continental Congress as a delegate from Massachusetts.

Late July 1775. Congress adjourns. John Adams goes to Watertown, Massachusetts, where the Provincial Congress is sitting.

August–early September 1775. Returns to Congress in Philadelphia.

November 1775. Appointed chief justice of the Massachusetts Superior Court, an office he considers but never fills.

December 1775–January 1776. Obtains leave to return home; visits Washington in the army camp in Cambridge, Massachusetts, then returns to Congress after a brief stay at home in Braintree.

March–April 1776. Writes *Thoughts on Government*.

June 12, 1776. Congress creates the Board of War and Ordnance and names John Adams as its president.

July 2, 1776. Congress votes for independence and subsequently approves the Declaration two days later.

July 12, 1776–September 2, 1776. Abigail Adams takes her children and servants to Boston to be inoculated for smallpox.

Early September 1776. John Adams, along with Benjamin Franklin and Edward Rutledge, travels to New York to meet with the British peace commissioners, who were only authorized to offer peace after American submission.

October 1776. Returns home for a nine-week visit.

January 1777. Returns to Congress, now meeting in Baltimore after British forces had occupied much of New Jersey. Congress returns to Philadelphia in March, but is forced to withdraw to York, Pennsylvania, in September.

November 1777. John Adams returns to Braintree, where he learns that he has been elected as a joint commissioner to treat with the French government.

February 15, 1778. Sails on the frigate *Boston* with his son John Quincy Adams for Bordeaux, France.

April 1778. Takes up residence with Franklin in Passy, outside of Paris.

June 17, 1779. Returns home with his son on board the French ship *La Sensible*.

August–November 1779. Takes part in the Massachusetts constitutional convention and drafts a constitution that is adopted after debate and revision in June 1780.

October 1779. Learns that Congress has appointed him as a minister plenipotentiary to negotiate an end to the War of Independence.

November 15, 1779. Sails on *La Sensible* for France, taking with him his sons John Quincy and Charles. The ship is forced to put in at El Ferrol, Spain, for repairs, and Adams and his party make a tortuous journey to Paris by land.

July–August 1780. Goes to Amsterdam in order to get loans for the American government and diplomatic recognition. Returns briefly to Paris in July 1781, but resides in the Netherlands until the following year.

October 1782. Returns to Paris for peace treaty negotiations.

January 28, 1783. Preliminary articles for a peace treaty between the United States, Britain, and France are signed.

Suggestions for Further Reading

Adair, Douglass. "Fame and the Founding Fathers," in *Fame and the Founding Fathers: Essays,* ed. Trevor Colbourn. New York: Norton, 1974.

Butterfield, L. H., et al., eds. *Adams Family Correspondence.* 6 vols. Cambridge: Harvard University Press, 1963–93.

———. *Diary and Autobiography of John Adams.* 4 vols. Cambridge: Harvard University Press, 1961.

Ferling, John. *John Adams: A Life.* Knoxville: University of Tennessee Press, 1992.

———. *Setting the World Ablaze: Washington, Adams, Jefferson, and the American Revolution.* New York: Oxford, 2000.

Gelles, Edith. *Abigail Adams: A Writing Life.* New York: Routledge, 2002.

———. *Portia: The World of Abigail Adams.* Bloomington: University of Indiana Press, 1992.

Haraszti, Zoltan. *John Adams and the Prophets of Progress.* Cambridge: Harvard University Press, 1952.

Howe, John R. *The Changing Political Thought of John Adams.* Princeton: Princeton University Press, 1966.

Keller, Rosemary. *Patriotism and the Female Sex: Abigail Adams and the American Revolution.* Brooklyn: Carlson Publishing, 1994.

Levin, Phyllis Lee. *Abigail Adams.* New York: St. Martin's Press, 1987.

McCullough, David. *John Adams.* New York: Simon and Schuster, 2001.

Ryerson, Richard Alan, ed. *John Adams and the Founding of the Republic.* Boston: Massachusetts Historical Society, 2001.

Shaw, Peter. *The Character of John Adams*. Chapel Hill: University of North Carolina Press, 1976.

Thompson, C. Bradley. *John Adams and the Spirit of Liberty*. Lawrence: University of Kansas Press, 1998.

Withey, Lynne. *Dearest Friend: A Life of Abigail Adams*. New York: Free Press, 1981.

A Note on the Text

The text reprinted here follows that of Charles Francis Adams's edition of *Familiar Letters of John Adams and His Wife Abigail Adams, During the Revolution* (New York: Hurd and Houghton, 1876). Charles Francis Adams was a careful and scrupulous editor by nineteenth-century standards, but he revised the manuscript text of the letters in various ways. Following editorial practice of the day, he standardized the spelling, capitalization, and punctuation of the texts according to modern standards with the intention of making them more accessible. This editing is particularly noticeable in Abigail Adams's letters, for she was a phonetic speller with a somewhat variable sense of orthography. In addition, New England dialect terms and pronunciations occasionally color her vocabulary and that of the children. Charles Francis smoothed all this out by correcting her "Phylidelphia" and "Canady," not necessarily a loss to the reader, but we do miss her reports of how the children asked "mar" about when "par" would return, showing that in the 1770s New Englanders were already adding an *r* to words ending in *a* like "ma" and "pa." He often silently changed familiar terms of address like these to more proper and genteel versions. References to daughter Abigail as "Nabby" became "Abby," for example. Since the younger Abigail is everywhere referred to in biographies of the Adams family as "Nabby," I have restored the original spelling here.

More problematic, Charles Francis silently cut passages that he thought were either irrelevant or too personal. These passages have been restored in this edition, including detailed accounts by Abigail of the family's experience with the dysentery epidemic of 1775 and their inoculation for smallpox in 1776. However, these

passages have been reedited for the most part to conform to
Charles Francis Adams's practice of regularizing spelling and
punctuation, although "mar" and "par" do make a reappearance
in a few inserted sentences. Interested readers who wish to sam-
ple Abigail's adventures in spelling and punctuation in their original form can consult the six-volume edition of the *Adams
Family Correspondence* (Cambridge: Harvard University Press,
1963–93).

I have placed in their correct chronological positions two letters that Charles Francis Adams misdated. Although a few of his
footnotes have been retained, the text is now extensively annotated, using endnotes, with the needs of the modern reader in
mind. Significant figures in the Adams's social and political cir-
cles have been identified, as well as the various books and historical and cultural events that John and Abigail refer to in many
of their letters. This edition also identifies for the first time most
of the literary allusions and quotations in the letters, mostly by
Abigail. For assistance in making some of these identifications,
I would like to thank Kevin Berland, Lisa Berglund, and Rose
Paprocki.

FAMILIAR LETTERS OF JOHN ADAMS AND HIS WIFE

1. JOHN ADAMS

Boston, 12 May 1774

I am extremely afflicted with the relation your father gave me of the return of your disorder. I fear you have taken some cold. We have had a most pernicious air a great part of this spring. I am sure I have reason to remember it. My cold is the most obstinate and threatening one I ever had in my life. However, I am unwearied in my endeavors to subdue it, and have the pleasure to think I have had some success. I rise at five, walk three miles, keep the air all day, and walk again in the afternoon. These walks have done me more good than anything, though I have been constantly plied with teas, and your specific. My own infirmities, the account of the return of yours, and the public news[1] coming altogether have put my utmost philosophy to the trial.

We live, my dear soul, in an age of trial. What will be the consequence, I know not. The town of Boston, for aught I can see, must suffer martyrdom. It must expire. And our principal consolation is, that it dies in a noble cause—the cause of truth, of virtue, of liberty, and of humanity, and that it will probably have a glorious resurrection to greater wealth, splendor, and power, than ever.

Let me know what is best for us to do. It is expensive keeping a family here, and there is no prospect of any business in my way in this town this whole summer. I don't receive a shilling a week. We must contrive as many ways as we can to save expenses; for we may have calls to contribute very largely, in proportion to our circumstances, to prevent other very honest worthy people from suffering for want, besides our own loss in point of business and profit.

Don't imagine from all this that I am in the dumps. Far otherwise. I can truly say that I have felt more spirits and activity since the arrival of this news than I had done before for years. I look upon this as the last effort of Lord North's despair,[2] and he will as surely be defeated in it, as he was in the project of the tea.

I am, with great anxiety for your health,

Your   JOHN ADAMS

2. JOHN ADAMS

York, 29 June 1774

I have a great deal of leisure, which I chiefly employ in scribbling, that my mind may not stand still or run back, like my fortune. There is very little business here, and David Sewall, David Wyer, John Sullivan and James Sullivan, and Theophilus Bradbury,[1] are the lawyers who attend the inferior courts, and consequently, conduct the causes at the superior.

I find that the country is the situation to make estates by the law. John Sullivan, who is placed at Durham in New Hampshire, is younger both in years and practice than I am. He began with nothing, but is now said to be worth ten thousand pounds lawful money, his brother James allows five or six or perhaps seven thousand pounds, consisting in houses and lands, notes, bonds, and mortgages. He has a fine stream of water, with an excellent corn mill, saw mill, fulling mill, scythe mill, and others, in all six mills, which are both his delight and his profit. As he has earned cash in his business at the bar, he has taken opportunities to purchase farms of his neighbors, who wanted to sell and move out farther into the woods, at an advantageous rate, and in this way has been growing rich; under the smiles and auspices of Governor Wentworth,[2] he has been promoted in the civil and military way, so that he is treated with great respect in this neighborhood.

James Sullivan, brother of the other, who studied law under him, without any academical education (and John was in the same case), is fixed at Saco, alias Biddeford, in our province. He began with neither learning, books, estate, nor anything but his head and hands, and is now a very popular lawyer and growing rich very fast, purchasing great farms, etc., and a justice of the peace and a member of the General Court. *the American Dream before America*

David Sewall, of this town, never practices out of this county; has no children; has no ambition nor avarice, they say (however, *quaere*).[3] His business in this county maintains him very handsomely, and he gets beforehand.

Bradbury, at Falmouth, they say, grows rich very fast.

I was first sworn in 1758. My life has been a continual scene of fatigue, vexation, labor, and anxiety. I have four children. I had a pretty estate from my father; I have been assisted by your father; I have done the greatest business in the province; I have had the very richest clients in the province. Yet I am poor, in comparison with others. → *compitition my friend*

This, I confess, is grievous and discouraging. I ought, however, to be candid enough to acknowledge that I have been imprudent. I have spent an estate in books. I have spent a sum of money indiscreetly in a lighter, another in a pew, and a much greater in a house in Boston. These would have been indiscretions, if the impeachment of the Judges,[4] the Boston Port Bill, etc., etc., had never happened; but by the unfortunate interruption of my business from these causes, those indiscretions became almost fatal to me; to be sure, much more detrimental.

John Lowell,[5] at Newburyport, has built himself a house like the palace of a nobleman, and lives in great splendor. His business is very profitable. In short, every lawyer who has the least appearance of abilities makes it do in the country. In town, nobody does, or ever can, who either is not obstinately determined never to have any connection with politics, or does not engage on the side of the Government, the Administration, and the Court.

Let us, therefore, my dear partner, from that affection which we feel for our lovely babes, apply ourselves, by every way we can, to the cultivation of our farm. Let frugality and industry be our virtues, if they are not of any others. And above all cares of this life, let our ardent anxiety be to mould the minds and manners of our children. Let us teach them not only to do virtuously, but to excel. To excel, they must be taught to be steady, active, and industrious.

3 . JOHN ADAMS

York, June 30 1774

I have nothing to do here but to take the air, inquire for news, talk politics, and write letters. This town has the best air I ever breathed. It is very level and there are no mountains or hills to obstruct the free course of the air upon any point of compass for eight or ten miles. It lies upon the sea on the south and has a river running through it. The weather has been inexpressibly fine all this week. The air is as clear, as bright, as springy, as you can conceive. Braintree air is thick and unelastic in comparison of this. What then is that of Boston?

I regret that I cannot have the pleasure of enjoying this fine weather with my family, and upon my farm. Oh, how often am I there! I have but a dull prospect before me. I have no hope of reaching Braintree under a fortnight from this day, if I should in twenty days.

I regret my absence from the county of Suffolk this week on another account. If I was there, I could converse with the gentlemen who are bound with me to Philadelphia;[1] I could turn the course of my reading and studies to such subjects of Law, and Politics, and Commerce, as may come in play at the Congress. I might be furbishing up my old reading in Law and History, that I might appear with less indecency before a variety of gentlemen, whose educations, travels, experience, family, fortune, and everything will give them a vast superiority to me, and I fear to some of my companions.

This town of York is a curiosity, in several views. The people here are great idolaters of the memory of their former minister, Mr. Moody. Dr. Sayward[2] says, and the rest of them generally think, that Mr. Moody was one of the greatest men and best saints who have lived since the days of the Apostles. He had an ascendency and authority over the people here, as absolute as that of any prince in Europe, not excepting his Holiness.

This he acquired by a variety of means. In the first place, he settled in the place without any contract. His professed principle was that no man should be hired to preach the gospel, but that the minister should depend upon the charity, generosity, and benevolence of the people. This was very flattering to their pride, and left room for their ambition to display itself in an emulation among them which should be most bountiful and ministerial.

In the next place, he acquired the character of firm trust in Providence. A number of gentlemen came in one day, when they had nothing in the house. His wife was very anxious, they say, and asked him what they should do. "Oh, never fear; trust Providence, make a fire in the oven, and you will have something." Very soon a variety of everything that was good was sent in, and by one o'clock they had a splendid dinner.

He had also the reputation of enjoying intimate communication with the Deity, and of having a great interest in the Court of Heaven by his prayers.

He always kept his musket in order, and was fond of hunting. On a time, they say, he was out of provisions. There came along two wild geese. He takes gun and cries, "If it please God I kill both, I will send the fattest to the poorest person in this parish." He shot, and killed both; ordered them plucked, and then sent the fattest to a poor widow, leaving the other, which was a very poor one, at home,—to the great mortification of his lady. But his maxim was, Perform unto the Lord thy vow.

But the best story I have heard yet was his doctrine in a sermon from this text: "Lord, what shall we do?" The doctrine was that when a person or people are in a state of perplexity, and know not what to do, they ought never to do they know not what. This is applicable to the times.

He brought his people into a remarkable submission and subjection to their spiritual rulers, which continues to this day. Their present parson[3] does and says what he pleases, is a great Tory, and as odd as Moody.

4 · JOHN ADAMS

York, 1 July 1774

I am so idle that I have not an easy moment without my pen in my hand. My time might have been improved to some purpose in mowing grass, raking hay, or hoeing corn, weeding carrots, picking or shelling pease. Much better should I have been employed in schooling my children, in teaching them to write, cipher, Latin, French, English, and Greek.

I sometimes think I must come to this—to be the foreman upon my own farm and the schoolmaster to my own children. I confess myself to be full of fears that the ministry and their friends and instruments will prevail, and crush the cause and friends of liberty. The minds of that party are so filled with prejudices against me that they will take all advantages, and do me all the damage they can. These thoughts have their turns in my mind, but in general my hopes are predominant.

In a trial of a cause here to-day, some facts were mentioned, which are worth writing to you. It was sworn, by Dr. Lyman, Elder [John] Bradbury, and others, that there had been a number of instances in this town of fatal accidents, happening from sudden noises striking the ears of babes and young children. A gun was fired near one child, as likely as any; the child fell immediately into fits, which impaired his reason, and is still living an idiot. Another child was sitting on a chamber floor. A man rapped suddenly and violently on the boards, which made the floor under the child [sound?]. The child was so startled, and frightened, that it fell into fits, which never were cured.

Dr. Gardiner,[1] arrived here to-day from Boston, brings us news of a battle at the town meeting, between Whigs and Tories, in which the Whigs, after a day and a half's obstinate engagement, were finally victorious by two to one. He says the Tories are preparing a flaming protest.

I am determined to be cool, if I can. I have suffered such torments in my mind heretofore as have almost overpowered my constitution, without any advantage. And now I will laugh and be easy if I can, let the contest of parties terminate as it will, let my own estate and interest suffer what it will, nay, whether I stand high or low in the estimation of the world, so long as I keep a conscience void of offense towards God and man. And this I am determined by the will of God to do, let what will become of me or mine, my country or the world.

I shall arouse myself erelong, I believe, and exert an industry, a frugality, a hard labor, that will serve my family, if I can't serve my country. I will not lie down in despair. If I cannot serve my children by the law, I will serve them by agriculture, by trade, by some way or other. I thank God I have a head, and heart, and hands, which, if once fully exerted altogether, will succeed in the world as well as those of the mean-spirited, low-minded, fawning, obsequious scoundrels who have long hoped that my integrity would be an obstacle in my way, and enable them to outstrip me in the race.

But what I want in comparison of them of villainy and servility, I will make up in industry and capacity. If I don't, they shall laugh and triumph. I will not willingly see blockheads, whom I have a right to despise, elevated above me and insolently triumphing over me. Nor shall knavery, through any negligence of mine, get the better of honesty, nor ignorance of knowledge, nor folly of wisdom, nor vice of virtue.

I must entreat you, my dear partner in all the joys and sorrows, prosperity and adversity of my life, to take a part with me in the struggle. I pray God for your health—entreat you to rouse your whole attention to the family, the stock, the farm, the dairy. Let every article of expense which can possibly be spared be retrenched; keep the hands attentive to their business, and the most prudent measures of every kind be adopted and pursued with alacrity and spirit.

5. JOHN ADAMS

York, 2 July 1774

I have concluded to mount my horse to-morrow morning at four, and ride to Wells to hear my old worthy, learned, ingenious friend Hemmenway,[1] whom I never was yet so happy as to hear. Mr. Winthrop[2] agrees to be my company. Wells is about fifteen miles from this place; from thence we propose to ride after the evening service is over to Saco, i.e., Biddeford, which is about thirty miles from here, which will leave us an easy journey to Falmouth for Monday.

Mr. Winthrop tells me that he has heard the late Governor Hutchinson,[3] while he was Chief Justice, frequently say for seven years together, that Salem was the most proper, convenient, and suitable place in the province for the seat of government; that he frequently complimented the gentlemen of Salem with the happiness and convenience of their situation for the seat of government, and with his prophecies that it would certainly be made such in a course of years. I mentioned this to Judge Trowbridge,[4] and he told me that he himself remembered to have heard him say the same thing. I am very much mistaken if I have not heard him say so too. And I remember I happened to be with Kent when he carried to Judge Lynde[5] his commission as Chief Justice, and Judge Lynde entertained me for some time with conversation about making Salem the seat of government, and with the probable effects of such a measure; one of which he said would be a translation of a great part of the trade from Boston to Salem. But he said he did not want to have troops in Salem.

Now let any one who knows these anecdotes judge who was the suggester, planner, and promoter of this wrongheaded and iniquitous measure.

Safford, my barber, tells me, that his Minister Lyman is bribed to be a Tory. He says that whenever Deacon Sayward has a vessel arrive, he sends the parson ten gallons of rum, two or three hundred of sugar, ten gallons of wine, a barrel of flour, etc., etc., etc. He says "he thinks that all Toryism grows out of bribery." I thought the barber's observation as just and as memorable as Parson Moody's doctrine "that when men knew not what to do, they ought not to do they knew not what."

I write you this tittle-tattle, my dear, in confidence. You must keep these letters to yourself, and communicate them with great caution and reserve. I should advise you to put them up safe and preserve them. They may exhibit to our posterity a kind of picture of the manners, opinions, and principles of these times of perplexity, danger, and distress.

Deacon Sayward said at table this week in my hearing that there was but one point in which he differed in opinion from the late Governor Hutchinson, and that was with regard to the reality of witchcraft and the existence of witches. The Governor, he said, would not allow there was any such thing. The Deacon said he was loath to differ from him in anything; he had so great a regard for him and his opinions, that he was willing to give up almost everything rather than differ with him. But in this he could not see with him.

Such is the cant of this artful, selfish, hypocritical man.

Pray remember me to my dear little babes, whom I long to see running to meet me and climb up upon me under the smiles of their mother.

6. JOHN ADAMS

Littlefield's, at Wells, 3 July 1774

Mr. Winthrop, Mr. Quincy,[1] and I came this morning from York before breakfast, fifteen miles, in order to hear my learned friend Hemmenway. Mr. Quincy brought me a letter from Williams,[2] in which he lets me know that you and the family were well. This is very refreshing news.

Patten's, at Arundel, 4 July

We went to meeting at Wells and had the pleasure of hearing my friend upon "Be not partakers in other men's sins. Keep yourselves pure." Mr. Hemmenway came and kindly invited us to dine, but we had engaged a dinner at Littlefield's, so we returned there, dined, and took our horses to meeting in the afternoon and heard the minister again upon "Seek first the kingdom of God and his righteousness, and all these things shall be added unto you." There is a great pleasure in hearing sermons so serious, so clear, so sensible and instructive as these.

We went to Mr. Hemmenway's, and as it rained a little he put out our horses, and we took a bed with him, i.e., Mr. Winthrop and I.

You know I never get or save anything by cozening or classmating. So I gave pistareens[3] enough among the children and servants to have paid twice for my entertainment.

Josiah Quincy,[4] always impetuous and vehement, would not stop, but drove forward; I suppose, that he might get upon the fishing ground before his brother Sam and me. I find that the divines and lawyers this way are all Tories. Brother Hemmenway is as impartial as any I have seen or heard of. James Sullivan seems half inclined to be a Whig.

Mr. Winthrop has been just making some observations which I think worth sending to you. Upon reading an observation in the Farmer's fourth letter,[5] that some of our (the Massachusetts) resolves and publications had better have been suppressed, Mr. Winthrop said that many things in our newspapers ought to have been suppressed, for example, whenever there was the least popular commotion or *disturbance,* it was instantly put in all the newspapers in this province. But in all the other provinces they took care to conceal and suppress every such thing.

Another thing, he says we ought to avoid all paragraphs in our papers about our own manufactures, especially all vaporing puffing advertisements about them, because such paragraphs only tend to provoke the ministers, merchants, and manufacturers in England to confine and restrain or prohibit our manufactures. But our presses in Boston, Salem, and Newburyport are under no regulation, nor any judicious, prudent care. Therefore it seems impracticable to keep out such imprudences. The printers are hot, indiscreet men, and they are under the influence of others as hot, rash, and injudicious as themselves, very often.

For my own part, it has long been my resolution to avoid being concerned in counseling, or aiding, or abetting any tumult or disorder; to avoid all exceptionable scribbling in the newspaper of every kind; to avoid all passion and personal altercation or reflections. I have found it difficult to keep these resolutions exactly; all but the last, however, I have religiously and punctiliously observed these six years.

5 July, Tuesday Morning

Arrived last evening at Falmouth, and procured a new place to lodge at, Mrs. Euston's. Quincy and I have taken a bed together. My brother Neg Freeman[6] came to pay his respects to me and to invite me to a bed in his house; but I was fixed before, and therefore thanked him and excused myself. It is a very neat house where we sleep. The desk and table shine like mirrors. The floors are clean and white and nicely sanded, etc.

But when shall I get home? This tedious journey will produce me very little profit. I never saw Falmouth before with such lean expectations and empty pockets. I am much concerned for my family. These Acts of Parliament and ministerial manoeuvres will injure me both in my property and business as much as any person whatever in proportion.

7. JOHN ADAMS

Falmouth, 5 July 1774

I can't be easy without my pen in my hand, yet I know not what to write.

I have this morning heard a dialogue between Will Gardiner and a Captain Pote,[1] of Falmouth. Gardiner says he can't subscribe the non-consumption agreement[2] because he has a hundred men coming from England to settle upon Kennebeck River, and he must supply them, which he can't do without English goods. That agreement he says may do at Boston, but not in the Eastern country. Pote said he never would sign it, and railed away at Boston mobs, drowning tea, and tarring Malcom.[3]

James Sullivan at dinner told us a story or two. One member of the General Court, he said, as they came down stairs after their dissolution at Salem said to him, "Though we are killed, we died scrabbling, did not we?"

This is not very witty, I think.

Another story was of a piece of wit of brother Porter,[4] of Salem. He came upon the floor and asked a member, "What state are you in now?" The member answered, "In a state of nature." "Aye," says Porter, "and you will be damned before you will get into a state of grace."

6 July

I spent an hour last evening at Mr. Wyer's, with Judge Cushing.[5] Wyer's father, who has a little place in the customs, came in. He began upon politics, and told us that Mr. Smith had a fast last week which he attended. Mr. Gilman[6] preached, he said, part of the day, and told them that the judgments of God upon the land were in consequence of the mobs and riots which had prevailed in the country; and then turning to me old Wyer said, "What do you think of that, Mr. Adams?"

I answered, "I can't say but mobs and violence may have been one cause of our calamities. I am inclined to think that they do come in for a share; but there are many other causes. Did not Mr. Gilman mention bribery and corruption as another cause? He ought to have been impartial, and pointed out the venality which prevails in the land as a cause, as well as tumults." "I think he did," says Wyer. I might have pursued my inquiry, whether he did not mention universal pilfering, robbery, and picking of pockets which prevails in the land,—as every man's pocket upon the continent is picked every day by taking from him duties without his consent. I might have inquired whether he mentioned the universal spirit of debauchery, dissipation, luxury, effeminacy, and gaming, which the late ministerial measures are introducing, etc., etc., etc., but I forbore.

How much profaneness, lewdness, intemperance, etc., have been introduced by the army and navy and revenue; how much servility, venality, artifice, and hypocrisy have been introduced among the ambitious and avaricious by the British politics of the last ten years. In short the original faulty causes of all the vices which have been introduced are the political innovations of the last ten years. This is no justification and a poor excuse for the girls who have been debauched, and for the injustice which has been committed in some riots; but surely the soldiers, sailors, and excisemen who have occasioned these vices ought not to reproach those they have corrupted. These Tories act the part of the devil. They tempt men and women into sin and then reproach them for it, and become soon their tormentors for it. A tempter and tormentor is the character of the devil. Hutchinson, Oliver,[7] and others of their circle, who for their own ends of ambition and avarice have pursued, promoted, encouraged, counseled, aided, and abetted the taxation of America, have been the real tempters of their countrymen and women into all the vices, sins, crimes, and follies which that taxation has occasioned. And now by themselves and their friends, dependents, and votaries, they are reproaching those very men and women with those vices and follies, sins and crimes.

There is not a sin which prevails more universally and has prevailed longer than prodigality in furniture, equipage, apparel, and diet. And I believe that this vice, this sin, has as large a share in drawing down the judgments of Heaven as any. And perhaps the punishment that is inflicted may work medicinally and cure the disease.

8. JOHN ADAMS

Falmouth, 6 July 1774

Mobs are the trite topic of declamation and invective among all
the ministerial people far and near. They are grown universally
learned in the nature, tendency, and consequences of them, and
very elegant and pathetic in descanting upon them. They are
sources of all kinds of evils, vices, and crimes, they say. They give
rise to profaneness, intemperance, thefts, robberies, murders, and
treason. Cursing, swearing, drunkenness, gluttony, lewdness, tres-
passes, maims, are necessarily involved in them and occasioned
by them. Besides, they render the populace, the rabble, the scum
of the earth, insolent and disorderly, impudent and abusive. They
give rise to lying, hypocrisy, chicanery, and even perjury among
the people, who are driven to such artifice and crimes to conceal
themselves and their companions from prosecutions in consequence of them. *> implying therefore false + propaganda*

This is the picture drawn by the Tory pencil; and it must be
granted to be a likeness. But this is declamation. What consequence is to be drawn from this description? Shall we submit to
Parliamentary taxation to avoid mobs? Will not Parliamentary
taxation, if established, occasion vices, crimes, and follies infinitely more numerous, dangerous, and fatal to the community?
Will not Parliamentary taxation, if established, raise a revenue
unjustly and wrongfully? If this revenue is scattered by the hand
of corruption among the public officers and magistrates and
rulers in the community, will it not propagate vices more numerous, more malignant and pestilential among them? Will it not
render magistrates servile and fawning to their vicious superiors,
and insolent and tyrannical to their inferiors? Are insolence,
abuse, and impudence more tolerable in a magistrate than in a
subject? Are they not more constantly and extensively pernicious? And does not the example of vice and folly in magistrates
descend and spread downwards among the people?

Besides, is not the insolence of officers and soldiers and sea-
men, in the army and navy, as mischievous as that of porters, or
of sailors in the merchant service? Are not riots raised and made
by armed men as bad as those by unarmed? Is not an assault

upon a civil officer, and a rescue of a prisoner from lawful authority, made by soldiers with swords or bayonets, as bad as if made by tradesmen with staves?

Are not the killing of a child by R.,[1] and the slaughter of half a dozen citizens by a party of soldiers, as bad as pulling down a house or drowning a cargo of tea, even if both should be allowed to be unlawful? Parties may go on declaiming, but it is not easy to say which party has excited most riots, which has published most libels, which has propagated most slander and defamation? Verbal scandal has been propagated in great abundance by both parties; but there is this difference, that one party have enjoyed almost all public offices, and therefore their defamation has been spread among the people more secretly, more maliciously, and more effectually. It has gone with greater authority, and been scattered by instruments more industrious. The ministerial newspapers have swarmed with as numerous and as malicious libels as the antiministerial ones. Fleet's paper, "Mein's Chronicle,"[2] etc., etc., have been as virulent as any that was ever in the province. These bickerings of opposite parties, and their mutual reproaches, their declamations, their sing-song, their triumphs and defiances, their dismals and prophecies, are all delusion.

We very seldom hear any solid reasoning. I wish always to discuss the question without all painting, pathos, rhetoric, or flourish of every kind. And the question seems to me to be, whether the American colonies are to be considered as a distinct community so far as to have a right to judge for themselves when the fundamentals of their government are destroyed or invaded, or whether they are to be considered as a part of the whole British empire, the whole English nation, so far as to be bound in honor, conscience, or interest by the general sense of the whole nation. However, if this was the rule, I believe it is very far from the general sense of the whole nation, that America should be taxed by the British parliament. If the sense of the whole of the empire could be fairly and truly collected, it would appear, I believe, that a great majority would be against taxing us against or without our consent. It is very certain that the sense of parliament is not the sense of the empire, nor a sure indication of it.

But, if all other parts of the empire were agreed unanimously in the propriety and rectitude of taxing us, this would not bind us. It is a fundamental, inherent, and unalienable right of the people, that they have some check, influence, or control in their supreme legislature. If the right of taxation is conceded to Parliament, the Americans have no check or influence at all left.

This reasoning never was nor can be answered.

9. JOHN ADAMS

Falmouth, 6 July 1774

Our Justice Hutchinson[1] is eternally giving his political hints. In a cause this morning, somebody named Captain Mackay as a referee. I said, "An honest man?" "Yes," says Hutchinson, "he's an honest man, only *misled*"—"he, he, he!"—blinking and grinning. At dinner today somebody mentioned determinations in the Lord's House (the Court sits in the meeting-house). "I've known many very bad determinations in the Lord's house of late," says he, meaning a fling upon the clergy. He is perpetually flinging about the Fasts, and ironically talking about getting home to the Fast. A gentleman told me that he had heard him say frequently that the Fast was perfect blasphemy. "Why don't you pay for the tea? Refuse to pay for the tea! and go to fasting and praying for direction! Perfect blasphemy!"

This is the moderation, candor, impartiality, prudence, patience, forbearance, and condescension of our Judge.

Samuel Quincy said yesterday, as Josiah told me, he was for staying at home and not going to meeting as they, i.e., the meetings, are so managed.

Such is the bitterness and rancor, the malice and revenge, the pride and vanity, which prevail in these men. And such minds are possessed of all the power of the province.

Samuel makes no fortune this court. There is very little business here, it is true, but S. gets but very little of that little—less than anybody.

Wyer retains his old good nature and good humor, his wit, such as it is, and his fancy, with its mildness. Bradbury retains his anxiety, and his plaintive, angry manner; David Sewall his softness and conceited modesty.

Bradbury and Sewall always roast Dr. Gardiner at these

courts, but they have done it more now than usual, as Gardiner had not me to protect him. See how I think of myself!

I believe it is time to think a little about my family and farm. The fine weather we have had for eight or ten days past I hope has been carefully improved to get in my hay. It is a great mortification to me that I could not attend every step of their progress in mowing, making, and carting. I long to see what burden. But I long more still to see to the procuring more sea-weed, and marsh mud, and sand, etc.

However, my prospect is interrupted again. I shall have no time. I must prepare for a journey to Philadelphia, a long journey indeed! But if the length of the journey were all, it would be no burden. But the consideration of what is to be done is of great weight. Great things are wanted to be done, and little things only I fear can be done. I dread the thought of the Congress' falling short of the expectations of the continent, but especially of the people of this province.

Vapors avaunt! I will do my duty, and leave the event. If I have the approbation of my own mind, whether applauded or censured, blessed or cursed, by the world, I will not be unhappy.

Certainly I shall enjoy good company, good conversation, and shall have a fine ride and see a little more of the world than I have seen before.

I think it will be necessary to make me up a couple of pieces of new linen. I am told they wash miserably at New York, the Jerseys, and Philadelphia too in comparison of Boston, and am advised to carry a great deal of linen. Whether to make me a suit of new clothes at Boston or to make them at Philadelphia, and what to make, I know not, nor do I know how I shall go—whether on horseback, in a curricle, a phaeton, or altogether in a stagecoach I know not.

The letters I have written, or may write, my dear, must be kept secret, or at least shown with great caution. Mr. Fairservice goes tomorrow: by him shall send a packet. Kiss my dear babes for me.

    Your   JOHN ADAMS

I believe I forgot to tell you one anecdote. When first came to this house it was late in the afternoon, and I had ridden thirty-five miles at least. "Madam," said I to Mrs. Huston, "is it lawful for a weary traveller to refresh himself with a dish of tea, provided it has been honestly smuggled, or paid no duties?" "No, sir," said she, "we have renounced all tea in this place, but I'll make you coffee." Accordingly I have drank coffee every afternoon since, and have borne it very well. Tea must be universally renounced, and I must be weaned, and the sooner the better.

10. JOHN ADAMS

Falmouth, 7 July 1774

Have you seen a list of the addressers of the late Governor?[1] There is one abroad, with the character, profession, or occupation of each person against his name. I have never seen it, but Judge Brown says against the name of Andrew Faneuil Phillips is "Nothing." And that Andrew, when he first heard of it, said, "Better be nothing with one side than everything with the other."

This was witty and smart, whether Andrew said it or what is more likely, it was made for him. A notion prevails among all parties that it is politest and genteelest to be on the side of administration; that the better sort, the wiser few, are on one side, and that the multitude, the vulgar, the herd, the rabble, the mob only, are on the other. So difficult is it for the frail, feeble mind of man to shake itself loose from all prejudice and habits. However, Andrew or his prompter is perfectly right in his judgment, and will finally be proved to be, so that the lowest on the Tory scale will make it more for his interest than the highest on the Whiggish. And as long as a man adheres immovably to his own interest and has understanding or luck enough to secure and promote it, he will have the character of a man of sense, and will be respected by a selfish world. I know of no better reason for it than this, that most men are conscious that they aim at their own interest only, and that if they fail it is owing to short sight or ill luck, and therefore they can't blame, but secretly applaud, admire, and sometimes envy those whose capacities have proved greater and fortunes more prosperous.

I am engaged in a famous cause,—the cause of King, of Scarborough,[2] *versus* a mob that broke into his house and rifled his papers and terrified him, his wife, children and servants in the night. The terror and distress, the distraction and horror of his family cannot be described by words or painted upon canvas. It is enough to move a statue, to melt a heart of stone, to read the story. A mind susceptible of the feelings of humanity, a heart which can be touched with sensibility for human misery and wretchedness, must reluct, must burn with resentment and indignation at such outrageous injuries. These private mobs I do and will detest. If popular commotions can be justified in opposition to attacks upon the Constitution, it can be only when fundamentals are invaded, nor then unless for absolute necessity, and with great caution. But these tarrings and featherings, this breaking open houses by rude and insolent rabble in resentment for private wrongs, or in pursuance of private prejudices and passions, must be discountenanced. It cannot be even excused upon any principle which can be entertained by a good citizen, a worthy member of society.

Dined with Mr. Collector Francis Waldo, Esquire,[3] in company with Mr. Winthrop, the two Quincys, and the two Sullivans, all very social and cheerful—full of politics. S. Quincy's tongue ran as fast as anybody's. He was clear in it, that the House of Commons had no right to take money out of our pockets more than any foreign state; repeated large paragraphs from a publication of Mr. Burke's in 1766, and large paragraphs from Junius Americanus,[4] etc. This is to talk and to shine before persons who have no capacity of judging, and who do not know that he is ignorant of every rope in the ship.

I shan't be able to get away till next week. I am concerned only in two or three cases, and none of them are come on yet. Such an Eastern circuit I never made. I shall bring home as much as I brought from home, I hope, and not much more, I fear. I go mourning in my heart all the day long, though I say nothing. I am melancholy for the public and anxious for my family. As for myself, a frock and trousers, a hoe and a spade would do for my remaining days.

For God's sake make your children *hardy, active,* and *industrious;* for strength, activity and industry will be their only resource and dependence.

11. JOHN ADAMS

9 July 1774

I never enjoyed better health in any of my journeys, but this has been the most irksome, the most gloomy and melancholy I ever made. I cannot with all my philosophy and Christian resignation keep up my spirits. The dismal prospect before me, my family, and my country, is too much for my fortitude.

> "Bear me, some god! Oh quickly bear me hence,
> To wholesome solitude, the nurse of sense;
> Where Contemplation prunes her ruffled wings,
> And the free soul looks down to pity kings."[1]

The day before yesterday a gentleman came and spoke to me, asked me to dine with him on Saturday; said he was very sorry I had not better lodgings in town; desired, if I came to town again, I would take a bed at his house and make his house my home; I should always be very welcome. I told him I had not the pleasure of knowing him. He said his name was Codman.[2] I said I was very much obliged to him, but I was very well accommodated where I lodged. I had a clean bed and a very neat house, a chamber to myself, and everything I wanted.

Saturday, I dined with him, in company with Brigadier Preble, Major Freeman[3] and his son, etc., and a very genteel dinner we had. Salt fish and all its apparatus, roast chickens, bacon, pease, as fine a salad as ever was made, and a rich meat pie. Tarts and custards, etc., good wine, and as good punch as ever you made. A large, spacious, elegant house, yard, and garden; I thought I had got into the palace of a nobleman. After dinner, when I was obliged to come away, he renewed his invitation to me to make his house my home whenever I shall come to town again.

Friday I dined with Colonel, Sheriff, alias Bill Tyng.[4] Mrs. Ross and her daughter Mrs. Tyng dined with us, and the court and clerk, and some of the bar. At table we were speaking about Captain MacCarty,[5] which led to the African trade. Judge Trowbridge said, "That was a very humane and Christian trade, to be sure, that of making slaves." "Aye," says I, "it makes no great odds; it is a trade that almost all mankind have been concerned in, all over the globe, since Adam, more or less, in one way and another." This occasioned a laugh.

At another time Judge Trowbridge said, "It seems, by Colonel Barré's speeches, that Mr. Otis has acquired honor by releasing his damages to Robinson."[6] "Yes," says I, "he has acquired honor with all generations." Trowbridge: "He did not make much profit, I think." Adams: "True, but the less profit, the more honor. He was a man of honor and generosity, and those who think he was mistaken will pity him."

Thus you see how foolish I am. I cannot avoid exposing myself before these high folks; my feelings will at times overcome my modesty and reserve, my prudence, policy, and discretion. I have a zeal at my heart for my country and her friends, which I cannot smother or conceal; it will burn out at times and in companies where it ought to be latent in my breast. This zeal will prove fatal to the fortune and felicity of my family, if it is not regulated by a cooler judgment than mine has hitherto been. Colonel Otis's phrase[7] is, "The zeal-pot boils over."

I am to wait upon brother Bradbury to meeting to-day, and to dine with brother Wyer. When I shall get home, I know not, but if possible, it shall be before next Saturday night. I long for that time to come, when my dear wife and my charming little prattlers will embrace me.

Your   JOHN ADAMS

12. ABIGAIL ADAMS

Braintree, 15 August 1774

I know not where this will find you, whether upon the road or at Philadelphia, but wherever it is, I hope it will find you in good health and spirits. Your journey, I imagine, must have been very tedious from the extreme heat of the weather and the dustiness of the roads. We are burnt up with the drought, having had no rain since you left us, nor is there the least appearance of any.

I was much gratified upon the return of some of your friends from Watertown,[1] who gave me an account of your social dinner and friendly parting. May your return merit and meet with the grateful acknowledgments of every well-wisher to their country. Your task is difficult and important. Heaven direct and prosper you. I find from Mr. A——r, of B——r,[2] that the Chief Justice is determined to take his seat and that the court shall proceed to business if possible; even though the sheriff should be obliged to return no other but the late addressers. He talks as he always used to; sometimes one thing, sometimes another; pretends the money would not be collected in that town for the Congress if he had not exerted himself, though it seems he stayed till the eleventh hour, and it did not get to town before you left it. I found by a hint he dropped that he used all his influence to suppress the non-consumption agreement which some of them had drawn up to sign, and that he has enlisted himself entirely under the influence of the Chief Justice. He also expresses great bitterness against C——l W——n, of P——h,[3] for encouraging young Morton[4] to settle there; seems gratified with the thought of his losing his place, etc.

So much for politics. Now for our own domestic affairs. Mr. Rice came this afternoon. He and Mr. Thaxter are settled over at the office. Crosby[5] has given up the school, and as it is to move to the other parish Mr. Rice cannot have it. I must therefore agree with them to take the care of John and school him with them, which will perhaps be better for him than going to the town school.

I shall reckon over every week as they pass, and rejoice at every Saturday evening. I hope to hear from you by Mr. Cunningham[6] when he returns, though I know not when that will be; but he was so kind as to send me word that he was going and would take a letter for me.

Our little ones send their duty to their papa, and that which at all times and in all places evermore attends you is the most affectionate regard of your   ABIGAIL ADAMS

13. ABIGAIL ADAMS

Braintree, 19 August 1774

The great distance between us makes the time appear very long to me. It seems already a month since you left me. The great anxiety I feel for my country, for you, and for our family renders the day tedious and the night unpleasant. The rocks and quicksands appear upon every side. What course you can or will take is all wrapped in the bosom of futurity. Uncertainty and expectation leave the mind great scope. Did ever any kingdom or state regain its liberty, when once it was invaded, without bloodshed? I cannot think of it without horror. Yet we are told that all the misfortunes of Sparta were occasioned by their too great solicitude for present tranquillity, and, from an excessive love of peace, they neglected the means of making it sure and lasting. They ought to have reflected, says Polybius,[1] that, "as there is nothing more desirable or advantageous than peace, when founded in justice and honor, so there is nothing more shameful, and at the same time more pernicious, when attained by bad measures and purchased at the price of liberty." I have received a most charming letter from our friend Mrs. Warren.[2] She desires me to tell you that her best wishes attend you through your journey, both as a friend and a patriot,—hopes you will have no uncommon difficulties to surmount, or hostile movements to impede you, but, if the Locrians[3] should interrupt you, she hopes that you will beware, that no future annals may say you chose an ambitious Philip for your leader, who subverted the noble order of the American Amphictyons, and built up a monarchy on the ruins of the happy institution.

I have taken a very great fondness for reading Rollin's Ancient History[4] since you left me. I am determined to go through with it, if possible, in these my days of solitude. I find great pleasure and entertainment from it, and I have persuaded Johnny to read me a page or two every day, and hope he will, from his desire to oblige me, entertain a fondness for it. We have had a charming rain, which lasted twelve hours and has greatly revived the dying fruits of the earth.

I want much to hear from you. I long impatiently to have you upon the stage of action. The first of September, or the month of September, perhaps, may be of as much importance to Great Britain as the Ides of March were to Caesar. I wish you every public as well as private blessing, and that wisdom which is profitable both for instruction and edification, to conduct you in this

difficult day. The little flock remember papa, and kindly wish to
see him; so does your most affectionate

ABIGAIL ADAMS

14. JOHN ADAMS

Princeton, New Jersey, 28 August 1774

I received your kind letter at New York, and it is not easy for you
to imagine the pleasure it has given me. I have not found a single
opportunity to write since I left Boston, excepting by the post,
and I don't choose to write by that conveyance, for fear of foul
play. But as we are now within forty-two miles of Philadelphia,
I hope there to find some private hand by which I can convey
this.

The particulars of our journey I must reserve, to be communicated after my return. It would take a volume to describe the
whole. It has been upon the whole an agreeable jaunt. We have
had opportunities to see the world and to form acquaintances
with the most eminent and famous men in the several colonies
we have passed through. We have been treated with unbounded
civility, complaisance, and respect. We yesterday visited Nassau
Hall College,[1] and were politely treated by the scholars, tutors,
professors, and president, whom we are this day to hear preach.
To-morrow we reach the theatre of action. God Almighty grant
us wisdom and virtue sufficient for the high trust that is devolved
upon us. The spirit of the people, wherever we have been, seems
to be very favorable. They universally consider our cause as their
own, and express the firmest resolution to abide by the determination of the Congress.

I am anxious for our perplexed, distressed province; hope they
will be directed into the right path. Let me entreat you, my dear,
to make yourself as easy and quiet as possible. Resignation to
the will of Heaven is our only resource in such dangerous times.
Prudence and caution should be our guides. I have the strongest
hopes that we shall yet see a clearer sky and better times.

Remember my tender love to little Nabby; tell her she must
write me a letter and inclose it in the next you send. I am charmed

with your amusement with our little Johnny. Tell him I am glad to hear he is so good a boy as to read to his mamma for her entertainment, and to keep himself out of the company of rude children. Tell him I hope to hear a good account of his accidence[2] and nomenclature when I return. Remember me to all inquiring friends, particularly to uncle Quincy, your papa and family, and Dr. Tufts[3] and family. Mr. Thaxter, I hope, is a good companion in your solitude. Tell him, if he devotes his soul and body to his books, I hope, notwithstanding the darkness of these days, he will not find them unprofitable sacrifices in future. I have received three very obliging letters from Tudor, Trumbull, and Hill.[4] They have cheered us in our wanderings and done us much service. My compliments to Mr. Wibird[5] and Colonel Quincy, when you see them.

Your account of the rain refreshed me. I hope our husbandry is prudently and industriously managed. Frugality must be our support. Our expenses in this journey will be very great. Our only reward will be the consolatory reflection that we toil, spend our time, and tempt dangers for the public good—happy indeed if we do any good.

The education of our children is never out of my mind. Train them to virtue. Habituate them to industry, activity, and spirit. Make them consider every vice as shameful and unmanly. Fire them with ambition to be useful. Make them disdain to be destitute of any useful or ornamental knowledge or accomplishment. Fix their ambition upon great and solid objects, and their contempt upon little, frivolous, and useless ones. It is time, my dear, for you to begin to teach them French. Every decency, grace, and honesty should be inculcated upon them.

I have kept a few minutes by way of journal,[6] which shall be your entertainment when I come home; but we have had so many persons and so various characters to converse with, and so many objects to view, that I have not been able to be so particular as I could wish. I am, with the tenderest affection and concern,

    Your wandering   JOHN ADAMS

15. ABIGAIL ADAMS

Braintree, 2 September 1774

I am very impatient to receive a letter from you. You indulged
me so much in that way in your last absence, that I now think I
have a right to hear as often from you as you have leisure and
opportunity to write. I hear that Mr. Adams wrote to his son,
and the Speaker[1] to his lady; but perhaps you did not know of
the opportunity. I suppose you have before this time received
two letters from me, and will write me by the same conveyance.
I judge you reached Philadelphia last Saturday night. I cannot
but felicitate you upon your absence a little while from this scene
of perturbation, anxiety, and distress. I own I feel not a little agitated with the accounts I have this day received from town;
great commotions have arisen in consequence of a discovery of a
traitorous plot of Colonel Brattle's,[2]—his advice to Gage to break
every commissioned officer and to seize the province's and town's
stock of gunpowder. This has so enraged and exasperated the
people that there is great apprehension of an immediate rupture.
They have been all in flames ever since the new-fangled counselors have taken their oaths. The importance, with which they
consider the meeting of the Congress, and the result thereof to
the community withholds the arm of vengeance already lifted,
but which would most certainly fall with accumulated wrath
upon Brattle, were it possible to come at him; but no sooner did
he discover that his treachery had taken air than he fled, not only
to Boston, but into the camp, for safety. You will, by Mr. Tudor,
no doubt have a much more accurate account than I am able to
give you; but one thing I can inform you of which perhaps you
may not have heard, namely, Mr. Vinton, our sheriff, it seems, received one of those twenty warrants which were issued by Messrs.
Goldthwait and Price,[3] which has cost them such bitter repentance and humble acknowledgments, and which has revealed the
great secret of their attachment to the liberties of their country,
and their veneration and regard for the good-will of their countrymen. See their address to Hutchinson and Gage. This warrant,
which was for Stoughtonham,[4] Vinton carried and delivered to a
constable there, but before he had got six miles he was overtaken

by sixty men on horseback, who surrounded him and told him unless he returned with them and demanded back that warrant and committed it to the flames before their faces, he must take the consequences of a refusal; and he, not thinking it best to endure their vengeance, returned with them, made his demand of the warrant, and consumed it, upon which they dispersed and left him to his own reflections. Since the news of the Quebec bill[5] arrived, all the Church people here have hung their heads and will not converse upon politics, though ever so much provoked by the opposite party. Before that, parties ran very high, and very hard words and threats of blows upon both sides were given out. They have had their town-meeting here, which was full as usual, chose their committee for the county meeting, and did business without once regarding or fearing for the consequences.

I should be glad to know how you found the people as you travelled from town to town. I hear you met with great hospitality and kindness in Connecticut. Pray let me know how your health is, and whether you have not had exceeding hot weather. The drought has been very severe. My poor cows will certainly prefer a petition to you, setting forth their grievances and informing you that they have been deprived of their ancient privileges, whereby they are become great sufferers, and desiring that they may be restored to them. More especially as their living, by reason of the drought, is all taken from them, and their property which they hold elsewhere is decaying, they humbly pray that you would consider them, lest hunger should break through stone walls.

Our little flock are well, and present their duty to their papa. My mother is in a very low state occasioned by a return of her old complaints. Nabby has enclosed a letter to you—would be glad I would excuse the writing, because of a sore thumb, which she has.

The tenderest regard evermore awaits you from your most affectionate   ABIGAIL ADAMS

16. JOHN ADAMS

Philadelphia, 8 September 1774

When or where this letter will find you I know not. In what scenes of distress and terror I cannot foresee. We have received a confused account from Boston of a dreadful catastrophe.[1] The particulars we have not heard. We are waiting with the utmost anxiety and impatience for further intelligence. The effect of the news we have, both upon the Congress and the inhabitants of this city, was very great. Great indeed! Every gentleman seems to consider the bombardment of Boston as the bombardment of the capital of his own province. Our deliberations are grave and serious indeed.

It is a great affliction to me that I cannot write to you oftener than I do. But there are so many hindrances that I cannot. It would fill volumes to give you an idea of the scenes I behold, and the characters I converse with. We have so much business, so much ceremony, so much company, so many visits to receive and return, that I have not time to write. And the times are such as to make it imprudent to write freely.

We cannot depart from this place until the business of the Congress is completed, and it is the general disposition to proceed slowly. When I shall be at home I can't say. If there is distress and danger in Boston, pray invite our friends, as many as possible, to take an asylum with you,—Mrs. Cushing and Mrs. Adams, if you can. There is in the Congress a collection of the greatest men upon this continent in point of abilities, virtues, and fortunes. The magnanimity and public spirit which I see here make me blush for the sordid, venal herd which I have seen in my own province. The addressers, and the new councillors,[2] are held in universal contempt and abhorrence from one end of the continent to the other.

Be not under any concern for me. There is little danger from anything we shall do at the Congress. There is such a spirit through the colonies, and the members of the Congress are such characters, that no danger can happen to us which will not involve the whole continent in universal desolation; and in that case, who would wish to live?

Make my Compliments to Mr. Thaxter and Mr. Rice—and to every other of my friends. My love to all my dear children—tell them to be good, and to mind their books. I shall come home and see them, I hope, the latter end of next month. Adieu.

P.S. You will judge how things are like to be in Boston, and whether it will not be best to remove the office entirely to Braintree. Mr. Hill and Williams may come up, if they choose, paying for their board.

17. JOHN ADAMS

Philadelphia, 14 September 1774

I have written but once to you since I left you. This is to be imputed to a variety of causes, which I cannot explain for want of time. It would fill volumes to give you an exact idea of the whole tour. My time is totally filled from the moment I get out of bed until I return to it. Visits, ceremonies, company, business, newspapers, pamphlets, etc., etc., etc.

The Congress will, to all present appearance, be well united, and in such measures as, I hope, will give satisfaction to the friends of our country. A Tory here is the most despicable animal in the creation. Spiders, toads, snakes are their only proper emblems. The Massachusetts councillors and addressers are held in curious esteem here, as you will see. The spirit, the firmness, the prudence of our province are vastly applauded, and we are universally acknowledged the saviours and defenders of American liberty. The designs and plans of the Congress must not be communicated until completed, and we shall move with great deliberation.

When I shall come home I know not, but at present I do not expect to take my leave of this city these four weeks. My compliments, love, service, where they are due. My babes are never out of my mind, nor absent from my heart. Adieu.

18. ABIGAIL ADAMS

Braintree, 14 September 1774

Five weeks have passed and not one line have I received. I would rather give a dollar for a letter by the post,[1] though the consequence should be that I ate but one meal a day these three weeks to come. Every one I see is inquiring after you, when did I hear. All my intelligence is collected from the newspaper, and I can only reply that I saw by that, you arrived such a day. I know your fondness for writing, and your inclination to let me hear from you by the first safe conveyance, which makes me suspect that some letter or other has miscarried; but I hope, now you have arrived at Philadelphia, you will find means to convey me some intelligence.

We are all well here. I think I enjoy better health than I have done these two years. I have not been to town since I parted with you there. The Governor is making all kinds of warlike preparations, such as mounting cannon upon Beacon Hill, digging intrenchments upon the Neck, placing cannon there, encamping a regiment there, throwing up breast-works, etc. The people are much alarmed, and the selectmen have waited upon him in consequence of it. The County Congress[2] have also sent a committee; all which proceedings you will have a more particular account of than I am able to give you, from the public papers. But as to the movements of this town, perhaps you may not hear them from any other person.

In consequence of the powder being taken from Charlestown, a general alarm spread through many towns and was caught pretty soon here. The report took here on Friday, and on Sunday a soldier was seen lurking about the Common, supposed to be a spy, but most likely a deserter. However, intelligence of it was communicated to the other parishes, and about eight o'clock Sunday evening there passed by here about two hundred men, preceded by a horsecart, and marched down to the powder-house, from whence they took the powder, and carried it into the other parish and there secreted it. I opened the window upon their return. They passed without any noise, not a word among them till they came against this house, when some of them, perceiving me, asked me if I wanted any powder. I replied, No, since it was in so good hands. The reason they gave for taking it was that we had so many Tories here, they dared not trust us with it; they had taken Vinton in their train, and upon their return they stopped between Cleverly's and Etter's, and called upon him to deliver two warrants. Upon his producing them, they put it to vote whether they should burn them, and it passed in the affirmative. They then made a circle and burnt them. They then called a vote whether they should huzza, but, it being Sunday evening, it passed in the negative. They called upon Vinton to swear that he would never be instrumental in carrying into execution any of these new acts. They were not satisfied with his answers; however, they let him rest. A few days afterwards, upon his making some foolish speeches, they assembled to the amount of two or three hundred, and swore vengeance upon him unless he took a solemn oath. Accordingly, they chose a committee and sent it with him to Major Miller's[3] to see that he complied; and they waited his return, which proving satisfactory, they dispersed. This town appears as high as you can well imagine, and, if necessary, would soon be in arms. Not a Tory but hides his head. The church parson thought they were coming after him, and ran up garret; they say another jumped out of his window and hid among the corn, whilst a third crept under his board fence and told his beads.

16 September 1774

I dined to-day at Colonel Quincy's. They were so kind as to send me and Nabby and Betsey an invitation to spend the day with them; and, as I had not been to see them since I removed to Braintree, I accepted the invitation. After I got there came Mr. Samuel Quincy's wife and Mr. Sumner, Mr. Josiah and wife.[4] A little clashing of parties, you may be sure. Mr. Sam's wife said she thought it high time for her husband to turn about; he had not done half so cleverly since he left her advice; said they both greatly admired the most excellent speech of the Bishop of St. Asaph,[5] which I suppose you have seen. It meets, and most certainly merits, the greatest encomiums.

Upon my return at night, Mr. Thaxter met me at the door with your letter, dated at Princeton, New Jersey. It really gave me such a flow of spirits that I was not composed enough to sleep until one o'clock. You make no mention of one I wrote you previous to that you received by Mr. Breck, and sent by Mr. Cunningham. I am rejoiced to hear you are well. I want to know many more particulars than you write me, and hope soon to hear from you again. I dare not trust myself with the thought how long you may perhaps be absent. I only count the weeks already past, and they amount to five. I am not so lonely as I should have been without my two neighbors;[6] we make a table-full at meal times. All the rest of their time they spend in the office. Never were two persons who gave a family less trouble than they do. It is at last determined that Mr. Rice keep the school here. Indeed, he has kept ever since he has been here, but not with any expectation that he should be continued; but the people, finding no small difference between him and his predecessor, chose he should be continued. I have not sent Johnny. He goes very steadily to Mr. Thaxter, who I believe takes very good care of him; and as they seem to have a liking to each other, I believe it will be best to continue him with him. However, when you return, we can consult what will be best. I am certain that, if he does not get so much good, he gets less harm; and I have always thought it of very great importance that children should, in the early part of life, be unaccustomed to such examples as would tend to corrupt the purity of their words and actions, that they may chill with horror at the sound of an oath, and blush with indignation at an obscene expression. These first principles, which grow with their growth, and strengthen with their strength, neither time nor custom can totally eradicate.

You will perhaps be tired. No. Let it serve by way of relaxation from the more important concerns of the day, and be such an amusement as your little hermitage used to afford you here. You have before you, to express myself in the words of the bishop, the greatest national concerns that ever came before any people; and if the prayers and petitions ascend unto heaven which are daily offered for you, wisdom will flow down as a stream, and righteousness as the mighty waters, and your deliberations will make glad the cities of our God.[7]

I was very sorry I did not know of Mr. Cary's going; it would have been so good an opportunity to have sent this, as I lament the loss of. You have heard, no doubt, of the people's preventing the court from sitting in various counties; and last week, in Taunton, Angier urged the court's opening and calling out the actions, but could not effect it. I saw a letter from Miss Eunice,[8] wherein she gives an account of it, and says there were two thousand men assembled round the court-house, and, by a committee of nine, presented a petition requesting that they would not sit, and with the utmost order waited two hours for their answer, when they dispersed.

Your family all desire to be remembered to you, as well as uncle Quincy who often visits me, to have an hour of sweet communion upon politics with me. Colonel Quincy desires his compliments to you. Dr. Tufts sends his love and your mother and brothers also. I have lived a very recluse life since your absence, seldom going anywhere except to my father's, who with my mother and sister desire to be remembered to you. My mother has been exceeding low, but is a little better.

How warm your climate may be I know not, but I have had my bed warmed these two nights.

I must request you to procure me some watermelon seeds and muskmelon, as I determine to be well stocked with them another year. We have had some fine rains, but as soon as the corn is gathered you must release me of my promise. The drought has rendered cutting a second crop impracticable; feeding a little cannot hurt it. However, I hope you will be at home to be convinced of the utility of the measure.—You will burn all these letters, lest they should fall from your pocket, and thus expose your most affectionate friend.

19. JOHN ADAMS

Philadelphia, 16 September 1774

Having a leisure moment, while the Congress is assembling, I gladly embrace it to write you a line.

When the Congress first met, Mr. Cushing made a motion that it should be opened with prayer. It was opposed by Mr. Jay, of New York, and Mr. Rutledge,[1] of South Carolina, because we were so divided in religious sentiments, some Episcopalians, some Quakers, some Anabaptists, some Presbyterians, and some Congregationalists, that we could not join in the same act of worship. Mr. Samuel Adams arose and said he was no bigot, and could hear a prayer from a gentleman of piety and virtue, who was at the same time a friend to his country. He was a stranger in Philadelphia, but had heard that Mr. Duché[2] (Dushay they pronounce it) deserved that character, and therefore he moved that Mr. Duché, an Episcopal clergyman, might be desired to read prayers to the Congress, to-morrow morning. The motion was seconded and passed in the affirmative. Mr. Randolph, our president, waited on Mr. Duché, and received for answer that if his health would permit he certainly would. Accordingly, next morning he appeared with his clerk and in his pontificals, and read several prayers in the established form; and then read the Collect for the seventh day of September, which was the thirty-fifth Psalm. You must remember this was the next morning after we heard the horrible rumor of the cannonade of Boston. I never saw a greater effect upon an audience. It seemed as if Heaven had ordained that Psalm to be read on that morning.

After this, Mr. Duché, unexpected to everybody, struck out into an extemporary prayer, which filled the bosom of every man present. I must confess I never heard a better prayer, or one so well pronounced. Episcopalian as he is, Dr. Cooper[3] himself never prayed with such fervor, such ardor, such earnestness and pathos, and in language so elegant and sublime—for America, for the Congress, for the Province of Massachusetts Bay, and especially the town of Boston. It has had an excellent effect upon everybody here. I must beg you to read that Psalm. If there was any faith in the sortes Virgilianae, or sortes Homericae, or especially the Sortes Biblicae,[4] it would be thought providential.

It will amuse your friends to read this letter and the thirty-fifth Psalm to them. Read it to your father and Mr. Wibird. I wonder what our Braintree Churchmen will think of this! Mr. Duché is one of the most ingenious men, and best characters, and greatest orators in the Episcopal order, upon this continent. Yet a zealous friend of Liberty and his country.

I long to see my dear family. God bless, preserve, and prosper it. Adieu.

20. JOHN ADAMS

Philadelphia, 18 September 1774

In your last you inquire tenderly after my health, and how we found the people upon our journey, and how we were treated.

I have enjoyed as good health as usual, and much more than I know how to account for, when I consider the extreme heat of the weather and the incessant feasting I have endured ever since I left Boston.

The people in Connecticut, New York, the Jerseys, and Pennsylvania we have found extremely well principled and very well inclined, although some persons in New York and Philadelphia wanted a little animation. Their zeal, however, has increased wonderfully since we began our journey.

When the horrid news was brought here of the bombardment of Boston, which made us completely miserable for two days, we saw proofs both of the sympathy and the resolution of the continent.

War! war! war! was the cry, and it was pronounced in a tone which would have done honor to the oratory of a Briton or a Roman.

If it had proved true, you would have heard the thunder of an American Congress.

I have not time nor language to express the hospitality and civility, the studied and expensive respect, with which we have been treated in every stage of our progress. If Camden, Chatham, Richmond, and St. Asaph[1] had travelled through the country, they could not have been entertained with greater demonstrations of respect than Cushing, Paine, and the brace of Adamses have been.

The particulars will amuse you when we return.

I confess, the kindness, the affection, the applause, which have been given to me, and especially to our province, have many a time filled my bosom and streamed from my eyes.

My best respects to Colonel Warren and his lady when you write to them. I wish to write to them. Adieu.

21. JOHN ADAMS

18 September 1774

I received your very agreeable letter by Mr. Marston, and have received two others, which gave me much pleasure. I have wrote several letters, but whether they have reached you I know not. There is so much rascality in the management of letters now come in fashion, that I am determined to write nothing of consequence, not even to the friend of my bosom, but by conveyances which I can be sure of. The proceedings of the Congress are all a profound secret as yet, except two votes which were passed yesterday, and ordered to be printed. You will see them from every quarter. These votes were passed in full Congress with perfect unanimity. The esteem, the affection, the admiration for the people of Boston and the Massachusetts which were expressed yesterday,[1] and the fixed determination that they should be supported, were enough to melt a heart of stone. I saw the tears gush into the eyes of the old grave pacific Quakers of Pennsylvania. You cannot conceive, my dear, the hurry of business, visits, ceremonies, which we are obliged to go through.

We have a delicate course to steer between too much activity and too much insensibility in our critical, interested situation. I flatter myself, however, that we shall conduct ourselves in such a manner as to merit the approbation of our country. It has taken us much time to get acquainted with the tempers, views, characters, and designs of persons, and to let them into the circumstances of our province. My dear, do entreat every friend I have to write me. Every line which comes from our friends is greedily inquired after, and our letters have done us vast service. Middlesex and Suffolk have acquired unbounded honor here.

There is no idea of submission here in anybody's head.

Thank my dear Nabby for her letter. Tell her it has given me great spirit. Kiss all my sweet ones for me.

Adieu.

22. JOHN ADAMS

Philadelphia, 20 September 1774

I am very well yet. Write to me as often as you can and send your letters to the office in Boston, or to Mr. Cranch's,[1] whence they will be sent by the first conveyance.

I am anxious to know how you can live without Government. But the experiment must be tried. The evils will not be found so dreadful as you apprehend them. Frugality, my dear, frugality, economy, parsimony, must be our refuge. I hope the ladies are every day diminishing their ornaments, and the gentlemen, too. Let us eat potatoes and drink water; let us wear canvas, and undressed sheepskins, rather than submit to the unrighteous and ignominious domination that is prepared for us.

Tell Brackett[2] I shall make him leave off drinking rum. We can't let him fight yet. My love to my dear ones. Adieu.

23. ABIGAIL ADAMS

Boston Garrison, 24 September 1774

I have just returned from a visit to my brother,[1] with my father, who carried me there the day before yesterday, and called here in my return, to see this much injured town. I view it with much the same sensations that I should the body of a departed friend— having only put off its present glory for to rise finally to a more happy state. I will not despair, but will believe that, our cause being good, we shall finally prevail. The maxim "In time of peace prepare for war" (if this may be called a time of peace) resounds throughout the country. Next Tuesday they are warned at Braintree, all above fifteen and under sixty, to attend with their arms; and to train once a fortnight from that time is a scheme which lies much at heart with many.

Scott[2] has arrived, and brings news that he expected to find all peace and quietness here, as he left them at home. You will have more particulars than I am able to send you, from much better hands.

There has been in town a conspiracy of the negroes. At present it is kept pretty private. It was discovered by one who endeavored to dissuade them from it. He, being threatened with his life, applied to Justice Quincy[3] for protection. They conducted in this way: got an Irishman to draw up a petition to the Governor, telling him they would fight for him, provided he would arm them and engage to liberate them if he conquered. And it is said that he attended so much to it as to consult Percy[4] upon it; and one Lieutenant Small has been very busy and active. There is but little said, and what steps they will take in consequence of it, I know not. I wish most sincerely there was not a slave in the province. It always appeared a most iniquitous scheme to me—to fight ourselves for what we are daily robbing and plundering from those who have as good a right to freedom as we have. You know my mind upon this subject.

I left all our little ones well, and shall return to them to-night. I hope to hear from you by the return of the bearer of this, and by Revere. I long for the day of your return, yet look upon you as much safer where you are—but I know it will not do for you. Not one action has been brought to this court; no business of any sort in your way. All law ceases and the gospel will soon follow, for they are supporters of each other. Adieu. My father hurries me.   Yours most sincerely.

24. JOHN ADAMS

Philadelphia, 25 September 1774

I would not lose the opportunity of writing to you, though I must be short. Tedious indeed is our business—slow as snails. I have not been used to such ways. We sit only before dinner. We dine at four o'clock. We are crowded with a levee in the evening.

Fifty gentlemen meeting together, all strangers, are not acquainted with each other's language, ideas, views, designs. They are, therefore, jealous of each other—fearful, timid, skittish.

25. JOHN ADAMS

Philadelphia, 29 September 1774

Sitting down to write you is a scene almost too tender for the state of my nerves.

It calls up to my view the anxious, distressed state you must be in, amidst the confusion and dangers which surround you. I long to return and administer all the consolation in my power, but when I shall have accomplished all the business I have to do here, I know not, and if it should be necessary to stay here till Christmas, or longer, in order to effect our purposes, I am determined patiently to wait.

Patience, forbearance, long-suffering, are the lessons taught here for our province, and, at the same time, absolute and open resistance to the new Government. I wish I could convince gentlemen of the danger or impracticability of this as fully as I believe it myself. The art and address of ambassadors from a dozen belligerent powers of Europe; nay, of a conclave of cardinals at the election of a Pope; or of the princes in Germany at the choice of an Emperor, would not exceed the specimens we have seen; yet the Congress all profess the same political principles. They all profess to consider our province as suffering in the common cause, and indeed they seem to feel for us as if for themselves. We have had as great questions to discuss as ever engaged the attention of men, and an infinite multitude of them.

I received a very kind letter from Deacon Palmer,[1] acquainting me with Mr. Cranch's designs of removing to Braintree, which I approve very much, and wish I had a house for every family in Boston, and abilities to provide for them in the country. I submit it to you, my dear, whether it would not be best to remove all the books and papers and furniture in the office at Boston up to Braintree. There will be no business there nor anywhere, I suppose, and my young friends can study there better than in Boston, at present.

I shall be killed with kindness in this place. We go to Congress at nine, and there we stay, most earnestly engaged in debates upon the most abstruse mysteries of state, until three in the afternoon; then we adjourn, and go to dine with some of the nobles of Pennsylvania at four o'clock, and feast upon ten thousand delicacies, and sit drinking Madeira, Claret, and Burgundy, till six or seven, and then go home fatigued to death with business, company, and care. Yet I hold it out surprisingly. I drink no cider, but feast upon Philadelphia beer, and porter. A gentleman, one Mr. Hare, has lately set up in this city a manufactory of porter, as good as any that comes from London. I pray we may introduce it into the Massachusetts. It agrees with me, infinitely better than punch, wine, or cider, or any other spirituous liquor.

My love to my dear children one by one. My compliments to Mr. Thaxter, and Rice, and everybody else.

Yours most affectionately.

26. JOHN ADAMS

Philadelphia, 7 October 1774

I thank you for all your kind favors. I wish I could write to you much oftener than I do. I wish I could write to you a dozen letters every day. But the business before me is so arduous, and takes up my time so entirely, that I cannot write oftener. I had the characters and tempers, the principles and views, of fifty gentlemen, total strangers to me, to study, and the trade, policy, and whole interest of a dozen provinces to learn, when I came here. I have multitudes of pamphlets, newspapers, and private letters to read. I have numberless plans of policy and many arguments to consider. I have many visits to make and receive, much ceremony to endure, which cannot be avoided, which, you know, I hate.

There is a great spirit in the Congress. But our people must be peaceable. Let them exercise every day in the week if they will, the more the better. Let them furnish themselves with artillery, arms, and ammunition. Let them follow the maxim which you say they have adopted, "In times of peace prepare for war." But let them avoid war *if possible—if possible,* I say.

Mr. Revere[1] will bring you the doings of the Congress, who are now all around me, debating what advice to give to Boston and the Massachusetts Bay.

We are all well; hope our family is so. Remember me to them all. I have advised you before to remove my office from Boston to Braintree. It is now, I think, absolutely necessary. Let the best care be taken of all books and papers. Tell all my clerks to mind their books and study hard, for their country will stand in need of able counselors. I must give you a general license to make my compliments to all my friends and acquaintances. I have not time to name them particularly. I wish they would all write to me. If they leave letters at Edes and Gill's,[2] they will soon be sent to me.

I long to be at home, but I cannot say when. I will never leave the Congress until it rises, and when it will rise, I cannot say. And indeed I cannot say but we are better here than anywhere. We have fine opportunities here to serve Boston and Massachusetts, by acquainting the whole continent with the true state of them. Our residence here greatly serves the cause. The spirit and principles of liberty here are greatly cherished by our presence and conversation. The elections of last week prove this. Mr. Dickinson was chosen, almost unanimously, a representative of the county. The broad-brims[3] began an opposition to your friend, Mr. Mifflin, because he was too warm in the cause. This instantly alarmed the friends of liberty, and ended in the election of Mr. Mifflin by eleven hundred votes out of thirteen, and in the election of our secretary, Mr. Charles Thomson, to be a burgess with him. This is considered here as a most complete and decisive victory in favor of the American cause. And it is said it will change the balance in the legislature against Mr. Galloway,[4] who has been supposed to sit on the skirts of the American advocates.

Mrs. Mifflin, who is a charming Quaker girl, often inquires kindly after your health.

Adieu, my dear wife. God bless you and yours; so wishes and prays, without ceasing, JOHN ADAMS

27. JOHN ADAMS

9 October 1774

I am wearied to death with the life I lead. The business of the Congress is tedious beyond expression. This assembly is like no other that ever existed. Every man in it is a great man, an orator, a critic, a statesman; and therefore every man upon every question must show his oratory, his criticism, and his political abilities. The consequence of this is that business is drawn and spun out to an immeasurable length. I believe if it was moved and seconded that we should come to a resolution that three and two make five, we should be entertained with logic and rhetoric, law, history, politics, and mathematics, and then—we should pass the resolution unanimously in the affirmative. The perpetual round of feasting, too, which we are obliged to submit to, makes the pilgrimage more tedious to me.

This day I went to Dr. Allison's meeting[1] in the forenoon, and heard the Dr.; a good discourse upon the Lord's supper. This is a Presbyterian meeting. I confess I am not fond of the Presbyterian meetings in this town. I had rather go to Church. We have better sermons, better prayers, better speakers, softer, sweeter music, and genteeler company. And I must confess that the Episcopal church is quite as agreeable to my taste as the Presbyterian. They are both slaves to the domination of the priesthood. I like the Congregational way best, next to that the Independent.

This afternoon, led by curiosity and good company, I strolled away to mother church, or rather to grandmother church. I mean the Romish chapel. I heard a good, short moral essay upon the duty of parents to their children, founded in justice and charity, to take care of their interests, temporal and spiritual. This afternoon's entertainment was to me most awful and affecting; the poor wretches fingering their beads, chanting Latin not a word of which they understood; their pater nosters and ave Marias; their holy water; their crossing themselves perpetually; their bowing to the name of Jesus, whenever they hear it; their bowings and kneelings and genuflections before the altar. The dress of the priest was rich with lace. His pulpit was velvet and gold. The altarpiece was very rich; little images and crucifixes about; wax candles lighted up. But how shall I describe the picture of our Saviour in a frame of marble over the altar, at full length, upon the cross in the agonies, and the blood dropping and streaming from his wounds! The music, consisting of an organ and a choir of singers, went all the afternoon except sermon time. And the assembly chanted most sweetly and exquisitely.

Here is everything which can lay hold of the eye, ear, and

imagination—everything which can charm and bewitch the simple and ignorant. I wonder how Luther ever broke the spell. Adieu.

28. ABIGAIL ADAMS

Braintree, 16 October 1774

MY MUCH LOVED FRIEND,—I dare not express to you, at three hundred miles' distance, how ardently I long for your return. I have some very miserly wishes, and cannot consent to your spending one hour in town, till, at least, I have had you twelve. The idea plays about my heart, unnerves my hand, whilst I write, awakens all the tender sentiments that years have increased and matured, and which, when with me were every day dispensing to you. The whole collected stock of ten weeks' absence knows not how to brook any longer restraint, but will break forth and flow through my pen. May the like sensations enter thy breast, and (spite of all the weighty cares of state) mingle themselves with those I wish to communicate; for, in giving them utterance, I have felt more sincere pleasure than I have known since the 10th of August.[1] Many have been the anxious hours I have spent since that day; the threatening aspect of our public affairs, the complicated distress of this province, the arduous and perplexed business in which you are engaged, have all conspired to agitate my bosom with fears and apprehensions to which I have heretofore been a stranger; and, far from thinking the scene closed, it looks as though the curtain was but just drawn, and only the first scene of the infernal plot disclosed. And whether the end will be tragical, Heaven alone knows. You cannot be, I know, nor do I wish to see you, an inactive spectator; but if the sword be drawn, I bid adieu to all domestic felicity, and look forward to that country where there is neither wars nor rumors of war, in a firm belief, that through the mercy of its King we shall both rejoice there together.

I greatly fear that the arm of treachery and violence is lifted over us, as a scourge and heavy punishment from Heaven for our numerous offenses, and for the misimprovement of our great advantages. If we expect to inherit the blessings of our fathers, we should return a little more to their primitive simplicity of manners, and not sink into inglorious ease. We have too many high-sounding words, and too few actions that correspond with them. I have spent one Sabbath in town since you left me. I saw no difference in respect to ornaments, etc.; but in the country you must look for that virtue, of which you find but small glimmerings in the metropolis. Indeed, they have not the advantages, nor the resolution, to encourage our own manufactories, which people in the country have. To the mercantile part, 'tis considered as throwing away their own bread; but they must retrench their expenses, and be content with a small share of gain, for they will find but few who will wear their livery. As for me, I will seek wool and flax, and work willingly with my hands; and indeed there is occasion for all our industry and economy. You mention the removal of our books, etc., from Boston; I believe they are safe there, and it would incommode the gentlemen to remove them, as they would not then have a place to repair to for study. I suppose they would not choose to be at the expense of boarding out. Mr. Williams, I believe, keeps pretty much with his mother. Mr. Hill's father had some thoughts of removing up to Braintree, provided he could be accommodated with a house, which he finds very difficult.

Mr. Cranch's last determination was to tarry in town unless anything new takes place. His friends in town oppose his removal so much that he is determined to stay. The opinion you have entertained of General Gage is, I believe, just. Indeed, he professes to act only upon the defensive. The people in the country begin to be very anxious for the Congress to rise; they have no idea of the weighty business you have to transact, and their blood boils with indignation at the hostile preparations they are constant witnesses of. Mr. Quincy's so secret departure[2] is matter of various speculation; some say he is deputed by the Congress, others that he is gone to Holland, and the Tories say he is gone to be hanged.

I rejoice at the favorable account you give me of your health. May it be continued to you. My health is much better than it was last fall; some folks say I grow very fat. I venture to write almost anything in this letter, because I know the care of the bearer.[3] He will be most sadly disappointed if you should be broken up before he arrives, as he is very desirous of being introduced by you to a number of gentlemen of respectable character. I almost envy him, that he should see you before I can. Mr. Thaxter and Mr. Rice present their regards to you. Uncle Quincy, too, sends his love to you. He is very good to call and see me, and so have many other of my friends been. Colonel Warren and lady were here on Monday, and send their love to you. The Colonel promised to write. Mrs. Warren will spend a day or two, on her return, with me.

Your mother sends her love to you; and all your family, too numerous to name, desire to be remembered. You will receive letters from two who are as earnest to write to papa as if the welfare of a kingdom depended upon it.* If you can give any guess, within a month, let me know when you think of returning.

Your most affectionate   ABIGAIL ADAMS

29. JOHN ADAMS

Hartford, 30 April 1775

New York has appointed an ample representation in our Congress, and has appointed a Provincial Congress. The people of the city have seized the city arms and ammunition out of the hands of the mayor, who is a creature of the Governor. Lord North will certainly be disappointed in his expectation of seducing New York. The Tories there durst not show their heads. The Jerseys are aroused, and greatly assist the friends of liberty in New York. North Carolina has done bravely; chosen the old del-

---

*[CFA note] One of these letters has been preserved. The writer was at this time seven years old. His subsequent career may make it interesting enough to print. It is written in a tolerably good, boy's hand, as follows:—

October 13, 1774

SIR, — I have been trying ever since you went away to learn to write you a letter. I shall make poor work of it; but, sir, mamma says you will accept my endeavors, and that my duty to you may be expressed in poor writing as well as good. I hope I grow a better boy, and that you will have no occasion to be ashamed of me when you return. Mr. Thaxter says I learn my books well. He is a very good master. I read my books to mamma. We all long to see you. I am, sir, your dutiful son,   JOHN QUINCY ADAMS

egates in Provincial Congress, and then confirmed the choice in
General Assembly, in opposition to all that Governor Martin[1]
could do. The Assembly of this colony is now sitting at Hartford. We are treated with great tenderness, sympathy, friendship,
and respect. Everything is doing by this colony that can be done
by men, both for New York and Boston. Keep your spirits composed and calm, and don't suffer yourself to be disturbed by idle
reports and frivolous alarms. We shall see better times yet. Lord
North is insuring us success. I am wounded to the heart with the
news, this moment told me, of Josiah Quincy's death.

30. JOHN ADAMS

Hartford, 2 May 1775

Our hearts are bleeding for the poor people of Boston. What will
or can be done for them I can't conceive. God preserve them.

I take this opportunity to write, by our committee who were
sent to this colony, just to let you know that I am comfortable,
and shall proceed this afternoon. Pray write to me, and get all
my friends to write, and let me be informed of everything that
occurs. Send your letters to Colonel Palmer or Dr. Warren,[1] who
will convey them. They will reach me sooner or later. This colony
is raising six thousand men. Rhode Island, fifteen hundred. New
York has shut up their port, seized the custom house, arms, ammunition, etc., called a Provincial Congress, and entered into an
association to stand by whatever shall be ordered by the Continental and their Provincial Congress. Dr. Cooper[2] fled on board
a man-of-war, and the Tories are humbled in the dust.

I have just made a visit to your cousin Austin, who is very
well. Tell my brothers I have bought some military books, and
intend to buy more, so that I shall come back qualified to make
them complete officers. Write me whether either of them intends
to take a command in the army. I won't advise them, but leave
them to their own inclinations and discretion. But, if they should
incline, they should apply to Colonel Palmer and Dr. Warren
soon.

31. JOHN ADAMS

Mr. Eliot, of Fairfield,[1] is this moment arrived, on his way to Boston. He read us a letter from the Dr., his father, dated yesterday sennight, being Sunday. The Dr.'s description of the melancholy of the town is enough to melt a stone. The trials of that unhappy and devoted people are likely to be severe indeed. God grant that the furnace of affliction may refine them. God grant that they may be relieved from their present distress.

It is arrogance and presumption, in human sagacity, to pretend to penetrate far into the designs of Heaven. The most perfect reverence and resignation becomes us, but I cannot help depending upon this, that the present dreadful calamity of that beloved town is intended to bind the colonies together in more indissoluble bonds, and to animate their exertions at this great crisis in the affairs of mankind. It has this effect in a most remarkable degree, as far as I have yet seen or heard. It will plead with all America with more irresistible persuasion than angels trumpet-tongued.

In a cause which interests the whole globe, at a time when my friends and country are in such keen distress, I am scarcely ever interrupted in the least degree by apprehensions for my personal safety. I am often concerned for you and our dear babes, surrounded, as you are, by people who are too timorous and too much susceptible of alarms. Many fears and jealousies and imaginary dangers will be suggested to you, but I hope you will not be impressed by them. In case of real danger, of which you cannot fail to have previous intimations, fly to the woods with our children. Give my tenderest love to them, and to all.

32. ABIGAIL ADAMS

Braintree, 4 May 1775

I have but little news to write you. Everything of that kind you will learn by a more accurate hand than mine. Things remain in much the same situation here that they were when you went away. There has been no descent upon the seacoast. Guards are regularly kept, and people seem more settled and are returning to their husbandry. I feel somewhat lonesome. Mr. Thaxter is gone home. Mr. Rice is going into the army, as captain of a company. We have no school. I know not what to do with John. As government is assumed, I suppose courts of justice will be established, and in that case there may be business to do. If so, would it not be best for Mr. Thaxter to return? They seem to be discouraged in the study of law, and think there never will be any business for them. I could have wished they had consulted you upon the subject, before you went away. Mr. Rice has asked my advice. I told him I would have him act his pleasure. I don't choose to advise him either way.

I suppose you will receive two or three volumes of that forlorn wretch Hutchinson's letters. Among many other things, I hear he wrote in 1772, that Deacon Phillips and you had like to have been chosen into the Council, but, if you had, you should have shared the same fate with Bowers.[1] May the fate of Mordecai be his.[2] There is nobody admitted into town yet. I have made two or three attempts to get somebody in, but cannot succeed; so have not been able to do the business you left in charge with me. I want very much to hear from you, how you stood your journey, and in what state you find yourself now. I felt very anxious about you; though I endeavored to be very insensible and heroic, yet my heart felt like a heart of lead. The same night you left me, I heard of Mr. Quincy's death, which, at this time, was a most melancholy event; especially as he wrote in minutes, which he left behind, that he had matters of consequence intrusted with him, which, for want of a confidant, must die with him. I went to see his distressed widow last Saturday, at the Colonel's; and in the afternoon, from an alarm they had, she and her sister, with three others of the family, took refuge with me and tarried all night. She desired me to present her regards to you, and let you know she wished you every blessing,—should always esteem you as a sincere friend of her deceased husband. Poor, afflicted woman; my heart was wounded for her. I must quit the subject, and entreat you to write me by every opportunity. Your mother desires to be remembered to you. She is with me now. The children send duty, and their mamma unfeigned love.

Yours,   PORTIA

33. ABIGAIL ADAMS

7 May 1775

I received by the Deacon two letters from you, this day, from Hartford. I feel a recruit of spirits upon the reception of them, and the comfortable news which they contain. We had not heard anything from North Carolina before, and could not help feeling anxious lest we should find a defection there, arising more from their ancient feuds and animosities than from any settled ill-will in the present contest; but the confirmation of the choice of their delegates by their Assembly leaves not a doubt of their firmness. Nor doth the eye say unto the hand, "I have no need of thee."[1] The Lord will not cast off his people, neither will He forsake his inheritance. Great events are most certainly in the womb of futurity; and, if the present chastisements which we experience have a proper influence upon our conduct, the event will certainly be in our favor. The distresses of the inhabitants of Boston are beyond the power of language to describe; there are but very few who are permitted to come out in a day; they delay giving passes, make them wait from hour to hour, and their counsels are not two hours together alike. One day, they shall come out with their effects; the next day, merchandise is not effects. One day, their household furniture is to come out; the next, only wearing apparel; the next, Pharaoh's heart is hardened, and he refuseth to hearken to them, and will not let the people go. May their deliverance be wrought out for them, as it was for the children of Israel. I do not mean by miracles, but by the interposition of Heaven in their favor. They have taken a list of all those who they suppose were concerned in watching the tea, and every other person whom they call obnoxious, and they and their effects are to suffer destruction. Poor Edes escaped out of town last night with one Ayers in a small boat, and was fired upon, but got safe and came up to Braintree to-day. His name it seems was upon the black list.

I find it impossible to get anybody in with any surety of their remaining again. I have sent to Waltham but cannot hear anything of Mr. Cushing's son. I wish you would write me whether

Mr. Cushing left any directions what should be done in that affair.

I hear that Mr. Bromfield has letters for you, and young Dr. Jarvis has more, but cannot get at them.

Pray write me every opportunity everything that transpires. Everybody desires to be remembered to you—it would fill the paper to name them. I wrote you once before. Let me know whether you have received it.

You don't say one word about your health. I hope it was comfortable and will continue so. It will be a great comfort to know that it is so to your   PORTIA ?

34. JOHN ADAMS

New York, May 8, 1775

I have an opportunity by Captain Beale to write you a line. We all arrived last night in this city. It would take many sheets of paper to give you a description of the reception we found here. The militia were all in arms, and almost the whole city out to meet us. The Tories are put to flight here as effectually as the Mandamus Council at Boston. They have associated to stand by Continental and Provincial Congresses, etc., etc., etc. Such a spirit was never seen in New York.

Jose Bass[1] met with a misfortune in the midst of some of the necessary parade that was made about us. My mare, being galled with an ugly buckle in the tackling, suddenly flinched and started in turning short round a rock, in a shocking bad road, overset the sulky, which frightened her still more. She ran and dashed the body of the sulky all to pieces. I was obliged to leave my sulky, slip my baggage on board Mr. Cushing's carriage, buy me a saddle, and mount on horseback. I am thankful that Bass was not killed. He was in the utmost danger, but not materially hurt.

I am sorry for this accident, both on account of the trouble and expense occasioned by it. I must pay your father for his sulky.[2] But in times like these such little accidents should not afflict us.

Let me caution you, my dear, to be upon your guard against the multitude of affrights and alarms which, I fear, will surround you. Yet I hope the people with you will grow more composed than they were.

Our prospect of a union of the colonies is promising indeed. Never was there such a spirit. Yet I feel anxious, because there is always more smoke than fire—more noise than music.

Our province is nowhere blamed. The accounts of the battle are exaggerated in our favor. My love to all. I pray for you all, and hope to be prayed for. Certainly there is a Providence; certainly we must depend upon Providence, or we fail; certainly the sincere prayers of good men avail much. But resignation is our duty in all events. I have this day heard Mr. Livingston in the morning, and Mr. Rogers[3] this afternoon—excellent men, and excellent prayers and sermons. My love to Nabby, Johnny, Charley, and Tommy. Tell them they must be good, and papa will come home, before long.

35. ABIGAIL ADAMS

Braintree, 24 May 1775

I suppose you have had a formidable account of the alarm we had last Sunday morning. When I rose, about six o'clock, I was told that the drums had been some time beating, and that three alarm guns were fired; that Weymouth bell had been ringing, and Mr. Weld's was then ringing. I immediately sent off an express to know the occasion, and found the whole town in confusion. Three sloops and one cutter had come out and dropped anchor just below Great Hill. It was difficult to tell their designs; some supposed they were coming to Germantown, others to Weymouth; people, women, children, from the iron-works, came flocking down this way; every woman and child driven off from below my father's; my father's family flying. The Dr.[1] is in great distress, as you may well imagine, for my aunt had her bed thrown into a cart, into which she got herself, and ordered the boy to drive her to Bridgewater, which he did. The report was to them that three hundred had landed, and were upon their march up into town. The alarm flew like lightning, and men from all parts came flocking down, till two thousand were collected. But it seems their expedition was to Grape Island for Levett's hay. There it was impossible to reach them, for want of boats; but the sight of so many persons, and the firing at them, prevented their getting more than three tons of hay, though they had carted much more down to the water. At last a lighter was mustered, and a sloop from Hingham, which had six port-holes. Our men eagerly jumped on board, and put off for the island. As soon as they perceived it, they decamped. Our people landed upon the island, and in an instant set fire to the hay, which, with the barn, was soon consumed,—about eighty tons, 'tis said. We expect soon to be in continual alarms, till something decisive takes place.

We wait, with longing expectation, in hopes to hear the best accounts from you, with regard to union and harmony, etc. We rejoice greatly on the arrival of Dr. Franklin, as he must certainly be able to inform you very particularly of the situation of affairs in England. I wish you would, if you can get time, be as particular as you *may*, when you write. Every one hereabouts comes to me, to hear what accounts I have. I was so unlucky as not to get the letter you wrote at New York. Captain Beale forgot it, and left it behind. We have a flying report here, with regard to New York, but cannot give any credit to it, as yet, that they had been engaged with the ships, which Gage sent there, and had taken them, with great loss upon both sides.

Yesterday we had an account of three ships coming into Boston. I believe it is true, as there was a salute from the other ships, though I have not been able to learn from whence they come. I suppose you have had an account of the fire, which did much damage to the warehouses, and added greatly to the distresses of the inhabitants, whilst it continued. The bad conduct of General Gage[2] was the means of its doing so much damage.

'Tis a fine growing season, having lately had a charming rain, which was much wanted as we had none before for a fortnight. Your meadow is almost fit to mow. Isaac talks of leaving you, and going into the army. I believe he will. Mr. Rice has a prospect of an *adjutant's* place in the army. I believe he will not be a very hardy soldier. He has been sick of a fever above this week, and has not been out of his chamber. He is upon the recovery now.

Our house has been, upon this alarm, in the same scene of confusion that it was upon the former. Soldiers coming in for a lodging, for breakfast, for supper, for drink, etc. Sometimes refugees from Boston, tired and fatigued, seek an asylum for a day, a night, a week. You can hardly imagine how we live; yet,—

> "To the houseless child of want,
>   Our doors are open still;
> And though our portions are but scant,
>   We give them with good will."[3]

I want to know how you do? How are your eyes? Is not the weather very hot where you are? The children are well and send duty to their papa. This day a month ago you set off. I have never once inquired when you think it possible to return; as I think you could not give me any satisfactory answer. I have according to your direction wrote to Mr. Dilly,[4] and given it to the care of Captain Beale, who will deliver it with his own hand; I got Mr. Thaxter to take a copy for me, as I had not time amidst our confusions; I send it to you for your approbation. You will be careful of it as I have no other copy. My best wishes attend you, both for your health and happiness, and that you may be directed into the wisest and best measures for our safety and the security of our posterity. I wish you were nearer to us; we know not what a day will bring forth, nor what distress one hour may throw us into. Hitherto I have been able to maintain a calmness and presence of mind, and hope I shall, let the exigency of the time be what it will. Mrs. Warren desires to be remembered to you with her sincere regards. Mr. Cranch and family send their love. He, poor man, has a fit of his old disorder. I have not heard one syllable from Providence since I wrote you last. I wait to hear from you, then shall act accordingly. I dare not discharge any debts with what I have except to Isaac, least you should be disappointed of the remainder. Adieu, breakfast calls your affectionate   PORTIA

Sister Betsey is with me, and desires her kindest wishes, and most affectionate regards, may be presented to you.

36. JOHN ADAMS

Philadelphia, 26 May 1775

I embrace an opportunity by two young gentlemen from Maryland[1] to write you a line, on friend Mifflin's table. The names of these gentlemen are Hall. They are of one of the best families in Maryland, and have independent fortunes—one a lawyer, the other a physician. If you have an opportunity, I beg you would show to these gentlemen all the civilities possible. Get them introduced to your uncle Quincy, and to your father and Dr. Tufts, and let everything be done to show them respect. They come five hundred miles to fight for you. They are volunteers to our camp, where they intend to spend the season.

My love and duty where they should be. I have not so good health as I had before, and I have harder service. Our business is more extensive and complicated, more affecting and hazardous. But our unanimity will not be less. We have a number of new and very ingenious members.

37. JOHN ADAMS

Philadelphia, 29 May 1775

Our amiable friend Hancock, who, by the way, is our president,[1] is to send his servant to-morrow for Cambridge. I am to send a few lines by him. If his man should come to you to deliver this letter, treat him very kindly, because he is a kind, humane, clever fellow. My friend Joseph Bass very cleverly caught the small-pox, in about two days after we arrived here, by inoculation and has walked about the streets every day since, and has got quite over it and quite well. He had about a dozen pimples upon the whole. Let his father and friends know this.

We are distressed here for want of intelligence and information from you and from Boston, Cambridge, etc., etc., etc. We have no regular advices. I received one kind letter from you in one from Colonel Warren. An excellent letter I had from him. It has done him great honor and me much good.

My duty and love to all. I have had miserable health and blind eyes ever since I left you. But I found Dr. Young[2] here, who, after scolding at me quantum sufficit[3] for not taking his advice, has pilled and electuaried me into pretty good order. My eyes are better, my head is better, and so are my spirits.

This Congress will support the Massachusetts. There is a good spirit here. But we have an amazing field of business before us. When I shall have the joy of meeting you and our little ones I know not.

The military spirit which runs through the continent is truly amazing. This city turns out two thousand men every day. Mr. Dickinson is a colonel, Mr. Reed[4] a lieutenant-colonel, Mr. Mifflin a major. He ought to have been a general, for he has been the animating soul of the whole.

Colonel Washington appears at Congress in his uniform, and, by his great experience and abilities in military matters, is of much service to us.

Oh that I was a soldier! I will be. I am reading military books. Everybody must, and will, and shall be a soldier.

38. JOHN ADAMS

Philadelphia, 2 June 1775

I had yesterday the pleasure of two letters from you, by Dr. Church.[1] We had been so long without any intelligence from our country, that the sight of the Dr. gave us great joy. I have received no letters from England, until the Doctor brought me one from Mr. Dilly.

Mr. Henly goes, to-morrow, to the camp at Cambridge. I am not so ill as I was when I left you, though not well. Bass has recovered of the small-pox.

Our debates and deliberations are tedious; from nine to four, five, and once near six—our determinations very slow—I hope sure. The Congress will support us, but in their own way. Not precisely in that way which I could wish, but in a better way than we could well expect, considering what a heterogeneous body it is.

The prospect of crops in all the Southern colonies never was exceeded. What will become of the immense quantities of provisions, when the non-exportation takes place, I can't conceive. Surely we shall not starve.

Poor Bostonians! My heart bleeds for them day and night. God preserve and bless them!

Was you frightened when the sheep-stealers got a drubbing at Grape Island? Father Smith prayed for our scow crew, I doubt not; but how did my dear friend Dr. Tufts sustain the shock? My duty and love to them and all others who justly claim them. My dear Nabby, and Johnny and Charley and Tommy are never out of my thoughts. God bless, preserve and prosper them. You need not send me any money; what I shall want will be supplied me here, by my colleagues, to be repaid after our return.

Dr. Warren writes me about my brother.[2] My love to both my brothers, my duty to my mother and your uncle Quincy. Tell him I hope our company continue their exercises. He would burst to see whole companies of armed Quakers in this city, in uniforms, going through the manual and manoeuvres like regular troops.

39. JOHN ADAMS

Philadelphia, 6 June 1775

I have received yours of 24 May, and a copy of your letter to Mr. Dilly, and one letter from him. Your letter to him is a very agreeable one. I hope you will continue to write him, whenever you have opportunity.

I am afraid you will have more alarms than are necessary, in consequence of the brush at Grape Island. But I hope you will maintain your philosophical composure.

Saturday last I took a little excursion, with Colonel Dyer and Mr. Deane,[1] down to Wilmington, a pretty village about thirty miles below this city, upon Delaware River, and kept Sabbath there. I find myself better for the ride.

We have a charming prospect here of a plentiful summer; hope it is so with you.

With yours, I had the pleasure of a letter from your uncle

Smith. I was rejoiced to find him and his family escaped from prison.[2]

Pray let me know whether your brother is in the army, and in what command. Let me know, too, about my brothers. My love to them. My love to my daughter and sons, and all the family. Tell Brackett I wish I was with him busied about the farm. Bass is well.

40. JOHN ADAMS

10 June 1775

Dr. Church returns to-day, and, with smarting eyes, I must write a few lines to you. I never had in my life such severe duty to do, and was never worse qualified to do it. My eyes depress my spirits, and my health is quite infirm. Yet I keep about, and attend Congress very constantly.

I wish I could write freely to you, my dear, but I cannot. The scene before me is complicated enough. It requires better eyes and better nerves than mine; yet I will not despond. I will lay all difficulties prostrate at my feet. My health and life ought to be hazarded in the cause of my country, as well as yours, and all my friends.

It is impossible to convey to you any adequate idea of the embarrassments I am under. I wish that you and our friends may not be in greater distress than I am. I fear you are. Pray let me know as often as possible. Our friends write to Mr. ———, not to me, this time. They don't let us know the state of Boston people, nor the state of the army in Boston, so exactly as I could wish.

Two days ago we saw a very wonderful phenomenon in this city: a field-day, on which three battalions of soldiers were reviewed, making full two thousand men, battalion men, light infantry, grenadiers, riflemen, light horse, artillery men with a fine train, all in uniforms, going through the manual exercise and the manoeuvres with remarkable dexterity. All this has been accomplished in this city since the 19th of April; so sudden a formation of an army never took place anywhere.

In Congress we are bound to secrecy. But, under the rose, I believe that ten thousand men will be maintained in the Massachusetts, and five thousand in New York, at the Continental expense.

We have a Major Skene, just arrived from London with a commission to be governor of Crown Point and Ticonderoga, and surveyor of the woods, etc., a close prisoner. He must dispute for his government with Arnold and Allen.[1] My love and duty where due.

41. JOHN ADAMS

Same date

Dr. Church has given me a lotion which has helped my eyes so much that I hope you will hear from me oftener than you have done. Pray write me as often and particularly as possible. Send your letters to the care of the Committee of Safety, who will forward them. I long to know how you fare, and whether you are often discomposed with alarms. Guard yourself against them, my dear, I think you are in no danger. Don't let the groundless fears and fruitful imaginations of others affect you. Let me know what guards are kept, and who were principally concerned in the battle at Grape Island, as well as that at Chelsea. The reputation of our countrymen for valor is very high. I hope they will maintain it, as well as that for prudence, caution, and conduct.

When I shall come home I know not. We have business enough before us, to detain us until the 31st of next December. No assembly ever had a greater number of great objects before them. Provinces, nations, empires are small things before us. I wish we were good architects.

Remember me to my dear brother and sister Cranch and to sister Betsey, to my parent and yours, to my children, and all. Bass sends his duty to his father—is quite recovered. Furnival sends his respects to Mr. Cranch and family. Fenno[1] prays to be remembered to Colonel Palmer, and wants something in the army.

42. ABIGAIL ADAMS

Weymouth, 15 June 1775[1]

I sat down to write to you on Monday, but really could not compose myself sufficiently; the anxiety I suffered from not hearing one syllable from you for more than five weeks, and the new distress arising from the arrival of recruits, agitated me more than I have been since the never-to-be-forgotten 14th of April. I have been much revived by receiving two letters from you last night; one by the servant of your friend, and the other by the gentlemen you mention, though they both went to Cambridge, and I have not seen them. I hope to send this as a return to you.

I feared much for your health, when you went away. I must entreat you to be as careful as you can consistently with the duty you owe your country. That consideration, alone, prevailed with me to consent to your departure in a time so perilous and so hazardous to your family, and with a body so infirm as to require the tenderest care and nursing. I wish you may be supported and divinely assisted in this most important crisis, when the fate of empire depends upon your wisdom and conduct. I greatly rejoice to hear of your union and determination to stand by us.

We cannot but consider the great distance you are from us as a very great misfortune, when our critical situation renders it necessary to hear from you every week, and will be more and more so, as difficulties arise. We now expect our seacoast ravaged; perhaps the very next letter I write will inform you that I am driven away from our yet quiet cottage. Necessity will oblige Gage to take some desperate steps. We are told for truth that he is now eight thousand strong. We live in continual expectation of alarms. Courage I know we have in abundance; conduct I hope we shall not want; powder,—where shall we get a sufficient supply? I wish we may not fail there. Every town is filled with the distressed inhabitants of Boston. Our house among others is deserted, and by this time, like enough, made use of as a barrack. Mr. Bowdoin and his lady are at present in the house of Mrs. Borland,[2] and are going to Middleborough, to the house of Judge Oliver. He, poor gentleman, is so low that I apprehend he is hastening to a house not made with hands; he looks like a mere skeleton, speaks faint and low, is racked with a violent cough, and, I think, far advanced in a consumption. I went to see him last Saturday. He is very inquisitive of every person with regard to the times; begged I would let him know of the first intelligence I had from you; is very unable to converse by reason of his cough. He rides every pleasant day, and has been kind enough to call at the door (though unable to get out) several times. He says the very name of Hutchinson distresses him. Speaking of him, the other day, he broke out, "Religious rascal! how I abhor his name!"

We have very dry weather, not a rainy day since you left us. The English grass will not yield half so great a crop as last year. Fruit promises well, but the caterpillars have been innumerable. I wrote you with regard to the money I had got from Providence. I have since obtained the rest. I have done as you directed with regard to the payment of some you mentioned, but it encroached some upon your stock. You will write me with regard to what you have necessity for and how I shall convey to you.

Mr. Rice is disappointed of his place in the army but has hopes of joining a company much talked of here under Mr. Hancock when he returns. I came here with some of my cousin Kents who came to see me a day or two ago, and have left company to write you this afternoon lest I should fail of conveyance. Pray be particular when you write as possible. Everybody wants to hear and to know what is doing, and what may be communicated do not fail to inform me. All our friends desire to be kindly remembered to you. Gage's proclamation you will receive by this conveyance. All the records of time cannot produce a blacker page. Satan, when driven from the regions of bliss, exhibited not more malice. Surely the father of lies is superseded. Yet we think it the best proclamation he could have issued.[3]

I shall, whenever I can, receive and entertain, in the best manner I am capable, the gentlemen who have so generously proffered their services in our army. Government is wanted in the army and elsewhere. We see the want of it more from so large a body being together, than when each individual was employed in his own domestic circle. My best regards attend every man you esteem. You will make my compliments to Mr. Mifflin and lady. I do not now wonder at the regard the ladies express for a sol-

dier. Every man who wears a cockade appears of double the importance he used to do, and I feel a respect for the lowest subal-
tern in the army. You tell me you know not when you shall see
me. I never trust myself long with the terrors which sometimes
intrude themselves upon me.

I hope we shall see each other again, and rejoice together in
happier days; the little ones are well, and send duty to papa.
Don't fail of letting me hear from you by every opportunity.
Every line is like a precious relic of the saints. Pray don't expose
me by a communication of any of my letters—a very bad sore
upon the middle finger of my right hand has prevented my writing for three weeks. This is the fifth letter I have wrote you. I
hope they have all come to hand.

I have a request to make of you; something like the barrel of
sand, I suppose you will think it, but really of much more importance to me. It is, that you would send out Mr. Bass, and purchase me a bundle of pins and put them in your trunk for me.
The cry for pins is so great that what I used to buy for seven
shillings and sixpence are now twenty shillings, and not to be
had for that. A bundle contains six thousand, for which I used to
give a dollar; but if you can procure them for fifty shillings, or three
pounds, pray let me have them. Mr. Welch, who carries this to
headquarters, waits, which prevents my adding more than that I
am, with the tenderest regard,

Your   PORTIA

43. JOHN ADAMS

Philadelphia, 11 June 1775

I have been this morning to hear Mr. Duffield,[1] a preacher in this
city, whose principles, prayers, and sermons more nearly resemble those of our New England clergy than any that I have heard.
His discourse was a kind of exposition on the thirty-fifth chap-
ter of Isaiah. America was the wilderness, and the solitary place,
and he said it would be glad, "rejoice and blossom as the rose."
He labored "to strengthen the weak hands and confirm the feeble knees." He "said to them that were of a fearful heart, Be
strong, fear not. Behold, your God will come with vengeance,

even God with a recompense; he will come and save you," "No
lion shall be there, nor any ravenous beast shall go up thereon,
but the redeemed shall walk there," etc. He applied the whole
prophecy to this country, and gave us as animating an entertainment as I ever heard. He filled and swelled the bosom of every
hearer. I hope you have received a letter, in which I inclosed you
a pastoral letter[2] from the synod of New York and Philadelphia;
by this you will see, that the clergy this way are but now beginning to engage in politics, and they engage with a fervor that will
produce wonderful effects.

17 June

I can now inform you that the Congress have made choice of the
modest and virtuous, the amiable, generous, and brave George
Washington, Esquire, to be General of the American army, and
that he is to repair, as soon as possible, to the camp before
Boston. This appointment will have a great effect in cementing
and securing the union of these colonies. The continent is really
in earnest, in defending the country. They have voted ten companies of riflemen to be sent from Pennsylvania, Maryland, and
Virginia, to join the army before Boston. These are an excellent
species of light infantry. They use a peculiar kind of musket,
called a rifle. It has circular or [?] grooves within the barrel, and
carries a ball with great exactness to great distances. They are
the most accurate marksmen in the world.

I begin to hope we shall not sit all summer. I hope the people
of our province will treat the General with all that confidence
and affection, that politeness and respect, which is due to one of
the most important characters in the world. The liberties of
America depend upon him, in a great degree. I have never been
able to obtain from our province any regular and particular intelligence, since I left it. Kent, Swift,[3] Tudor, Dr. Cooper, Dr.
Winthrop, and others wrote me often last fall; not a line from
them this time.

I have found this Congress like the last. When we first came
together, I found a strong jealousy of us from New England, and
the Massachusetts in particular; suspicions were entertained of
designs of independency; an American republic; Presbyterian
principles, and twenty other things. Our sentiments were heard

in Congress with great caution, and seemed to make but little impression; but the longer we sat, the more clearly they saw the necessity of pushing vigorous measures. It has been so now. Every day we sit, the more we are convinced that the designs against us are hostile and sanguinary, and that nothing but fortitude, vigor, and perseverance can save us.

But America is a great, unwieldy body. Its progress must be slow. It is like a large fleet sailing under convoy. The fleetest sailors must wait for the dullest and slowest. Like a coach and six, the swiftest horses must be slackened, and the slowest quickened, that all may keep an even pace.

It is long since I heard from you. I fear you have been kept in continual alarms. My duty and love to all. My dear children, come here and kiss me. We have appointed a Continental fast. Millions will be upon their knees at once before their great Creator, imploring his forgiveness and blessing; his smiles on American councils and arms.

My duty to your uncle Quincy; your papa, mamma, and mine; my brothers and sisters, and yours. Adieu.

44. JOHN ADAMS

18 June 1775

This letter, I presume, will go by the brave and amiable General Washington. Our army will have a group of officers equal to any service. Washington, Ward, Lee, Gates, Gridley,[1] together with all the other New England officers, will make a glorious council of war.

This Congress are all as deep as the delegates from the Massachusetts, and the whole continent as forward as Boston. We shall have a redress of grievances or an assumption of all the powers of government, legislative, executive, and judicial, throughout the whole continent, very soon. Georgia is bestirring itself; I mean the whole of it. The parish of St. John's, which is one third of it, was with us before.

45. ABIGAIL ADAMS

Sunday, 18 June

The day—perhaps the decisive day—is come, on which the fate of America depends. My bursting heart must find vent at my pen. I have just heard that our dear friend, Dr. Warren, is no more, but fell gloriously fighting for his country; saying, <u>Better to die honorably in the field, than ignominiously hang upon the gallows</u>. Great is our loss. He has distinguished himself in every engagement, by his courage and fortitude, by animating the soldiers, and leading them on by his own example. A particular account of these dreadful, but I hope glorious days, will be transmitted you, no doubt, in the exactest manner.

[biblical reference]

"The race is not to the swift, nor the battle to the strong; but the God of Israel is He that giveth strength and power unto his people. Trust in him at all times, ye people, pour out your hearts before him; God is a refuge for us."[1] Charlestown is laid in ashes. The battle began upon our intrenchments upon Bunker's Hill, Saturday morning about three o'clock, and has not ceased yet, and it is now three o'clock Sabbath afternoon.

It is expected they will come out over the Neck to-night, and a dreadful battle must ensue. Almighty God, cover the heads of our countrymen, and be a shield to our dear friends! How many have fallen, we know not. The constant roar of the cannon is so distressing that we cannot eat, drink, or sleep. May we be supported and sustained in the dreadful conflict. I shall tarry here till it is thought unsafe by my friends, and then I have secured myself a retreat at your brother's, who has kindly offered me part of his house. I cannot compose myself to write any further at present. I will add more as I hear further.

[→ literally living in a war-zone]

Tuesday Afternoon

I have been so much agitated, that I have not been able to write since Sabbath day. When I say that ten thousand reports are passing, vague and uncertain as the wind, I believe I speak the truth. I am not able to give you any authentic account of last Saturday, but you will not be destitute of intelligence. Colonel Palmer has just sent me word that he has an opportunity of conveyance. Incorrect as this scrawl will be, it shall go. I ardently pray that you may be supported through the arduous task you have before you. I wish I could contradict the report of the Dr.'s death;[2] but it is a lamentable truth, and the tears of multitudes pay tribute to his memory; those favorite lines of Collins continually sound in my ears:—

> "How sleep the brave who sink to rest
> By all their country's wishes blest!
> When Spring, with dewy fingers cold,
> Returns to deck their hallowed mold,
> She there shall dress a sweeter sod
> Than Fancy's feet have ever trod.
>
> By fairy hands their knell is rung,
> By forms unseen their dirge is sung;
> There Honor comes, a pilgrim gray,
> To bless the turf that wraps their clay,
> And Freedom shall awhile repair,
> To dwell a weeping hermit there!"[3]

I rejoice in the prospect of plenty you inform me of, but cannot say we have the same agreeable view here. The drought is very severe, and things look but poorly. Mr. Rice and Mr. Thaxter, uncle Quincy, Colonel Quincy, Mr. Wibird all desire to be remembered, so do all our family. Nabby will write by the next conveyance.

I must close, as the Deacon waits. I have not pretended to be particular with regard to what I have heard, because I know you will collect better intelligence. The spirit of the people are very good; the loss of Charlestown affects them no more than a drop in the bucket.

I am, most sincerely, yours,   PORTIA

46. ABIGAIL ADAMS

22 June 1775

I received yours of June 10th, for which I thank you. I want you to be more particular. Does every member feel for us? Can they realize what we suffer? And can they believe with what patience and fortitude we endure the conflict? Nor do we even tremble at the frowns of power.

You inquire of me who were at the engagement at Grape Island. I may say, with truth, all Weymouth, Braintree, Hingham, who were able to bear arms, and hundreds from other towns within twenty, thirty, and forty miles of Weymouth. Our good friend, the Dr., is in a miserable state of health, has the jaundice to a very great degree, is a mere skeleton and hardly able to go from his own house to my father's. Danger, you know, sometimes makes timid men bold. He stood that day very well, and generously attended, with drink, biscuit, flints, etc., five hundred men, without taking any pay. He has since been chosen one of the committee of correspondence for that town, and has done much service by establishing a regular method of alarm from town to town. Both your brothers were there; your younger brother, with his company, who gained honor by their good order that day. He was one of the first to venture on board a schooner to land upon the island. As to Chelsea, I cannot be so particular, as I know only in general that Colonel Putnam commanded there, and had many gentlemen volunteers. We have two companies stationed in this town: at Germantown, Captain Turner; at Squantum, Captain Vinton;[1] in Weymouth, one; in Hingham, two, etc. I believe I shall remove your books this week to your brother's. We think it advisable. Colonel Quincy has procured his family a retreat at Deacon Holbrook's. Mr. Cranch has one at Major Bass's, in case of necessity, to which we hope not to be driven. We hear that the troops destined for New York are all expected here; but we have got to that pass that a whole legion of them would not intimidate us. I think I am very brave, upon the whole. If danger comes near my dwelling, I suppose I shall shudder. We want powder, but, with the blessing of Heaven, we fear them not. Write every opportunity you can. The state we are in at present is intrenching and fortifying. 'Tis said we have lost forty-four men, and the regulars near a thousand, sixty-four officers amongst them.

God bless and preserve us. I am, yours,   PORTIA

47. JOHN ADAMS

Philadelphia, 23 June

I have this morning been out of town to accompany our generals, Washington, Lee, and Schuyler,[1] a little way on their journey to the American camp before Boston. The three generals were all mounted on horse-back, accompanied by Major Mifflin, who is gone in the character of aide-de-camp. All the delegates from the Massachusetts, with their servants and carriages, attended; many others of the delegates from the Congress; a large troop of light horse in their uniforms; many officers of militia besides, in theirs, music playing, etc., etc. Such is the pride and pomp of war. I, poor creature, worn out with scribbling for my bread and my liberty, low in spirits and weak in health, must leave others to wear the laurels which I have sown; others to eat the bread which I have earned; a common case.

We had, yesterday, by the way of New York and New London, a report which distresses us almost as much as that we had last fall of the cannonade of Boston. A battle at Bunker's Hill and Dorchester Point. Three colonels wounded, Gardner mortally.[2] We wait to hear more particulars. Our hopes and fears are alternately very strong. If there is any truth in this account, you must be in great confusion. God Almighty's providence preserve, sustain, and comfort you.

27 June

This moment received two letters from you. Courage, my dear. We shall be supported in life or comforted in death. I rejoice that my countrymen behaved so bravely, though not so skillfully conducted as I could wish. I hope this defect will be remedied by the new modeling of the army.

My love everywhere.

48. ABIGAIL ADAMS

Braintree, 25 June 1775

My father has been more afflicted by the destruction of Charles-town than by anything which has heretofore taken place. Why should not his countenance be sad, when the city, the place of his father's sepulchre, lieth waste, and the gates thereof are consumed with fire? Scarcely one stone remaineth upon another; but in the midst of sorrow we have abundant cause of thankfulness, that so few of our brethren are numbered with the slain, whilst our enemies were cut down like the grass before the scythe. But one officer of all the Welsh fusileers remains to tell his story. Many poor wretches die for want of proper assistance and care of their wounds.

Every account agrees in fourteen or fifteen hundred slain and wounded upon their side, nor can I learn that they dissemble the number themselves. We had some heroes that day, who fought with amazing intrepidity and courage.

> "Extremity is the trier of spirits;
> —common chances common men can bear."
> And, "When the sea is calm, all boats alike
> Show mastership in floating: fortune's blows
> When most struck home, being *bravely* warded, crave
> A noble cunning."[1]

I hear that General Howe said that the battle upon the Plains of Abram was but a bauble to this. When we consider all the circumstances attending this action, we stand astonished that our people were not all cut off. They had but one hundred foot intrenched, the number who were engaged did not exceed eight hundred, and they with not half ammunition enough; the reinforcement not able to get to them seasonably. The tide was up, and high, so that their floating batteries came upon each side of the causeway, and their row-galleys kept a continual fire. Added to this, the fire from Copp's Hill, and from the ships; the town in flames, all around them, and the heat from the flames so intense as scarcely to be borne; the day one of the hottest we have had this season, and the wind blowing the smoke in their faces,— only figure to yourself all these circumstances, and then consider that we do not count sixty men lost. My heart overflows at the recollection.

We live in continual expectation of hostilities. Scarcely a day that does not produce some; but, like good Nehemiah, having made our prayer unto God, and set the people with their swords, their spears, and their bows, we will say unto them, "Be not ye afraid of them; remember the Lord, who is great and terrible, and fight for your brethren, your sons, and your daughters, your wives and your houses."

I have just received yours of the 17th of June, in seven days only; every line from that far country is precious; you do not tell me how you do, but I will hope better. Alas, you little thought what distress we were in the day you wrote. They delight in molesting us upon the Sabbath. Two Sabbaths we have been in such alarm that we have had no meeting; this day we have sat under our own vine in quietness; have heard Mr. Taft,[2] from Psalms, "The Lord is good to all, and his tender mercies are over all his works." The good man was earnest and pathetic; I could forgive his weakness for the sake of his sincerity, but I long for a Cooper and an Eliot. I want a person who has feeling and sensibility, who can take one up with him,—

> And "in his duty prompt, at every call,"
> Can "watch, and weep, and pray, and feel for all."[3]

Mr. Rice joins General Heath's regiment[4] to-morrow, as adjutant. Your brother is very desirous of being in the army, but your good mother is really violent against it. I cannot persuade nor reason her into a consent. Neither he nor I dare let her know that he is trying for a place. My brother has a captain's commission, and is stationed at Cambridge. I thought you had the best of intelligence, or I should have taken pains to be more particular. As to Boston, there are many persons yet there who would be glad to get out if they could. Mr. Boylston, and Mr. Gill, the printer, with his family, are held upon the black list, it is said. 'Tis certain they watch them so narrowly that they cannot escape, nor your brother Swift and family. Mr. Mather[5] got out a day or two before Charlestown was destroyed, and had lodged his papers and what else he got out at Mr. Carey's, but they were all consumed; so were many other people's, who thought they might trust their little there till teams could be procured to remove them. The people from the almshouse and workhouse were sent to the lines, last week, to make room for their wounded, they say. Medford people are all removed. Every seaport seems in motion. O North, may the groans and cries of the injured and oppressed harrow up thy soul. We have a prodigious army, but we lack many accommodations which we need. I hope the appointment of these new Generals will give satisfaction; they must be proof against calumny. In a contest like this, continual reports are circulated by our enemies, and they catch with the unwary and the gaping crowd, who are ready to listen to the marvelous without considering of consequences, even though their best friends are injured.

I have not ventured to inquire one word of you about your return. I do not know whether I ought to wish for it; it seems as if your sitting together was absolutely necessary, whilst every day is big with events.

Mr. Bowdoin called Friday and took his leave of me, desiring I would present his affectionate regards to you. I have hopes that he will recover; he has mended a good deal. He wished he could have stayed in Braintree, but his lady was fearful. I have often heard that fear makes people loving. I never was so much noticed *by some people* as I have been since you went out of town, or rather since the 19th of April. Mr. W——w's family are determined to be sociable. Mr. A——n's are quite friendly.

Nabby, Johnny, Charley, Tommy all send duty. Tom says I wish I could see *par*. You would laugh to see them all run upon the sight of a letter—like chickens for a crumb, when the hen clucks. Charles says, "*Mar*, what is it, any good news?" And "Who is for us and who against us," is the continual inquiry. Brother and sister Cranch send their love. He has been very well since he removed, for him, and has full employ in his business. Uncle Quincy calls to hear most every day, and as for the parson, he determines I shall not make the same complaint I did last time, for he comes every other day. 'Tis exceeding dry weather.

We have not had any rain for a long time. Brackett has mowed
the meadow and over the way, but it will not be last year's crop.

Pray let me hear from you by every opportunity till I have the
joy of once more meeting you.

Yours evermore,   PORTIA

P.S. Tell Bass his father and family is well.

49. ABIGAIL ADAMS

5 July 1775

I have received a good deal of paper from you. I wish it had been
more covered; the writing is very scant, yet I must not grumble.
I know your time is not yours nor mine. Your labors must be
great and your mouth closed; but all you may communicate, I
beg you would. There is a pleasure, I know not whence it arises,
nor can I stop now to find it out, but I say there is a degree of
pleasure in being able to tell news, especially any which so nearly
concerns us, as all your proceedings do.

I should have been more particular, but I thought you knew
everything that passed here. The present state of the inhabitants
of Boston is that of the most abject slaves, under the most cruel
and despotic of tyrants. Among many instances I could mention,
let me relate one. Upon the 17th of June, printed handbills were
posted up at the corners of the streets, and upon houses, forbid-
ding any inhabitants to go upon their houses, or upon any eminence, on pain of death; the inhabitants dared not to look out of
their houses, nor to be heard or seen to ask a question. Our prisoners were brought over to the Long Wharf, and there lay all
night, without any care of their wounds, or any resting-place but
the pavements, until the next day, when they exchanged it for
the jail, since which we hear they are civilly treated. Their living
cannot be good, as they can have no fresh provisions; their beef,
we hear, is all gone, and their own wounded men die very fast,
so that they have a report that the bullets were poisoned. Fish
they cannot have, they have rendered it so difficult to procure;
and the admiral is such a villain as to oblige every fishing
schooner to pay a dollar every time it goes out. The money that

people of Boston are starving.

has been paid for passes is incredible. Some have given ten, twenty, thirty, and forty dollars, to get out with a small proportion of their things. It is reported and believed that they have taken up a number of persons and committed them to jail, we know not for what in particular. Master Lovell[1] is confined in the dungeon; a son of Mr. Edes is in jail, one Mr. Wendle who married a Hunt, and one Wiburt, a ship-carpenter, is now upon trial for his life. God alone knows to what length these wretches will go, and will, I hope, restrain their malice.

I would not have you be distressed about me. Danger, they say, makes people valiant. Hitherto I have been distressed, but not dismayed. I have felt for my country and her sons. I have bled with them and for them. Not all the havoc and devastation they have made has wounded me like the death of Warren. We want him in the Senate; we want him in his profession; we want him in the field. We mourn for the citizen, the senator, the physician, and the warrior. May we have others raised up in his room.

a common America an imagined community

I have had a very kind and friendly visit from our dear friends Colonel Warren, lady, and son. Mrs. Warren spent a week almost with me, and he came and met her here, and kept Sabbath with me. I suppose she will write to you, though she says you are in her debt.

You scarcely make mention of Dr. Franklin. Surely he must be a valuable member. Pray what is become of your Judas?[2] I see he is not with you upon the list of delegates. I wish I could come and see you. I never suffer myself to think you are about returning soon. Can it, will it be? May I ask, may I wish for it? When once I expect you, the time will crawl till I see you. But hush! Do you know it is eleven o'clock at night? We have had some very fine rains since I wrote you last. I hope we shall not now have famine added to war. Grain, grain is what we want here. Meat we have enough, and to spare. Pray don't let Bass forget my pins. Hardwick has applied to me for Mr. Bass to get him a hundred of needles, number six, to carry on his stocking weaving. We shall very soon have no coffee, nor sugar, nor pepper, here; but huckleberries and milk we are not obliged to commerce for. All the good folks here send their regards. Uncle Quincy is just gone from here, sends his love. You don't say in the two last letters I received how you do. I hope I have not felt unwell by sympathy, but I have been very unwell for this week, though better now. I saw a letter of yours to Colonel Palmer, by General Washington. I hope I have one too. Good night. With thoughts of thee do I close my eyes. Angels guard and protect thee; and may a safe return erelong bless thy   PORTIA

so sweet

50. JOHN ADAMS

Philadelphia, 7 July 1775

I have received your very agreeable favors of June 22 and 25. They contain more particulars than any letters I had before received from anybody.

It is not at all surprising to me, that the wanton, cruel, and infamous conflagration of Charlestown, the place of your father's nativity, should afflict him. Let him know that I sincerely condole with him on that melancholy event. It is a method of conducting war long since become disreputable among civilized nations. But every year brings us fresh evidence that we have nothing to hope for from our loving mother country, but cruelties more abominable than those which are practiced by the savage Indians. *compares England to Native Americans*

The account you give me of the numbers slain on the side of our enemies is affecting to humanity, although it is a glorious proof of the bravery of our worthy countrymen. Considering all the disadvantages under which they fought, they really exhibited prodigies of valor. Your description of the distresses of the worthy inhabitants of Boston and the other seaport towns is enough to melt a heart of stone. *pity* Our consolation must be this, my dear, that cities may be rebuilt, and a people reduced to poverty may acquire fresh property. But a constitution of government, once changed from freedom, can never be restored. Liberty, once lost, is lost forever. When the people once surrender their share in the legislature, and their right of defending the limitations upon the Government, and of resisting every encroachment upon them, they can never regain it. *freedom to be free*

The loss of Mr. Mather's library, which was a collection of books and manuscripts made by himself, his father, his grandfather, and great-grandfather, and was really very curious and valuable, is irreparable. The family picture you draw is charming indeed. My dear Nabby, Johnny, Charley, and Tommy, I long to see you, and to share with your mamma the pleasures of your conversation. I feel myself much obliged to Mr. Bowdoin, Mr. Wibird, and the two families you mention, for their civilities to you. My compliments to them. Does Mr. Wibird preach against oppression and the other cardinal vices of the times? Tell him the clergy here of every denomination, not excepting the Episcopalian, thunder and lighten every Sabbath. They pray for Boston and the Massachusetts. They thank God most explicitly and fervently for our remarkable successes. They pray for the American army. They seem to feel as if they were among you.

You ask if every member feels for us? Every member says he does, and most of them really do. But most of them feel more for themselves. In every society of men, in every club I ever yet saw, you find some who are timid, their fears hurry them away upon every alarm, some who are selfish and avaricious, on whose callous hearts nothing but interest and money can make impression. There are some persons in New York and Philadelphia to whom a ship is dearer than a city, and a few barrels of flour than a thousand lives—other men's lives, I mean.

You ask, Can they realize what we suffer? I answer, No. They can't. They don't. And, to excuse them as well as I can, I must confess, I should not be able to do it myself, if I was not more acquainted with it by experience than they are.

I am grieved for Dr. Tufts's ill-health, but rejoiced exceedingly at his virtuous exertions in the cause of his country. I am happy to hear that my brothers were at Grape Island, and behaved well. My love to them, and duty to my mother.

It gives me more pleasure than I can express, to learn that you sustain with so much fortitude the shocks and terrors of the times. You are really brave, my dear. You are a heroine, and you have reason to be. For the worst that can happen can do you no harm. A soul as pure, as benevolent, as virtuous and pious as yours, has nothing to fear, but everything to hope and expect from the last of human evils. I am glad you have secured an asylum, though I hope you will not have occasion for it. Love to brother Cranch and sister and children.

There is an amiable, ingenious hussy, named Betsey Smith,[1] for whom I have a very great regard. Be pleased to make my love acceptable to her, and let her know that her elegant pen cannot be more usefully employed than in writing letters to her brother at Philadelphia, though it may be more agreeably, in writing billets-doux to young gentlemen.

The other day, after I had received a letter of yours, with one or two others, Mr. William Barrell[2] desired to read them. I put them into his hand, and the next morning had them returned in a large bundle packed up with two great heaps of pins, with a very polite card requesting Portia's acceptance of them. I shall bring them with me when I return. But when that will be is uncertain. I hope not more than a month hence.

I have really had a very disagreeable time of it. My health, and especially my eyes, have been so very bad that I have not been so fit for business as I ought; and if I had been in perfect health, I should have had, in the present condition of my country and my friends, no taste for pleasure. But Dr. Young has made a kind of cure of my health, and Dr. Church of my eyes.

I have received two kind letters from your uncle Smith. Do thank him for them. I shall forever love him for them. I love everybody that writes to me.

I am forever yours.

another example of sacrifice

51. ABIGAIL ADAMS

Braintree, 16 July 1775

I have this afternoon had the pleasure of receiving your letter by your friends Mr. Collins and Kaighn and an English gentleman, his name I do not remember. It was next to seeing my dearest friend. Mr. Collins could tell me more particularly about you and your health than I have been able to hear since you left me. I rejoice in his account of your better health, and of your spirits, though he says I must not expect to see you till next spring. I hope he does not speak the truth. I know (I think I do, for am I not your bosom friend?) your feelings, your anxieties, your exertions, etc., more than those before whom you are obliged to wear the face of cheerfulness.

I have seen your letters to Colonels Palmer and Warren. I pity

IS THIS A SARCASTIC TONE?

your embarrassments. How difficult the task to quench the fire and the pride of private ambition, and to sacrifice ourselves and all our hopes and expectations to the public weal! How few have souls capable of so noble an undertaking! How often are the laurels worn by those who have had no share in earning them! But there is a future recompense of reward, to which the upright man looks, and which he will most assuredly obtain, provided he perseveres unto the end.

The appointment of the generals Washington and Lee gives universal satisfaction. The people have the highest opinion of Lee's abilities, but you know the continuation of the popular breath depends much upon favorable events. I had the pleasure of seeing both the generals and their aides-de-camp soon after their arrival, and of being personally made known to them. They very politely express their regard for you. Major Mifflin said he had orders from you to visit me at Braintree. I told him I should be very happy to see him there, and accordingly sent Mr. Thaxter to Cambridge with a card, to him and Mr. Reed, to dine with me. Mrs. Warren and her son were to be with me. They very politely received the message, and lamented that they were not able to come, upon account of expresses which they were on that day to get in readiness to send off.

I was struck with General Washington. You had prepared me to entertain a favorable opinion of him, but I thought the half was not told me. Dignity with ease and complacency, the gentleman and soldier, look agreeably blended in him. Modesty marks every line and feature of his face. Those lines of Dryden instantly occurred to me:—

> "Mark his majestic fabric; he's a temple
> Sacred by birth, and built by hands divine;
> His soul's the deity that lodges there;
> Nor is the pile unworthy of the god."[1]

General Lee looks like a careless, hardy veteran, and by his appearance brought to my mind his namesake, Charles the Twelfth, of Sweden. The elegance of his pen far exceeds that of his person. I was much pleased with your friend Collins. I persuaded them to stay coffee with me, and he was as unreserved and social as if we had been old acquaintances, and said he was very loath to leave the house. I would have detained them till morning, but they were very desirous of reaching Cambridge.

You have made frequent complaints that your friends do not write to you. I have stirred up some of them. Dr. Tufts, Colonel Quincy, Mr. Tudor, and Mr. Thaxter all have wrote to you now, and a lady whom I am willing you should value preferable to all others save one. May not I in my turn make complaints? All the letters I receive from you seem to be written in so much haste that they scarcely leave room for a social feeling. They let me know that you exist, but some of them contain scarcely six lines. I want some sentimental effusions of the heart. I am sure you are not destitute of them. Or are they all absorbed in the great public? Much is due to that, I know, but, being part of the public, I lay claim to a larger share than I have had. You used to be more communicative on Sundays. I always loved a Sabbath day's letter, for then you had a greater command of your time; but hush to all complaints.

I am much surprised that you have not been more accurately informed of what passes in the camps. As to intelligence from Boston, it is but very seldom we are able to collect anything that may be relied on; and to report the vague flying rumors would be endless. I heard yesterday, by one Mr. Roulstone, a goldsmith, who got out in a fishing schooner, that their distress increased upon them fast. Their beef is all spent; their malt and cider all gone. All the fresh provisions they can procure they are obliged to give to the sick and wounded. Nineteen of our men who were in jail,[2] and were wounded at the battle of Charlestown, were dead. No man dared now to be seen talking to his friend in the street. They were obliged to be within, every evening, at ten o'clock, according to martial law; nor could any inhabitant walk any street in town after that time, without a pass from Gage. He has ordered all the molasses to be distilled into rum for the soldiers; taken away all licenses, and given out others, obliging to a forfeiture of ten pounds, if any rum is sold without written orders from the General. He gives much the same account of the killed and wounded we have from others. The spirit, he says, which prevails among the soldiers, is a spirit of malice and revenge; there is no true courage and bravery to be observed among them.

Their duty is hard; always mounting guard with their packs at their backs, ready for an alarm, which they live in continual hazard of. Dr. Eliot is not on board a man-of-war, as has been reported, but perhaps was left in town, as the comfort and support of those who cannot escape. He was constantly with our prisoners. Messrs. Lovell and Leach, with others, are certainly in jail. A poor milch cow was last week killed in town, and sold for a shilling sterling per pound. The transports arrived last week from York, but every additional man adds to their distress. There has been a little expedition[3] this week to Long Island. There have been, before, several attempts to go on, but three men-of-war lay near, and cutters all round the island, so that they could not succeed. A number of whaleboats lay at Germantown. Three hundred volunteers, commanded by one Captain Tupper, came on Monday evening and took the boats, went on, and brought off seventy odd sheep, fifteen head of cattle, and sixteen prisoners, thirteen of whom were sent by (Simple Sapling)[4] to mow the hay, which they had very badly executed. They were all asleep in the house and barn. When they were taken, there were three women with them. Our heroes came off in triumph, not being observed by their enemies. This spirited up others. They could not endure the thought that the house and barn should afford them any shelter; they did not destroy them the night before for fear of being discovered. Captain Wild, of this town, with about twenty-five of his company, Captain Gold, of Weymouth, with as many of his, and some other volunteers, to the amount of a hundred, obtained leave to go on and destroy the hay, together with the house and barn; and in open day, in full view of the men-of-war, they set off from the Moon, so called, covered by a number of men who were placed there, went on and set fire to the buildings and hay. A number of armed cutters immediately surrounded the island and fired upon our men. They came off with a hot and continued fire upon them, the bullets flying in every direction, and the men-of-war's boats plying them with small arms. Many in this town, who were spectators, expected every moment our men would all be sacrificed, for sometimes they were so near as to be called and damned by their enemies, and ordered to surrender; yet they all returned in safety, not one man even wounded. Upon the Moon we lost one man, from the cannon on board the man-of-war. On the evening of the same day, a man-of-war came and anchored near Great Hill, and two cutters came to Pig Rocks. It occasioned an alarm in this town, and we were up all night. They remain there yet, but have not ventured to land any men.

This town have chosen their representative. Colonel Palmer is the man. There was a considerable muster upon Thayer's side, and Vinton's company marched up in order to assist, but got sadly disappointed. Newcomb[5] insisted upon it that no man should vote who was in the army. He had no notion of being under the military power; said we might be so situated as to have the greater part of the people engaged in the military, and then all power would be wrested out of the hands of the civil magistrate. He insisted upon its being put to vote, and carried his point immediately. It brought Thayer to his speech, who said all he could against it.

As to the situation of the camps, our men are in general healthy, much more so at Roxbury than at Cambridge, and the camp is in vastly better order. General Thomas[6] has the character of an excellent officer. His merit has certainly been overlooked, as modest merit generally is. I hear General Washington is much pleased with his conduct.

Every article here in the West India way is very scarce and dear. In six weeks we shall not be able to purchase any article of the kind. I wish you would let Bass get me one pound of pepper and two yards of black calamanco[7] for shoes. I cannot wear leather, if I go barefoot, the reason I need not mention. Bass may make a fine profit if he lays in a stock for himself. You can hardly imagine how much we want many common small articles, which are not manufactured amongst ourselves; but we will have them in time; not one pin to be purchased for love or money. I wish you could convey me a thousand by any friend travelling this way. It is very provoking to have such a plenty so near us, but, Tantalus-like, not to be able to touch. I should have been glad to have laid in a small stock of the West India articles, but I cannot get one copper; no person thinks of paying anything, and I do not choose to run in debt. I endeavor to live in the most frugal manner possible, but I am many times distressed.

Mr. Trott[8] I have accommodated by removing the office into my own chamber, and after being very angry and sometimes persuading I obtained the mighty concession of the bedroom, but I am now so crowded as not to have a lodging for a friend that calls to see me. I must beg you would give them warning to seek a place before winter. Had that house been empty I could have had a hundred a year for it. Many persons had applied before Mr. Trott, but I wanted some part of it myself, and the other part of it seems I have no command of.

We have, since I wrote you, had many fine showers, and, although the crops of grass have been cut short, we have a fine prospect of Indian corn and English grain. Be not afraid, ye beasts of the field, for the pastures of the wilderness do spring, the tree beareth her fruit, the vine and the olive yield their increase. We have not yet been much distressed for grain. Everything at present looks blooming. Oh that peace would once more extend her olive branch!

> "This day be bread and peace my lot;
>   All else beneath the sun
> Thou knowest if best bestowed or not,
>   And let thy will be done."

> "But is the Almighty ever bound to please,
> Build by my wish, or studious of my ease?
> Shall I determine where his frowns shall fall,
> And fence my grotto from the lot of all?
> Prostrate, his sovereign wisdom I adore,
> Intreat his mercy, but I dare no more."[9]

Our little ones send duty to papa. You would smile to see them all gather round mamma upon the reception of a letter to hear from papa, and Charles with open mouth, What does par say—did not he write no more? And little Tom says I wish I could see par. Upon Mr. Rice's going into the army he asked Charles if he should get him a place; he catched at it with great eagerness and insisted upon going. We could not put him off, he cried and begged, no obstacle we could raise was sufficient to satisfy him, till I told him he must first obtain your consent. Then he insisted that I must write about it, and has been every day these three weeks insisting upon my asking your consent. At last I have promised to write to you, and am obliged to be as good as my word. I have now written you all I can collect from every quarter. 'Tis fit for no eyes but yours, because you can make all necessary allowances. I cannot copy.

There are yet in town four of the selectmen and some thousands of inhabitants, 'tis said. I hope to hear from you soon. Do let me know if there is any prospect of seeing you. Next Wednesday is thirteen weeks since you went away. I must bid you adieu.

You have many friends, though they have not noticed you by writing. I am sorry they have been so negligent. I hope no share of that blame lies upon

Your most affectionate   PORTIA

Mr. Cranch has in his possession a barrel of Mrs. Wilkin's beer, which belonged to the late Dr. Warren. He does not know what to do with it. Suppose you should take it and give credit for it, as there will be neither wine, lemons or anything else to be had but what we make ourselves. Write me your pleasure about it.

52. JOHN ADAMS

Philadelphia, 23 July 1775

You have more than once in your letters mentioned Dr. Franklin, and in one intimated a desire that I should write you something concerning him.

Dr. Franklin has been very constant in his attendance on Congress from the beginning. His conduct has been composed and grave, and, in the opinion of many gentlemen, very reserved. He has not assumed anything, nor affected to take the lead; but has seemed to choose that the Congress should pursue their own principles and sentiments, and adopt their own plans. Yet he has not been backward; has been very useful on many occasions, and discovered a disposition entirely American. He does not hesitate at our boldest measures, but rather seems to think us too irresolute and backward. He thinks us at present in an odd state, neither in peace nor war, neither dependent nor independent; but he thinks that we shall soon assume a character more decisive.

He thinks that we have the power of preserving ourselves; and that even if we should be driven to the disagreeable necessity of assuming a total independency, and set up a separate state, we can maintain it. The people of England have thought that the opposition in America was wholly owing to Dr. Franklin; and I suppose their scribblers will attribute the temper and proceedings of Congress to him; but there cannot be a greater mistake. He has had but little share, further than to cooperate and to assist. He is, however, a great and good man. I wish his colleagues from this city were all like him; particularly one, whose abilities and virtues, formerly trumpeted so much in America, have been found wanting.[1] There is a young gentleman from Pennsylvania, whose name is Wilson, whose fortitude, rectitude, and abilities too, greatly outshine his master's. Mr. Biddle, the Speaker, has been taken off by sickness, Mr. Mifflin is gone to the camp, Mr. Morton is ill too, so that this province has suffered by the timidity of two overgrown fortunes.[2] The dread of confiscation or caprice, I know not what, has influenced them too much; yet they were for taking arms, and pretended to be very valiant.

This letter must be secret, my dear; at least communicated with great discretion.

Yours,   JOHN ADAMS

53. JOHN ADAMS

Same date

Have only time to send by this opportunity a token of remembrance.

The fast was observed here with a decorum and solemnity never before seen on a Sabbath. The clergy of all denominations here preached upon politics and war in a manner that I never heard in New England. They are a flame of fire. It is astonishing to me that the people are so cool here. Such sermons in our country would have a much greater effect.

I hope to see you erelong. You have stirred up my friends to write to me. Austin, Tudor, Rice, have wrote. Dr. Tufts wrote me an excellent letter, and very particular intelligence.

My love to all the children.

54. JOHN ADAMS

24 July 1775[1]

It is now almost three months since I left you, in every part of which, my anxiety about you and the children, as well as our country, has been extreme. The business I have had upon my mind has been as great and important as can be entrusted to man, and the difficulty and intricacy of it prodigious. When fifty or sixty men have a Constitution to form for a great empire, at the same time that they have a country of fifteen hundred miles in extent to fortify, millions to arm and train, a naval power to begin, an extensive commerce to regulate, numerous tribes of Indians to negotiate with, a standing army of twenty-seven thousand men to raise, pay, victual, and officer, I really shall pity those fifty or sixty men. I must see you erelong. Rice has wrote me a very good letter. So has Thaxter, for which I thank them both. Love to the children.   J. A.

P.S.—I wish I had given you a complete history, from the beginning to the end of the journey, of the behavior of my compatriots. No mortal tale can equal it. I will tell you in future, but you shall keep it secret. The fidgets, the whims, the caprice, the vanity, the superstition, the irritability of some of us is enough to ———
    Yours.

55. ABIGAIL ADAMS

Braintree, 25 July 1775

DEAREST FRIEND, — I received yours of July 7th, for which I heartily thank you. It was the longest and best letter I have had; the most leisurely, and therefore the most sentimental. Previous to your last, I had written you, and made some complaints of you, but I will take them all back again. Only continue your obliging favors, whenever your time will allow you to devote one moment to your absent Portia.

This is the 25th of July. Gage has not made any attempts to

march out since the battle at Charlestown. Our army are rest-
less, and wish to be doing something to rid themselves and the
land of the vermin and locusts which infest it. Since I wrote you
last, the companies stationed upon the coast, both in this town,
Weymouth, and Hingham, were ordered to Nantasket, to reap
and bring off the grain, which they accomplished, all except a
field or two which was not ripe; and having whaleboats, they undertook to go to the Lighthouse and set fire to it, which they effected in open day, and in fair sight of several men-of-war. Upon
their return came down upon them eight barges, one cutter, and
one schooner, all in battle-array, and poured whole broadsides
upon them; but our men all reached the shore, and not one life
lost, two only slightly wounded in their legs. They marched up a
hill, and drew into order in hopes the marines would land; but
they chose rather to return without a land engagement, though
'tis thought they will burn the town down as soon as our forces
leave it. I had this account from Captain Vinton, who with his
company were there. These little skirmishes seem trifling, but
they serve to inure our men, and harden them to danger. I hear
the rebels are very wroth at the destruction of the Lighthouse.

    There has been an offer from Gage to send the poor of Boston
to Salem, by water, but not complied with on our part; they returned for answer, they would receive them upon the lines. Dr.
Tufts saw a letter from Deacon Newall, in which he mentions
the death of John Cotton;[1] he says it is very sickly in town. Every
fishing vessel is now obliged to enter and clear out, as though she
was going a foreign voyage. No inhabitant is suffered to partake,
but obliged to wait till the army is supplied, and then, if one
[fish] remains, they are allowed to purchase it. An order has been
given out in town that no person shall be seen to wipe his face
with a white handkerchief. The reason I hear is, that it is a signal
of mutiny. General Burgoyne[2] lives in Mr. Sam Quincy's house.
A lady, who lived opposite, says she saw raw meat cut and
hacked upon her mahogany tables, and her superb damask curtain and cushions exposed to the rain, as if they were of no
value. How much better do the Tories fare than the Whigs? I
suppose this worthy, good man was put in with all confidence
that nothing should be hurt.

I was very much pleased with General Lee's letter,[3] and really entertained a more favorable opinion of Burgoyne than I before had imbibed from his speech; but a late letter from London, written to Mr. Josiah Quincy, and, in case of his absence, to be opened either by you or Mr. Samuel Adams, or either of the Warrens, has left me no room to think that he is possessed either of generosity, virtue, or humanity. His character runs thus:—

"As to Burgoyne, I am not master of language sufficient to give you a true idea of the horrible wickedness of the man. His designs are dark; his dissimulation of the deepest dye; for, not content with deceiving mankind, he practices deceit on God himself, by assuming the appearance (like Hutchinson) of great attention to religious worship, when every action of his life is totally abhorrent to all ideas of true religion, virtue, or common honesty. An abandoned, infamous gambler, of broken fortune, and the worst and most detestable of the Bedford gang, who are wholly bent on blood, tyranny, and spoil, and therefore the darling favorite of our unrivaled ruler, Lord Bute."[4]

The character of Howe is not drawn much more favorably, but Clinton's general character very good, and 'tis said he does not relish the service he is sent upon. I am ready to believe this of Clinton,[5] as I have never heard of any speeches of his since his arrival, nor scarcely any mention of him. That such characters as Burgoyne and Howe should engage in such a cause is not to be wondered at; but it is really to be lamented, when a man possessed of one spark of virtue should be drawn aside, and disgrace himself and posterity by adding one more to the already infamous list. I suppose you have heard of Derby's arrival,[6] and the intelligence he brings. I could not refrain wishing them everlasting fetters; "the news received with some symptoms of pleasure," and "our friends increased," and a few more such sugar plums. Were they suffering as we are, could Americans sit thus coldly whilst Britons were bleeding? How is it possible that the love of gain and the lust of domination should render the human mind so callous to every principle of honor, generosity, and benevolence?

May that day be far distant from America, when "trade's unfeeling train" shall "usurp this land, and dispossess the swain."

> "Ill fares the land, to hastening ills a prey,
>   Where wealth accumulates, and men decay;
>   Princes and lords may flourish, or may fade;
>   A breath can make them, as a breath has made;
>   But a bold peasantry, their country's pride,
>   When once destroyed, can never be supplied."[7]

Your address[8] meets with general approbation here; your petitioning the King again pleases (forgive me if I say the timid and the weak) those persons who were esteemed the lukewarm, and who think no works of supererogation can be performed to Great Britain; whilst others say you heap coals of fire upon the heads of your enemies. You know you are considered here as a most perfect body; if one member is by any means rendered incapable of acting, 'tis supposed the deficiency will be made up. The query is, why your President[9] left the Congress so long as to make it necessary to choose another member,—whether he declined returning to you again.

I suppose you have a list of our Council. It was generally thought that Gage would make an attempt to come out either Election day or upon the Fast; but I could not believe we should be disturbed upon that day. Even "the devils believe and tremble," and I really believe they are more afraid of the Americans' prayers than of their swords. I could not bear to hear our inanimate old bachelor.[10] Mrs. Cranch and I took our chaise and went to hear Mr. Haven, of Dedham,[11] and we had no occasion to repent eleven miles' ride; especially as I had the pleasure of spending the day with my namesake and sister delegate. Why should we not assume your titles when we give you up our names? I found her comfortably situated in a little country cottage, with patience, perseverance, and fortitude for her companions, and in better health than she has enjoyed for many months past.

I fear General Thomas being overlooked, and Heath placed over him, will create much uneasiness. I know not who was to blame, but it is likely to make a great and fatal gap in the army. If Thomas resigns, all his officers resign; and Mr. Thomas cannot with honor hold under Heath. The camp will evince to every eye how good an officer he has been; but this is out of my sphere. I only say what others say, and what the general disposition of the people is.

I believe you will not complain that I do not write often enough, and at length enough. When you are tired, tell me. Pray make my compliments to Mr. Barrell for his great civility to Portia. I really feel very anxious at being exposed to any eyes but yours, whose partiality I have so often experienced to cover a multitude of faults, that I rely upon it with the utmost security. You will not fail letting me hear from you by every opportunity. All our little folks send duty to papa. Johnny says, "Do you think, mamma, papa will write to me—has not he so many things to do that he will forget me?" Brother and sister Cranch send their love. My mother says I must always remember to add hers to you when I write.

I need not say how much I want to see you, but no one will credit my story of your returning in a month. I hope to have the best of proofs to convince them.

It cannot need any to convince you how sincerely

I am your affectionate   PORTIA

56. JOHN ADAMS

Philadelphia, 30 July 1775

This letter is intended to go by my friend Mr. William Barrell, whom I believe you have seen in Boston. If he calls at our house you will please to receive him complaisantly and thank him for your present of pins. I have been treated by him with great civility both at this and the former Congress.

This day I have heard my parish priest, Mr. Duffield, from 2 Chronicles xv. 1, 2. This gentleman never fails to adapt his discourse to the times. He pressed upon his audience the necessity of piety and virtue, in the present times of adversity, and held up to their view the army before Boston as an example. He understood, he said, that the voice of the swearer was scarcely heard; that the Sabbath was well observed, and all immoralities discountenanced. No doubt there were vicious individuals, but the general character was good. I hope this good man's information is true, and that this will become more and more the true character of that camp. You may well suppose that this language was exceedingly pleasing to me.

We have nothing new but the arrival of some powder. Three little vessels have certainly arrived, making about ten tons in the whole, and four or five tons have arrived from South Carolina. A supply I think now we shall certainly obtain. Congress have taken measures for this end which I hope to have the pleasure of explaining to you in person within a few days, as Congress has determined to adjourn to some time in September. I could not vote for this myself, because I thought it might be necessary to keep together, but I could not blame those who did; for really we have been all so assiduous in business in this exhausting, debilitating climate, that our lives are more exposed than they would be in camp.

Love to the children.

57. ABIGAIL ADAMS

Braintree, 31 July 1775

I do not feel easy more than two days together without writing to you. If you abound, you must lay some of the fault upon yourself, who have made such sad complaints for letters, but I really believe I have written more than all my sister delegates. There is nothing new transpired since I wrote you last, but the sailing of some transports, and five deserters having come into our camp. One of them is gone, I hear, to Philadelphia. I think I should be cautious of him. No one can tell the secret designs of such fellows, whom no oath binds. He may be sent with assassinating designs. I can credit any villainy that a Caesar Borgia would have been guilty of, or Satan himself would rejoice in. Those who do not scruple to bring poverty, misery, slavery, and death upon thousands will not hesitate at the most diabolical crimes; and this is Britain! Blush, O Americans, that ever you derived your origin from such a race.

We learn from one of these deserters that our ever-valued friend Warren, dear to us even in death, was not treated with any more respect than a common soldier; but the savage wretches, called officers, consulted together, and agreed to sever his head from his body and carry it in triumph to Gage, who no doubt would have "grinned horribly a ghastly smile," instead of imitating Caesar, who, far from being gratified with so horrid a spectacle as the head even of his enemy, turned away from Pompey's with disgust, and gave vent to his pity in a flood of tears. How much does Pagan tenderness put Christian benevolence to shame! What humanity could not obtain, the rites and ceremonies of a Mason demanded. An officer, who it seems was one of the brotherhood, requested that as a Mason he might have the body unmangled, and find a decent interment for it. He obtained his request, but upon returning to secure it, he found it already thrown into the earth, only with the ceremony of being first placed there with many bodies over it.[1]

"Nor writ his name, whose tomb should place the skies."

> "Glows my resentment into guilt?   What guilt
> Can equal violations of the dead?
> The dead how sacred! Sacred is the dust
> Of this heaven-labored form, erect, divine!
> This heaven-assumed, majestic robe of earth."[2]

2 August

Thus far I wrote, and broke off; hearing there was a probability of your return I thought not to send it; but the reception of yours this morning, of July 23d, makes me think the day further off than I hoped. I therefore will add a few lines, though very unfit. I have had a very ill night. Just recovered from the rash, I went out yesterday to attend the funeral of the poor fellow who, the night before, fell in battle, as they were returning from the Lighthouse. I caught some cold. Sabbath evening there was a warm fire from Prospect Hill and Bunker's Hill, begun first by the riflemen taking off their guard. Two men upon our side were killed; five of their guards were killed, two taken. I believe my account will be very confused, but I will relate it as well as I am able. Sabbath evening a number of men, in whaleboats, went off from Squantum and Dorchester to the Lighthouse, where the General, Gage, had again fixed up a lamp, and sent twelve carpenters to repair it. Our people went on amidst a hot fire from thirty marines, who were placed there as a guard to the Tory carpenters, burnt the dwelling-house, took the Tories and twenty-eight marines, killed the lieutenant and one man, brought off all the oil and stores which were sent, without the loss of a man, until they were upon their return, when they were so closely pursued that they were obliged to run one whaleboat ashore, and leave her to them; the rest arrived safe, except the unhappy youth whose funeral I yesterday attended, who received a ball through the temple as he was rowing the boat. He belonged to Rhode Island. His name was Griffin. He, with four wounded marines, was brought by Captain Turner to Germantown, and buried from there with the honors of war. Mr. Wibird upon the occasion, made the best oration (he never prays, you know) I ever heard from him. The poor wounded fellows (who were all wounded in their arms) desired they might attend. They did, and he very pathetically addressed them, with which they appeared affected. I spoke with them,—I told them it was very unhappy that they should be obliged to fight their best friends. They said they were sorry; they hoped in God an end would be speedily put to the unhappy contest; when they came, they came in the way of their duty, to relieve Admiral Montague,[3] with no thought of fighting, but their situation was such as obliged them to obey orders; but they wished, with all their souls, that they that sent them here had been in the heat of the battle; expressed gratitude at the kindness they received; and said, in that they had been deceived, for they were told, if they were taken alive they would be sacrificed by us. Dr. Tufts dressed their wounds.

I had a design to write something about a talked-of appointment[4] of a friend of mine to a judicial department, but hope soon to see that friend before his acceptance may be necessary. I inclose a compliment, copied by a gentleman from a piece in the Worcester paper, signed "Lycurgus."

I can add no more, as the good Colonel Palmer waits. Only my compliments to Mrs. Mifflin, and tell her I do not know whether her husband is safe here. Bellona and Cupid have a contest about him. You hear nothing from the ladies but about Major Mifflin's easy address, politeness, complaisance, etc. 'Tis well he has so agreeable a lady at Philadelphia. They know nothing about forts, intrenchments, etc., when they return,[5] or, if they do, they are all forgotten and swallowed up in his accomplishments.

Adieu, my dearest friend, and always believe me

Unalterably yours,   PORTIA

58. ABIGAIL ADAMS

Braintree, 10 August 1775

DEAREST FRIEND, — 'Tis with a sad heart I take my pen to write to you, because I must be the bearer of what will greatly afflict and distress you. Yet I wish you to be prepared for the event. Your brother Elihu lies very dangerously sick with a dysentery. He has been very bad for more than a week. His life is despaired of. Ere I close this letter, I fear I shall write you that he is no more.

We are all in great distress. Your father is with him in great anguish. I hear this morning that he is sensible of his danger, and calmly resigned to the will of Heaven, which is a great satisfaction to his mourning friends. I cannot write more at present than to assure you of the health of your own family. Mr. Elisha Niles lies very bad with the same disorder.

11 August

I have this morning occasion to sing of mercies and judgments. May I properly notice each. A mixture of joy and grief agitates my bosom. The return of thee, my dear partner, after a four months' absence, is a pleasure I cannot express; but the joy is overclouded, and the day is darkened, by the mixture of grief,— the sympathy I feel for the loss of your brother, cut off in the pride of life and the bloom of manhood, in the midst of his usefulness. Heaven sanctify this affliction to us, and make me properly thankful that it is not my sad lot to mourn the loss of a husband in the room of a brother.

May thy life be spared and thy health confirmed for the benefit of thy country and the happiness of thy family, is the constant supplication of thy friend.

59. ABIGAIL ADAMS

Braintree, 8 September

Since you left me I have passed through great distress both of body and mind, and whether greater is to be my portion, Heaven only knows.

You may remember Isaac[1] was unwell when you went from home. His disorder increased, till a violent dysentery was the consequence of his complaints. There was no resting-place in the house, for his terrible groans. He continued in this state near a week, when his disorder abated, and we have now hopes of his recovery. Two days after he was sick, I was seized with the same disorder in a violent manner. Had I known you were at Watertown, I should have sent Brackett for you. I suffered greatly between my inclination to have you return and my fear of sending lest you should be a partaker of the common calamity. After three days an abatement of my disease relieved me from anxiety. The next person in the same week was Susy; her we carried home,—hope she will not be very bad. Our little Tommy was the next, and he lies very ill now. There is no abatement at present of his disorder. I hope he is not dangerous. Yesterday Patty was seized, and took a puke. Our house is a hospital in every part; and what with my own weakness and distress of mind for my family, I have been unhappy enough.

And such is the distress of the neighborhood, that I can scarcely find a well person to assist in looking after the sick. Mrs. Randall has one child that is not expected to live out the night. Mrs. Belcher has another; Joseph Bracket, another; Deacon Adams has lost one, but is on the recovery himself, and so are the rest of his family. Mr. Wibird lies bad; Major Miller is dangerous, and Mr. Gay is not expected to live.

So sickly and so mortal a time the oldest man does not remember. I am anxious for you. Pray let me hear from you soon. I thought you would have left me a letter at Watertown, as you stayed so long there. I was disappointed that you did not. As to politics, I know nothing about them. The distresses of my own family are so great that I have not thought of them. I have written as much as I am able to, being very weak. I hope to add a more pleasing account ere I close.

Sunday, 10 September

'Tis now two days since I wrote. As to my own health, I mend but very slowly; have been fearful of a return of my disorder today, but feel rather better now. Hope it is only owing to my having been fatigued with looking after Tommy, as he is unwilling any one but mamma should do for him; and, if he was, I could not find anybody that is worth having, but what is taken up already for the sick. Tommy, I hope, is mending. His fever has abated, his bowels are better, but were you to look in upon him, you would not know him. From a hearty, hale, corn-fed boy, he has become pale, lean, and wan. Isaac is getting better, but very slowly. Patty is very bad. We cannot keep anything down that she takes; her situation is very dangerous. Mr. Trott and one of his children are taken with the disorder. I shall write every day if I am able.

Pray let me hear from you often. Heaven preserve both your life and health, and all my suffering will be but small. By the first safe conveyance be kind enough to send me one ounce of Turkey rhubarb, the root, and to procure me one quarter of a pound of nutmegs, for which here I have to give 2*s.* 8*d.* lawful; one ounce of cloves, two of cinnamon. You may send me only a few of the nutmegs till Bass returns. I should be glad of one ounce of Indian root. So much sickness has occasioned a scarcity of medicine.

Destroy this. Such a doleful tale it contains can give no pleasure to any one. Our other children are well, and send duty to papa. Brackett has been complaining, but has got better. The small-pox in the natural way was not more mortal than this distemper has proved in this and many neighboring towns. Eighteen have been buried since you left us, in Mr. Weld's parish. Four, three, and two funerals in a day, for many days, Hitherto our family has been greatly favored. Heaven still preserve us. 'Tis a melancholy time with us. I hope you will not think me in the dismals; but public and private judgments ought to be noticed by every one.

I am, most affectionately, yours,   PORTIA

60. ABIGAIL ADAMS

Braintree, Sunday, 16 September 1775

I set myself down to write with a heart depressed with the melancholy scenes around me. My letter will be only a bill of mortality; though thanks be to that Being who restraineth the pestilence, that it has not yet proved mortal to any of our family, though we live in daily expectation that Patty will not continue many hours. A general putrefaction seems to have taken place, and we cannot bear the house only as we are constantly cleansing it with hot vinegar. I had no idea of the distemper producing such a state as hers, till now. Yet we take all possible care by shifting her bed every day. Two of the children, John and Charles, I have sent out of the house, finding it difficult to keep them out of the chamber. Nabby continues well. Tommy is better, but entirely stripped of the hardy, robust countenance, as well as of all the flesh he had, save what remains for to keep his bones together. Jonathan is the only one who remains in the family who has not had a turn of the disorder. Mrs. Randall has lost her daughter. Mrs. Brackett, hers. Mr. Thomas Thayer, his wife. Two persons belonging to Boston have died this week in this parish. I know of eight this week who have been buried in this town.

In Weymouth, it is very sickly, but not mortal. Dr. Tufts tells me he has between sixty and seventy patients now sick with this disorder. Mr. Thaxter has been obliged to go home, as it was not possible for me to accommodate him. Mr. Mason[1] came this week, but if he had been inclined, I could not have taken him now. But the general sickness in the towns determined him to return home for the present. The dread upon the minds of people of catching the distemper is almost as great as if it was the smallpox. I have been disturbed more than ever I was in my life to procure watchers and to get assistance.

I hear Mr. Tudor has been dangerously sick, but is now upon the recovery. Mr. Wibird is very low indeed, scarcely able to walk a step. We have been four Sundays without any meeting. Thus does pestilence travel in the rear of war, to remind us of our entire dependence upon that Being who not only directeth the arrow by day, but has also at his command that which flieth in darkness. So uncertain and so transitory are all the enjoyments of life, that were it not for the tender connections which bind us, would it not be folly to wish for continuance here? I think I shall never be wedded to the world, and were I to lose about a dozen of my dearest connections, I should have no further relish for life.

But perhaps I deceive myself and know but little of my own heart.

> "To bear and suffer is our portion here."

And unto Him who mounts the whirlwind and directs the storm I will cheerfully leave the ordering of my lot, and whether adverse or prosperous days should be my future portion, I will trust in his right hand to lead me safely through, and, after a short rotation of events, fix me in a state immutable and happy.

You will think me melancholy. 'Tis true, I am much affected by the distressed scenes around me, but I have some anxieties in my mind which I do not think it prudent to mention at present to any one. Perhaps when I hear from you, I may in my next letter tell you.

In the mean time I wish you would tell me whether the intercepted letters have reached Philadelphia, and what effect they have there. There is a most infamous versification[2] of them, I hear, sent out. I have not been able to get it.

As to politics, there seems to be a dead calm upon all sides. Some of the Tories have been sending out their children. Colonel Chandler has sent out his, and Mr. Winslow[3] has sent out his daughter. People appear to be gratified with the Remonstrance, Address, and Petition,[4] and most earnestly long for further intelligence.

God helps them that help themselves, as King Richard says; and if we can obtain the Divine aid by our own virtue, fortitude, and perseverance, we may be sure of relief.

To-morrow will be three weeks since you left home; in all which time I have not heard one word from you. Patience is a lesson I have not to learn, so can wait your own time, but hope it will not be long ere my anxious heart is relieved.

Adieu! I need not say how sincerely I am

Your affectionate   PORTIA

61 · JOHN ADAMS

Philadelphia, 17 September 1775

This is the first time that I have attempted to write since I left you. I arrived here in good health, after an agreeable journey, last Wednesday. There had not been members enough to make a House, several colonies being absent, so that I was just in time. The next day an adequate number appeared, and Congress has sat ever since. Georgia is now fully represented, and united to the other twelve. Their delegates are Doctor Zubly,[1] a clergyman of the Independent persuasion, who has a parish in that colony, and a good deal of property. He is a native of Switzerland; is a man of learning and ingenuity. It is said he is master of several languages—Greek, Latin, French, Dutch, and English; in the latter it is said he writes tolerably. He is a man of zeal and spirit, as we have already seen upon several occasions. However, as he is the first gentleman of the cloth who has appeared in Congress, I cannot but wish he may be the last. Mixing the sacred character with that of the statesman, as it is quite unnecessary at this time of day, in these colonies, is not attended with any good effects. The clergy are universally too little acquainted with the world and the modes of business, to engage in civil affairs with any advantage. Besides, those of them who are really men of learning, have conversed with books so much more than men as to be too much loaded with vanity to be good politicians. Mr. Bullock is another of the Georgia delegates—a sensible man— a planter, I suppose. Mr. Houston is the third, a young lawyer, of modesty as well as sense and spirit, which you will say is uncommon.

Mr. Jones and Doctor Hall[2] are not yet arrived.

Mr. Henry is made a General in Virginia, and therefore could not come. Mr. Pendleton and Colonel Bland excused themselves on account of age and ill-health. Messrs. Nelson, Wythe, and Lee[3] are chosen, and are here in the stead of the other three. Wythe and Lee are inoculated. You shall hear more about them. Although they come in the room of very good men, we have lost nothing by the change, I believe. Remember me in the tenderest language to all our little folks. I am yours.

62. JOHN ADAMS

Philadelphia, 1 October 1775

This morning I received your two letters, of 8 September and 16 September. What shall I say? The intelligence they contain came upon me by surprise, as I never had the least intimation before that any of my family was ill, excepting in a card from Mrs. Warren, received a few days ago, in which she informed me that "Mrs. Adams had been unwell, but was better."

You may easily conceive the state of mind in which I am at present. Uncertain and apprehensive at first, I suddenly thought of setting off immediately for Braintree, and I have not yet determined otherwise. Yet the state of public affairs is so critical that I am half afraid to leave my station, although my presence here is of no great consequence.

I feel, I tremble for you. Poor Tommy! I hope, by this time, however, he has recovered his plump cheeks and his fine bloom. By your account of Patty I fear, but still I will hope she has been supported, and is upon the recovery. I rejoice to learn that Nabby and her brothers have hitherto escaped, and pray God that His goodness may be still continued to them. Your description of the distressed state of the neighborhood is affecting indeed. It is not uncommon for a train of calamities to come together. Fire, sword, pestilence, famine, often keep company and visit a country in a flock.

At this distance I can do no good to you nor yours. I pray God to support you. I hope our friends and neighbors are kind as usual. I feel for them in the general calamity. I am so far from thinking you melancholy, that I am charmed with that admirable fortitude and that divine spirit of resignation which appear in your letters. I cannot express the satisfaction it gives me, nor how much it contributes to support me.

You have alarmed me, however, by mentioning anxieties which you do not think it prudent to mention to any one. I am wholly at a loss to conjecture what they can be. If they arise from the letters, be assured that you may banish them forever. These letters[1] have reached Philadelphia, but have produced effects very different from those which were expected from the publication of them. These effects I will explain to you sometime or other. As to the versification of them, if there is wit or humor in it, laugh; if ill-nature, sneer; if mere dullness, why, you may even yawn or nod. I have no anger at it, nay even scarcely contempt. It is impotent.

As to politics, we have nothing to expect but the whole wrath and force of Great Britain. But your words are as true as an oracle, "God helps them who help themselves, and if we obtain the divine aid by our own virtue, fortitude, and perseverance, we may be sure of relief." It may amuse you to hear a story. A few days ago, in company with Dr. Zubly, somebody said there was nobody on our side but the Almighty. The Doctor, who is a native of Switzerland, and speaks but broken English, quickly replied, "Dat is enough! Dat is enough!" And turning to me, says he, "It puts me in mind of a fellow who once said, The Catholics have on their side the Pope, and the King of France, and the King of Spain, and the King of Sardinia, and the King of Poland, and the Emperor of Germany, etc., etc., etc.; but as to those poor devils, the Protestants, they have nothing on their side but God Almighty."

63. ABIGAIL ADAMS

Weymouth, 1 October 1775

Have pity upon me. Have pity upon me, O thou my beloved, for the hand of God presseth me sore.[1]

Yet will I be dumb and silent, and not open my mouth, because Thou, O Lord, hast done it.

How can I tell you (O my bursting heart!) that my dear mother has left me? This day, about five o'clock, she left this world for an infinitely better.

After sustaining sixteen days' severe conflict, nature fainted, and she fell asleep. Blessed spirit! where art thou? At times I am almost ready to faint under this severe and heavy stroke, separated from *thee*, who used to be a comforter to me in affliction; but, blessed be God, his ear is not heavy that He cannot hear, but He has bid us call upon Him in time of trouble.

I know you are a sincere and hearty mourner with me, and

will pray for me in my affliction. My poor father, like a firm believer and a good Christian, sets before his children the best of examples of patience and submission. My sisters send their love to you and are greatly afflicted. You often expressed your anxiety for me when you left me before, surrounded with terrors; but my trouble then was as the small dust in the balance, compared to what I have since endured. I hope to be properly mindful of the correcting hand, that I may not be rebuked in anger.

You will pardon and forgive all my wanderings of mind; I cannot be correct.

'Tis a dreadful time with the whole province. Sickness and death are in almost every family. I have no more shocking and terrible idea of any distemper, except the plague, than this.

Almighty God! restrain the pestilence which walketh in darkness and wasteth at noonday, and which has laid in the dust one of the dearest of parents. May the life of the other be lengthened out to his afflicted children.

From your distressed   PORTIA

64. JOHN ADAMS

Philadelphia, 2 October 1775

Everything here is in as good a way as I could wish, considering the temper and designs of Administration. I assure you the letters have had no such bad effects as the Tories intended, and as some of our short-sighted Whigs apprehended; so far otherwise, that I see and hear every day fresh proofs that everybody is coming fast into every political sentiment contained in them. I assure you I could mention compliments passed upon them, and if a serious decision could be had upon them, the public voice would be found in their favor.

But I am distressed with cares of another kind. Your two letters are never out of my thoughts. I should have mounted my horse this day for Braintree if I had not hopes of hearing further from you in a day or two. However, I will hope that your prospects are more agreeable than they were, and that the children are all better, as well as the rest of the family, and the neighbors. If I should hear more disagreeable advices from you, I shall certainly come home, for I cannot leave you in such affliction without endeavoring to lessen it, unless there was an absolute necessity of my staying here to do a duty to the public, which I think there is not.

I must beg to be excused, my dear, from hinting at anything for the future, of public persons or things. Secrecy is so much exacted. But thus much I may say, that I never saw so serious and determined a spirit. I must also beseech you to be cautious what you write to me and by whom you send. Letters sent to the care of Colonel Warren will come safe. My regards, with all proper distinctions, to my relations and yours, my friends and yours, my acquaintances and yours.

This will go by Major Bayard,[1] a gentleman of the Presbyterian persuasion in this city, of excellent character, to whom I am indebted for a great many civilities.

65. JOHN ADAMS

7 October 1775

Yesterday, by the post, I received yours of 25 September. And it renewed a grief and anxiety that were before almost removed from my mind. Two days before, I had the pleasure of a very valuable letter from Colonel Quincy, in which he kindly informed me that you and our family were so much better that you and my dear Nabby had made a visit at his house; and Mr. Williams, who brought the letter, acquainted me that he had been to Braintree after the date of it, that you was in good spirits, that Tommy was so much better as to be playing abroad, and that he hoped Patty was not in danger. You will easily believe that this information gave me great pleasure and fine spirits. It really relieved me from a heavy load. But your last letter has revived my concern. I will still hope, however, that your excellent mother will yet be spared for a blessing to her family, and an example to the world. I build my hopes of her recovery upon the advantage of a constitution which has hitherto sustained so many attacks, and upon a long course of exact temperance, which, I hope, has deprived the distemper of its most dangerous food and fuel. However, our lives are not in our own power. It is our duty to submit. "The ways of Heaven are dark and intricate," its designs are often inscrutable, but are always wise and just and good.

It was long before I had the least intimation of the distress of the family, and I fear that your not receiving so many letters from me as usual may have been one cause of infelicity to you. Really, my dear, I have been more cautious than I used to be. It is not easy to know whom to trust in these times; and if a letter from any person in the situation I am in can be laid hold of, there are so many lies made and told about it, so many false copies taken and dispersed, and so many false constructions put, that one ought to be cautious.

The situation of things is so alarming, that it is our duty to prepare our minds and hearts for every event, even the worst. From my earliest entrance into life, I have been engaged in the public cause of America; and from first to last I have had upon my mind a strong impression that things would be wrought up to their present crisis. I saw from the beginning that the controversy was of such a nature that it never would be settled, and every day convinces me more and more. This has been the source of all the disquietude of my life. It has lain down and risen up with me these twelve years. The thought that we might be driven to the sad necessity of breaking our connection with Great Britain, exclusive of the carnage and destruction, which it was easy to see must attend the separation, always gave me a great deal of grief. And even now I would cheerfully retire from public life forever, renounce all chance for profits or honors from the public, nay, I would cheerfully contribute my little property, to obtain peace and liberty. But all these must go, and my life too, before I can surrender the right of my country to a free Constitution. I dare not consent to it. I should be the most miserable of mortals ever after, whatever honors or emoluments might surround me.

66. ABIGAIL ADAMS

Braintree, 9 October 1775

I have not been composed enough to write you since last Sabbath, when in the bitterness of my soul I wrote a few confused lines, since which it has pleased the great disposer of all events to add breach to breach.

> "Rare are solitary woes, they leave a train
> And tread each other's heel."[1]

The day week that I was called to attend a dying parent's bed I was again called to mourn the loss of one of my own family. I have just returned from attending Patty to the grave. No doubt, long before this will reach you, you have received a melancholy train of letters, in some of which I mention her as dangerously sick. She has lain five weeks, wanting a few days, so bad that we had little hope of her recovery. The latter part of the time she was the most shocking object my eyes ever beheld, and so loathsome that it was with the utmost difficulty we could bear the house. A mortification took place a week before she died, and rendered her a most pitiable object. We have yet great sickness in the town. She made the fourth corpse that was this day committed to the ground. We have many others now so bad as to despair of their lives.

But blessed be the Father of mercies, all our family are now well, though I have my apprehension lest the malignancy of the air in the house may have infected some of them. We have fevers of various kinds, the throat distemper as well as the dysentery prevailing in this and the neighboring towns.

How long, O Lord, shall the whole land say, I am sick![2] Oh, show us wherefore it is that Thou art thus contending with us! In a very particular manner I have occasion to make this inquiry, who have had breach upon breach—nor has one wound been permitted to be healed ere it is made to bleed afresh. In six weeks I count five of my near connections laid in the grave. Your aunt Simpson[3] died at Milton about ten days ago, with the dysentery.

But the heavy stroke which most of all disturbs me is my dear mother. I cannot overcome my too selfish sorrow. All her tenderness towards me, her care and anxiety for my welfare at all times; her watchfulness over my infant years, her advice and instruction in maturer age,—all, all endear her memory to me and heighten my sorrow for her loss. At the same time, I know a patient submission is my duty. I will strive to obtain it, but the lenient hand of time alone can blunt the keen edge of sorrow. He who deigned to weep over a departed friend will surely forgive a sorrow which at all times desires to be bounded and restrained by a firm belief that a Being of infinite wisdom and unbounded goodness will carve out my portion in tender mercy to me. Yea, though He slay me, I will trust in Him, said holy Job. What though His corrective hand hath been stretched against me; I will not murmur. Though earthly comforts are taken away, I will not repine. He who gave them has surely a right to limit their duration, and He has continued them to me much longer than I deserve. I might have been stripped of my children, as many others have been. I might,—oh, forbid it Heaven,—I might have been left a solitary widow!

Still I have many blessings left, many comforts thankful for and rejoice in. I am not left to mourn as one without hope. My dear parent knew in whom she had believed, and from the first attack of the distemper she was persuaded it would prove fatal to her. A solemnity possessed her soul, nor could you force a smile from her till she died. The violence of her disease soon weakened her so that she was unable to converse, but whenever she could speak, she testified her willingness to leave the world and an entire resignation to the Divine Will. She retained her senses to the last moment of her existence, and departed the world with an easy tranquillity, trusting in the merits of a Redeemer. Her passage to immortality was marked with a placid smile upon her countenance, nor was there to be seen scarcely a vestige of the king of terrors.

> "The sweet remembrance of the just
> Shall flourish when they sleep in Dust."

'Tis by soothing grief that it can be healed.

"Give sorrow words. The grief that cannot speak
Whispers the o'erfraught heart and bids it break."[4]

Forgive me for thus dwelling upon a subject sweet to me, but I fear painful to you. Oh, how I have longed for your bosom, to pour forth my sorrows there and find a healing balm; but perhaps that has been denied me that I might be led to a higher and a more permanent consolator who has bid us all call upon Him in the day of trouble.

As this is the first day since your absence that I could write you that we were all well, I desire to mark it with particular gratitude and humbly hope that all my warnings and corrections are not in vain.

I most thankfully received your kind favor of the 26th, yesterday. It gives me much pleasure to hear of your health. I pray Heaven for the continuance of it. I hope for the future to be able to give you more intelligence with regard to what passes out of my own little circle, but such has been my distress that I know nothing of the political world.

You have doubtless heard of the villainy of one who has professed himself a patriot.[5] But let not that man be trusted who can violate private faith and cancel solemn covenants, who can leap over moral law and laugh at Christianity. How is he to be bound whom neither honor nor conscience holds? We have here a rumor that Rhode Island has shared the fate of Charlestown. Is this the day we read of, when Satan was to be loosed?

I do not hear of any inhabitants getting out of town. 'Tis said Gage is superseded and Howe in his place, and that Howe released the prisoners from jail. 'Tis also said, though not much credited, that Burgoyne is gone to Philadelphia.

I hope to hear from you soon. Adieu, 'tis almost twelve o'clock at night. I have had so little sleep lately that I must bid you goodnight.   PORTIA

67. JOHN ADAMS

Philadelphia, 10 October 1775

I am much concerned lest you should feel an addition to your anxieties, from your having so seldom heard from me. But I pray you to dismiss all concern about me. I am happier far than I was before the adjournment. My health is better, and business and conversation are much more to my taste.

The surprising intelligence we have in private letters concerning the Director of the Hospital, has made me more cautious of writing than ever. I must be excused from writing a syllable of anything of any moment. My letters have been and will be nothing but trifles. I don't choose to trust the post. I am afraid to trust private travellers. They may peep. Accidents may happen. And I would avoid, if I could, even ridicule, but especially mischief.

Pray, bundle up every paper, not already hid, and conceal them in impenetrable darkness. Nobody knows what may occur.

My love to those who are dearest to us both. Send yours to the care of the gentleman whose care has hitherto been successful.[1] Date them in time but not place, and assume a now fictitious name.

68. JOHN ADAMS

13 October 1775

I this day received yours of the 29th of September and the 1st of October. Amidst all your afflictions, I am rejoiced to find that you all along preserve so proper and so happy a temper; that you are sensible "the consolations of religion are the only sure comforters." It is the constitution under which we are born, that if we live long ourselves, we must bury our parents and all our elder relations, and many of those who are younger. I have lost parent, a child, and a brother, and each of them left a lasting impression on my mind. But you and I have many more relations and very good friends to follow to the house appointed for all flesh, or else we must be followed by them. In your last you make no mention of Patty, poor distressed girl! I fear the next news I shall hear will be of her departure, yet I will hope that youth, and a strong constitution which has lasted so long, will finally survive. If not we must submit. I bewail, more than I can express, the loss of your excellent mother. I mourn the loss of so much purity, and unaffected piety and virtue, to the world. I know of no better character left in it. I grieve for you, and your brother and sisters. I grieve for your father, whose age will need the succor of so excellent a companion. But I grieve for nobody more than my children, and brothers Smith's and Mr. Cranch's. Her most amiable and discreet example, as well as her kind skill and care, I have ever relied upon, in my own mind, for the education of these little swarms. Not that I have not a proper esteem for the capacity and disposition of the mother, but I know that the efforts of the grandmother are of great importance, when they second those of the parent. And I am sure that my children are the better for the forming hand of their grandmother. It gives me great joy to learn that ours are well. Let us be thankful for this, and many other blessings yet granted us. Pray, my dear, cherish in the minds of my Nabby and Johnny and Charley and Tommy the remembrance of their grandmamma, and remind them of her precepts and example. God Almighty grant to you and to every branch of the family all the support that you want.

You and I, my dear, have reason, if ever mortals had, to be thoughtful; to look forward beyond the transitory scene. Whatever is preparing for us, let us be prepared to receive. It is time for us to subdue our passions of every kind. The prospect before us is an ocean of uncertainties, in which no pleasing objects appear. We have few hopes, excepting that of preserving our honor and our consciences untainted, and a free Constitution to our country. Let me be sure of these, and, amidst all my weaknesses, I cannot be overcome. With these, I can be happy in extreme poverty, in humble insignificance, nay I hope and believe, in death. Without them, I should be miserable with a crown upon my head, millions in my coffers, and a gaping, idolizing multitude at my feet.

My heart is too full of grief for you and our friends, to whom I wish you to present my regards, to say anything of news or politics. Yet the affair of the Surgeon-general is so strange and

important an event that I cannot close this gloomy letter without adding a sigh for this imprudent, unfortunate man. I know
not whether the evidence will support the word treachery, but
what may we not expect after treachery to himself, his wife and
children?

69. JOHN ADAMS

19 October 1775

It is some time since I wrote you, and I have nothing now to
write but repetitions of respect and affection. I am anxious to
hear from you. I hope the family is better; that your grief for the
great loss we have all sustained is somewhat abated. I hope your
father and sister Betsey are well, though they must be greatly afflicted. Give my love to Betsey, and let her know that I feel most
intimately for her, as well as for myself and the rest. I consider
the stroke must fall heavier upon her, as it was nearer to her. Her
prosperity is near my heart. I wish her every blessing which she
can possibly wish for herself.

Really, it is very painful to be four hundred miles from one's
family and friends, when we know they are in affliction. It seems
as if it would be a joy to me to fly home, even to share with you
your burdens and misfortunes. Surely, if I were with you, it
would be my study to allay your griefs, to mitigate your pains,
and to divert your melancholy thoughts. When I shall come
home, I know not. We have so much to do, and it is so difficult
to do it right, that we must learn patience. Upon my word, I
think, if ever I were to come here again, I must bring you with
me. I could live here pleasantly, if I had you with me. Will you
come and have the small-pox[1] here? I wish I could remove all the
family, our little daughter and sons, and all go through the distemper here. What if we should? Let me please myself with the
thought, however.

Congress has appointed Mr. Wythe, Mr. Deane, and me a
committee to collect an account of the hostilities committed by
the troops and ships, with proper evidence of the number and
value of the houses and other buildings destroyed or damaged,
the vessels captivated, and the cattle, sheep, hogs, etc., taken. We

are about writing to all the General Assemblies of New England, and to many private gentlemen in each colony, to assist us in making the collections. The gentlemen with me are able men. Deane's character you know. He is a very ingenious man and an able politician. Wythe is a new member from Virginia, a lawyer of the highest eminence in that province, a learned and very laborious man; so that we may hope this commission will be well executed. A tale of woe it will be! Such a scene of distress and destruction, and so patiently and magnanimously borne! Such a scene of cruelty and barbarity, so unfeelingly committed! I mention this to you, my dear, that you may look up, and transmit to me, a paper which Colonel Palmer lent me, containing a relation of the Charlestown battle, which was transmitted to England by the Committee of Safety. This paper I must have, or a copy of it.

I wish I could collect, from the people of Boston or others, a proper set of paintings of the scenes of distress and misery brought upon that town from the commencement of the Port Bill. Posterity must hear a story that shall make their ears to tingle.

Yours, yours, yours.

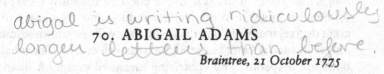

70. ABIGAIL ADAMS

Braintree, 21 October 1775

'Tis ten days since I have wrote you a line; I have received one letter since dated 27 of September. You do not mention having heard from me although I have wrote six letters. I thought I should have heard oftener from you in this absence than I had ever done before, but it has been quite otherwise. I never found the communication so difficult, and 'tis only in my night visions that I know anything about you. I have now the pleasure to tell you that we are all well. Charley has had an ill turn since I wrote, but soon got better. Mr. Thaxter and Mr. Mason are returned to me, and my family begins again to appear as it used to. Hayden does not stir. Says he will not go out of the parish unless he is carried out—and here nobody will let him come in. I have offered him part of the house that Field is in if he will but go out, but nowhere suits, and it is not to be wondered at as he has wood at free cost and has plundered pretty well from the family they live with many articles. I have a great mind to send a sheriff and put him out.

The sickness has abated here and in the neighboring towns. In Boston, I am told, it is very sickly among the inhabitants and the soldiery. By a man, one Haskins, who came out the day before yesterday, I learn that there are but about twenty-five hundred soldiers in town. How many there are at Charlestown, he could not tell. He had been in irons three weeks, some malicious fellow having said that he saw him at the battle of Lexington; but he proved that he was not out of Boston that day, upon which he was released, and went with two other men out in a small boat, under their eye, to fish. They played about near the shore, while catching small fish, till they thought they could possibly reach Dorchester Neck; no sooner were they perceived attempting to escape, than they had twenty cannons discharged at them, but they all happily reached the shore. He says no language can paint the distress of the inhabitants; most of them destitute of wood and of provisions of every kind. The bakers say, unless they have a new supply of wood they cannot bake above one fortnight longer; their biscuit are not above one half the former size; the soldiers are obliged to do very hard duty, and are uneasy to a great degree, many of them declaring they will not continue much longer in such a state, but at all hazards will escape. The inhabitants are desperate, and contriving means of escape. A floating battery of ours went out two nights ago, and rowed near the town, and then discharged their guns. Some of the balls went into the workhouse, some through the tents in the Common, and one through the sign of the Lamb Tavern. He says it drove them all out of the Common, men, women, and children screaming, and threw them into the utmost distress; but, very unhappily for us, in the discharge of one of the cannon, the ball not being properly rammed down, it split and killed two men, and wounded seven more, upon which they were obliged to return. He also says that the Tories are much distressed about the fate of Dr. Church, and very anxious to obtain him, and would exchange Lovell for him.

This man is so exasperated at the ill usage he has received from them, that he is determined to enlist immediately. They almost starved him whilst he was in irons. He says he hopes it will be in his power to send some of them to heaven for mercy. They are building a fort by the hay-market, and rending down houses for timber to do it with. In the course of the last week, several persons have found means to escape. One of them says it is talked in town that Howe will issue a proclamation, giving liberty to all who will not take up arms, to depart the town, and making it death to have any intercourse with the country afterwards.

At present it looks as if there was no likelihood of peace; the ministry are determined to proceed at all events; the people are already slaves, and have neither virtue nor spirit to help themselves nor us. The time is hastening when George, like Richard, may cry, "My kingdom for a horse!" and want even that wealth to make the purchase. I hope by degrees we shall be inured to hardships, and become a virtuous, valiant people, forgetting our former luxury, and each one apply with industry and frugality to manufactory and husbandry, till we rival all other nations by our virtues.

I thank you for your amusing account of the Quakers; their great stress with regard to color in their dress, etc., is not the only ridiculous part of their sentiments with regard to religious matters.

> "There's not a day but to the man of thought
> Betrays some secret, that throws new reproach
> On life, and makes him sick of seeing more."[1]

What are your thoughts with regard to Dr. Church? Had you much knowledge of him? I think you had no intimate acquaintance with him.

> "A foe to God was ne'er true friend to man;
> Some sinister intent taints all he does."[2]

It is matter of great speculation what will be his punishment; the people are much enraged against him; if he is set at liberty, even after he has received a severe punishment, I do not think he will be safe. He will be despised and detested by every one, and many suspicions will remain in the minds of people in regard to our rulers; they are for supposing *this* person is not sincere, and *that* they have jealousy of.

Have you any prospect of returning? I hoped to have heard from you by the gentlemen who came as a committee here;[3] but they have been here a week, and I have not any letters.

My father and sister Betsey desire to be remembered to you. He is very disconsolate. It makes my heart ache to see him, and I know not how to go to the house. He said to me the other day, "Child, I see your mother, go to what part of the house I will." I think he has lost almost as much flesh as if he had been sick; and Betsey, poor girl, looks broken and worn with grief. These near connections, how they twist and cling about the heart, and, when torn off, draw the best blood from it.

> "Each friend by fate snatched from us is a plume
> Plucked from the wing of human vanity."[4]

Be so good as to present my regards to Mrs. Hancock. I hope she is very happy. Mrs. Warren called upon me on her way to Watertown. I wish I could as easily come to you as she can go to Watertown. But it is my lot. In the twelve years we have been married, I believe we have not lived together more than six.

If you could, with any conveniency, procure me the articles I wrote for, I should be very glad, more especially the needles and cloth; they are in such demand that we are really distressed for want of them.

We have had abundance of rain since you left us. I hope the sickness with which we have been exercised has not reached Philadelphia. Mr. Wibird has not been able to preach since you left us, and is in a very low state. Our little ones are well. Tommy is so fat he can scarcely see out of his eyes, but is still exercised with the fits. Dr. Tufts's son is sick with a slow fever.

Adieu. I think of nothing further to add, but that I am, with the tenderest regard, your   PORTIA

P.S. Since I wrote the above I have received a letter by Mr. Bayard for which I thank you. It gives me great pleasure to find you in so good health. I have heard this evening that a man-of-war has been sent to Falmouth to make a demand of wood, upon which an express was sent off to our camp, and the express says a few hours after he set out, he heard a smart cannonade. The truth has not yet reached us. We are anxious to hear from Canada.

If you can procure me some Carolina pinkroot from any of the apothecaries I wish you would for Tommy. We think knots of worms is the occasion of his fits. I have tried wormseed, but it has no effect.

Write if you can to my father and sister. Send the newspapers; they are very acceptable.

71. ABIGAIL ADAMS

Braintree, 22 October 1775

Mr. Lothrop[1] called here this evening, and brought me yours of the 1st of October,—a day which will ever be remembered by me, for it was the most distressing one I ever experienced. That morning I rose, and went into my mother's room, not apprehending her so near her exit; went to her bed with a cup of tea in my hand, and raised her head to give it to her. She swallowed a few drops, gasped, and fell back upon her pillow, opening her eyes with a look that pierced my heart, and which I shall never forget; it was the eagerness of a last look;

> "And oh, the last sad silence of a friend!"

Yet she lived till five o'clock that day, but I could not be with her. My dear father prayed twice beside her bed that day. God Almighty was with him and supported him that day, and enabled him to go through the services of it. It was his communion day,[2] he had there a tender scene to pass through—a young granddaughter, Betsey Cranch, joining herself to the church, and a beloved wife dying, to pray for. Weeping children, weeping and mourning parishioners all round him, for every eye streamed, his own heart almost bursting as he spoke. How painful is the recollection, and yet how pleasing!

I know I wound your heart. Why should I? Ought I to give relief to my own by paining yours? Yet

"the grief that cannot speak
Whispers the o'erfraught heart and bids it break."

My pen is always freer than my tongue. I have written many things to you that I suppose I never could have talked. My heart is made tender by repeated affliction; it never was a hard heart. The death of Patty came very near me, having lived four years with me under my care. I hope it will make me more continually mindful and watchful of all those who are still committed to my charge. 'Tis a great trust; I daily feel more and more of the weight and importance of it, and of my own inability. I wish I could have more of the assistance of my dearest friend, but these perilous times swallow him up.

Mr. Lothrop has given me this account of the demand upon Falmouth. A man-of-war and two tenders went down, and sent to the inhabitants to demand their arms and require them to stand neuter. They required time to consider; they had until nine o'clock the next day, which time they employed in removing the women, children, and *the rest of their most valuable effects,* out of danger, when they sent their answer in the negative. Upon this, the enemy began a cannonade, and were continuing it when the express came away. Hichborne[3] and another gentleman got out of town in a small boat, one of the foggy nights we have had this week. I have not heard what intelligence he brings. Another person says that Howe enlarged all the prisoners but Lovell, and he would not come out.

I have since seen the Paraphrase,[4] as it is called; but 'tis as low as the mock oration, though no reflection upon your private character, further than immoderately whipping your scholars when you kept school, a crime any one will acquit you of who knows you. As a specimen of the wit and humor it contained I will give you the title: "A Paraphrase upon the Second Epistle of John the Roundhead, to James, the Prolocutor of the Rump Parliament. Dear Devil," etc. I had it, but it was when I was in so much distress that I cared nothing about it. I will mention, when I see you, the foolish conjectures of some who want always to be finding out something extraordinary in whatever happens.

Mr. Cranch's family are well and send love to you. Your mother, too, is anxious for you, and is so apprehensive lest a fleet should be sent to bombard Philadelphia that she has not much comfort. Brother's family are well except young Crosby, who had the dysentery very bad, and has left him bereaved of his reason. Isaac is so far recovered as to return after six weeks and Susy is returned to me again. Our neighbors are now all getting well. I hope to hear often from you, which is all the alleviation I have in your absence, and is, next to seeing you, the greatest comfort of your   PORTIA

72. JOHN ADAMS

Philadelphia, 23 October 1775

Yesterday yours of October 9th came to hand. Your letters never failed to give me pleasure. The greatest pleasure that I take is in receiving them. And although every one which has yet come to hand is replete with melancholy tidings, yet I can truly say I never was so earnest to receive them. I rejoice in the happy principles and the happy temper which apparently dictated them all.

I feel myself much affected with the breach upon the family. But we can count a mother, a brother, an aunt, and a brother's child among the slain by this cruel pestilence. May God Almighty put a stop to its rage, and humble us under the ravages already made by it. The sorrows of all our friends, on the loss of your mother, are never out of my mind. I pray God to spare my parent, whose life has been prolonged by his goodness hitherto, as well as yours that survives. The tremendous calamities already felt, of fire, sword, and pestilence, may be only harbingers of greater still. We have no security against calamity here. This planet is its region. The only principle is to be prepared for the worst events.

If I could write as well as you, my sorrow would be as eloquent as yours, but, upon my word, I cannot.

The unaccountable event which you allude to has reached this place and occasioned a fall.[1] I would be glad, however, that the worst construction might not be put. Let him have fair play; though I doubt.

The man who violates private faith, cancels solemn obligations, whom neither honor nor conscience holds, shall never be knowingly trusted by me. Had I known, when I first voted for a Director of an Hospital, what I heard afterwards, when I was down, I would not have voted as I did. Open, barefaced immorality ought not to be so countenanced. Though I think a fatality attends us in some instances, yet a divine protection and favor is visible in others; and let us be cheerful, whatever happens. Cheerfulness is not a sin in any times.

I am afraid to hear again, almost, lest some other should be sick in the house. Yet I hope better, and that you will reassume your wonted cheerfulness and write again upon news and politics. Send your letters to Warren for conveyance. I won't trust any other.

73. JOHN ADAMS

29 October

I cannot exclude from my mind your melancholy situation. The griefs of your father and sisters, your uncles and aunts, as well as the remoter connections, often crowd in upon me, when my whole attention ought to be directed to other subjects. Your uncle Quincy, my friend as well as uncle, must regret the loss of a beloved sister. Dr. Tufts, my other friend, I know bewails the loss of a friend, as well as an aunt and a sister. Mr. Cranch, the friend of my youth as well as of my riper years, whose tender heart sympathizes with his fellow-creatures in every affliction and distress, in this case feels the loss of a friend, a fellow-Christian, and a mother. But, alas! what avail these mournful reflections? The best thing we can do, the greatest respect we can show to the memory of our departed friend, is to copy into our own lives those virtues which, in her lifetime, rendered her the object of our esteem, love, and admiration. I must confess I ever felt a veneration for her, which seems increased by the news of her translation.

Above all things, my dear, let us inculcate these great virtues and bright excellences upon our children.

Your mother had a clear and penetrating understanding, and a profound judgment, as well as an honest, and a friendly, and a charitable heart. There is one thing, however, which you will forgive me if I hint to you. Let me ask you, rather, if you are not of my opinion? Were not her talents and virtues too much confined to private, social, and domestic life? My opinion of the duties of religion and morality comprehends a very extensive connection with society at large and the great interests of the public. Does not natural morality and much more Christian benevolence make it our indispensable duty to lay ourselves out to serve our fellow-creatures, to the utmost of our power, in promoting and supporting those great political systems and general regulations upon which the happiness of multitudes depends? The benevolence, charity, capacity, and industry which, exerted in private life, would make a family, a parish, or a town happy, employed upon a larger scale, in support of the great principles of virtue and freedom of political regulations, might secure whole nations and generations from misery, want, and contempt. Public virtues and political qualities, therefore, should be incessantly cherished in our children.

> how we should treat our families + how we should treat our government

74. JOHN ADAMS

Philadelphia, 29 October 1775

Human nature, with all its infirmities and deprivation, is still capable of great things. It is capable of attaining to degrees of wisdom and of goodness which, we have reason to believe, appear respectable in the estimation of superior intelligences. Education makes a greater difference between man and man, than nature has made between man and brute. The virtues and powers to which men may be trained, by early education and constant discipline, are truly sublime and astonishing. Newton and Locke are examples of the deep sagacity which may be acquired by long habits of thinking and study. Nay, your common mechanics and artisans are proofs of the wonderful dexterity acquired by use; a watchmaker, in finishing his wheels and springs; a pin or needle-maker, etc. I think there is a particular occupation in Europe, which is called a paper-stainer or linen-stainer. A man who has been long habituated to it shall sit for a whole day, and draw upon paper fresh figures to be imprinted upon the papers for rooms, as fast as his eye can roll and his fingers move, and no two of his draughts shall be alike. The Saracens, the Knights of

virtues can be taught

[handwritten: ROUSSEAU! ROUSSEAU]

Malta, the army and navy in the service of the English republic, among many others, are instances to show to what an exalted height valor, or bravery, or courage may be raised by artificial means.

It should be your care, therefore, and mine, to elevate the minds of our children and exalt their courage; to accelerate and animate their industry and activity; to excite in them an habitual contempt of meanness, abhorrence of injustice and inhumanity, and an ambition to excel in every capacity, faculty, and virtue. If we suffer their minds to grovel and creep in infancy, they will grovel all their lives.

But their bodies must be hardened, as well as their souls exalted. Without strength and activity and vigor of body, the brightest mental excellences will be eclipsed and obscured.

[handwritten: they're trying to institue the principals of the nation in their children]

75. JOHN ADAMS

Same date

There is in the human breast a social affection which extends to our whole species, faintly indeed, but in some degree. The nation, kingdom, or community to which we belong is embraced by it more vigorously. It is stronger still towards the province to which we belong, and in which we had our birth. It is stronger and stronger as we descend to the county, town, parish, neighborhood, and family, which we call our own. And here we find it often so powerful as to become partial, to blind our eyes, to darken our understandings, and pervert our wills.

It is to this infirmity in my own heart that I must perhaps attribute that local attachment, that partial fondness, that overweening prejudice in favor of New England, which I feel very often, and which, I fear, sometimes leads me to expose myself to just ridicule.

New England has, in many respects, the advantage of every other colony in America, and, indeed, of every other part of the world that I know anything of.

1. The people are purer English blood; less mixed with Scotch, Irish, Dutch, French, Danish, Swedish, etc., than any other; and

descended from Englishmen, too, who left Europe in purer times than the present, and less tainted with corruption than those they left behind them.

2. The institutions in New England for the support of religion, morals, and decency exceed any other; obliging every parish to have a minister, and every person to go to meeting, etc.

3. The public institutions in New England for the education of youth, supporting colleges at the public expense, and obliging towns to maintain grammar schools, are not equaled, and never were, in any part of the world.

4. The division of our territory, that is, our counties, into townships; empowering towns to assemble, choose officers, make laws, mend roads, and twenty other things, gives every man an opportunity of showing and improving that education which he received at college or at school, and makes knowledge and dexterity at public business common.

5. Our law for the distribution of intestate estates occasions a frequent division of landed property, and prevents monopolies of land.

But in opposition to these we have labored under many disadvantages. The exorbitant prerogative of our Governors, etc., which would have overborne our liberties if it had not been opposed by the five preceding particulars.

76. JOHN ADAMS

4 November 1775

I have but yesterday received yours of October 21. Your letters of the following dates I have received: 8 and 10, 16, 29 September; 1, 9, 21, and 22 October. These letters, and indeed every line from you, give me inexpressable pleasure, notwithstanding the melancholy scenes described in most of them of late. I am happy to learn that the family is in health once more, and hope it will continue. My duty to my mother. I wish she would not be concerned about me. She ought to consider that a dysentery can kill as surely as a cannon. This town is as secure from the cannon and men-of-war as the moon is. I wish she had a little of your fortitude. I had rather be killed by a ball than live in such continual fears as she does.

I can't write as often as I wish. I am engaged from seven in the morning till eleven at night.

Two pair of colors, belonging to the Seventh Regiment, were brought here last night from Chambly,[1] and hung up in Mrs. Hancock's chamber with great splendor and elegance. That lady sends her compliments and good wishes. Among a hundred men, almost, at this house, she lives and behaves with modesty, decency, dignity, and discretion, I assure you. Her behavior is easy and genteel. She avoids talking upon politics. In large and mixed companies she is totally silent, as a lady ought to be. But whether her eyes are so penetrating, and her attention so quick to the words, looks, gestures, sentiments, etc., of the company, as yours would be, saucy as you are this way, I won't say.

But to resume a more serious subject. You ask me to write to your father and sister, and my heart wishes and longs to do it, but you can have no conception what there is to prevent me. I really fear I shall ruin myself for want of exercise.

77. ABIGAIL ADAMS

5 November 1775

I have been prevented writing you for more than a week past by a whitlow upon the forefinger of my right hand. 'Tis now so tender that I can manage a pen but poorly. I hope you have received several letters from me in this fortnight past. I wrote by Mr. Lynch and by Dr. Franklin, the latter of whom I had the pleasure of dining with, and of admiring him, whose character from my infancy I had been taught to venerate. I found him social, but not talkative, and when he spoke, something useful dropped from his tongue. He was grave, yet pleasant and affable. You know I make some pretensions to physiognomy, and I thought I could read in his countenance the virtues of his heart, among which patriotism shone in its full lustre, and with that is blended every virtue of a Christian: for a true patriot must be a religious man. I have been led to think from a late defection, that he who neglects his duty to his Maker may well be expected to be deficient and insincere in his duty towards the public. Even suppose him to possess a large share of what is called honor and public spirit, yet do not these men, by their bad example, by a loose, immoral conduct, corrupt the minds of youth and vitiate the morals of the age, and thus injure the public more than they can compensate by intrepidity, generosity, and honor? Let revenge or ambition, pride, lust, or profit, tempt these men to a base and vile action, you may as well hope to bind up a hungry tiger with a cobweb, as to hold such debauched patriots in the visionary chains of decency, or to charm them with the intellectual beauty of truth and reason.

But where am I running? I mean to thank you for all your obliging favors lately received; and, though some of them are very laconic, yet, were they to contain only two lines to tell me that you were well, they would be acceptable to me. I think, however, you are more apprehensive than you need be; the gentleman to whose care they have always been directed has been very kind in his conveyance, and very careful. I hope that it will not now be long before we shall have nearer interviews. You must tell me that you will return next month; a late appointment[1] will make it inconvenient (provided you accept) for you to go again to Congress.

The little flock in receiving papa's letters have been more gratified than they could have been by any other present. They are very proud of being thus noticed. I am much obliged by the sermons lately received. The dedication of Dr. Zubly's is both spirited and zealous. I was greatly pleased with it, but suppose it will be casting of pearl before swine.

It seems human nature is the same in all ages and countries. Ambition and avarice reign everywhere, and where they predominate, there will be bickerings after places of honor and profit. There is an old adage, "Kissing goes by favor," that is daily verified. I inclose to you the paper you sent for. Your business in collecting facts will be very difficult, and the sufferings of this people cannot be described with pen, ink, and paper. Besides, these ministers of Satan are rendering it every day more and more difficult, by their ravages and devastation, to tell a tale which will freeze the young blood of succeeding generations, as well as harrow up the souls of the present.

Nothing new has transpired since I wrote you last. I have not heard of one person's escape out of town, nor of any manoeuvre of any kind.

Master John is very anxious to write, but has been confined for several days with a severe cold, which has given him sore eyes, but he begs me to make his excuse and say that he has wrote twice before, but it did not please him well enough to send it. Nabby has been with her aunt Betsey ever since her grand-mamma's death. Charley and Tommy beg mamma to thank papa for their letters, and wish they could write to tell him so. Brother and sister Cranch send their love. Mrs. Cranch's disorder left her soon, and the sickness has greatly abated all round us. Your mother speaks pathetically of you, and always sends her love to you. I will only ask you to measure by your own the affectionate regard of your nearest friend.

78. ABIGAIL ADAMS

Braintree, 12 November 1775

I received yours of 23d October. I want to hear from you every day, and I always feel sorry when I come to the close of a letter. Your time must be greatly engrossed—but little of it to spare to the calls of private friendship, and I have reason to think I have the largest share of it. Winter makes its approaches fast. I hope I shall not be obliged to spend it without my dearest friend. I know not how to think of it.

The intelligence you will receive before this reaches you will, I should think, make a plain path, though a dangerous one, for you. I could not join to-day in the petitions of our worthy pastor, for a reconciliation between our no longer parent state, but tyrant state, and these colonies. Let us separate; they are unworthy to be our brethren. Let us renounce them; and instead of supplications, as formerly, for their prosperity and happiness, let us beseech the Almighty to blast their counsels and bring to nought all their devices.

I have nothing remarkable to write you. A little skirmish happened last week. The particulars I have endeavored to collect, but whether I have the facts right, I am not certain. A number of

ABIGAL IS OBVIOUSLY VERY PRO INDEPENDENT

cattle were kept at Lechmere's Point, where two sentinels were placed. In a high tide 'tis an island. The regulars had observed this, and a scheme was laid to send a number of them over and take off the stock. Accordingly, a number of boats and about four hundred men were sent. They landed, it seems, unperceived by the sentinels, who were asleep; one of whom they killed, and the other took prisoner. As soon as they were perceived, they fired the cannon from Prospect Hill upon them, which sunk one of their boats; but, as the tide was very high, it was difficult getting over, and some time before any alarm was given. A Colonel Thompson, of the riflemen, marched instantly with his men; and, though a very stormy day, they regarded not the tide nor waited for boats, but marched over neck-high in water, and discharged their pieces, when the regulars ran, without waiting to get off their stock, and made the best of their way to the opposite shore. The General sent his thanks[1] in a public manner to the brave officer and his men. Major Mifflin, I hear, was there, and flew about as though he would have raised the whole army. May they never find us deficient in courage and spirit.

Our army is exceedingly well supplied with every article but wood and provender, which is very scarce. As to provisions we should find no difficulty to victual an army full as large. 'Tis now very healthy both in the army, and country. We have had very long tedious rains for six weeks past; sometimes not more than one fair day in a week. All our friends are well. My father seems to be much broke by his great affliction, seems to have his care and anxiety doubled. I can perceive it in numberless instances. I hope you will be able to get his sulky repaired, as he wants it now it comes cold weather very much.

Dr. Franklin invited me to spend the winter in Philadelphia. I shall wish to be there unless you return. I have been like a nun in a cloister, ever since you went away, and have not been into any other house than my father's and sister's, except once to Colonel Quincy's. Indeed, I have had no inclination for company. My evenings are lonesome and melancholy. In the daytime family affairs take off my attention, but the evenings are spent with my departed parent. I then ruminate upon all her care and tenderness, and am sometimes lost and absorbed in a flood of tender-

ness ere I am aware of it, or can call to my aid my only prop and
support. I must bid you adieu; 'tis late at night.

Most affectionately yours.

79. ABIGAIL ADAMS

27 November 1775

great, good stuff, thanks Abigail

'Tis a fortnight to-night since I wrote you a line, during which I
have been confined with the jaundice, rheumatism, and a most
violent cold; I yesterday took a puke, which has relieved me, and
I feel much better to-day. Many, very many people who have had
the dysentery, are now afflicted with the jaundice and rheumatism; some it has left in hectics, some in dropsies. The great and
incessant rains we have had this fall (the like cannot be recollected) may have occasioned some of the present disorders. The
jaundice is very prevalent in the camp. We have lately had a
week of very cold weather, as cold as January, and a flight of
snow, which I hope will purify the air of some of the noxious vapors. It has spoilled many hundreds of bushels of apples, which
were designed for cider, and which the great rains had prevented
people from making up. Suppose we have lost five barrels by it.

Colonel Warren returned last week to Plymouth, so that I
shall not hear anything from you until he goes back again, which
will not be till the last of this month. He damped my spirits
greatly by telling me that the Court[1] had prolonged your stay another month. I was pleasing myself with the thought that you
would soon be upon your return. It is in vain to repine. I hope
the public will reap what I sacrifice.

I wish I knew what mighty things were fabricating. If a form
of government is to be established here, what one will be assumed? Will it be left to our Assemblies to choose one? And will
not many men have many minds? And shall we not run into dis-
sensions among ourselves?

I am more and more convinced that man is a dangerous creature; and that power, whether vested in many or a few, is ever
grasping, and, like the grave, cries, "Give, give!" The great fish
swallow up the small; and he who is most strenuous for the

worried about men being inherently selfish

rights of the people, when vested with power, is as eager after the prerogatives of government. You tell me of degrees of perfection to which human nature is capable of arriving, and I believe it, but at the same time lament that our admiration should arise from the scarcity of the instances.

yep

The building up a great empire, which was only hinted at by my correspondent, may now, I suppose, be realized even by the unbelievers. Yet, will not ten thousand difficulties arise in the formation of it? The reins of government have been so long slackened, that I fear the people will not quietly submit to those restraints which are necessary for the peace and security of the community. If we separate from Britain, what code of laws will be established? How shall we be governed so as to retain our liberties? Can any government be free which is not administered by general stated laws? Who shall frame these laws? Who will give them force and energy? 'Tis true, your resolutions, as a body, have hitherto had the force of laws; but will they continue to have? → *all good questions*

When I consider these things, and the prejudices of people in favor of ancient customs and regulations, I feel anxious for the fate of our monarchy, or democracy, or whatever is to take place. I soon get lost in a labyrinth of perplexities; but, whatever occurs, may justice and righteousness be the stability of our times, and order arise out of confusion. Great difficulties may be surmounted by patience and perseverance.

I believe I have tired you with politics. As to news, we have not any at all. I shudder at the approach of winter, when I think I am to remain desolate. Suppose your weather is warm yet. Mr. Mason and Mr. Thaxter live with me, and render some part of my time less disconsolate. Mr. Mason is a youth who will please you, he has spirit, taste and sense. His application to his studies is constant, and I am much mistaken if he does not make a very good figure in his profession. I have with me now the only daughter of your brother; I feel a tenderer affection for her as she has lost a kind parent. Though too young to be sensible of her own loss, I can pity her. She appears to be a child of a very good disposition—only wants to be a little used to company. Our little ones send duty to papa and want much to see him. Tom says he won't come home till the battle is over—some strange notion he has got into his head. He has got a political creed to say to him when he returns.

I must bid you good-night; 'tis late for me, who am much of an invalid. I was disappointed last week in receiving a packet by the post, and, upon unsealing it, finding only four newspapers. I think you are more cautious than you need be. All letters, I believe, have come safe to hand. I have sixteen from you, and wish I had as many more.

    Adieu.   Yours.

80. JOHN ADAMS

Philadelphia, 3 December 1775

MY BEST FRIEND, — Yours of November 12th is before me. I wish I could write you every day, more than once, for although I have a number of friends and many relations who are very dear to me, yet all the friendship I have for others is far unequal to that which warms my heart for you. The most agreeable time that I spend here is in writing to you, and conversing with you, when I am alone. But the call of friendship and of private affection must give place to that of duty and honor. Even private friendship and affections require it.

I am obliged, by the nature of the service I am in, to correspond with many gentlemen, both of the army and of the two houses of Assembly, which takes up much of my time. How I find time to write half the letters I do, I know not, for my whole time seems engrossed with business. The whole Congress is taken up, almost, in different committees, from seven to ten in the morning. From ten to four or sometimes five, we are in Congress, and from six to ten in committees again. I don't mention this to make you think me a man of importance, because it is not I alone,[1] but the whole Congress is thus employed, but to apologize for not writing to you oftener.

Indeed, I know not what to write that is worth your reading. I send you the papers, which inform you of what is public. As to what passes in Congress, I am tied fast by my honor to communicate nothing. I hope the Journal of the Session will be published soon, and then you will see what we have been about in one view, excepting what ought to be excepted. If I could visit the coffee-houses in the evening, and the coffee-tables of the ladies in the afternoon, I could entertain you with many smart remarks upon dress and air, etc., and give you many sprightly conversations, but my fate, you know, is to be moping over books and papers all the leisure time I have, when I have any.

I hope I shall be excused from coming to Philadelphia again, at least until other gentlemen have taken their turns. But I never will come here again without you, if I can persuade you to come with me. Whom God has joined together ought not to be put asunder so long, with their own consent. We will bring master Johnny with us; you and he shall have the small-pox here, and we will be as happy as Mr. Hancock and his lady. Thank Nabby and John for their letters, and kiss Charles and Tom for me. John writes like a hero, glowing with ardor for his country and burning with indignation against her enemies. When I return I will get the sulky back to New Haven, and there leave it to be repaired, to be brought home by the first post after it is done.

As to coming home, I have no thoughts of it; shall stay here till the year is out, for what I know. Affairs are in a critical state, and important steps are now taking every day, so that I could not reconcile it to my own mind to be absent from this place at present. Nothing is expected from the Commissioners, yet we are waiting for them in some respects. The Tories and timids pretend to expect great things from them. But the generality expect nothing but more insults and affronts. Privateering is licensed, and the ports are wide open. As soon as the resolves are printed, which will be to-morrow, I will send them.

I have had a long conversation with ———.[2] He seems to be in a better temper, and I live on terms of decency and civility with him and he with me. And I am determined to live so. Have lived in more decency with him and another, since my last return than ever, at least since last August when the sin of precedence was committed. There's the rub. But what can't be cured must be endured.

81. ABIGAIL ADAMS

Braintree, 10 December 1775

I received your obliging favor by Mrs. Morgan, with the papers and the other articles you sent, which were very acceptable to me, as they are not to be purchased here. I shall be very choice of them.

I have, according to your desire, been upon a visit to Mrs. Morgan,[1] who keeps at Major Mifflin's. I had received a message from Mrs. Mifflin some time ago, desiring I would visit her. My papa who, you know, is very obliging in this way, accompanied me, and I had the pleasure of drinking coffee with the Doctor and his lady, the Major and his lady, and a Mr. and Mrs. Smith from New York, a daughter of the famous son of liberty, Captain Sears; Generals Gates and Lee; a Dr. M'Henry[2] and a Mr. Elwyn, with many others who were strangers to me. I was very politely entertained, and noticed by the generals; more especially General Lee, who was very urgent with me to tarry in town, and dine with him and the ladies present, at Hobgoblin Hall, but I excused myself. The General was determined that I should not only be acquainted with him, but with his companions too, and therefore placed a chair before me, into which he ordered Mr. Spada[3] to mount and present his paw to me for a better acquaintance. I could not do otherwise than accept it. "That, Madam," says he, "is the dog which Mr. ―――― has rendered famous."

I was so little while in company with these persons, and the company so mixed, that it was almost impossible to form any judgment of them. The Doctor appeared modest, and his lady affable and agreeable. Major Mifflin, you know, I was always an admirer of, as well as of his delicate lady. I believe Philadelphia must be an unfertile soil, or it would not produce so many unfruitful women. I always conceive of these persons as wanting one addition to their happiness; but in these perilous times, I know not whether it ought to be considered as an infelicity, since they are certainly freed from the anxiety every parent must feel for their rising offspring.

I drank coffee one day with General Sullivan upon Winter Hill.

He appears to be a man of sense and spirit. His countenance denotes him of a warm constitution, not to be very suddenly moved, but, when once roused, not very easily lulled,—easy and social,— well calculated for a military station, as he seems to be possessed of those popular qualities necessary to attach men to him.

By the way, I congratulate you upon our late noble acquisition of military stores.[4] 'Tis a most grand mortar, I assure you. Surely Heaven smiles upon us, in many respects, and we have continually to speak of mercies, as well as of judgments. I wish our gratitude may be anyways proportionate to our benefits. I suppose, in Congress, you think of everything relative to trade and commerce, as well as other things; but, as I have been desired to mention to you some things, I shall not omit them. One is, that there may be something done, in a Continental way, with regard to excise upon spirituous liquors, that each of the New England colonies may be upon the same footing; whereas we formerly used to pay an excise, and the other colonies none, or very little, by which means they drew away our trade. An excise is necessary, though it may be objected to by the mercantile interest, as a too frequent use of spirits endangers the well-being of society. Another article is, that some method may be devised to keep among us our gold and silver, which are now every day shipped off to the West Indies for molasses, coffee, sugar, etc. This I can say of my own knowledge, that a dollar in silver is now become a great rarity, and our traders will give you a hundred pounds of paper for ninety of silver, or nearly that proportion. If any trade is allowed to the West Indies, would it not be better to carry some commodity of our own produce in exchange? Medicines, cotton-wool, and some other articles, we are in great want of. Formerly we used to purchase cotton-wool at one shilling, lawful money, per bag; now it is three, and the scarcity of that article distresses us, as it was wrought up with less trouble than any other article of clothing. Flax is now from a shilling, to one and sixpence per pound, sheep's wool eighteenpence, and linens not to be had at any price. I cannot mention the article in the English goods way which is not double; and in the West India molasses by retail I used formerly to purchase at one and eightpence, now it is two and eightpence; rum, three shillings; coffee, one and threepence, and all other things in proportion. Corn is four shillings per bushel; rye, five; oats, three and eightpence; hay, five and six shillings per hundred; wood, twenty shillings per cord; but meat of all kinds cheap.

I inclose a memorandum of Dr. Tufts requesting you to procure for him those articles if you can bring them with any convenience. The Dr. takes it a little hard that you have never wrote him a line, as he has wrote you several times. If it was but a few lines he would receive it kindly. I am very loath to trouble you about articles of conveniency for myself, especially as they are so much out of your way of business. I will only mention two or three, which if you can direct Bass to get for me will much oblige me—one black Barcelona handkerchief, two or three yards of black calamanco for shoes and binding for the same—he knows how much will be proper—and three or four common Manchester check handkerchiefs for the pocket. Not a handkerchief of any kind can be purchased here, but out of the store for the army, and they are allowed only to those who enlist. My papa would be glad if you would send him a sermon of Dr. Zubly's.

My uncle Quincy desires to be remembered to you; he inquired when you talked of coming home. I told him you had not fixed any time. He says, if you don't come soon, he would advise me to procure another husband. He, of all persons, ought not to give me such advice, I told him, unless he set a better example himself. Be kind enough to burn this letter. 'Tis written in great haste, and a most incorrect scrawl it is. But I can not conclude without telling you we are all very angry with your House of Assembly for their instructions.[5] They raise prejudices in the minds of people, and serve to create in their minds a terror at a separation from a people wholly unworthy of us. We are a little of the spaniel kind; though so often spurned, still to fawn argues a meanness of spirit, that, as an individual, I disclaim, and would rather endure any hardship than submit to it. Our little folks are all well and long for papa's return, in which wish their mamma most sincerely joins them.   Yours.

I often meet with a bundle, open a cover with eager expectations and find only a newspaper, but I know your avocations will not suffer you to write so often as you wish.

82. JOHN ADAMS

Watertown, 24 January 1776

MY DEAR, — I am determined not to commit a fault which escaped me the last time I set out for the southward. I waited on General Thomas at Roxbury, this morning, and then went to Cambridge, where I dined at Colonel Mifflin's with the General and lady, and a vast collection of other company, among whom were six or seven sachems and warriors of the French Caghnawaga Indians with several of their wives and children. A savage feast they made of it, yet were very polite in the Indian style. One of these sachems is an Englishman, a native of this colony, whose name was Williams,[1] captivated in infancy with his mother, and adopted by some kind squaw; another, I think, is half French blood.

I was introduced to them by the General, as one of the grand council fire at Philadelphia, which made them prick up their ears. They came and shook hands with me, and made me low bows and scrapes, etc. In short, I was much pleased with this day's entertainment.

The General is to make them presents in clothes and trinkets. They have visited the lines at Cambridge, and are going to see those at Roxbury.

To-morrow we mount for the grand council fire, where I shall think often of my little brood at the foot of Penn's Hill. Remember me particularly to Nabby, Johnny, Charley, and Tommy. Tell them I charge them to be good, honest, active, and industrious, for their own sakes as well as ours.

83. JOHN ADAMS

Philadelphia, 11 February 1776

Here I am again. Arrived last Thursday, in good health, although I had a cold journey. The weather, a great part of the way, was very severe, which prevented our making very quick progress, and by an accident which happened to one of my horses, which obliged me to leave her at Brookfield and hire another, was delayed two days. A horse broke loose in the barn and corked mine under the foreshoulder. I hope that Bass upon his return will find her well. My companion[1] was agreeable and made the journey much less tedious than it would have been.

I can form no judgment of the state of public opinions and principles here, as yet, nor any conjectures of what an hour may bring forth.

Have been to meeting, and heard Mr. Duffield from Jeremiah ii. 17: "Hast thou not procured this unto thyself, in that thou hast forsaken the Lord thy God, when He led thee by the way?" He prayed very earnestly for Boston and New York, supposing the latter to be in danger of destruction. I, however, am not convinced that Vandeput[2] will fire upon that town. It has too much Tory property to be destroyed by Tories. I hope it will be fortified and saved. If not, the question may be asked, "Hast thou not procured this?" etc.

To-morrow Dr. Smith is to deliver an oration in honor of the brave Montgomery.[3] I will send it, as soon as it is out, to you. There is a deep anxiety, a kind of thoughtful melancholy, and in some, a lowness of spirits approaching to despondency, prevailing through the southern colonies, at present, very similar to what I have often observed in Boston, particularly on the first news of the Port Bill, and last year about this time, or a little later, when the bad news arrived which dashed their fond hopes, with which they had deluded themselves through the winter. In this or a similar condition we shall remain, I think, until late in the spring, when some critical event will take place, perhaps sooner. But the arbiter of events, the sovereign of the world, only knows which way the torrent will be turned. Judging by experience, by probabilities, and by all appearances, I conclude it will roll on to dominion and glory, though the circumstances and consequences may be bloody.

In such great changes and commotions, individuals are but atoms. It is scarcely worth while to consider what the consequences will be to us. What will be the effects upon present and future millions, and millions of millions, is a question very interesting to benevolence, natural and Christian. God grant they may, and I firmly believe they will, be happy.

84. JOHN ADAMS

Philadelphia, [13] February 1776

Lee is at York,[1] and we have requested a battalion of Philadelphia associators, together with a regiment of Jersey minute-men, to march to his assistance. Lord Stirling[2] was there before with his regiment, so that there will be about a thousand men with Lee from Connecticut, about six hundred with Lord Stirling from the Jerseys, one battalion of about seven hundred and twenty minute-men from Jersey, and one of the same number from Philadelphia. We shall soon have four battalions more, raised in Pennsylvania, to march to the same place, and one more in the Jerseys. Mr. Dickinson, being the first Colonel and commander of the first battalion too, claimed it as his right to march upon this occasion. Mr. Reed, formerly General Washington's secretary, goes his lieutenant-colonel. Mr. Dickinson's alacrity and spirit upon this occasion, which certainly becomes his character and sets a fine example, is much talked of and applauded. This afternoon, the four battalions of the militia were together, and Mr. Dickinson mounted the rostrum to harangue them, which he did with great vehemence and pathos, as it is reported.

I suppose, if I could have made interest enough to have been chosen more than a lieutenant, I should march too, upon some such emergency; and possibly a contingency may happen when it will be proper for me to do it still, in rank and file. I will not fail to march, if it should. In the beginning of a war, in colonies like this and Virginia, where the martial spirit is but just awakened and the people are unaccustomed to arms, it may be proper and necessary for such popular orators as Henry and Dickinson to assume a military character. But I really think them both better statesmen than soldiers, though I cannot say they are not very good in the latter character. Henry's principles and systems are much more conformable to mine than the other's, however.

I feel, upon some of these occasions, a flow of spirits and an effort of imagination, very like an ambition to be engaged in the more active, gay, and dangerous scenes; (dangerous, I say, but recall that word, for there is no course more dangerous than that which I am in). I have felt such passions all my lifetime, particularly in the year 1757, when I longed more ardently to be a soldier than I ever did to be a lawyer. But I am too old, and too much worn with fatigues of study in my youth, and there is too little need, in my province, of such assistance, for me to assume a uniform.

> "Non tali auxilio, nec defensoribus istis
> Tempus eget."[3]

I believe I must write you soon Lord Stirling's character, because I was vastly pleased with him. For the future I shall draw no characters but such as I like. Pimps destroy all freedom of correspondence.

85. JOHN ADAMS

Philadelphia, 18 February

I sent you from New York a pamphlet intituled "Common Sense,"[1] written in vindication of doctrines which there is reason to expect that the further encroachments of tyranny and depredations of oppression will soon make the common faith; unless the cunning ministry, by proposing negotiations and terms of reconciliation, should divert the present current from its channel.

Reconciliation if practicable, and peace if attainable, you very well know, would be as agreeable to my inclinations, and as advantageous to my interest, as to any man's. But I see no prospect, no probability, no possibility. And I cannot but despise the understanding which sincerely expects an honorable peace, for its credulity, and detest the hypocritical heart which pretends to expect it, when in truth it does not. The newspapers here are full of free speculations, the tendency of which you will easily discover. The writers reason from topics which have been long in contemplation and fully understood by the people at large in New England, but have been attended to in the southern colonies only by gentlemen of free spirits and liberal minds, who are very few. I shall endeavor to inclose to you as many of the papers and pamphlets as I can, as long as I stay here. Some will go by this conveyance.

Dr. Franklin, Mr. Chase,[2] and Mr. Charles Carroll of Carrollton, in Maryland, are chosen a committee to go into Canada. The characters of the two first you know. The last is not a member of Congress, but a gentleman of independent fortune, perhaps the largest in America, a hundred and fifty or two hundred thousand pounds sterling; educated in some university in France, though a native of America, of great abilities and learning, complete master of the French language, and a professor of the Roman Catholic religion, yet a warm, a firm, a zealous supporter of the rights of America, in whose cause he has hazarded his all. Mr. John Carroll, of Maryland, a Roman Catholic priest and a Jesuit, is to go with the committee, the priests in Canada having refused baptism and absolution to our friends there. General Lee is to command in that country, whose address, experience, and abilities, added to his fluency in the French language, will give him great advantages.

The events of war are uncertain. We cannot insure success, but we can deserve it. I am happy in this provision for that important department, because I think it the best that could be made in our circumstances. Your prudence will direct you to communicate the circumstances of the priest, the Jesuit, and the Romish religion, only to such persons as can judge of the measure upon large and generous principles, and will not indiscreetly divulge it. The step was necessary, for the anathemas of the Church are very terrible to our friends in Canada.

I wish I understood French as well as you. I would have gone to Canada, if I had. I feel the want of education every day, particularly of that language. I pray, my dear, that you would not suffer your sons or your daughter ever to feel a similar pain. It is in your power to teach them French, and I every day see more and more that it will become a necessary accomplishment of an American gentleman or lady. Pray write me in your next the name of the author of your thin French grammar, which gives you the pronunciation of the French words in English letters, that is, which shows you how the same sounds would be signified by English vowels and consonants.

Write me as often as you can. Tell me all the news. Desire the children to write to me, and believe me to be theirs and yours.

86. ABIGAIL ADAMS

Saturday Evening, 2 March 1776

I was greatly rejoiced at the return of your servant, to find you had safely arrived, and that you were well. I had never heard a word from you after you had left New York, and a most ridiculous story had been industriously propagated in this and the neighboring towns to injure the cause and blast your reputation; namely, that you and your President[1] had gone on board of a man-of-war from New York, and sailed for England. I should not mention so idle a report, but that it had given uneasiness to some of your friends; not that they in the least credited the report, but because the gaping vulgar swallowed the story. One man had deserted them and proved a traitor, another might, etc. I assure you, such high disputes took place in the public-house of this parish, that some men were collared and dragged out of the shop with great threats, for reporting such scandalous lies, and an uncle of ours offered his life as a forfeit for you, if the report proved true. However, it has been a nine days' marvel, and will now cease. I heartily wish every Tory was extirpated from America; they are continually, by secret means, undermining and injuring our cause.

I am charmed with the sentiments of "Common Sense," and wonder how an honest heart, one who wishes the welfare of his country and the happiness of posterity, can hesitate one moment at adopting them. I want to know how these sentiments are received in Congress. I dare say there would be no difficulty in procuring a vote and instructions from all the Assemblies in New England for Independency. I most sincerely wish that now, in the lucky minute, it might be done.

I have been kept in a continual state of anxiety and expectation ever since you left me. It has been said "to-morrow" and "to-morrow," for this month, but when the dreadful to-morrow will be, I know not. But hark! The house this instant shakes with the roar of cannon. I have been to the door, and find it is a cannonade from our army. Orders, I find, are come for all the remaining militia to repair to the lines Monday night by twelve o'clock. No sleep for me to-night. And if I cannot, who have no guilt upon my soul with regard to this cause, how shall the miserable wretches who have been the procurers of this dreadful scene, and those who are to be the actors, lie down with the load of guilt upon their souls?

Sunday Evening, 3 March

I went to bed after twelve, but got no rest; the cannon continued firing, and my heart beat pace with them all night. We have had a pretty quiet day, but what to-morrow will bring forth, God only knows.

Monday Evening

Tolerable quiet. To-day the militia have all mustered, with three days' provision, and are all marched by three o'clock this afternoon, though their notice was no longer ago than eight o'clock, Saturday. And now we have scarcely a man, but our regular guards, either in Weymouth, Hingham, Braintree, or Milton, and the militia from the more remote towns are called in as seacoast guards. Can you form to yourself an idea of our sensations? Palmer is chief colonel, Bass is lieutenant-colonel, and Soper major and Hall captain.

I have just returned from Penn's Hill, where I have been sitting to hear the amazing roar of cannon, and from whence I could see every shell which was thrown. The sound, I think, is one of the grandest in nature, and is of the true species of the sublime. 'Tis now an incessant roar; but oh! the fatal ideas which are connected with the sound! How many of our dear countrymen must fall!

Tuesday Morning

I went to bed about twelve, and rose again a little after one. I could no more sleep than if I had been in the engagement; the rattling of the windows, the jar of the house, the continual roar of twenty-four pounders, and the bursting of shells, give us such ideas, and realize a scene to us of which we could form scarcely any conception. About six, this morning, there was quiet. I rejoiced in a few hours' calm. I hear we got possession of Dorchester Hill last night; four thousand men upon it to-day; lost but one man. The ships are all drawn round the town. To-night we shall realize a more terrible scene still. I sometimes think I cannot stand it. I wish myself with you, out of hearing, as I cannot assist them. I hope to give you joy of Boston, even if it is in ruins, before I send this away. I am too much agitated to write as I ought, and languid for want of rest.

Thursday, Fast-day

All my anxiety and distress is at present at an end. I feel disappointed. This day our militia are all returning without effecting anything more than taking possession of Dorchester Hill. I hope it is wise and just, but, from all the muster and stir, I hoped and expected more important and decisive scenes. I would not have suffered all I have for two such hills. Ever since the taking of that, we have had a perfect calm; nor can I learn yet what effect it has had in Boston. I do not hear of one person's escaping since.

I was very much pleased with your choice of a committee for Canada. All those to whom I have ventured to show that part of your letter, approve the scheme of the priest as a master-stroke of policy. I feel sorry that General Lee has left us, but his presence at New York was no doubt of great importance, as we have reason to think it prevented Clinton from landing and gathering together such a nest of vermin as would at least have distressed us greatly. But how can you spare him from here? Can you make his place good? Can you supply it with a man equally qualified to save us? How do the Virginians relish the troops said to be destined for them? Are they putting themselves into a state of defense? I inclose to you a copy of a letter sent by Captain Furnance, who is in Mr. Ned Church's employ,[2] and who came into the Cape about ten days ago. You will learn the sentiments of our cousin[3] by it. Some of which may be true, but I hope he is a much better divine than politician. I hear that in one of his letters he mentions certain intercepted letters which he says have made much noise in England, and laments that you ever wrote them. I cannot bear to think of your continuing in a state of supineness this winter.

> "There is a tide in the affairs of men,
>   Which, taken at the flood, leads on to fortune;

Omitted, all the voyage of their life
Is bound in shallows and in miseries.
On such a full sea are we now afloat;
And we must take the current when it serves,
Or lose our ventures."[4]

Sunday Evening, 10 March

I had scarcely finished these lines when my ears were again assaulted by the roar of cannon. I could not write any further. My hand and heart will tremble at this "domestic fury and fierce civil strife," which "cumber all" our "parts"; though "blood and destruction" are "so much in use," "and dreadful objects so familiar," yet is not "pity choked,"[5] nor my heart grown callous. I feel for the unhappy wretches who know not where to fly for safety. I feel still more for my bleeding countrymen, who are hazarding their lives and their limbs. A most terrible and incessant cannonade from half after eight till six this morning. I hear we lost four men killed, and some wounded, in attempting to take the hill nearest the town, called Nook's Hill. We did some work, but the fire from the ships beat off our men, so that they did not secure it, but retired to the fort upon the other hill.

I have not got all the particulars; I wish I had; but, as I have an opportunity of sending this, I shall endeavor to be more particular in my next. All our little ones send duty. Tommy has been very sick with what is called the scarlet or purple fever, but has got about again.

If there are reinforcements here, I believe we shall be driven from the seacoast; but, in whatever state I am, I will endeavor to be therewith content.

"Man wants but little here below,
Nor wants that little long."[6]

You will excuse this very incorrect letter. You see in what perturbation it has been written, and how many times I have left off. Adieu.

Yours.

P.S. Took's grammar is the one you mention.

87. ABIGAIL ADAMS

B——e, 16 March 1776

I last evening received yours of March 8. I was in continual expectation that some important event would take place to give me a subject worth writing upon. Before this reaches you, I imagine you will have received two letters from me; the last I closed this day week. Since that time there have been some movements amongst the ministerial troops, as if they meant to evacuate the town of Boston. Between seventy and eighty vessels of various sizes are gone down, and lie in a row in fair sight of this place, all of which appear to be loaded; and by what can be collected from our own observations, and from deserters, they have been plundering the town. I have been very faithless with regard to their quitting Boston, and know not how to account for it; nor am I yet satisfied that they will leave it, though it seems to be the prevailing opinion of most people.

We are obliged to place the militia upon guard every night upon the shores, through fear of an invasion. There has been no firing since last Tuesday till about twelve o'clock last night, when I was waked out of my sleep with a smart cannonade, which continued till nine o'clock this morning, and prevented any further repose for me. The occasion I have not yet heard; but before I close this letter I may be able to give you some account of it.

By the accounts in the public papers, the plot thickens, and some very important crisis seems near at hand. Perhaps Providence sees it necessary, in order to answer important ends and designs, that the seat of war should be changed from this to the southern colonies, that each may have a proper sympathy with the other, and unite in a separation. The refuge of the believer, amidst all the afflictive dispensations of Providence, is that the Lord reigneth, and that He can restrain the arm of man.

Orders are given to our army to hold themselves in readiness to march at a moment's warning. "I'll meet you at Philippi," said the ghost of Caesar to Brutus.

↳ allusion to Caesar.

Sunday Noon

Being quite sick with a violent cold, I have tarried at home to-day. I find the firing was occasioned by our people's taking possession of Nook's Hill, which they kept in spite of the cannonade, and which has really obliged our enemy to decamp this morning on board the transports, as I hear by a messenger just come from headquarters. Some of the selectmen have been to the lines, and inform that they have carried away everything they could possibly take; and what they could not, they have burnt, broke, or hove into the water. This is, I believe, fact; many articles of good household furniture having in the course of the week come on shore at Great Hill, both upon this and Weymouth side,—lids of desks, mahogany chairs, tables, etc. Our people, I hear, will have liberty to enter Boston,—those who have had the small-pox.

The enemy have not yet come under sail. I cannot help suspecting some design, which we do not yet comprehend. To what quarter of the world they are bound is wholly unknown; but 'tis generally thought to New York. Many people are elated with their quitting Boston. I confess I do not feel so. 'Tis only lifting the burden from one shoulder to the other, which is perhaps less able or less willing to support it. To what a contemptible situation are the troops of Britain reduced! I feel glad, however, that Boston is not destroyed. I hope it will be so secured and guarded as to baffle all future attempts against it. I hear that General Howe said, upon going on some eminence in town to view our troops, who had taken Dorchester Hill, unperceived by them till sunrise, "My God, these fellows have done more work in one night than I could make my army do in three months." And he might well say so; for in one night two forts and long breastworks were sprung up, besides several barracks. Three hundred and seventy teams were employed, most of which went three loads in the night, besides four thousand men, who worked with good hearts.

From Penn's Hill we have a view of the largest fleet ever seen in America. You may count upwards of a hundred and seventy sail. They look like a forest. It was very lucky for us that we got possession of Nook's Hill. They had placed their cannon so as to fire upon the top of the hill, where they had observed our people marking out the ground; but it was only to elude them; for they began lower upon the hill and nearer the town. It was a very dark, foggy evening, and they had possession of the hill six hours before a gun was fired; and when they did fire, they overshot our people, so that they were covered before morning, and not one man lost, which the enemy no sooner discovered, than Bunker Hill was abandoned, and every man decamped as soon as he could. They found they should not be able to get away if we once got our cannon mounted. Our General may say with Caesar, "*Veni, vidi, et vici.*"

What effect does the expectation of Commissioners have with you? Are they held in disdain as they are here? It is come to that pass now, that the longest sword must decide the contest; and the sword is less dreaded here than the Commissioners.

You mention threats upon B———e. I know of none, nor ever heard of any till you mentioned them. The Tories look a little crestfallen. As for Cleverly, he looks like the knight of the woful countenance. I hear all the mongrel breed are left in Boston, and our people who were prisoners are put in irons and carried off. As to all your own private affairs I generally avoid mentioning them to you; I take the best care I am capable of them. I have found some difficulty attending the only man I have upon the place, being so often taking off. John and Jonathan have taken all the care in his absence, and performed very well. Bass got home very well. My father's horse came home in fine order and much to his satisfaction. Your own very poor.

Cannot you hire a servant where you are? I am sorry you are put to so much difficulty for want of one.

I suppose you do not think one word about coming home, and how you will get home I know not.

I made a mistake in the name of the grammar. It is Tandon's instead of Took's. I wish you could purchase Lord Chesterfield's Letters.[1] I have lately heard them very highly spoken of. I smiled at your couplet of Latin. Your daughter may be able in time to construe it, as she has already made some considerable proficiency in her accidence; but her mamma was obliged to get it translated. Pray write Lord Stirling's character.

I want to know whether you live in any harmony with ———,[2] and how you settled matters. I think he seems in better humor.

I think I do not admire the speech from the rostrum.[3] 'Tis a heavy, inelegant, verbose performance, and did not strike my fancy at all. I am very saucy, I suppose you will say. 'Tis a liberty I take with you. Indulgence is apt to spoil one. Adieu.

P.S. Pray convey me a little paper. I have but enough for one letter more.

Monday Morning

A fine, quiet night. No alarms—no cannon. The more I think of our enemies quitting Boston, the more amazed I am that they should leave such a harbor, such fortifications, such intrench-ments, and that we should be in peaceable possession of a town which we expected would cost us a river of blood, without one drop shed. Surely it is the Lord's doings, and it is marvelous in our eyes. Every foot of ground which they obtain now they must fight for, and may they purchase it at a Bunker Hill price.

88. JOHN ADAMS

Philadelphia, 17 March 1776

Our worthy friend, Frank Dana,[1] arrived here last evening from New York, to which place he came lately from England in the packet. In company with him is a gentleman by the name of Wrixon,[2] who has been a field-officer in the British army, served all the last war in Germany, and has seen service in every part of Europe. He left the army some time ago, and studied law in the Temple, in which science he made a great proficiency. He wrote, lately, a pamphlet under the title of "The Rights of Britons," which he has brought over with him. He is a friend of liberty, and thinks justly of the American question. He has great abili-ties, as well as experience in the military science, and is an able engineer. I hope we shall employ him.

The Baron de Woedtke[3] we have made a Brigadier-general, and ordered him to Canada. The testimonials in his favor I shall inclose to you. Mr. Dana's account, with which Mr. Wrixon's

agrees, ought to extinguish, in every mind, all hopes of reconciliation with Great Britain. This delusive hope has done us great
injuries, and, if ever we are ruined, will be the cause of our fall.
A hankering after the leeks of Egypt makes us forget the cruelty
of her task-masters.

I shall suffer many severe pains on your account for some
days. By a vessel from Salem a cannonade was heard from dark
till nine o'clock, last night was a week ago. Your vicinity to such
scenes of carnage and desolation as, I fear, are now to be seen in
Boston and its environs, will throw you into much distress, but I
believe in my conscience, I feel more here than you do. The
sound of cannon was not so terrible when I was at Braintree as
it is here, though I hear it at four hundred miles distance.

You can't imagine what a mortification I sustain in not having
received a single line from you since we parted. I suspect some
villainy in conveyance. By the relation of Mr. Dana, Mr. Wrixon,
and Mr. Temple, Mr. Hutchinson, Mr. Sewall,[4] and their associates are in great disgrace in England. Persons are ashamed to be
seen to speak to them. They look despised and sunk.

I shall inclose an extract of a letter from Mons. Dubourg[5] in
Paris, and a testimonial in favor of our Prussian General. Adieu.

89. JOHN ADAMS

Philadelphia, 19 March

Yesterday I had the long expected and much wished pleasure of
a letter from you, of various dates from the 2d to the 10th
March. This is the first line I have received since I left you. I
wrote you from Watertown, I believe, relating my feast at the
Quartermaster-general's with the Caghnawaga Indians, and
from Framingham an account of the ordnance there, and from
New York I sent you a pamphlet. Hope you received these. Since
I arrived here I have written to you as often as I could.

I am much pleased with your caution in your letter, in avoid-
ing names both of persons and places, or any other circumstances which might designate to strangers the writer, or the
person written to, or the persons mentioned. Characters and description will do as well.

The lie which you say occasioned such disputes at the tavern was curious enough. Who could make and spread it? I am much obliged to an uncle for his friendship. My worthy fellow-citizens may be easy about me. I never can forsake what I take to be their interests. My own have never been considered by me in competition with theirs. My ease, my domestic happiness, my rural pleasures, my little property, my personal liberty, my reputation, my life, have little weight and ever had in my own estimation, in comparison with the great object of my country. I can say of it with great sincerity, as Horace says of virtue, "To America only and her friends a friend."

You ask what is thought of "Common Sense." Sensible men think there are some whims, some sophisms, some artful addresses to superstitious notions, some keen attempts upon the passions, in this pamphlet. But all agree there is a great deal of good sense delivered in clear, simple, concise, and nervous style. His sentiments of the abilities of America, and of the difficulty of a reconciliation with Great Britain, are generally approved. But his notions and plans of continental government are not much applauded. Indeed, this writer has a better hand in pulling down than building. It has been very generally propagated through the continent that I wrote this pamphlet. But although I could not have written anything in so manly and striking a style, I flatter myself I should have made a more respectable figure as an architect, if I had undertaken such a work. This writer seems to have very inadequate ideas of what is proper and necessary to be done in order to form constitutions for single colonies, as well as a great model of union for the whole.

Your distresses, which you have painted in such lively colors, I feel in every line as I read. I dare not write all that I think upon this occasion. I wish our people had taken possession of Nook's Hill at the same time when they got the other heights, and before the militia was dismissed.

Poor cousin! I pity him. How much soever he may lament certain letters,[1] I don't lament. I never repent of what was no sin. Misfortunes may be borne without whining. But if I can believe Mr. Dana, those letters were much admired in England. I can't help laughing when I write it, because they were really such hasty, crude scraps. If I could have foreseen their fate, they should have been fit to be seen, and worth all the noise they have made. Mr. Dana says they were considered in England as containing a comprehensive idea of what was necessary to be done, and as showing resolution enough to do it. Wretched stuff as they really were, according to him they have contributed somewhat towards making certain persons to be thought the greatest statesmen in the world. So much for vanity.

My love, duty, respects, and compliments wherever they belong. Virginia will be well defended. So will New York. So will South Carolina. America will erelong raise her voice aloud and assume a bolder air.

90. JOHN ADAMS

Philadelphia, 29 March 1776

I give you joy of Boston and Charlestown, once more the habitation of Americans. I am waiting with great impatience for letters from you, which I know will contain many particulars. We are taking precautions to defend every place that is in danger, the Carolinas, Virginia, New York, Canada. I can think of nothing but fortifying Boston harbor. I want more cannon than are to be had. I want a fortification upon Point Alderton, one upon Lovell's Island, one upon George's Island, several upon Long Island, one upon the Moon, one upon Squantum. I want to hear of half a dozen fire-ships, and two or three hundred fire-rafts prepared. I want to hear of row-galleys, floating batteries built, and booms laid across the channel in the narrows, and *Vaisseaux de Frise* sunk in it. I wish to hear that you are translating Braintree commons into the channel. No efforts, no expense are too extravagant for me to wish for, to fortify that harbor so as to make it impregnable. I hope everybody will join and work until it is done.

We have this week lost a very valuable friend of the colonies in Governor Ward, of Rhode Island, by the small-pox[1] in the natural way. He never would hearken to his friends, who have been constantly advising him to be inoculated, ever since the first Congress began. But he would not be persuaded. Numbers, who have been inoculated, have gone through this distemper without any danger, or even confinement, but nothing would do. He must take it in the natural way and die. He was an amiable and a sensible man, a steadfast friend to his country upon very pure principles. His funeral was attended with the same solemnities as Mr. Randolph's. Mr. Stillman[2] being the Anabaptist minister here, of which persuasion was the Governor, was desired by Congress to preach a sermon, which he did with great applause.

Remember me as you ought.

91. ABIGAIL ADAMS

Braintree, 31 March 1776

I wish you would ever write me a letter half as long as I write you, and tell me, if you may, where your fleet are gone; what sort of defense Virginia can make against our common enemy; whether it is so situated as to make an able defense. Are not the gentry lords, and the common people vassals? Are they not like the uncivilized vassals Britain represents us to be? I hope their riflemen, who have shown themselves very savage and even blood-thirsty, are not a specimen of the generality of the people. I am willing to allow the colony great merit for having produced a Washington; but they have been shamefully duped by a Dunmore.[1]

I have sometimes been ready to think that the passion for liberty cannot be equally strong in the breasts of those who have been accustomed to deprive their fellow-creatures of theirs. Of this I am certain, that it is not founded upon that generous and Christian principle of doing to others as we would that others should do unto us.

Do not you want to see Boston? I am fearful of the small-pox, or I should have been in before this time. I got Mr. Crane to go to our house and see what state it was in. I find it has been occupied by one of the doctors of a regiment; very dirty, but no other damage has been done to it. The few things which were left in it are all gone. Cranch has the key, which he never delivered up. I have wrote to him for it and am determined to get it cleaned as soon as possible and shut it up. I look upon it as a new acquisition of property—a property which one month ago I did not value at a single shilling, and would with pleasure have seen it in flames.

The town in general is left in a better state than we expected; more owing to a precipitate flight than any regard to the inhabitants; though some individuals discovered a sense of honor and justice, and have left the rent of the houses in which they were, for the owners, and the furniture unhurt, or, if damaged, sufficient to make it good. Others have committed abominable ravages. The mansion-house of your President is safe, and the furniture unhurt; while the house and furniture of the Solicitor General[2] have fallen a prey to their own merciless party. Surely the very fiends feel a reverential awe for virtue and patriotism, whilst they detest the parricide and traitor.

I feel very differently at the approach of spring from what I did a month ago. We knew not then whether we could plant or sow with safety, whether where we had tilled we could reap the fruits of our own industry, whether we could rest in our own cottages or whether we should be driven from the seacoast to seek shelter in the wilderness; but now we feel as if we might sit under our own vine and eat the good of the land.

I feel a *gaieté de cœur* to which before I was a stranger. I think the sun looks brighter, the birds sing more melodiously, and Nature puts on a more cheerful countenance. We feel a temporary peace, and the poor fugitives are returning to their deserted habitation.

Though we felicitate ourselves, we sympathize with those who are trembling lest the lot of Boston should be theirs. But they cannot be in similar circumstances unless pusillanimity and cowardice should take possession of them. They have time and warning given them to see the evil and shun it.

I long to hear that you have declared an independency. And, by the way, in the new code of laws which I suppose it will be necessary for you to make, I desire you would remember the ladies and be more generous and favorable to them than your ancestors. Do not put such unlimited power into the hands of the husbands. Remember, all men would be tyrants if they could. If particular care and attention is not paid to the ladies, we are determined to foment a rebellion, and will not hold ourselves bound by any laws in which we have no voice or representation.

That your sex are naturally tyrannical is a truth so thoroughly established as to admit of no dispute; but such of you as wish to be happy willingly give up the harsh title of master for the more tender and endearing one of friend. Why, then, not put it out of the power of the vicious and the lawless to use us with cruelty and indignity with impunity? Men of sense in all ages abhor those customs which treat us only as the vassals of your sex; regard us then as beings placed by Providence under your protection, and in imitation of the Supreme Being make use of that power only for our happiness.

April 5

Not having an opportunity of sending this I shall add a few lines more; though not with a heart so gay. I have been attending the sick chamber of our neighbor Trott whose affliction I most sensibly feel but cannot describe, stripped of two lovely children in one week. George the eldest died on Wednesday and Billy the youngest on Friday, with the canker fever, a terrible disorder so much like the throat distemper that it differs but little from it. Betsy Cranch has been very bad, but upon the recovery. Becky Peck they do not expect will live out the day. Many grown persons are now sick with it, in this street. It rages much in other towns. The mumps too are very frequent. Isaac is now confined with it. Our own little flock are yet well. My heart trembles with anxiety for them. God preserve them.

I want to hear much oftener from you than I do. March 8th was the last date of any that I have yet had. You inquire of me whether I am making saltpetre.[3] I have not yet attempted it, but after soap-making believe I shall make the experiment. I find as much as I can do to manufacture clothing for my family, which would else be naked. I know of but one person in this part of the town who has made any. That is Mr. Tertius Bass, as he is called, who has got very near a hundred-weight which has been found to be very good. I have heard of some others in the other parishes. Mr. Reed, of Weymouth, has been applied to, to go to Andover to the mills which are now at work, and he has gone.

I have lately seen a small manuscript describing the proportions of the various sorts of powder fit for cannon, small arms, and pistols. If it would be of any service your way I will get it transcribed and send it to you. Every one of your friends sends regards, and all the little ones. Your brother's youngest child lies bad with con-

vulsion fits. Adieu. I need not say how much I am your ever
faithful friend.

92. ABIGAIL ADAMS

Braintree, 7 April 1776

I have received two letters from you this week. One of the 17th
and the other the 19th of March. I know not where one of my
letters is gone, unless you have since received it. I certainly wrote
you in February, and the first letter I wrote I mention that I had
not written before. I have written four letters before this. I believe I have received all yours except one you mention writing
from Framingham, which I never heard of before. I have received all the papers you have sent, the oration, and the magazines. In the small papers I sometimes find pieces begun and
continued (for instance, Johnstone's speech),[1] but am so unlucky
as not to get the papers in order, and miss of seeing the whole.

The removal of the army seems to have stopped the current of
news. I want to know to what part of America they are now wandering. It is reported and credited that Manly has taken a schooner
belonging to the fleet, richly laden with money, plate, and English goods, with a number of Tories. The particulars I have not
yet learned. Yesterday the remains of our worthy General Warren were dug up upon Bunker's Hill, and carried into town, and
on Monday are to be interred with all the honors of war.

10 April

The Dr. was buried on Monday; the Masons walking in procession from the State House, with the military in uniforms, and a
large concourse of people attending. He was carried into the
Chapel, and there a funeral dirge was played, an excellent prayer
by Dr. Cooper, and an oration by Mr. Morton,[2] which I hope
will be printed. I think the subject must have inspired him. A
young fellow could not have wished a finer opportunity to display his talents. The amiable and heroic virtues of the deceased,
recent in the minds of the audience; the noble cause to which he
fell a martyr; their own sufferings and unparalleled injuries, all
fresh in their minds, must have given weight and energy to what-

ever could be delivered upon the occasion. The dead body, like that of Caesar, before their eyes, whilst each wound,—

> "Like dumb mouths, did ope their ruby lips,
> To beg the voice and utterance of a tongue.
> Woe to the hands that shed this costly blood!
> A curse shall light upon their line.
> Domestic fury, and fierce civil strife
> Shall cumber all the parts of Britton."[3]

11 April

I take my pen and write just as I can get time; my letters will be a strange mixture. I really am "cumbered about many things," and scarcely know which way to turn myself. I miss my partner, and find myself unequal to the cares which fall upon me. I find it necessary to be the directress of our husbandry. Hands are so scarce, that I have not been able to procure one, and add to this that Isaac has been sick with a fever this fortnight, not able to strike a stroke, and a multiplicity of farming business pouring in upon us. In this dilemma I have taken Belcher into pay, and must secure him for the season, as I know not what better course to steer. I hope in time to have the reputation of being as good a *farmeress* as my partner has of being a good statesman. To ask you anything about your return would, I suppose, be asking a question which you cannot answer.

Retirement, rural quiet domestic pleasures, all, all must give place to the weighty cares of state. It would be—

> "Meanly poor in solitude to hide
> An honest zeal, unwarped by party rage."

> "Though certain pains attend the cares of state,
> A good man owes his country to be great,
> Should act abroad the high distinguished part,
> And show, at least, the purpose of his heart."[4]

I hope your Prussian General[5] will answer the high character which is given of him. But we, who have been bred in a land of liberty, scarcely know how to give credit to so unjust and arbitrary a mandate of a despot. To cast off a faithful servant, only for being the unhappy bearer of ill news, degrades the man and dishonors the prince. The Congress, by employing him, have shown a liberality of sentiment not confined to colonies or continents, but, to use the words of "Common Sense," have "carried their friendship on a larger scale, by claiming brotherhood with every European Christian, and may justly triumph in the generosity of the sentiment."

Yesterday, was taken and carried into Cohasset, by three whale-boats, which went from the shore on purpose, a snow from the Grenadas, laden with three hundred and fifty-four puncheons of West India rum, forty-three barrels of sugar, twelve thousand and five hundred-weight of coffee; a valuable prize. A number of Eastern sloops have brought wood into town since the fleet sailed. We have a rumor of Admiral Hopkins[6] being engaged with a number of ships and tenders off Rhode Island, and are anxious to know the event.

Be so good as to send me a list of the vessels which sail with Hopkins, their names, weight of metal, and number of men; all the news you know, etc.

I hear our jurors refuse to serve, because the writs are issued in the King's name. Surely they are for independence.

Write me how you do this winter. I want to say many things I must omit. It is not fit "to wake the soul by tender strokes of art," or to ruminate upon happiness we might enjoy, lest absence become intolerable. Adieu.

Yours.

I wish you would burn all my letters.

93. JOHN ADAMS

12 April 1776

I inclose a few sheets of paper, and will send more as fast as opportunities present.

Chesterfield's letters are a chequered set. You would not choose to have them in your library. They are like Congreve's plays, stained with libertine morals and base principles.

You will see by the papers the news, the speculations, and the political plans of the day. The ports are opened wide enough at last, and privateers are allowed to prey upon British trade. This is not independency, you know. What is? Why, government in every colony, a confederation among them all, and treaties with foreign nations to acknowledge us a sovereign state, and all that. When these things will be done, or any of them, time must discover. Perhaps the time is near, perhaps a great way off.

94. JOHN ADAMS

14 April

You justly complain of my short letters, but the critical state of things and the multiplicity of avocations must plead my excuse. You ask where the fleet is? The inclosed papers will inform you. You ask what sort of defense Virginia can make? I believe they will make an able defense. Their militia and minute-men have been some time employed in training themselves, and they have nine battalions of regulars, as they call them, maintained among them, under good officers, at the Continental expense. They have set up a number of manufactories of fire-arms, which are busily employed. They are tolerably supplied with powder, and are successful and assiduous in making saltpetre. Their neighboring sister, or rather daughter colony of North Carolina, which is a warlike colony, and has several battalions at the Continental expense, as well as a pretty good militia, are ready to assist them, and they are in very good spirits and seem determined to make a brave resistance. The gentry are very rich, and the common people very poor. This inequality of property gives an aristocratical turn to all their proceedings, and occasions a strong aversion in their patricians to "Common Sense." But the spirit of these Barons is coming down, and it must submit. It is very true, as you observe, they have been duped by Dunmore. But this is a common case. All the colonies are duped, more or less, at one time and another. A more egregious bubble was never blown up than the story of Commissioners coming to treat with the Congress, yet it has gained credit like a charm, not only with, but against the clearest evidence. I never shall forget the delusion which seized our best and most sagacious friends, the dear inhabitants of Boston, the winter before last. Credulity and the want of foresight are imperfections in the human character, that no politician can sufficiently guard against.

You give me some pleasure by your account of a certain house in Queen Street. I had burned it long ago in imagination. It rises now to my view like a phoenix. What shall I say of the Solicitor General? I pity his pretty children. I pity his father and his sisters. I wish I could be clear that it is no moral evil to pity him and his lady. Upon repentance, they will certainly have a large share in the compassions of many. But let us take warning, and give it to our children. Whenever vanity and gayety, a love of pomp and dress, furniture, equipage, buildings, great company, expensive diversions, and elegant entertainments get the better of the principles and judgments of men or women, there is no knowing where they will stop, nor into what evils, natural, moral, or political, they will lead us.

Your description of your own *gaieté de cœur* charms me. Thanks be to God, you have just cause to rejoice, and may the bright prospect be obscured by no cloud. As to declarations of independency, be patient. Read our privateering laws and our commercial laws. What signifies a word?

As to your extraordinary code of laws, I cannot but laugh. We have been told that our struggle has loosened the bands of government everywhere; that children and apprentices were disobedient; that schools and colleges were grown turbulent; that Indians slighted their guardians, and negroes grew insolent to their masters. But your letter was the first intimation that another tribe, more numerous and powerful than all the rest, were grown discontented. This is rather too coarse a compliment, but you are so saucy, I won't blot it out. Depend upon it, we know better than to repeal our masculine systems. Although they are in full force, you know they are little more than theory. We dare not exert our power in its full latitude. We are obliged to go fair and softly, and, in practice, you know we are the subjects. We have only the name of masters, and rather than give up this, which would completely subject us to the despotism of the petticoat, I hope General Washington and all our brave heroes would fight; I am sure every good politician would plot, as long as he would against despotism, empire, monarchy, aristocracy, oligarchy, or ochlocracy. A fine story, indeed! I begin to think the ministry as deep as they are wicked. After stirring up Tories, land-jobbers, trimmers, bigots, Canadians, Indians, negroes, Hanoverians, Hessians, Russians, Irish Roman Catholics, Scotch renegadoes, at last they have stimulated the ———— to demand new privileges and threaten to rebel.

95. ABIGAIL ADAMS

Braintree, 14 April 1776

I have missed my good friend Colonel Warren from Watertown in the conveyance of my letters. You make no mention of more than one. Write me how many you have had and what the dates were.

I wrote you, upon the 17th of March.[1] Particulars it was not then possible to obtain; and after that, I thought every pen would be employed in writing to you a much more accurate account than I could give you.

The fleet lay in the road almost a fortnight after the town was evacuated. In that time Major Tupper came with a body of men to Germantown, and procured two lighters, and fitted them with every sort of combustible matter, hand grenades, etc., in order to set fire to the fleet. But the very day he was ready, they sailed. And it was said that they had intelligence from Boston of the design. However, he carried the lighters up to town for the next fleet that appears.

Fort Hill is a-fortifying, I suppose, in the best manner. Committees have been appointed to survey the islands, etc., but we are scanty of men. It is said we have not more than two thousand effective men left, and the General thought it necessary to take the heavy cannon with him. We have many pieces spiked up, which they are employed in clearing. About a hundred pieces, I have heard, were left at the castle with their trunnels broken, or spiked. The castle, you have no doubt heard, was burnt by the troops before they sailed, and an attempt was made to blow up the walls, in which, however, they did not succeed any further than to shatter them. There are so many things necessary to be done, that I suppose business moves slowly. At present we all seem to be so happy and so tranquil, that I sometimes think we want another fleet to give some energy and spirit to our motions. But there has been a great overturn that people seem to be hardly recovered from their amazement. Many buildings in town sustained great damages, more particularly at the south end. The furniture of many houses was carried off or broken in pieces. Dr. Gardiner left all his furniture and medicine, valued, it is said, at four hundred sterling. Dr. Lloyd is still in town; Dr. Whitworth too. Both ought to be transported. Mr. Goldthwait[2] is in town. All the records of which he had the care safe, though it seems part of them were carried into Boston. All the papers relating to the Probate Courts are missing. Mr. Lovell, and all the prisoners taken at the Charlestown battle, are carried off. The bells are all in town; never were taken down. The officers and Tories have lived a life of dissipation. Inclosed is a prologue of Burgoyne's,[3] with a parody written in Boston, soon after it was acted. Burgoyne is a better poet than soldier.

As to goods of any kind, we cannot tell what quantity there is. Only two or three shops open. Goods at most extravagant prices. All the better to promote manufactures. The small-pox prevents my going to town; several have broke out with it in the army since they went into Boston. I cannot help wishing that it would spread. I think the country is in more danger than ever. I am anxious about it. If it should spread there is but one thing would prevent my going down to our own house and having it with all our children, and I don't know but I should be tempted to run you in debt for it. There is talk of raising another regiment. If they should, I fear we shall suffer in our husbandry. Labor is very high. I cannot hire a man for six months under twenty pounds lawful money. The works upon the Neck are leveling. We keep guards upon the shores yet. Manly has taken a vessel-load of Tories. Among them is Black, the Scotchman, and Brazen-head Jackson, Hill, the baker, etc. What can be done with them? I think they ought to be transported to England. I would advertise for Tory transports.

Hanover has made large quantities of saltpetre. This week we are to hold court here, but I do not imagine anything will be done. I have a letter from you the 29th of March. It is said there is one from Mr. Gerry the 3d of April, acquainting us with your opening trade. Who is the writer of "Common Sense"? of "Cato"? of "Cassandra"?[4] I wish you would, according to promise, write me an account of Lord Stirling. We know nothing about him here.

All the Tories look crest-fallen. Several deserters from on board the commodore's ship say that it is very sickly on board. We have only that and two or three cutters besides. We fear that a brig, laden with seventy tons of powder, which sailed from Newburyport, has fallen into the enemy's hands upon her return.

I rejoice in the Southern victories. The oration was a very elegant performance, but not without much art,—a few strokes which to me injure it. I know not anything further which I ought to say but that I am most affectionately yours.

96. JOHN ADAMS

15 April

I send you every newspaper that comes out, and I send you, now and then, a few sheets of paper, but this article is as scarce here as with you. I would send a quire, if I could get a conveyance.

I write you now and then a line, as often as I can, but I can tell you no news but what I send in the public papers.

We are waiting, it is said, for Commissioners;[1] a messiah that will never come. This story of Commissioners is as arrant an illusion as ever was hatched in the brain of an enthusiast, a politician, or a maniac. I have laughed at it, scolded at it, grieved at it, and I don't know but I may, at an unguarded moment, have rip'd at it. But it is vain to reason against such delusions. I was very sorry to see, in a letter from the General, that he had been bubbled with it; and still more, to see, in a letter from my sagacious friend W.,[2] at Plymouth, that he was taken in too.

My opinion is that the Commissioners and the commission have been here (I mean in America), these two months. The Governors, Mandamus Councillors, Collectors and Comptrollers, and Commanders of the army and navy, I conjecture, compose the list, and their power is to receive submissions. But we are not in a very submissive mood. They will get no advantage of us. We shall go on to perfection, I believe. I have been very busy for some time; have written about ten sheets of paper[3] with my own hand, about some trifling affairs, which I may mention some time or other—not now, for fear of accidents.

What will come of this labor, time will discover. I shall get nothing by it, I believe, because I never get anything by anything that I do. I am sure the public or posterity ought to get something. I believe my children will think I might as well have thought and labored a little, night and day, for their benefit. But I will not bear the reproaches of my children. I will tell them that I studied and labored to procure a free constitution of government for them to solace themselves under, and if they do not prefer this to ample fortune, to ease and elegance, they are not my children, and I care not what becomes of them. They shall live upon thin diet, wear mean clothes, and work hard with cheerful hearts and free spirits, or they may be the children of the earth, or of no one, for me.

John has genius, and so has Charles. Take care that they don't go astray. Cultivate their minds, inspire their little hearts, raise their wishes. Fix their attention upon great and glorious objects. Root out every little thing. Weed out every meanness. Make them great and manly. Teach them to scorn injustice, ingratitude, cowardice, and falsehood. Let them revere nothing but religion, morality, and liberty.

Nabby and Tommy are not forgotten by me, although I did not mention them before. The first, by reason of her sex, requires a different education from the two I have mentioned. Of this, you are the only judge. I want to send each of my little pretty flock some present or other. I have walked over this city twenty times, and gaped at every shop, like a countryman, to find something, but could not. Ask every one of them what they would choose to have, and write it to me in your next letter. From this I shall judge of their taste and fancy and discretion.

97. JOHN ADAMS TO JOHN Q. ADAMS

Philadelphia, 18 April 1776

I thank you for your agreeable letter of the 24th of March. I rejoice with you that our friends are once more in possession of the town of Boston; am glad to hear that so little damage is done to our house.

I hope you and your sister and brothers will take proper notice of these great events, and remember under whose wise and kind Providence they are all conducted. Not a sparrow falls, nor a hair is lost, but by the direction of infinite wisdom. Much less are cities conquered and evacuated. I hope that you will all remember how many losses, dangers, and inconveniences have been borne by your parents, and the inhabitants of Boston in general, for the sake of preserving freedom for you and yours, and I hope you will all follow the virtuous example, if, in any future time, your country's liberties shall be in danger, and suffer every human evil rather than give them up. My love to your mamma, your sister and brothers, and all the family. I am your affectionate father.

98. ABIGAIL ADAMS

18 April 1776

I cannot omit so good an opportunity as offers by Mr. Church of telling you that we are all well. I wrote you two letters last week, which I sent to Watertown. In those I said everything that occurred to my mind. Nothing since of any importance has taken place. The 19th of April, ever memorable for America as the Ides of March to Rome and to Caesar, is fixed upon for the examination of the Tories by a committee from the General Court. I could have wished that some other persons in the room of one or two might have been chosen. It is so dangerous mentioning names that I refer you to Mr. Church for the names of the committee, and then you will easily guess who I mean.

I wish I could tell you that business in the fortification way went on briskly; but a western member[1] of the General Court, who has great influence there, has got it into his head that Fort Hill and Noddle's Island are sufficient, and though a man possessed of a very good heart, is sometimes obstinately wrong.

The Court of Sessions sat yesterday, and went on with business very smoothly.

We hear that Congress has declared a free trade; and I give you joy of the success of Admiral Hopkins, not only in his expedition, but in his success upon his return. Great Britain, I think, is not quite omnipotent at sea any more than upon the land.

You promised to come and see me in May or June. Shall I expect you, or do you determine to stay out the year? I very well remember when the eastern circuits of the courts, which lasted a month, were thought an age, and an absence of three months intolerable. But we are carried from step to step, and from one degree to another, to endure that which at first we think impossible.

But I assure you I am obliged to make use of reason and philosophy in addition to custom, to feel patient. Be assured I always remember you as I ought, that is, with the kindest affection.

PORTIA

99. ABIGAIL ADAMS

21 April 1776

I have to acknowledge the receipt of a very few lines dated the 12th of April. You make no mention of the whole sheets I have wrote to you, by which I judge you either never received them, or that they were so lengthy as to be troublesome; and in return you have set me an example of being very concise. I believe I shall not take the hint, but give as I love to receive. Mr. Church talked a week ago of setting off for Philadelphia. I wrote by him, but suppose it has not yet gone. You have perhaps heard that the bench is filled by Messrs. Foster and Sullivan,[1] so that a certain person is now excluded. I own I am not of so forgiving a disposition as to wish to see him holding a place which he refused merely from a spirit of envy.

I give up my request for Chesterfield's "Letters," submitting entirely to your judgment, as I have ever found you ready to oblige me in this way whenever you thought it would contribute either to my entertainment or improvement. I was led to the request from reading the following character of him in my favorite Thomson, from some spirited and patriotic speeches of his in the reign of George II:—

> "O thou whose wisdom, solid yet refined,
>   Whose patriot-virtues and consummate skill
>   To touch the finer springs that move the world,

Joined to whate'er the Graces can bestow,
And all Apollo's animating fire,
Give thee with pleasing dignity to shine
At once the guardian, ornament, and joy
Of polished life. Permit the rural muse,
O Chesterfield! to grace thee with her song,
Ere to the shades again she humbly flies;
Indulge her fond ambition, in thy train
(For every muse has in thy train a place)
To mark thy various, full accomplished mind,—
To mark that spirit which, with British scorn,
Rejects th' allurements of corrupted power;
That elegant politeness which excels,
Even in the judgment of presumptuous France,
The boasted manner of her shining court;
That wit, the vivid energy of sense,
The truth of nature, which, with Attic point,
And kind, well-tempered satire, smoothly keen,
Steals through the soul, and, without pain, corrects."[2]

I think the speculations you inclose prove that there is full liberty of the press. Cato shows he has a bad cause to defend; whilst the Forester writes with a spirit peculiar to himself, and leads me to think that he has an intimate acquaintance with "Common Sense."

We have intelligence of the arrival of some of the Tory fleet at Halifax; that they are much distressed for want of houses,—obliged to give six dollars per month for one room; provisions scarce and dear. Some of them with six or eight children around them, sitting upon the rocks, crying, not knowing where to lay their heads.

Just Heaven has given them to taste of the same cup of affliction which they one year ago administered with such callous hearts to thousands of their fellow-citizens; but with this difference, that they fly from the injured and enraged country, whilst pity and commiseration received the sufferers whom they inhumanly drove from their dwellings.

I would fain hope that the time may not be far distant when those things you hint at may be carried into execution.

"Oh! are ye not those patriots in whose power
    That best, that godlike luxury is placed
    Of blessing thousands, thousands yet unborn
    Thro' late posterity? Ye large of soul,
    Cheer up dejected industry, and give
    A double harvest to the pining swain.
    Teach thou, the laboring hand the sweets of toil
    How, by the finest art, the native robe
    To weave; how, white as Hyperborean snow,
    To form the lucid lawn; with venturous oar
    How to dash wide the billow; nor look on,
    Shamefully passive, while Britannia's fleets
    Defraud us of the glittering finny swarms
    That heave our friths and swarm upon our shores
    How all-enlivening trade to rouse, and wing
    The prosperous sail from every growing port
    Uninjured round the sea-encircled globe."[3]

It is rumored here that Admiral Hopkins is blocked up in Newport harbor by a number of men-of-war. If so, 'tis a very unlucky circumstance. As to fortifications, those who preside in the Assembly can give you a much better account than I.

I heard yesterday that a number of gentlemen who were together at Cambridge thought it highly proper that a committee of ladies should be chosen to examine the Tory ladies, and proceeded to the choice of three—Mrs. Winthrop, Mrs. Warren, and your humble servant.

I could go on and give you a long list of domestic affairs, but they would only serve to embarrass you and noways relieve me. I hope it will not be long before things will be brought into such a train as that you may be spared to your family.

Your brother has lost his youngest child with convulsion fits. Your mother is well and always desires to be remembered to you. Nabby is sick with the mumps,—a very disagreeable disorder. You have not once told me how you do. I judge you are well, as you seem to be in good spirits. I bid you good night. All the little flock send duty, and want to see p——a.

Adieu. Shall I say, remember me as you ought?

100. JOHN ADAMS

Philadelphia, 23 April 1776

This is St. George's day, a festival celebrated by the English, as St. Patrick's is by the Irish, St. David's by the Welsh, and St. Andrew's by the Scotch. The natives of Old England in this city heretofore formed a society, which they called St. George's Club or St. George's Society. Upon the 23d of April, annually, they had a great feast. But the Tories and politics have made a schism in the society, so that one part of them are to meet and dine at the City Tavern, and the other at the Bunch of Grapes, Israel Jacobs's,[1] and a third party go out of town. One set are stanch Americans, another stanch Britons, and a third, half-way men, neutral beings, moderate men, prudent folks; for such is the division among men upon all occasions and every question. This is the account which I have from my barber, who is one of the society, and zealous on the side of America, and one of the Philadelphia Associators.[2]

This curious character of a barber I have a great inclination to draw, for your amusement. He is a little, dapper fellow, short and small, but active and lively. A tongue as fluent and voluble as you please, wit at will, and a memory or an invention which never leaves him at a loss for a story to tell you for your entertainment. He has seen great company. He has dressed hair and shaved faces at Bath, and at Court. He is acquainted with several of the nobility and gentry, particularly Sir William Meredith. He married a girl, the daughter of a Quaker in this place, of whom he tells many droll stories. He is a serjeant in one of the companies of some battalion or other here. He frequents, of evenings, a beer house kept by one Weaver, in the city, where he has many curious disputes and adventures, and meets many odd characters.

I believe you will think me very idle to write you so trifling a letter, upon so uninteresting a subject, at a time when my country is fighting *pro aris et focis*.[3] But I assure you I am glad to chat with this barber, while he is shaving and combing me, to divert myself from less agreeable thoughts. He is so sprightly and good-humored that he contributes, more than I could have imagined, to my comfort in this life. Burne has prepared a string of toasts for the club to drink to-day at Israel's.

The thirteen united colonies.

The free and independent States of America.

The Congress for the time being.

The American army and navy.

The Governor and Council of South Carolina, etc., etc., etc.

A happy election for the Whigs on the first of May, etc.

101. JOHN ADAMS

Philadelphia, 28 April 1776

Yesterday I received two letters from you from the 7th to the 14th of April. I have received all your letters, and I am not certain I wrote one from Framingham. The one I mean contains an account of my dining with the Indians at Mr. Mifflin's. It gives me concern to think of the many cares you must have upon your mind. Am glad that you have taken [Belcher] into play, and that Isaac is well before now, I hope. Your reputation as a farmer, or anything else you undertake, I dare answer for. Your partner's character as a statesman is much more problematical.

As to my return, I have not a thought of it. Journeys of such a length are tedious, and expensive both of time and money, neither of which is my own. I hope to spend the next Christmas where I did the last, and after that I hope to be relieved; for by that time, I shall have taken a pretty good trick at helm, whether the vessel has been well steered or not. But if my countrymen should insist upon my serving them another year, they must let me bring my whole family with me. Indeed, I could keep house here, with my partner, four children, and two servants, as cheap as I maintain myself here with two horses and a servant at lodgings.

Instead of domestic felicity, I am destined to public contentions. Instead of rural felicity, I must reconcile myself to the smoke and noise of a city. In the place of private peace, I must be distracted with the vexation of developing the deep intrigues of politicians, and must assist in conducting the arduous operations of war, and think myself well rewarded if my private pleasure and interests are sacrificed, as they ever have been and will be, to the happiness of others.

You tell me our jurors refuse to serve, because the writs are issued in the King's name. I am very glad to hear that they discover so much sense and spirit. I learn, from another letter, that the General Court have left out of their bills the year of his reign, and that they are making a law that the same name shall be left out of all writs, commissions, and all law processes. This is good news too. The same will be the case in all the colonies, very soon.

You ask me, how I have done, the winter past. I have not enjoyed so good health as last fall. But I have done complaining of anything. Of ill-health I have no right to complain, because it is given me by Heaven. Of meanness, of envy, of littleness, of ———, of ———, of ———, I have reason and right to complain, but I have too much contempt to use that right. There is such a mixture of folly, littleness, and knavery in this world, that I am weary of it, and although I behold it with unutterable contempt and indignation, yet the public good requires that I should take no notice of it by word or by letter. And to this public good I will conform.

You will see an account of the fleet in some of the papers I have sent you. I give you joy of the Admiral's success. I have vanity enough to take to myself a share in the merit of the American navy. It was always a measure that my heart was much engaged in, and I pursued it for a long time against the wind and tide, but at last obtained it.

Is there no way for two friendly souls to converse together although the bodies are four hundred miles off? Yes, by letter. But I want a better communication. I want to hear you think or to see your thoughts. The conclusion of your letter makes my heart throb more than a cannonade would. You bid me burn your letters. But I must forget you first. In yours of April 14 you say you miss our friend in the conveyance of your letters. Don't hesitate to write by the post. Seal well. Don't miss a single post. You take it for granted that I have particular intelligence of everything from others, but I have not. If any one wants a vote for a commission he vouchsafes me a letter, but tells me very little news. I have more particulars from you than any one else. Pray keep me constantly informed what ships are in the harbor and what fortifications are going on. I am quite impatient to hear of more vigorous measures for fortifying Boston harbor. Not a moment should be neglected. Every man ought to go down, as they did after the battle of Lexington, and work until it is done. I would willingly pay half a dozen hands myself, and subsist them, rather than it should not be done immediately. It is of more importance than to raise corn. You say "inclosed is a prologue and a parody," but neither was inclosed. If you did not forget it, the letter has been opened, and the inclosures taken out. If the small-pox spreads, run me in debt. I received, a post or two past, a letter from your uncle at Salem, containing a most friendly and obliging invitation to you and yours to go and have the distemper at his house if it should spread. He has one or two in his family to have it.

The writer of "Common Sense" and "The Forester" is the same person. His name is Paine, a gentleman about two years ago from England, a man who, General Lee says, has genius in his eyes. The writer of "Cassandra" is said to be Mr. James Cannon, a tutor in the Philadelphia College. "Cato" is reported here to be Doctor Smith—a match for Brattle. The oration[1] was an insolent performance. A motion was made to thank the orator, and ask a copy, but opposed with great spirit and vivacity from every part of the room, and at last withdrawn, lest it should be rejected, as it certainly would have been, with indignation. The orator then printed it himself, after leaving out or altering some offensive passages. This is one of the many irregular and extravagant characters of the age. I never heard one single person speak well of anything about him but his abilities, which are generally allowed to be good. The appointment of him to make the oration was a great oversight and mistake.

The late act of Parliament[2] has made so deep an impression upon people's minds throughout the colonies, it is looked upon as the last stretch of oppression, that we are hastening rapidly to great events. Governments will be up everywhere before midsummer, and an end to royal style, titles, and authority. Such mighty revolutions make a deep impression on the minds of men, and set many violent passions at work. Hope, fear, joy, sorrow, love, hatred, malice, envy, revenge, jealousy, ambition, avarice, resentment, gratitude, and every other passion, feeling, sentiment, principle, and imagination were never in more lively exercise than they are now from Florida to Canada inclusively. May God in his providence overrule the whole for the good of mankind. It requires more serenity of temper, a deeper understanding, and more courage than fell to the lot of Marlborough to ride in this whirlwind.

102. ABIGAIL ADAMS

Braintree, 7 May 1776

How many are the solitary hours I spend ruminating upon the past and anticipating the future, whilst you, overwhelmed with the cares of state, have but a few moments you can devote to any individual. All domestic pleasures and enjoyments are absorbed in the great and important duty you owe your country, "for our country is, as it were, a secondary god, and the first and greatest parent. It is to be preferred to parents, wives, children, friends, and all things,—the gods only excepted; for, if our country perishes, it is as impossible to save an individual as to preserve one of the fingers of a mortified hand." Thus do I suppress every wish, and silence every murmur, acquiescing in a painful separation from the companion of my youth and the friend of my heart.

I believe 'tis near ten days since I wrote you a line. I have not felt in a humor to entertain you. If I had taken up my pen perhaps some unbecoming invective might have fallen from it. The eyes of our rulers have been closed, and a lethargy has seized almost every member. I fear a fatal security has taken possession of them. Whilst the building is on flame, they tremble at the expense of water to quench it. In short, two months have elapsed since the evacuation of Boston, and very little has been done in that time to secure it, or the harbor, from future invasion. The people are all in a flame, and no one among us, that I have heard of, even mentions expense. They think, universally, that there has been an amazing neglect somewhere. Many have turned out as volunteers to work upon Noddle's Island, and many more would go upon Nantasket, if it was once set on foot. " 'Tis a maxim of state, that power and liberty are like heat and moisture. Where they are well mixed, everything prospers; where they are single, they are destructive."[1]

A government of more stability is much wanted in this colony, and they are ready to receive it from the hands of the Congress. And since I have begun with maxims of state, I will add another, namely, that a people may let a king fall, yet still remain a people; but, if a king let his people slip from him, he is no longer a king. And as this is most certainly our case, why not proclaim to the world, in decisive terms, your own importance?

Shall we not be despised by foreign powers, for hesitating so long at a word?

I cannot say that I think you are very generous to the ladies; for, whilst you are proclaiming peace and good-will to men, emancipating all nations, you insist upon retaining an absolute power over wives. But you must remember that arbitrary power is like most other things which are very hard, very liable to be broken; and, notwithstanding all your wise laws and maxims, we have it in our power, not only to free ourselves, but to subdue our masters, and, without violence, throw both your natural and legal authority at our feet;—

> "Charm by accepting, by submitting sway,
> Yet have our humor most when we obey."

I thank you for several letters which I have received since I wrote last; they alleviate a tedious absence, and I long earnestly for a Saturday evening, and experience a similar pleasure to that which I used to find in the return of my friend upon that day after a week's absence. The idea of a year dissolves all my philosophy.

Our little ones, whom you so often recommend to my care and instruction, shall not be deficient in virtue or probity, if the precepts of a mother have their desired effect; but they would be doubly enforced, could they be indulged with the example of a father alternately before them. I often point them to their sire,—

> "engaged in a corrupted state,
> Wrestling with vice and faction."[2]

9 May

I designed to have finished the sheet, but, an opportunity offering, I close, only just informing you that, May the 7th, our privateers took two prizes in the bay, in fair sight of the man-of-war; one, a brig from Ireland; the other from Fayal, loaded with wine, brandy, etc.; the other with beef, etc. The wind was east, and a flood tide, so that the tenders could not get out, though they tried several times; the lighthouse fired signal guns, but all would not do. They took them in triumph, and carried them into Lynn. Johnny and Charles have the mumps, a bad disorder, but they are not very bad. Pray be kind enough to remember me at all times, and write, as often as you possibly can, to your

PORTIA

103. ABIGAIL ADAMS

9 May 1776

I this day received yours of the 20th of April, accompanied with a letter upon government. Upon reading it I somehow or other felt an uncommon affection for it. I could not help thinking it was a near relation of a very intimate friend of mine. If I am mistaken in its descent, I know it has a near affinity to the sentiments of that person. And though I cannot pretend to be an adept in the art of government, yet it looks rational that a government of good laws well administered should carry with them the fairest prospect of happiness to a community, as well as to individuals. But as this is a prerogative to which your sex lay an almost exclusive claim, I shall quit the subject after having quoted a passage in favor of a republic, from an anonymous author entitled "Essays on the Genius and Writings of Pope."[1]

"The fine arts in short, are naturally attendant upon power and luxury. But the sciences require unlimited freedom to raise them to their full vigor and growth. In a monarchy there may be poets, painters, and musicians, but orators, historians, and philosophers can exist in a republic alone. The Roman nation, by their unjust attempt upon the liberty of the world, justly lost their

own, and with their liberty they lost not only their force of eloquence, but even their style and language itself."

This province is not in the most agreeable situation at present.
It wants a poise, a stability, which it does not possess. The Council have recommended it to the Superior Court to sit at Ipswich
next term. Judge Cushing called upon me yesterday with his lady,
and made me a very friendly visit; said he wished earnestly for the
presence of the Chief Justice. He had many things he wished to
say to him. I requested him to write, and he has promised to.

The spirit of fortification has just waked, and we are now pursuing with vigor what ought before this time to have been completed. Fort Hill, the Castle, Dorchester Points, Noddle's Island
are almost completed. A committee are sent down to Nantasket,
and orders are given to fortify the Moon, George's Island, etc. I
believe Noddle's Island has been done by subscription. Six hundred inhabitants of the town meet every morning in the town
house, from whence they march with fife and drum, with Mr.
Gordon, Mr. Skilman, and Mr. Lothrop[2] at their head, to the
Long Wharf, where they embark for the island; and it comes to
the subscribers' turn to work two days in a week.

You have no doubt heard of the appointment of your friend[3]
as judge. He seems loath to accept, and his lady I think loath that
he should. Surely it does not look well to have those offices
bandied about from hand to hand; if they could not obtain one
from the bar, that gentleman will fill the place with honor to
himself and his brethren. But Mr. Lowell[4] ought to have come in,
instead of some others; but there are some in Council who require more than Heaven: that demands only repentance and
amendment.

Let me hear from you often.   Yours unfeignedly.

104. JOHN ADAMS

Philadelphia, 12 May 1776

Yours of 21 April came to hand yesterday. I send you regularly
every newspaper, and write as often as I can; but I feel more skittish about writing than I did, because, since the removal of
headquarters[1] to New York, we have no express, and very few

individual travellers; and the post I am not quite confident in; however, I shall write as I can.

What shall I do with my office?[2] I want to resign it for a thousand reasons. Would you advise me?

There has been a gallant battle in Delaware River between the galleys and two men-of-war, the *Roebuck* and *Liverpool,* in which the men-of-war came off second best; which has diminished, in the minds of the people on both sides of the river, the terror of a man-of-war.

I long to hear a little of my private affairs; yet I dread it, too, because I know you must be perplexed and distressed. I wish it was in my power to relieve you. It gives me great pleasure to learn that our rulers are, at last, doing something towards the fortification of Boston. But I am inexpressibly chagrined to find that the enemy is fortifying on George's Island. I never shall be easy until they are completely driven out of that harbor, and effectually prevented from ever getting in again. As you are a politician and now elected into an important office, that of judgess of the Tory ladies, which will give you, naturally, an influence with your sex, I hope you will be instant, in season and out of season, in exhorting them to use their influence with the gentlemen, to fortify upon George's Island, Lovell's, Pettick's, Long, or wherever else it is proper. Send down fire ships and rafts, and burn to ashes those pirates. I am out of patience with the languid, lethargic councils of the province, at such a critical, important moment, puzzling their heads about twopenny fees, and confession bills, and what not, when the harbor of Boston is defenseless. If I was there, I should storm and thunder like Demosthenese or scold like a tooth-drawer. Do ask Mr. Wibird and Mr. Weld and Mr. Taft to preach about it. I am ashamed, vexed, angry to the last degree. Our people, by their torpitude, have invited the enemy to come to Boston again, and I fear they will have the civility and politeness to accept the invitation.

Your uncle has never answered my letter. Thank the Dr.; he has written me a most charming letter, full of intelligence and very sensible and useful remarks. I will pay the debt, as far as my circumstances will admit, and as soon. But I hope my friends will not wait for regular returns from me. I have not yet left off pitying "the fifty or sixty men";[3] and if my friends knew all that I do,

they would pity too. Betsey Smith, lazy hussy, has not written me
a line, a great while. I wish she was married—then she would
have some excuse. Duty to Pa. Love to all. How is the family
over against the church?

105. JOHN ADAMS

17 May 1776

I have this morning heard Mr. Duffield, upon the signs of the
times. He ran a parallel between the case of Israel and that of
America; and between the conduct of Pharaoh and that of
George. Jealousy that the Israelites would throw off the government of Egypt made him issue his edict that the midwives should
cast the children into the river, and the other edict, that the men
should make a large revenue of bricks without straw. He concluded, that the course of events indicated strongly the design of
Providence that we should be separated from Great Britain, etc.

Is it not a saying of Moses, "Who am I, that I should go in and
out before this great people"? When I consider the great events
which are passed, and those greater which are rapidly advanc-
ing, and that I may have been instrumental in touching some
springs and turning some small wheels, which have had and
will have such effects, I feel an awe upon my mind which is not
easily described. Great Britain has at last driven America to the
last step, a complete separation from her; a total, absolute
independence, not only of her Parliament, but of her crown, for
such is the amount of the resolve of the 15th.[1] Confederation
among ourselves, or alliances with foreign nations, are not necessary to a perfect separation from Britain. That is effected by
extinguishing all authority under the crown, Parliament, and nation, as the resolution for instituting governments has done, to
all intents and purposes. Confederation will be necessary for our
internal concord, and alliances may be so for our external defense.

I have reasons to believe that no colony, which shall assume a
government under the people, will give it up. There is something
very unnatural and odious in a government a thousand leagues
off. A whole government of our own choice, managed by per-

sons whom we love, revere, and can confide in, has charms in it for which men will fight. Two young gentlemen from South Carolina in this city, who were in Charlestown when their new constitution was promulgated, and when their new Governor and Council and Assembly walked out in procession, attended by the guards, company of cadets, light horse, etc., told me that they were beheld by the people with transports and tears of joy. The people gazed at them with a kind of rapture. They both told me that the reflection that these were gentlemen whom they all loved, esteemed, and revered, gentlemen of their own choice, whom they could trust, and whom they could displace, if any of them should behave amiss, affected them so that they could not help crying. They say their people will never give up this government. One of these gentlemen is a relation of yours, a Mr. Smith, son of Mr. Thomas Smith. I shall give him this letter or another to you.

A privateer fitted out here by Colonel Roberdeau and Major Bayard since our resolves for privateering, I am this moment informed, has taken a valuable prize. This is encouragement at the beginning.

In one or two of your letters, you remind me to think of you as I ought. Be assured, there is not an hour of the day in which I don't think of you as I ought, that is, with every sentiment of tenderness, esteem, and admiration.

106. JOHN ADAMS

Philadelphia, 22 May 1776

When a man is seated in the midst of forty people, some of whom are talking, and others whispering, it is not easy to think what is proper to write. I shall send you the newspapers, which will inform you of public affairs, and the particular flickerings of parties in this colony. I am happy to learn from your letter that a flame is at last raised among the people, for the fortification of the harbor. Whether Nantasket or Point Alderton would be proper posts to be taken, I can't say. But I would fortify every place which is proper, and which cannon could be obtained for. Generals Gates and Mifflin are now here. General Washington will be here to-morrow, when we shall consult and deliberate concerning the operations of the ensuing campaign.

We have dismal accounts from Europe of the preparations against us. This summer will be very important to us. We shall have a severe trial of our patience, fortitude, and perseverance. But I hope we shall do valiantly, and tread down our enemies.

I have some thoughts of petitioning the General Court for leave to bring my family here. I am a lonely, forlorn creature here. It used to be some comfort to me that I had a servant and some horses. They composed a sort of family for me. But now, there is not one creature here that I seem to have any kind of relation to. It is a cruel reflection, which very often comes across me, that I should be separated so far from those babes whose education and welfare lie so near my heart. But greater misfortunes than these must not divert us from superior duties.

Your sentiments of the duties we owe to our country are such as become the best of women and the best of men. Among all the disappointments and perplexities which have fallen to my share in life, nothing has contributed so much to support my mind as the choice blessing of a wife whose capacity enabled her to comprehend, and whose pure virtue obliged her to approve, the views of her husband. This has been the cheering consolation of my heart in my most solitary, gloomy, and disconsolate hours. In this remote situation, I am deprived in a great measure of this comfort. Yet I read and read again your charming letters, and they serve me, in some faint degree, as a substitute for the company and conversation of the writer. I want to take a walk with you in the garden, to go over to the common, the plain, the meadow. I want to take Charles in one hand and Tom in the other, and walk with you, Nabby on your right hand and John upon my left, to view the corn fields, the orchards, etc.

Alas, poor imagination! how faintly and imperfectly do you supply the want of originality and reality. But instead of these pleasing scenes of domestic life, I hope you will not be disturbed with the alarms of war. I hope, yet I fear.

107. JOHN ADAMS

Philadelphia, 27 May 1776

I have three of your favors before me, one of May 7, another of May 9, and a third of May 14th. The last has given me relief from many anxieties. It relates wholly to private affairs, and contains such an account of wise and prudent management as makes me very happy. I begin to be jealous that our neighbors will think affairs more discreetly conducted in my absence than at any other time. Whether your suspicions concerning a letter under a marble cover[1] are just or not, it is best to say little about it. It is a hasty, hurried thing, and of no great consequence, calculated for a meridian at a great distance from New England. If it has done no good, it will do no harm. It has contributed to set people thinking upon the subject, and in this respect has answered its end. The manufacture of governments having, since the publication of that letter, been as much talked of as that of saltpetre was before.

I rejoice at your account of the spirit of fortification, and the good effects of it. I hope by this time you are in a tolerable posture of defense. The inhabitants of Boston have done themselves great honor by their laudable zeal, the worthy clergymen, especially.

I think you shine as a stateswoman of late, as well as a farmeress. Pray where do you get your maxims of state? They are very apropos. I am much obliged to Judge Cushing and his lady for their polite visit to you. I should be very happy to see him, and converse with him about many things, but cannot hope for that pleasure very soon. The affairs of America are in so critical a state, such great events are struggling into birth, that I must not quit this station at this time. Yet I dread the melting heats of a Philadelphia summer, and know not how my frail constitution will endure it. Such constant care, such incessant application of mind, drinking up and exhausting the finer spirits, upon which life and health so essentially depend, will wear away a stronger man than I am. Yet I will not shrink from this danger or this toil. While my health shall be such that I can discharge, in any tolerable manner, the duties of this important post, I will not desert it.

I am pleased to hear that the Superior Court is to sit at Ipswich in June. This will contribute to give stability to the government, I hope, in all its branches. But I presume other steps will be taken for this purpose. A Governor and Lieutenant-governor, I hope, will be chosen, and the Constitution a little more fixed. I hope too, that the Council will, this year, be more full, and augmented by the addition of good men. I hope Mr. Bowdoin will be Governor, if his health will permit, and Dr. Winthrop[2] Lieutenant-governor. These are wise, learned, and prudent men. The first has a great fortune and wealthy connections. The other has the advantage of a name and family which is much reverenced, besides his personal abilities and virtues, which are very great.

Our friend, I sincerely hope, will not refuse his appointment. For although I have ever thought that the bench should be filled from the bar, and once labored successfully to effect it, yet as the gentlemen have seen fit to decline, I know of no one who would do more honor to the station than my friend. None would be so agreeable to me, whether I am to sit by him or before him. I suppose it must be disagreeable to him and his lady, because he loves to be upon his farm, and they both love to be together. But you must tell them of a couple of their friends, who are as fond of living together, who are obliged to sacrifice their rural amusements and domestic happiness to the requisitions of the public.

The Generals, Washington, Gates, and Mifflin, are all here, and we shall derive spirit, unanimity, and vigor from their presence and advice. I hope you will have some general officers at Boston soon. I am, with constant wishes and prayers for your health and prosperity, forever yours.

108. ABIGAIL ADAMS

What can be the reason I have not heard from you since the 20th of April, and now 'tis the 27th of May. My anxious, foreboding heart fears every evil, and my nightly slumbers are tortured. I have sent and sent again to the post-office, which is now kept in Boston at the office of the former Solicitor General. Not one line for me, though your handwriting is to be seen to several others. Not a scrip have I had since the General Assembly rose, and our worthy friend W——n left Watertown. I fear you are sick. The very idea casts such a gloom upon my spirits that I cannot recover them for hours, nor reason myself out of my fears. Surely if letters are delivered to any other hand than those to whose care they are directed, 'tis cruel to detain them. I believe for the future you had better direct them to be left in the post-office, from whence I shall be sure of obtaining them.

I am desired by sister A——s to ask you if you will take twenty-eight acres of woodland which she mentioned to you. It must be sold, has a very fine growth of walnut wood upon it, as well as other wood, 'tis prized at forty shillings per acre, which by looking into his deed of it, I find to be the same he gave for it. The distance which it lies from us is the chief objection in my mind. You will be so good as to send me word as soon as you receive this. They are about settling the estate as soon as possible. What can be done with or about the lighter I know not. I was told that she was taken for a fire ship, but was misinformed. There is no regular account of anything but the ropes, cable, and sails, nor anything which appears to show the cost of her. I think it can only be left to those who built about that time to say what they believe she cost. They have prized on half of her very low £33.8.4. I have asked my uncle Q——y to assist in your stead. The watch, she says, you desired to have. I know nothing about it; not having heard you mention it. She sets it at six pounds.

I wrote you two letters about a fortnight ago which were both covered together. Hope you have received them. We have no news here but what you will be informed of long before this reaches you, unless it is the politics of the town. At our May meeting Mr. Wibird was desired to preach a sermon previous to the choice, which he did to great acceptation. The debates were not who, but how many should be sent. They agreed upon three: Mr. Bass for the upper precinct, Colonel Thayer for the middle, and an uncle of ours[1] for this; but he begged to be excused as his state of health was so infirm, and so subject to a nervous headache that he was sure he could not stand it to sit in so numerous an assembly. The next vote was for your brother, and a tie took place between him and Colonel Palmer; but the latter declaring that he would tarry in the House if chosen there, the vote fell upon him.

The disagreeable news we have from Quebec is a great damper to our spirits, but shall we receive good and not evil? Upon this occasion you will recollect the sentiments of your favorite, Sully:[2] "Without attempting to judge of the future, which depends upon too many accidents, much less to subject it to our precipitation in bold and difficult enterprises, we should endeavor to subdue one obstacle at a time, nor suffer ourselves to be depressed by their greatness and their number. We ought never to despair at *what has once been accomplished.* How many things have had the idea of impossible annexed to them, that have become easy to those who knew how to take advantage of time, opportunity, lucky moments, the faults of others, different dispositions and an infinite number of other circumstances."

These are sentiments worthy of the man who could execute what he planned. I sincerely wish we had the spirit of Sully animating our counsels.

27 May

My heart is as light as a feather and my spirits are dancing. I received this afternoon a fine parcel of letters and papers by Colonel Thayer. It was a feast to me. I shall rest in quiet, I hope, this night. The papers I have not read, but sit down to write you, for Mr. Bass has just been here to let me know that Harry will call upon him to-morrow and take this letter for me. I would not have you anxious about me. I make out better than I did.

I have hired a negro fellow for six months, am to give him ten pounds, which is much lower than I had any prospect of getting help, and Belcher is exceedingly assiduous and I believe faithful in what he undertakes. If he should purloin a little I must bear that; he is very diligent, and being chief engineer is ambitious. If you could find a few moments leisure just to write him a few lines and let him know that I had wrote you that he had the care of the place, and that you should be glad of his best services upon it, of his constant care and attention, I believe it would go a good way towards insuring it.

You will find by one of the letters which I mention as having sent an account of some of your affairs. My best endeavors will not be wanting in every department. I wish my abilities were equal to my wishes. My father and your mother desire to be remembered to you in very particular terms. The family you mention are well. So is your brother's; your own are tolerably comfortable. Charles has the mumps and has been very sick but is now better. Can you tell how I feel when they come to me as the two youngest often do, with a *mar,* when will *par* come home? Charley's grandmamma tells this story of him. She was carrying him to meeting the Sabbath the regulars left Boston when a person stopped her upon the road to tell her the news. Gone from Boston says he with his eyes just ready to run over. "What gone away themselves?" "Yes," replied his grandmamma. "Then I say they are cowards, for they have stood it but one year and we would have stood it three."

I took a ride last week, and ventured just as far as the stump of Liberty Tree. Roxbury looks more injured than Boston. That is, the houses look more torn to pieces. I was astonished at the extent of our lines and their strength.

We have taken a most noble prize, the inventory of which you will have in the paper. The poor Captain[3] has since lost his life in a desperate engagement with thirteen boats from the men-of-war, which attacked and attempted to board him; but by a most brave resistance they sunk four of the boats and fought so warmly with their spears and small arms as to oblige them to quit him, though he had but twenty-seven men and they five times his number. He unhappily fell, and was the only one who did. Many dead bodies have since been taken up, among whom is an officer.

We have now in fair sight of my uncle's the commodore,[4] a thirty-six gun frigate, another large vessel, and six small craft. I hope after election we shall have ways and means devised to drive off these torments. Providence seems to have delivered into our hands the very articles most needed, and at a time when we were weak and not so well provided for as we could wish. We have two row-galleys building, and men of spirit to use them I dare say will be found. One engagement only whets their appetite for another.

I heard last night that we had three regiments coming back to us, with General Gates to head them; at which I most sincerely rejoiced. I think he is the man we want. Believe you may venture letters safely by the post. Mine go that way, and for the future I will send to the post-office for yours.

You ask my advice with regard to your office.[5] If I was to consult only my own private satisfaction and pleasure, I should request you to resign it; but alas, that is of small moment when compared to the whole, and I think you qualified and know you disposed to serve your country. I must advise you to hold it, at least for the present year. And in saying this I make a sacrifice which those only can judge of whose hearts are one.

I was much affected, the other day, by a letter which I saw from the lady of the late worthy General Montgomery. Speaking of him, she says, "Suffer me to repeat his last words to me: 'You shall never blush for your Montgomery.' Nobly has he kept his word. As a wife I must ever mourn the husband, friend, and lover of a thousand virtues, of all domestic bliss, the idol of my warmest affections, and, in one word, my every dream of happiness. Methinks I am like the poor widow in the Gospel; having given my mite, I sit down disconsolate."

These are only detached parts of the letter, to which I fear I have not done justice, as I have only my memory to serve me; but it was a very fine letter. Our worthy friends are in great trouble, their eldest son is disordered in his mind. I have not had a line since he was carried home, and I know not the cause. I want to hear from them, but know not how to write to them. I bid you good-night. Oh that I could annihilate space.

Yours.

You have been misinformed. The regulars have not made any fortifications anywhere. It was so reported but was not true. The season promises very fair for grass, and a fine bloom upon the trees. Warm weather we want, which will make everything look finely. I wish you could be here to enjoy it.

109. JOHN ADAMS

2 June 1776

Yesterday I dined with Captain Richards, the gentleman who made me the present of the brass pistols. We had cherries, strawberries, and green peas in plenty. The fruits are three weeks earlier here than with you. Indeed, they are a fortnight earlier on the east than on the west side of Delaware River. We have had green peas this week past, but they were brought over the river, from New Jersey, to this market. There are none grown in the city or on the west side of the river yet. The reason is, the soil of New Jersey is a warm sand; that of Pennsylvania a cold clay. So much for peas and berries.

Now for something of more importance. In all the correspondence I have maintained, during a course of twenty years, at least, that I have been a writer of letters, I never kept a single copy. This negligence and inaccuracy has been a great misfortune to me on many occasions. I have now purchased a folio book, in the first page of which, expecting one blank leaf, I am writing this letter, and intend to write all my letters to you in it, from this time forward. This will be an advantage to me in several respects. In the first place, I shall write more deliberately. In the second place, I shall be able, at all times, to review what I have written. Third, I shall know how often I write. Fourth, I shall discover by this means whether any of my letters to you miscarry. If it were possible for me to find a conveyance, I would send you such another blank book as a present, that you might begin the practice at the same time, for I really think that your letters are much better worth preserving than mine. Your daughter and sons will very soon write so good hands that they will copy the letters for you from your book, which will improve them, at the same time that it relieves you.

110. ABIGAIL ADAMS

3 June 1776

I received by Mr. Church a few lines from you. I wish to hear from you every opportunity, though you say no more than that you are well. I feel concerned lest your clothes should go to rags, having nobody to take any care of you in your long absence; and then, you have not with you a proper change for the seasons. However, you must do the best you can. I have a suit of homespun for you whenever you return. I cannot avoid sometimes repining that the gifts of fortune were not bestowed upon us, that I might have enjoyed the happiness of spending my days with my partner, but as it is, I think it my duty to attend with frugality and economy to our own private affairs; and if I cannot add to our little substance, yet see it that it is not diminished. I should enjoy but little comfort in a state of idleness and uselessness. Here I can serve my partner, my family, and myself, and enjoy the satisfaction of your serving your country.

I wish you would write me what I had best do with our house at Boston. I would advertise it if you think best. There are so many houses torn to pieces and so many others abused, that I might stand a chance of letting it, perhaps, as it is in so good repair.

My brother is desirous of joining the army again, but would choose to be a field-officer. I have mentioned him to some of the House, and suppose he will be recommended to Congress for a commission. I hardly know where you will find men to form the regiments required. I begin to think population a very important branch in the American manufactories.

I inclose a list of the Council. The House consists of more than two hundred and fifty members. Your former pupil Angier comes from Bridgewater, and five others. I hope they will proceed in business with a little more spirit than heretofore. They are procuring two row-galleys, but when they will be finished I know not. I thought they were near done, but find to-day they are not yet contracted for. All our gentry are gone from Nantasket Road except the commodore and one or two small craft.

Everything bears a very great price. The merchant complains of the farmer and the farmer of the merchant—both are extravagant. Living is double what it was one year ago.

I find you have licensed tea, but I am determined not to be a purchaser unless I can have it at Congress price, and in that article the venders pay no regard to Congress, asking ten, eight, and the lowest is seven and sixpence per pound. I should like a little green, but they say there is none to be had here. I only wish it for a medicine, as a relief to a nervous pain in my head to which I am sometimes subject. Were it as plenty as ever, I would not practice the use of it.

Our family are all well. It has been reported here that Congress were going to remove forty miles beyond Philadelphia. I gave no credit to the report. I heard no reason assigned for it. I had much rather they would come a hundred miles nearer here.

Adieu.   Yours.

111. JOHN ADAMS

Philadelphia, 16 June 1776

Yesterday was to me a lucky day, as it brought me two letters from you. One dated May 27, and the other June 3d. Don't be concerned about me, if it happens now and then that you don't hear from me for some weeks together. If anything should injure my health materially, you will soon hear of it. But I thank God I am in much better health than I expected to be. But this cannot last long under the load that I carry. When it becomes too great for my strength, I shall ask leave to lay it down, and come home. But I will hold it out a good while yet, if I can. I am willing to take the woodland sister mentions, and the watch and the sword. As to the lighter, it cost more than five hundred dollars in hard cash.

I wish your uncle[1] had as much ambition as he has virtue and ability. A deficiency of ambition is as criminal and injurious as an excess of it. Tell him I say so. How shall we contrive to make so wise and good a man ambitious? Is it not a sin to be so modest? Ask him how he can answer it? So! Then it seems the brigadier was obliged to step downstairs in order to keep my brother out of the lower room. . . . I am sorry for it. Thanks for your quotation from Sully. It is extremely apropos. I am very glad you are so well provided with help. Give my respects to Mr. Belcher and his family. Tell him I am obliged to him for his kind care of the farm. I wish I could go out with him and see the business go on, but I can't. Thank your father and my mother for their kind remembrance of me. Return my duty to both. Charles's young heroism charms me. Kiss him. Poor Mugford, yet glorious Mugford. How beautiful and sublime it is to die for one's country! What a fragrant memory remains!

The rumor you heard of General Gates will prove premature.

I endeavored both here and with the General to have it so, and should have succeeded, if it had not been for the loss of General Thomas. Cruel small-pox! worse than the sword! But now, I fear we must part with Gates for the sake of Canada. Mrs. Montgomery is a lady, like all the family, of refined sentiments and elegant accomplishments. Her letter, as you quote it, is very pathetic. Do you mean that our Plymouth friends are in trouble for a disordered son! If so, I am grieved to the heart. God grant them support under so severe an affliction. But this world is a scene of afflictions. I rejoice to hear that the enemy have not fortified, and hope they will not be suffered to attempt it.

Don't think about my clothes. I do well enough in that respect. As to your house at Boston, do with it as you please. Sell it, if you will, but not for a farthing less than it cost me. Let it, if you please, but take care who your tenant is, both of his prudence to preserve the house and his ability to pay the rent. Your brother, I hope will be promoted. He is fit for it, and has deserved it. If his name comes recommended from the General Court, he will have a commission for a field-officer, and I will recommend him to the General for his notice. My pupil, if he pleases, will do Honor to his preceptor, and important service to his country. I hope his zeal and fidelity will be found equal to his abilities.

I send you all the news in the papers. Great things are on the tapis. These throes will usher in the birth of a fine boy. We have no thoughts of removing from hence. There is no occasion for it.

112. ABIGAIL ADAMS

Plymouth, 17 June 1776, a remarkable day

I this day received by the hands of our worthy friend a large packet, which has refreshed and comforted me. Your own sensations have ever been similar to mine. I need not then tell you how gratified I am at the frequent tokens of remembrance with which you favor me, nor how they rouse every tender sensation of my soul, which sometimes will find vent at my eyes. Nor dare I describe how earnestly I long to fold to my fluttering heart the object of my warmest affections; the idea soothes me. I feast upon it with a pleasure known only to those whose hearts and hopes are one.

The approbation you give to my conduct in the management of our private affairs is very grateful to me, and sufficiently compensates for all my anxieties and endeavors to discharge the many duties devolved upon me in consequence of the absence of my dearest friend. Were they discharged according to my wishes, I should merit the praises you bestow.

You see I date from Plymouth. I came upon a visit to our amiable friends, accompanied by my sister Betsey, a day or two ago. It is the first night I have been absent since you left me. Having determined upon this visit for some time, I put my family in order and prepared for it, thinking I might leave it with safety. Yet, the day I set out I was under many apprehensions, by the coming in of ten transports, which were seen to have many soldiers on board, and the determination of the people to go and fortify upon Long Island, Pettick's Island, Nantasket, and Great Hill. It was apprehended they would attempt to land somewhere, but the next morning I had the pleasure to hear they were all driven out, commodore and all; not a transport, a ship, or a tender to be seen. This shows what might have been long ago done. Had this been done in season, the ten transports, with many others, in all probability would have fallen into our hands; but the progress of wisdom is slow.

Since I arrived here I have really had a scene quite novel to me. The brig *Defence,* from Connecticut, put in here for ballast. The officers, who are all from thence, and who are intimately acquainted at Dr. Lothrop's,[1] invited his lady to come on board, and bring with her as many of her friends as she could collect. She sent an invitation to our friend, Mrs. Warren, and to us. The brig lay about a mile and a half from town. The officers sent their barge, and we went. Every mark of respect and attention which was in their power, they showed us. She is a fine brig, mounts sixteen guns, twelve swivels, and carries one hundred and twenty men. A hundred and seventeen were on board, and no private family ever appeared under better regulation than the crew. It was as still as though there had been only half a dozen; not a profane word among any of them. The captain himself is an exemplary man (Harden his name);[2] has been in nine sea engagements; says if he gets a man who swears, and finds he cannot reform him, he turns him on shore, yet is free to confess that it was the sin of his youth. He has one lieutenant, a very fine fellow, Smelden by name. We spent a very agreeable afternoon, and drank tea on board. They showed us their arms, which were sent by Queen Anne, and everything on board was a curiosity to me. They gave us a mock engagement with an enemy, and the manner of taking a ship. The young folks went upon the quarter-deck and danced. Some of their Jacks played very well upon the violin and German flute. The brig bears the Continental colors, and was fitted out by the Colony of Connecticut. As we set off from the brig, they fired their guns in honor to us, a ceremony I would very readily have dispensed with.

I pity you, and feel for you under all the difficulties you have to encounter. My daily petitions to Heaven for you are that you may have health, wisdom, and fortitude sufficient to carry you through the great and arduous business in which you are engaged, and that your endeavors may be crowned with success. Canada seems a dangerous and ill-fated place. It is reported here that General Thomas is no more, that he took the small-pox, and died with it. Every day some circumstance arises which shows me the importance of having that distemper in youth. Dr. Bulfinch[3] has petitioned the General Court for leave to open a hospital somewhere, and it will be granted him. I shall, with all the children, be one of the first class, you may depend upon it.

I have just this moment heard that the brig which I was on board of on Saturday, and which sailed yesterday morning from this place, fell in with two transports, having each of them a hundred and fifty men on board, and took them, and has brought them into Nantasket Road, under cover of the guns which are mounted there. I will add further particulars as soon as I am informed.

I am now better informed, and will give you the truth. The brig *Defence*, accompanied by a small privateer, sailed in concert Sunday morning. About twelve o'clock they discovered two transports, and made for them. Two privateers, who were small, had been in chase of them, but finding the enemy was of much larger force, had run under Cohasset rocks. The *Defence* gave a signal gun to bring them out. Captain Burk,[4] who accompanied the *Defence,* being a prime sailer, he came up first, and poured a broadside on board a sixteen gun brig. The *Defence* soon attacked her upon her bows. An obstinate engagement ensued. There was a continual blaze upon all sides for many hours, and it was near midnight before they struck. In the engagement, the *Defence* lost one man, and five wounded. With Burk, not one man received any damage; on board the enemy, fourteen killed, among whom was a major, and sixty wounded. They are part of the Highland soldiers. The other transport mounted six guns. When the fleet sailed out of this harbor last week, they blew up the lighthouse. They met six transports coming in, which they carried off with them. I hope we shall soon be in such a posture of defense as to bid them defiance.

I feel no great anxiety at the large armament designed against us. The remarkable interpositions of Heaven in our favor cannot be too gratefully acknowledged. He who fed the Israelites in the wilderness, who clothes the lilies of the field, and feeds the young ravens when they cry, will not forsake a people engaged in so righteous a cause, if we remember his loving-kindness. We wanted powder,—we have a supply. We wanted arms,—we have been favored in that respect. We wanted hard money,—twenty-two thousand dollars, and an equal value in plate, are delivered into our hands.

You mention your peas, your cherries, and your strawberries, etc. Ours are but just in blossom. We have had the coldest spring I ever knew. Things are three weeks back of what they generally used to be. The corn looks poor. The season now is rather dry. Our friend has refused his appointment. I am very sorry. I said everything I could think to persuade him, but his lady was against it. I need say no more. I believe I did not understand you, when in a former letter you said, "I want to resign my office, for a thousand reasons." If you mean that of judge, I know not what to say. I know it will be a difficult and arduous station; but, divesting myself of private interest, which would lead me to be against your holding that office, I know of no person who is so well calculated to discharge the trust, or who I think would act a more conscientious part. My paper is full. I have only room to thank you for it.

113. JOHN ADAMS

Philadelphia, 26 June 1776

I have written so seldom to you, that I am really grieved at the recollection. I wrote you a few lines June 2, and a few more June 16. These are all that I have written to you since this month began. It has been the busiest month that ever I saw. I have found time to inclose all the newspapers, which I hope you will receive in due time.

Our misfortunes in Canada are enough to melt a heart of stone. The small-pox is ten times more terrible than Britons, Canadians, and Indians, together. This was the cause of our precipitate retreat from Quebec. This the cause of our disgraces at the Cedars.[1] I don't mean that this was all. There has been want approaching to famine, as well as pestilence. And these discouragements have so disheartened our officers that none of them seem to act with prudence and firmness. But these reverses of fortune don't discourage me. It was natural to expect them, and we ought to be prepared in our minds for greater changes and more melancholy scenes still. It is an animating cause, and brave spirits are not subdued with difficulties.

Amidst all our gloomy prospects in Canada, we receive some pleasure from Boston. I congratulate you on your victory over your enemies in the harbor. This has long lain near my heart, and it gives me great pleasure to think that what was so much wished is accomplished. I hope our people will now make the lower harbor impregnable, and never again suffer the flag of a tyrant to fly within any part of it.

The Congress have been pleased to give me more business than I am qualified for, and more than, I fear, I can go through, with safety to my health. They have established a board of war and ordnance and made me President of it, an honor to which I never aspired, a trust to which I feel myself vastly unequal. But I am determined to do as well as I can, and make industry supply, in some degree, the place of abilities and experience. The Board sits every morning and every evening. This with constant attendance in Congress will so entirely engross my time, that I fear I shall not be able to write you so often as I have. But I will steal time to write to you.

The small-pox! the small-pox! what shall we do with it? I could almost wish that an inoculating hospital was opened in every town in New England. It is some small consolation that the scoundrel savages have taken a large dose of it. They plundered the baggage and stripped off the clothes of our men who had the small-pox out full upon them at the Cedars.

114. JOHN ADAMS

3 July 1776

Your favor of 17 June, dated at Plymouth, was handed me by yesterday's post. I was much pleased to find that you had taken a journey to Plymouth, to see your friends, in the long absence of one whom you may wish to see. The excursion will be an amusement, and will serve your health. How happy would it have made me to have taken this journey with you!

I was informed, a day or two before the receipt of your letter, that you was gone to Plymouth, by Mrs. Polly Palmer, who was obliging enough, in your absence, to send me the particulars of the expedition to the lower harbor against the men-of-war. Her narration is executed with a precision and perspicuity, which would have become the pen of an accomplished historian.

I am very glad you had so good an opportunity of seeing one of our little American men-of-war. Many ideas now to you must have presented themselves in such a scene; and you will, in future, better understand the relations of sea engagements.

I rejoice extremely at Dr. Bulfinch's petition to open a hospital. But I hope the business will be done upon a larger scale. I hope that one hospital will be licensed in every county, if not in every town. I am happy to find you resolved to be with the children in the first class. Mr. Whitney and Mrs. Katy Quincy are cleverly through inoculation in this city. I have one favor to ask, and that is, that in your future letters, you would acknowledge the receipt of all those you may receive from me, and mention their dates. By this means I shall know if any of mine miscarry.

The information you give me of our friend's refusing his appointment has given me much pain, grief, and anxiety. I believe I shall be obliged to follow his example. I have not fortune enough to support my family, and, what is of more importance, to support the dignity of that exalted station. It is too high and lifted up for me, who delight in nothing so much as retreat, solitude, silence, and obscurity. In private life, no one has a right to censure me for following my own inclinations in retirement, simplicity, and frugality. In public life, every man has a right to remark as he pleases. At least he thinks so.

Yesterday, the greatest question was decided which ever was debated in America, and a greater, perhaps, never was nor will be decided among men. A Resolution was passed without one dissenting Colony "that these United Colonies are, and of right ought to be, free and independent States, and as such they have, and of right ought to have, full power to make war, conclude peace, establish commerce, and to do all other acts and things which other States may rightfully do." You will see, in a few days, a Declaration setting forth the causes which have impelled us to this mighty revolution, and the reasons which will justify it in the sight of God and man. A plan of confederation will be taken up in a few days.

When I look back to the year 1761, and recollect the argument concerning writs of assistance in the superior court, which I have hitherto considered as the commencement of this controversy between Great Britain and America, and run through the whole period from that time to this, and recollect the series of political events, the chain of causes and effects, I am surprised at the suddenness as well as greatness of this revolution. Britain has been filled with folly, and America with wisdom; at least, this is my judgment. Time must determine. It is the will of Heaven that the two countries should be sundered forever. It may be the will of Heaven that America shall suffer calamities still more wasting, and distresses yet more dreadful. If this is to be the case, it will have this good effect at least. It will inspire us with many virtues which we have not, and correct many errors, follies, and vices which threaten to disturb, dishonor, and destroy us. The furnace of affliction produces refinement in states as well as individuals. And the new Governments we are assuming in every part will require a purification from our vices, and an augmentation of our virtues, or they will be no blessings. The people will have unbounded power, and the people are extremely addicted to corruption and venality, as well as the great. But I must submit all my hopes and fears to an overruling Providence, in which, unfashionable as the faith may be, I firmly believe.

115. JOHN ADAMS

Philadelphia, 3 July 1776

Had a Declaration of Independency been made seven months ago, it would have been attended with many great and glorious effects. We might, before this hour, have formed alliances with foreign states. We should have mastered Quebec, and been in possession of Canada. You will perhaps wonder how such a declaration would have influenced our affairs in Canada, but if I could write with freedom, I could easily convince you that it would, and explain to you the manner how. Many gentlemen in high stations, and of great influence, have been duped by the ministerial bubble of Commissioners to treat. And in real, sincere expectation of this event, which they so fondly wished, they have been slow and languid in promoting measures for the reduction of that province. Others there are in the Colonies who really wished that our enterprise in Canada would be defeated, that the Colonies might be brought into danger and distress between two fires, and be thus induced to submit. Others really wished to defeat the expedition to Canada, lest the conquest of it should elevate the minds of the people too much to hearken to those terms of reconciliation which, they believed, would be offered us. These jarring views, wishes, and designs occasioned an opposition to many salutary measures which were proposed for the support of that expedition, and caused obstructions, embarrassments, and studied delays, which have finally lost us the province.

All these causes, however, in conjunction would not have disappointed us, if it had not been for a misfortune which could not be foreseen, and perhaps could not have been prevented; I mean the prevalence of the small-pox among our troops. This fatal pestilence completed our destruction. It is a frown of Providence upon us, which we ought to lay to heart.

But, on the other hand, the delay of this Declaration to this time has many great advantages attending it. The hopes of reconciliation which were fondly entertained by multitudes of honest and well-meaning, though weak and mistaken people, have been gradually, and at last totally extinguished. Time has been given for the whole people maturely to consider the great question of independence, and to ripen their judgment, dissipate their fears, and allure their hopes, by discussing it in newspapers and pamphlets, by debating it in assemblies, conventions, committees of safety and inspection, in town and county meetings, as well as in private conversations, so that the whole people, in every colony of the thirteen, have now adopted it as their own act. This will cement the union, and avoid those heats, and perhaps convulsions, which might have been occasioned by such a Declaration six months ago.

But the day is past. The second day of July, 1776,[1] will be the most memorable epocha in the history of America. I am apt to believe that it will be celebrated by succeeding generations as the great anniversary festival. It ought to be commemorated as the day of deliverance, by solemn acts of devotion to God Almighty. It ought to be solemnized with pomp and parade, with shows, games, sports, guns, bells, bonfires, and illuminations, from one end of this continent to the other, from this time forward forevermore.

You will think me transported with enthusiasm, but I am not. I am well aware of the toil and blood and treasure that it will cost us to maintain this Declaration and support and defend these States. Yet, through all the gloom, I can see the rays of ravishing light and glory. I can see that the end is more than worth all the means. And that posterity will triumph in that day's transaction, even although we should rue it, which I trust in God we shall not.

116. JOHN ADAMS

Philadelphia, 7 July 1776

I have this moment folded up a magazine and an "Evening Post," and sent them off by an express who could not wait for me to write a single line. It always goes to my heart to send off a packet of pamphlets and newspapers without a letter, but it sometimes unavoidably happens, and I suppose you had rather receive a pamphlet or newspaper than nothing.

The design of our enemy now seems to be a powerful invasion of New York and New Jersey. The Halifax fleet and army is arrived, and another fleet and army under Lord Howe is expected to join them. We are making great preparations to meet them by marching the militia of Maryland, Pennsylvania, and New Jersey down to the scene of action, and have made large requisitions upon New England. I hope, for the honor of New England and the salvation of America, our people will not be backward in marching to New York. We must maintain and defend that important post, at all events. If the enemy get possession there, it will cost New England very dear. There is no danger of the small-pox at New York. It is carefully kept out of the city and the army. I hope that your brother and mine too will go into the service of their country at this critical period of its distress.

Our army at Crown Point is an object of wretchedness enough to fill a humane mind with horror; disgraced, defeated, discontented, dispirited, diseased, naked, undisciplined, eaten up with vermin, no clothes, beds, blankets, no medicines, no victuals but salt pork and flour. A chaplain from that army preached a sermon here the other day from "Cursed is he that doeth the work of the Lord deceitfully." I knew, better than he did, who the persons were who deserved these curses. But I could not help myself, nor my poor country, any more than he. I hope that measures will be taken to cleanse the army at Crown Point from the small-pox, and that other measures will be taken in New England, by tolerating and encouraging inoculation, to render that distemper less terrible.

I am solicitous to hear what figure our new Superior Court made in their eastern circuit; what business they did; whether the grand juries and petit juries were sworn; whether they tried any criminals, or any civil actions; how the people were affected at the appearance of Courts again; how the judges were treated; whether with respect or cold neglect, etc. Every colony upon the continent will soon be in the same situation. They are erecting governments as fast as children build cob-houses; but, I conjecture, they will hardly throw them down again so soon.

The practice we have hitherto been in, of ditching round about our enemies, will not always do. We must learn to use other weapons than the pick and the spade. Our armies must be disciplined, and learn to fight. I have the satisfaction to reflect that our Massachusetts people, when they have been left to themselves, have been constantly fighting and skirmishing, and always with success. I wish the same valor, prudence, and spirit had been discovered everywhere.

117. JOHN ADAMS

Philadelphia, 7 July 1776

It is worth the while of a person, obliged to write as much as I do, to consider the varieties of style. The epistolary is essentially different from the oratorical and the historical style. Oratory abounds with figures. History is simple, but grave, majestic, and formal. Letters, like conversation, should be free, easy, and familiar. Simplicity and familiarity are the characteristics of this kind of writing. Affectation is as disagreeable in a letter as in conversation, and therefore studied language, premeditated method, and sublime sentiments are not expected in a letter. Notwithstanding which, the sublime, as well as the beautiful and the novel, may naturally enough appear in familiar letters among friends. Among the ancients there are two illustrious examples of the epistolary style, Cicero and Pliny, whose letters present you with models of fine writing, which have borne the criticism of almost two thousand years. In these you see the sublime, the beautiful, the novel, and the pathetic, conveyed in as much simplicity, ease, freedom, and familiarity as language is capable of.

Let me request you to turn over the leaves of "The Preceptor"[1] to a letter of Pliny the Younger, in which he has transmitted to these days the history of his uncle's philosophical curiosity, his heroic courage, and his melancholy catastrophe. Read it, and say whether it is possible to write a narrative of facts in a better manner. It is copious and particular in selecting the circumstances most natural, remarkable, and affecting. There is not an incident omitted which ought to have been remembered, nor one inserted that is not worth remembrance. It gives you an idea of the scene, as distinct and perfect as if a painter had drawn it to the life before your eyes. It interests your passions as much as if you had been an eye-witness of the whole transaction. Yet there are no figures or art used. All is as simple, natural, easy, and familiar as if the story had been told in conversation, without a moment's premeditation.

Pope and Swift have given the world a collection of their letters; but I think in general they fall short, in the epistolary way, of their own eminence in poetry and other branches of literature. Very few of their letters have ever engaged much of my attention. Gay's letter concerning the pair of lovers killed by lightning is worth more than the whole collection, in point of simplicity and elegance of composition, and as a genuine model of the epistolary style. There is a book, which I wish you owned,—I mean Rollin's "Belles Lettres,"[2]—in which the variations of style are explained.

Early youth is the time to learn the arts and sciences, and especially to correct the ear and the imagination, by forming a style. I wish you would think of forming the taste and judgment of your children now, before any unchaste sounds have fastened on their ears, and before any affectation or vanity is settled on their minds, upon the pure principles of nature. Music is a great advantage; for style depends, in part, upon a delicate ear. The faculty of writing is attainable by art, practice, and habit only. The sooner, therefore, the practice begins, the more likely it will be to succeed. Have no mercy upon an affected phrase, any more than an affected air, gait, dress, or manners.

Your children have capacities equal to anything. There is a vigor in the understanding and a spirit and fire in the temper of every one of them, which is capable of ascending the heights of art, science, trade, war, or politics. They should be set to compose descriptions of scenes and objects, and narrations of facts and events. Declamations upon topics and other exercises of various sorts should be prescribed to them. Set a child to form a description of a battle, a storm, a siege, a cloud, a mountain, a lake, a city, a harbor, a country seat, a meadow, a forest, or almost anything that may occur to your thoughts. Set him to compose a narration of all the little incidents and events of a day, a journey, a ride, or a walk. In this way a taste will be formed, and a facility of writing acquired.

For myself, as I never had a regular tutor, I never studied anything methodically, and consequently never was completely accomplished in anything. But, as I am conscious of my own deficiency in these respects, I should be the less pardonable if I neglected the education of my children. In grammar, rhetoric, logic, my education was imperfect, because immethodical. Yet I have perhaps read more upon these arts, and considered them in a more extensive view, than some others.

118. JOHN ADAMS

10 July

You will see, by the newspapers which I from time to time inclose, with what rapidity the colonies proceed in their political manoeuvres. How many calamities might have been avoided if these measures had been taken twelve months ago, or even no longer ago than last December?

The colonies to the south are pursuing the same maxima which have heretofore governed those to the north. In constituting their new governments, their plans are remarkably popular, more so than I could ever have imagined; even more popular than the "Thoughts on Government"; and in the choice of their rulers, capacity, spirit, and zeal in the cause supply the place of fortune, family, and every other consideration which used to have weight with mankind. My friend Archibald Bullock, Esquire, is Governor of Georgia. John Rutledge, Esquire, is Governor of South Carolina. Patrick Henry, Esquire, is Governor of Virginia, etc. Dr. Franklin will be Governor of Pennsylvania. The new members of this city are all in this taste, chosen because of their inflexible zeal for independence. All the old members left out because they opposed independence, or at least were luke-warm about it. Dickinson, Morris, Allen, all fallen, like grass be-fore the scythe, notwithstanding all their vast advantages in point of fortune, family, and abilities. I am inclined to think, however, and to wish, that these gentlemen may be restored at a fresh election, because, although mistaken in some points, they are good characters, and their great wealth and numerous connec-tions will contribute to strengthen America and cement her union.

I wish I were at perfect liberty to portray before you all these characters in their genuine lights, and to explain to you the course of political changes in this province. It would give you a great idea of the spirit and resolution of the people, and show you, in a striking point of view, the deep roots of American in-dependence in all the colonies. But it is not prudent to commit to writing such free speculations in the present state of things. Time, which takes away the veil, may lay open the secret springs of this surprising revolution. But I find, although the colonies have differed in religion, laws, customs, and manners, yet in the great essentials of society and government they are all alike.

119. JOHN ADAMS

Philadelphia, 11 July 1776

You seem to be situated in the place of greatest tranquillity and security of any upon the continent. I may be mistaken in this particular, and an armament may have invaded your neighbor-hood, before now. But we have no intelligence of any such design, and all that we now know of the motions, plans, operations, and designs of the enemy indicates the contrary. It is but just that you should have a little rest, and take a little breath.

I wish I knew whether your brother and mine have enlisted in the army, and what spirit is manifested by our militia for march-ing to New York and Crown Point. The militia of Maryland, New Jersey, Pennsylvania, and the lower counties are marching with much alacrity, and a laudable zeal to take care of Howe and his army at Staten Island. The army in New York is in high spirits, and seems determined to give the enemy a serious reception. The unprincipled and unfeeling and unnatural inhabitants of Staten Island are cordially receiving the enemy, and, deserters say, have engaged to take arms. They are an ignorant, cowardly pack of scoundrels. Their numbers are small, and their spirit less.

It is some time since I received any letter from you. The Plymouth one was the last. You must write me every week, by the post, if it is but a few lines. It gives me many spirits. I design to write to the General Court requesting a dismission, or at least a furlough. I think to propose that they choose four more members, or at least three more, that so we may attend here in rotation. Two or three or four may be at home at a time, and the Colony properly represented notwithstanding. Indeed, while the Congress were employed in political regulations, forming the sentiments of the people of the Colonies into some consistent system, extinguishing the remainders of authority under the crown, and gradually erecting and strengthening governments under the authority of the people, turning their thoughts upon the principles of polity and the forms of government, framing constitutions for the Colonies separately, and a limited and a defined Confederacy for the United Colonies, and in some other measures, which I do not choose to mention particularly, but which are now determined, or near the point of determination, I flattered myself that I might have been of some little use here. But now, these matters will be soon completed, and very little business will be to be done here but what will be either military or commercial; branches of knowledge and business for which hundreds of others in our province are much better qualified than I am. I shall therefore request my masters to relieve me.

I am not a little concerned about my health, which seems to have been providentially preserved to me, much beyond my expectations. But I begin to feel the disagreeable effects of unremitting attention to business for so long a time, and a want of exercise, and the bracing quality of my native air; so that I have the utmost reason to fear an irreparable injury to my constitution, if I do not obtain a little relaxation. The fatigues of war are much less destructive to health than the painful, laborious attention to debates and to writing, which drinks up the spirits and consumes the strength.   I am, etc.

120. ABIGAIL ADAMS

Boston, 13 July 1776

I must begin with apologizing to you for not writing since the 17th of June. I have really had so many cares upon my hands and mind, with a bad inflammation in my eyes, that I have not been able to write. I now date from Boston, where I yesterday arrived and was with all of our little ones inoculated for the small-pox.[1] My uncle and aunt were so kind as to send me an invitation with my family. Mr. Cranch and wife and family, my sister Betsey and her little niece, Cotton Tufts and Mr. Thaxter, a maid who has had the distemper and my old nurse compose our family. A boy too I should have added. Seventeen in all. My uncle's maid with his little daughter and a negro man are here. We had our bedding, etc., to bring. A cow we have driven down from Braintree and some hay I have had put into the stable, wood, etc., and we have really commenced housekeepers here. The house was furnished with almost every article (except beds), which we have free use of, and think ourselves much obliged by the fine accommodations and kind offer of our friends. All our necessary stores we purchase jointly. Our little ones stood the operation manfully. Dr. Bulfinch is our physician. Such a spirit of inoculation never before took place; the town and every house in it are as full as they can hold. I believe there are not less than thirty persons from Braintree. Mrs. Quincy, Mrs. Lincoln, Miss Betsy, and Nancy are our near neighbors. God grant that we may all go comfortably through the distemper; the physic part is bad enough I know. I knew your mind so perfectly upon the subject that I thought nothing but our recovery would give you equal pleasure, and as to safety there was none. The soldiers inoculated privately, so did many of the inhabitants and the paper currency spread it everywhere. I immediately determined to set myself about it, and get ready with my children. I wish it was so you could have been with us, but I submit. I received some letters from you last Saturday night the 26th of June. You mention a letter of the 16th which I have never received, and I suppose must relate something to private affairs which I wrote about in May and sent by Harry.

As to news, we have taken several prizes since I wrote you, as you will see by the newspapers. The present report is of Lord Howe's coming with unlimited powers. However, suppose it is so, I believe he little thinks of treating with us as Independent States. How can any person yet dream of a settlement, accommodations, etc.? They have neither the spirit nor the feeling of men. Yet I see some who never were called Tories gratified with the idea of Lord Howe's being upon his passage with such powers!

Sunday, 14 July

By yesterday's post I received two letters dated 3d and 4th of July, and though your letters never fail to give me pleasure, be the subject what it will, yet it was greatly heightened by the prospect of the future happiness and glory of our country. Nor am I a little gratified when I reflect that a person so nearly connected with me has had the honor of being a principal actor in laying a foundation for its future greatness.

May the foundation of our new Constitution be Justice, Truth, and Righteousness! Like the wise man's house, may it be founded upon these rocks, and then neither storms nor tempests will overthrow it!

I cannot but feel sorry that some of the most manly sentiments in the Declaration are expunged from the printed copy. Perhaps wise reasons induced it.[2]

Poor Canada, I lament Canada, but we ought to be in some measure sufferers for the past folly of our conduct. The fatal effects of the small-pox there has led almost every person to consent to hospitals in every town. In many towns already around Boston the selectmen have granted liberty for inoculation. I hope the necessity is now fully seen. I had many disagreeable sensations at the thoughts of coming myself, but to see my children through it I thought my duty, and all those feelings vanished as soon as I was inoculated, and I trust a kind Providence will carry me safely through. Our friends from Plymouth came into town yesterday. We have enough upon our hands in the morning. The little folks are very sick then and puke every morning but after that they are comfortable.

I shall write you now very often. Pray inform me constantly of every important action. Every expression of tenderness is a cordial to my heart. Important as they are to the rest of the world, to me they are *everything*.

We have had during all the month of June a most severe drought, which cut off all our promising hopes of English grain and the first crop of grass, but since July came in we have had a plenty of rain and now everything looks well. There is one misfortune in our family which I have never mentioned in hopes it would have been in my power to have remedied it, but all hopes of that kind are at an end. It is the loss of your gray horse. About two months ago, I had occasion to send Jonathan of an errand to my uncle Quincy's (the other horse being a plowing). Upon his return a little below the church she trod upon a rolling stone and lamed herself to that degree that it was with great difficulty that she could be got home. I immediately sent for Tirrell, and everything was done for her by baths, ointments, polticing, bleeding, etc., that could be done. Still she continued extremely lame, though not so bad as at first. I then got her carried to Domet, but he pronounces her incurable, as a callus is grown upon her fetlock joint. She was not with foal, as you imagined, but I hope she is now as care has been taken in that respect.

I suppose you have heard of a fleet which came up pretty near the Light and kept us all with our mouths open, ready to catch them, but after staying near a week, and making what observations they could, set sail and went off to our great mortification, who were [?] for them in every respect. If our ship of thirty-two guns which was built at Portsmouth, and waiting only for guns, and another at Plymouth in the same state, had been in readiness, we should in all probability have been masters of them. Where the blame lies in that respect, I know not. 'Tis laid upon Congress, and Congress is also blamed for not appointing us a General. But Rome was not built in a day.

I hope the multiplicity of cares and avocations which envelop you will not be too powerful for you. I have many anxieties upon that account. Nabby and Johnny send duty and desire mamma to say that an inflammation in their eyes, which has been as much of a distemper as the small-pox, has prevented their writing, but they hope soon to be able to acquaint papa of their happy recovery from the distemper.

Mr. Cranch and wife, sister Betsey, and all our friends desire

to be remembered to you, and foremost in that number stands
your   PORTIA

A little India herb would have been mighty agreeable now.

121. JOHN ADAMS

15 July

My very deserving friend, Mr. Gerry, sets off to-morrow for
Boston, worn out of health by the fatigues of this station. He is
an excellent man, and an active, able statesman. I hope he will
soon return hither. I am sure I should be glad to return with him,
but I cannot. I must wait to have the guard relieved.

There is a most amiable, laudable, and gallant spirit prevailing
in these middle colonies. The militia turn out in great numbers
and in high spirits, in New Jersey, Pennsylvania, Maryland, and
Delaware, so that we hope to resist Howe and his myrmidons.

Independence is, at last, unanimously agreed to in the New
York Convention. You will see, by the newspapers inclosed,
what is going forward in Virginia and Maryland and New Jersey. Farewell! farewell! infatuated, besotted step-dame. I have
not time to add more than that I receive letters from you but seldom of late. To-morrow's post, I hope, will bring me some. So I
hoped of last Saturday's and last Tuesday's.

122. JOHN ADAMS

20 July

I cannot omit the opportunity of writing you a line by this post.
This letter will, I suppose, find you, in some degree or other, under the influence of the small-pox. The air is of very great importance. I don't know your physician, but I hope he won't
deprive you of air more than is necessary.

We had yesterday an express from General Lee in Charleston,
South Carolina, with an account of a brilliant little action between the armament under Clinton and Cornwallis, and a bat-

tery on Sullivan's Island, which terminated very fortunately for America. I will endeavor to inclose with this a printed account of it. It has given us good spirits here, and will have a happy effect upon our armies at New York and Ticonderoga. Surely our northern soldiers will not suffer themselves to be outdone by their brethren so nearly under the sun. I don't yet hear of any Massachusetts men at New York. Our people must not flinch at this critical moment, when their country is in more danger than it ever will be again, perhaps. What will they say if the Howes should prevail against our forces at so important a post as New York, for want of a few thousand men from the Massachusetts? I will likewise send you by this post Lord Howe's letter[1] and proclamation, which has let the cat out of the bag. These tricks deceive no longer. Gentlemen here, who either were or pretended to be deceived heretofore, now see or pretend to see through such artifices. I apprehend his Lordship is afraid of being attacked upon Staten Island, and is throwing out his barrels to amuse Leviathan until his reinforcements shall arrive.

20 July

This has been a dull day to me. I waited the arrival of the post with much solicitude and impatience, but his arrival made me more solicitous still. "To be left at the Post Office," in your handwriting on the back of a few lines from the Dr. was all that I could learn of you and my little folks. If you was too busy to write, I hoped that some kind hand would have been found to let me know something about you. Do my friends think that I have been a politician so long as to have lost all feeling? Do they suppose I have forgotten my wife and children? Or are they so panic-struck with the loss of Canada as to be afraid to correspond with me? Or have they forgotten that you have a husband, and your children a father? What have I done, or omitted to do, that I should be thus forgotten and neglected in the most tender and affecting scene of my life? Don't mistake me. I don't blame you. Your time and thoughts must have been wholly taken up with your own and your family's situation and necessities; but twenty other persons might have informed me.

I suspect that you intended to have run slyly through the small-pox with the family, without letting me know it, and then have sent me an account that you were all well. This might be a kind intention, and if the design had succeeded, would have made me very joyous. But the secret is out, and I am left to conjecture. But as the faculty have this distemper so much under command, I will flatter myself with the hope and expectation of soon hearing of your recovery.

123. ABIGAIL ADAMS

Boston, 21 July 1776

I have no doubt that my dearest friend is anxious to know how his Portia does, and his little flock of children under the operation of a disease once so formidable. I have the pleasure to tell him that they are all comfortable, though some of them complaining. Nabby has been very ill, but the eruption begins to make its appearance upon her, and upon Johnny. Tommy is so well that the Dr. inoculated him again today fearing that it had not taken. Charley has no complaints yet, though his arm has been very sore.

I have been out to meeting this forenoon, but have so many disagreeable sensations this afternoon that I thought it prudent to tarry at home. The Dr. says they are very good feelings. Mr. Cranch has passed through the preparation, and the eruption is coming out cleverly upon him without any sickness at all. Mrs. Cranch is cleverly and so are all her children. Those who are broke out are pretty full for the new method, as 'tis called the Suttonian they profess to practice upon. I hope to give you a good account when I write next, but our eyes are very weak and the Dr. is not fond of either writing or reading for his patients. But I must transgress a little.

I received a letter from you by Wednesday's post, the 7th of July, and though I think it is a choice one in the literary way, containing many useful hints and judicious observations which will greatly assist me in the future instruction of the little ones, yet it lacked some essential ingredients to make it compleat. Not one word respecting yourself, your health or your present situation.

My anxiety for your welfare will never leave me but with my parting breath, 'tis of more importance to me than all this world contains besides. The cruel separation to which I am necessitated cuts off half the enjoyments of life, the other half are comprised in the hope I have that what I do and what I suffer may be serviceable to you, to our little ones and our country. I must beseech you therefore for the future never to omit what is so essential to my happiness.

Last Thursday, after hearing a very good sermon, I went with the multitude into King Street to hear the Proclamation for Independence read and proclaimed. Some field-pieces with the train were brought there. The troops appeared under arms, and all the inhabitants assembled there (the small-pox prevented many thousand from the country), when Colonel Crafts[1] read from the balcony of the State House the proclamation. Great attention was given to every word. As soon as he ended, the cry from the balcony was, "God save our American States," and then three cheers which rended the air. The bells rang, the privateers fired, the forts and batteries, the cannon were discharged, the platoons followed, and every face appeared joyful. Mr. Bowdoin then gave a sentiment, "Stability and perpetuity to American independence." After dinner, the King's Arms were taken down from the State House, and every vestige of him from every place in which it appeared, and burnt in King Street. Thus ends royal authority in this State. And all the people shall say, Amen.

I have been a little surprised that we collect no better accounts with regard to the horrid conspiracy at New York, and that so little mention has been made of it here. It made a talk for a few days, but now seems all hushed in silence. The Tories say that it was not a conspiracy, but an association. And pretend that there was no plot to assassinate the General.[2] Even their hardened hearts feel the discovery we have in George a match for a Borgia or a Catiline, a wretch callous to every humane feeling. Our worthy preacher told us that he believed one of our great sins, for which a righteous God has come out in judgment against us, was our bigoted attachment to so wicked a man. May our repentance be sincere.

I omitted many things yesterday in order to be better informed. I have got Mr. Cranch to inquire and write you, con-

cerning a French schooner from Martinique which came in yesterday and a prize from Ireland. My own infirmities prevent my
writing. A most excruciating pain in my head and every limb and
joint I hope portends a speedy eruption and prevents my saying
more than that I am forever yours. The children are not yet
broke out. 'Tis the eleventh day with us.

124. JOHN ADAMS

29 July

How are you all this morning? Sick, weak, faint, in pain, or
pretty well recovered? By this time, you are well acquainted with
the small-pox. Pray, how do you like it?

We have no news. It is very hard that half a dozen or half a
score armies can't supply us with news. We have a famine, a perfect dearth of this necessary article. I am, at this present writing,
perplexed and plagued with two knotty problems in politics.
You love to pick a political bone. So I will even throw it to you.

If a confederation should take place, one great question is,
how we shall vote. Whether each colony shall count one; or
whether each shall have a weight in proportion to its numbers,
or wealth, or exports and imports, or a compound ratio of all.
Another is, whether Congress shall have authority to limit the
dimensions of each colony, to prevent those, which claim by
charter, or proclamation, or commission to the south sea, from
growing too great and powerful, so as to be dangerous to the
rest?

Shall I write you a sheet upon each of these questions? When
you are well enough to read, and I can find leisure enough to
write, perhaps I may.

Gerry carried with him a canister for you. But he is an old
bachelor, and what is worse, a politician, and what is worse still,
a kind of soldier; so that I suppose he will have so much curiosity to see armies and fortifications, and assemblies, that you will
lose many a fine breakfast at a time when you want them most.

Tell Betsey that this same Gerry is such another as herself, sex
excepted. How is my brother and friend Cranch? How is his
other self and their little selves, and ours? Don't be in the dumps,

above all things. I am hard put to it to keep out of them, when I look at home. But I will be gay if I can.   Adieu.

125. JOHN ADAMS

3 August 1776

The post was later than usual to-day, so that I had not yours of July 24[1] till this evening. You have made me very happy by the particular and favorable account you give me of all the family. But I don't understand how there are so many who have no eruptions and no symptoms. The inflammation in the arm might do, but without these there is no small-pox. I will lay a wager, that your whole hospital has not had so much small-pox as Mrs. Katy Quincy. Upon my word, she has had an abundance of it, but is finally recovered, looks as fresh as a rose, but pitted all over as thick as ever you saw any one. I this evening presented your compliments and thanks to Mr. Hancock for his polite offer of his house, and likewise your compliments to his lady and Mrs. Katy.

4 August

Went this morning to the Baptist meeting, in hopes of hearing Mr. Stillman, but was disappointed. He was there, but another gentleman preached. His action was violent to a degree bordering on fury; his gestures unnatural and distorted. Not the least idea of grace in his motions, or elegance in his style. His voice was vociferous and boisterous, and his composition almost wholly destitute of ingenuity. I wonder extremely at the fondness of our people for scholars educated at the southward, and for southern preachers. There is no one thing in which we excel them more than in our University, our scholars and preachers. Particular gentlemen here, who have improved upon their education by travel, shine; but in general, old Massachusetts outshines her younger sisters. Still in several particulars they have more wit than we. They have societies, the Philosophical Society particularly, which excites a scientific emulation, and propagates their fame. If ever I got through this scene of politics and war, I will spend the remainder of my days in endeavoring to instruct my countrymen in the art of making the most of their abilities and virtues; an art which they have hitherto too much neglected. A philosophical society shall be established at Boston, if I have wit and address enough to accomplish it, sometime or other. Pray set brother Cranch's philosophical head to plodding upon this project. Many of his lucubrations would have been published and preserved, for the benefit of mankind and for his honor, if such a club had existed.

My countrymen want art and address. They want knowledge of the world. They want the exterior and superficial accomplishment of gentlemen, upon which the world has set so high a value. In solid abilities and real virtues they vastly excel, in general, any people upon this continent. Our New England people are awkward and bashful, yet they are pert, ostentatious, and vain; a mixture which excites ridicule and gives disgust. They have not the faculty of showing themselves to the best advantage, nor the art of concealing this faculty; an art and faculty which some people possess in the highest degree. Our deficiencies in these respects are owing wholly to the little intercourse we have with strangers, and to our inexperience in the world. These imperfections must be remedied, for New England must produce the heroes, the statesmen, the philosophers, or America will make no great figure for some time.

Our army is rather sickly at New York, and we live in daily expectation of hearing of some great event. May God Almighty grant it may be prosperous for America. Hope is an anchor and a cordial. Disappointment, however, will not disconcert us.

If you will come to Philadelphia in September, I will stay as long as you please. I should be as proud and happy as a bridegroom.   Yours.

126. JOHN ADAMS

Philadelphia, 12 August 1776

Mr. A.[1] sets off to-day, if the rain should not prevent him, with Colonel Whipple,[2] of Portsmouth, a brother of the celebrated Miss Hannah Whipple, a sensible and worthy man. By him I have sent you two bundles of letters, which I hope you will be careful of. I thought I should not be likely to find a safer opportunity. By them you will see that my private correspondence alone is business enough for a lazy man. I think I have answered all but a few of those large bundles.

A French vessel, a pretty large brigantine, deeply laden, arrived here yesterday from Martinique. She had fifty barrels of limes, which are all sold already, at such prices that the amount of them will be sufficient to load the brig with flour. The trade, we see, even now, in the midst of summer, is not totally interrupted by all the efforts of our enemies. Prizes are taken in no small numbers. A gentleman told me, a few days ago, that he had summed up the sugar which has been taken, and it amounted to three thousand hogsheads, since which two other ships have been taken and carried into Maryland. Thousands of schemes for privateering are afloat in American imaginations. Some are for taking the Hull ships, with woolens, for Amsterdam and Rotterdam; some are for the tin ships; some for the Irish linen ships; some for outward bound, and others for inward bound Indiamen; some for the Hudson's Bay ships, and many for West India sugar ships. Out of these speculations, many fruitless and some profitable projects will grow.

We have no news from New York. All is quiet as yet. Our expectations are raised. The eyes of the world are upon Washington and Howe, and their armies. The wishes and prayers of the virtuous part of it, I hope, will be answered. If not, yet virtues grow out of affliction. I repeat my request that you would ask some of the members of the General Court if they can send me horses; and if they cannot, that you would send them. I can live no longer without a servant and a horse.

127. JOHN ADAMS

Philadelphia, 12 August 1776

Mr. A. and Colonel Whipple are at length gone. Colonel Tudor went off with them. They went away about three o'clock this afternoon. I wrote by A., and Colonel Whipple too; by the latter I sent two large bundles, which he promised to deliver to you. These middle States begin to taste the sweets of war. Ten thousand difficulties and wants occur, which they had no conception of before. Their militia are as clamorous, and impatient of discipline, and mutinous as ours, and more so. There has been seldom less than four thousand men in this city at a time, for a fortnight past, on their march to New Jersey. Here they wait, until we grow very angry about them, for canteens, camp kettles, blankets, tents, shoes, hose, arms, flints, and other dittoes, while we are under a very critical solicitude for our army at New York, on account of the insufficiency of men.

I want to be informed of the state of things with you; whether there is a scarcity of provisions of any kind, of West India articles, of clothing. Whether any trade is carried on, any fishery. Whether any vessels arrive from abroad, or whether any go to sea upon foreign voyages. I wish to know, likewise, what posture of defense you are in. What fortifications are at Nantasket, at Long Island, Pettick's Island, etc., and what men and officers there are to garrison them. We hear nothing from the Massachusetts, lately, in comparison of what we did when the army was before Boston.

I must not conclude without repeating my request that you would ask some of the members of the General Court to send me horses, and if they cannot, to send them yourself.

128. JOHN ADAMS

Philadelphia, 14 August 1776

This is the anniversary of a memorable day[1] in the history of America. A day when the principle of American resistance and independence was first asserted and carried into action. The stamp office fell before the rising spirit of our countrymen. It is not impossible that the two grateful brothers[2] may make their grand attack this very day. If they should, it is possible it may be more glorious for this country than ever; it is certain it will become more memorable.

Your favors of August 1 and 5 came by yesterday's post. I congratulate you all upon your agreeable prospects. Even my pathetic little hero Charles, I hope will have the distemper finely. It is very odd that the Dr. can't put infection enough into his veins;

nay, it is unaccountable to me that he has not taken it, in the natural way before now. I am under little apprehension, prepared as he is, if he should. I am concerned about you, much more. So many persons about you, sick. The children troublesome—your mind perplexed—yourself weak and relaxed. The situation must be disagreeable. The country air, and exercise, however, will refresh you.

I am put upon a committee to prepare a device for a golden medal, to commemorate the surrender of Boston to the American arms, and upon another to prepare devices for a great seal for the confederated States. There is a gentleman here of French extraction, whose name is Du Simitiere,[3] a painter by profession, whose designs are very ingenious, and his drawings well executed. He has been applied to for his advice. I waited on him yesterday, and saw his sketches. For the medal he proposes, Liberty, with her spear and pileus, leaning on General Washington. The British fleet in Boston harbor with all their sterns towards the town, the American troops marching in. For the seal, he proposes the arms of the several nations from whence America has been peopled, as, English, Scotch, Irish, Dutch, German, etc., each in a shield. On one side of them, Liberty with her pileus, on the other, a rifler in his uniform, with his rifle-gun in one hand and his tomahawk in the other; this dress and these troops, with this kind of armor, being peculiar to America, unless the dress was known to the Romans. Dr. Franklin showed me yesterday a book containing an account of the dresses of all the Roman soldiers, one of which appeared exactly like it. This M. du Simitiere is a very curious man. He has begun a collection of materials for a history of this revolution. He begins with the first advices of the tea ships. He cuts out of the newspapers every scrap of intelligence and every piece of speculation, and pastes it upon clean paper, arranging them under the head of that State to which they belong, and intends to bind them up in volumes. He has a list of every speculation and pamphlet concerning independence, and another of those concerning forms of government.

Dr. F. proposes a device for a seal: Moses lifting up his wand and dividing the Red Sea, and Pharaoh in his chariot overwhelmed with the waters. This motto, "Rebellion to tyrants is obedience to God."

Mr. Jefferson proposed the children of Israel in the wilderness, led by a cloud by day and a pillar of fire by night; and on the other side, Hengist and Horsa, the Saxon chiefs from whom we claim the honor of being descended, and whose political principles and form of government we have assumed.

I proposed the choice of Hercules, as engraved by Gribelin,[4] in some editions of Lord Shaftesbury's works. The hero resting on his club. Virtue pointing to her rugged mountain on one hand, and persuading him to ascend. Sloth, glancing at her flowery paths of pleasure, wantonly reclining on the ground, displaying the charms both of her eloquence and person, to seduce him into vice. But this is too complicated a group for a seal or medal, and it is not original.

I shall conclude by repeating my request for horses and a servant. Let the horses be good ones. I can't ride a bad horse so many hundred miles. If our affairs had not been in so critical a state at New York, I should have run away before now. But I am determined now to stay until some gentleman is sent here in my room, and until my horses come. But the time will be very tedious.

The whole force is arrived at Staten Island.

129. ABIGAIL ADAMS

Boston, 14 August 1776

Mr. Smith[1] called upon me to-day and told me he should set out to-morrow for Philadelphia; desired I would write by him. I have shown him all the civility in my power, since he has been here, though not all I have wished to. I was much pleased with the account he gave us of the universal joy of his province upon the establishment of their new government, and the harmony subsisting between every branch of it. This State seems to behindhand of their neighbors. We want some master workman here. Those who are capable seem backward in this work, and some who are so tenacious of their own particular plan as to be loath to give it up. Some who are for abolishing both House and Council, affirming business was never so well done as in the provincial Congress, and they perhaps never so important.

Last Sunday, after service, the Declaration of Independence was read from the pulpit by order of Council. The Dr.[2] concluded with asking a blessing "upon the United States of America even until the final restitution of all things."

Dr. Chauncy's address[3] pleased me. The good man after having read it, lifted his eyes and hands to heaven. "God bless the United States of America, and let all the people say Amen."

One of his audience told me it universally struck them.

I have no news to write you. I am sure it will be none to tell you I am ever

Yours   PORTIA

130. ABIGAIL ADAMS

14 August 1776

I wrote you to-day by Mr. Smith but as I suppose this will reach you sooner, I omitted mentioning anything of my family in it. Nabby has enough of the small-pox for all the family beside. She is pretty well covered, not a spot but what is so sore that she can neither walk, sit, stand, or lay with any comfort. She is as patient as one can expect, but they are a very sore sort. If it was a disorder to which we should be subject more than once I would go as far as it was possible to avoid it. She is swelled a good deal. You will receive a particular account before this reaches you of the uncommon manner in which the small-pox acts; it baffles the skill of the most experienced here. Billy Cranch is now out with about forty, as so well as not to be detained at home for an hour for it. Charley remains in the same state he did.

Your letter of August 3 came by this day's post. I find it very convenient to be so handy. I can receive a letter at night, sit down and reply to it, and send it off in the morning.

You remark upon the deficiency of education in your countrymen. It never, I believe, was in a worse state, at least for many years. The college is not in the state one could wish. The scholars complain that their professor in philosophy[1] is taken off by public business, to their great detriment. In this town I never saw so great a neglect of education. The poorer sort of children are wholly neglected, and left to range the streets, without schools, without business, given up to all evil. The town is not, as formerly, divided into wards. There is either too much business left upon the hands of a few, or too little care to do it. We daily see the necessity of a regular government.

You speak of our worthy brother.[2] I often lament it, that a man so peculiarly formed for the education of youth, and so well qualified as he is in many branches of literature, excelling in philosophy and the mathematics, should not be employed in some public station. I know not the person who would make half so good a successor to Dr. Winthrop. He has a peculiar, easy manner of communicating his ideas to youth; and the goodness of his heart and the purity of his morals, without an affected austerity, must have a happy effect upon the minds of pupils.

If you complain of neglect of education in sons, what shall I say with regard to daughters, who every day experience the want of it? With regard to the education of my own children, I find myself soon out of my depth, destitute and deficient in every part of education.

I most sincerely wish that some more liberal plan might be laid and executed for the benefit of the rising generation, and that our new Constitution may be distinguished for encouraging learning and virtue. If we mean to have heroes, statesmen, and philosophers, we should have learned women. The world perhaps would laugh at me and accuse me of vanity, but you, I know, have a mind too enlarged and liberal to disregard the sentiment. If much depends, as is allowed, upon the early education of youth, and the first principles which are instilled take the deepest root, great benefit must arise from literary accomplishments in women.

Excuse me. My pen has run away with me. I have no thoughts of coming to Philadelphia. The length of time I have and shall be detained here would have prevented me, even if you had no thoughts of returning till December; but I live in daily expectation of seeing you here. Your health, I think, requires your immediate return. I expected Mr. Gerry would have set off before now, but he perhaps finds it very hard to leave his mistress. I won't say harder than some do to leave their wives. Mr. Gerry stood very high in my esteem. What is meat for one is not for another. No accounting for fancy. She is a queer dame and leads people wild dances.

But hush! Post, don't betray your trust and lose my letter. Nabby is poorly this morning. The pocks are near the turn, six or seven hundred boils are no agreeable feeling. You and I know not what a feeling it is. Miss Katy can tell. I had but three; they were very clever and filled nicely. The town instead of being clear of this distemper are now in the height of it, hundreds having it in the natural way through the deceitfulness of inoculation. Adieu ever yours. Breakfast waits.   PORTIA

131. JOHN ADAMS

18 August 1776

My letters to you are an odd mixture. They would appear to a stranger like the dish which is sometimes called *omnium gatherum*. This is the first time, I believe, that these two words were ever put together in writing. The literal interpretation I take to be "a collection of all things." But, as I said before, the words having never before been written, it is not possible to be very learned in telling you what the Arabic, Syriac, Chaldaic, Greek, and Roman commentators say upon the subject. Amidst all the rubbish that constitutes the heap, you will see a proportion of affection for my friends, my family, and country, that gives a complexion to the whole. I have a very tender, feeling heart. This country knows not, and never can know, the torments I have endured for its sake. I am glad it never can know, for it would give more pain to the benevolent and humane than I could wish even the wicked and malicious to feel.

I have seen in this world but a little of that pure flame of patriotism which certainly burns in some breasts. There is much of the ostentation and affectation of it. I have known a few who could not bear to entertain a selfish design, nor to be suspected by others of such a meanness; but these are not the most respected by the world. A man must be selfish, even to acquire great popularity. He must grasp for himself, under specious pretenses for the public good, and he must attach himself to his relations, connections, and friends, by becoming a champion for their interests, in order to form a phalanx about him for his own defense, to make them trumpeters of his praise, and sticklers for his fame, fortune, and honor.

My friend Warren, the late Governor Ward, and Mr. Gadsden[1] are three characters in which I have seen the most generous disdain of every spice and species of such meanness. The two last had not great abilities, but they had pure hearts. Yet they had less influence than many others, who had neither so considerable parts nor any share at all of their purity of intention. Warren has both talents and virtues beyond most men in this world, yet his character has never been in proportion. Thus it always is and has been and will be. Nothing has ever given me more mortification than a suspicion that has been propagated of me, that I am actuated by private views and have been aiming at high places. The office of Chief Justice has occasioned this jealousy, and it never will be allayed until I resign it. Let me have my farm, family, and goosequill, and all the honors and offices this world has to bestow may go to those who deserve them better and desire them more. I covet them not. There are very few people in this world with whom I can bear to converse. I can treat all with decency and civility, and converse with them, when it is necessary, on points of business. But I am never happy in their company. This has made me a recluse and will one day make me a hermit. I had rather build stone wall upon Penn's Hill, than to be the first Prince in Europe, or the first General or first Senator in America.

Our expectations are very high of some great affair at New York.

132. JOHN ADAMS

21 August 1776

Yesterday morning I took a walk into Arch Street to see Mr. Peale's painter's room.[1] Peale is from Maryland, a tender, soft, affectionate creature. He showed me a large picture containing a group of figures, which, upon inquiry, I found were his family: his mother and his wife's mother, himself and his wife, his brothers and sisters, and his children, sons and daughters, all young.

There was a pleasant, a happy cheerfulness in their countenances, and a familiarity in their air towards each other.

He showed me one moving picture. His wife, all bathed in tears, with a child about six months old laid out upon her lap. This picture struck me prodigiously. He has a variety of portraits, very well done, but not so well as Copley's portraits. Copley is the greatest master that ever was in America. His portraits far exceed West's. Peale has taken General Washington, Dr. Franklin, Mrs. Washington, Mrs. Rush, Mrs. Hopkinson, Mr. Blair McClenachan and his little daughter in one picture, his lady and her little son in another. Peale showed me some books upon the art of painting. Among the rest one by Sir Joshua Reynolds, the President of the English Academy of Painters, by whom the pictures of General Conway and Colonel Barré, in Faneuil Hall, were taken. He showed me, too, a great number of miniature pictures. Among the rest, Mr. Hancock and his lady, Mr. Smith, of South Carolina, whom you saw the other day in Boston, Mr. Custis, and many others.

He showed me, likewise, draughts, or rather sketches, of gentlemen's seats in Virginia, where he had been, Mr. Corbin's, Mr. Page's, General Washington's, etc. Also a variety of rough drawings made by great masters in Italy, which he keeps as models. He showed me several imitations of heads, which he had made in clay, as large as the life, with his hands only. Among the rest, one of his own head and face, which was a great likeness. He is ingenious. He has vanity, loves finery, wears a sword, gold lace, speaks French, is capable of friendship, and strong family attachments and natural affections.

At this shop I met Mr. Francis Hopkinson, late a Mandamus Counsellor of New Jersey, now a member of the Continental Congress, who, it seems, is a native of Philadelphia, a son of a prothonotary of this county, who was a person much respected. The son was liberally educated, and is a painter and a poet. I have a curiosity to penetrate a little deeper into the bosom of this curious gentleman, and may possibly give you some more particulars concerning him. He is one of your pretty, little, curious, ingenious men. His head is not bigger than a large apple, less than our friend Pemberton, or Dr. Simon Tufts. I have not met with anything in natural history more amusing and entertaining than his personal appearance; yet he is genteel and well bred, and is very social.

I wish I had leisure and tranquillity of mind to amuse myself with those elegant and ingenious arts of painting, sculpture, statuary, architecture, and music. But I have not. A taste in all of them is an agreeable accomplishment. Mr. Hopkinson has taken in crayons with his own hand a picture of Miss Keys, a famous New Jersey beauty. He talks of bringing it to town, and in that case, I shall see it, I hope.

133. JOHN ADAMS

Philadelphia, 25 August 1776

The day before yesterday, and yesterday, we expected letters and papers by the post, but by some accident or mismanagement of the riders no post is arrived yet which has been a great disappointment to me. I watch with longing eyes for the post, because you have been very good, of late, in writing by every one. I long to hear that Charles is in as fair a way through the distemper as the rest of you.

Poor Barrell is violently ill, in the next chamber to mine, of an inflammatory fever. I hear every cough, sigh, and groan. His fate hangs in a critical suspense. The least thing may turn the scale against him. Miss Quincy is here, very humanely employed in nursing him. This goodness does her honor. Mr. Paine has recovered of his illness, and, by present appearances, is in better health than before. I hope it will not be my fate to be sick here. Indeed, I am not much afraid of these acute disorders: mine are more chronical, nervous, and slow. I must have a ride. I cannot make it do without it.

We are now approaching rapidly to the autumnal equinox, and no great blow has yet been struck, in the martial way, by our enemies, nor by us. If we should be blessed, this year, with a few storms as happy as those which fell out last year in the beginning of September, they will do much for us. The British fleet, where they now lie, have not a harbor so convenient or safe as they had last year. Another winter will do much for us too. We shall have more and better soldiers. We shall be better armed. We shall have a greater force at sea. We shall have more trade. Our artillery will be greatly increased, our officers will have more experience and our soldiers more discipline, our politicians more courage and confidence, and our enemies less hope. Our American commonwealths will be all completely formed and organized, and everything, I hope, will go on with greater vigor.

After I had written thus far, the post came in and brought me your favor of the 14th of August. Nabby by this time, I conclude, is well, and Charles, I hope, is broken out. Don't you recollect, upon this occasion, Dr. Byles's benediction[1] to me when I was inoculated? As you will see the piquancy of it now, more than ever you could before, I will tell the story.

After having been ten or eleven days inoculated, I lay lolling on my bed in Major Cunningham's chamber, under the tree of liberty, with half a dozen young fellows as lazy as myself, all waiting and wishing for symptoms and eruptions; all of a sudden appeared at the chamber door the reverend Doctor with his rosy face, many-curled wig, and pontifical air and gait. "I have been thinking," says he, "that the clergy of this town ought, upon this occasion, to adopt the benediction of the Romish clergy, and, when we enter the apartment of the sick, to say in the foreign pronunciation, '*Pax tecum.*'" These words are spoken by foreigners, as the Dr. pronounced them, *Pox take 'em.* One would think Sir Isaac Newton's discovery of the system of gravitation did not require a deeper reach of thought than this frivolous pun.

Your plan of making our worthy brother, professor, would be very agreeable to me.

Your sentiments of the importance of education in women are exactly agreeable to my own. Yet the *femmes savantes* are contemptible characters. So is that of a pedant universally, how muchsoever of a male he may be. In reading history, you will generally observe, when you light upon a great character, whether a general, a statesman, or philosopher, some female about him, either in the character of a mother, wife, or sister, who has knowledge and ambition above the ordinary level of women, and that much of his eminence is owing to her precepts, example, or instigation, in some shape or other. Let me mention an example or two. Sempronius Gracchus and Caius Gracchus, two great though unfortunate men, are said to have been instigated to their great actions by their mother, who, in order to stimulate their ambition, told them that she was known in Rome by the title of the mother-in-law of Scipio, not the mother of the Gracchi. Thus she excited their emulation and put them upon reviving the old project of an equal division of the conquered lands (a genuine republican measure, though it had been too long neglected to be then practicable), in order to make their names as illustrious as Scipio's.

The great Duke who first excited the Portuguese to revolt from the Spanish monarchy was spurred on to his great enterprise by a most artful and ambitious wife, and thus indeed you will find it very generally. What tale have you heard of Gerry? What mistress is he courting?

134. ABIGAIL ADAMS

Boston, 25 August 1776

I sent Johnny last evening to the post-office for letters. He soon returned, and pulling one from under his gown gave it me. The young rogue, smiling and watching mamma's countenance, draws out another and then another, highly gratified to think he had so many presents to bestow.

Our friends are very kind. My father sends his horse, and Dr. Tufts has offered me another one he had of uncle Quincy, about five years old. He has never been on journeys, but is able enough. Mr. Bass is just come, and says he cannot set out till to-morrow week without great damage to his business. He has been a long time out of stock, and about a week ago obtained a quantity and has engaged twenty pair of shoes which will be equal to twenty dollars to him, which he must lose if I will not consent to his tarrying till then. Though I urged him to set out to-morrow, yet the horses will be in a better state, as they will not be used, and more able to perform the journey. I am obliged to consent to his tarrying till then, when you may certainly expect him.

Bass is afraid that the Dr.'s horse will not be able to travel so fast as he must go. He will go and see him, and in case he is not, your brother has promised to let one of his go. I only have to regret that I did not sooner make trial of my friends, and have sent for you three weeks ago. I fear you will think me negligent, and inattentive. If I had been at home, I should have been sooner in a capacity to have assisted you. I was talking of sending for you and trying to procure horses for you when little Charles, who lay upon the couch covered over with small-pox, and nobody knew that he heard or regarded anything which was said, lifted up his head and says, "Mamma, take my dollar and get a horse for papa." Poor fellow has had a tedious time of it as well as I, but 'tis now upon the turn, and he is much easier and better. I hope I shall be able to get out of town a Saturday next.

Mr. and Mrs. Cranch with their children went out a Friday. I feel rather lonely. Such a change from one or two and twenty to only five or six is a great alteration.

I took the liberty of sending my compliments to General Lincoln,[1] and asking him some questions which you proposed to me, but which I was totally unable to answer, and he has promised a particular reply to them.

As to provisions, there is no scarcity. 'Tis true they are high, but that is more owing to the advanced price of labor than the scarcity. English goods of every kind are not purchasable, at least by me. They are extravagantly high. West India goods articles are very high, all except sugars, which have fallen half since I came into town. Our New England rum is four shillings per gallon; molasses the same price; loaf sugar two and fourpence; cotton-wool four shillings per pound; sheep's wool two shillings; flax one and sixpence. In short, one hundred pounds two years ago would purchase more than two will now.

House rent in this town is very low. Some of the best and genteelest houses rent for twenty pounds a year. Ben Hallowell's has been offered for ten, and Mr. Chardon's for thirteen pounds six shillings and eight pence.

The privateer *Independence,* which sailed from Plymouth about three weeks ago, has taken a Jamaica-man laden with sugars, and sent her into Marblehead last Saturday. I hear the *Defence* has taken another. I think we make a fine hand at prizes.

Colonel Quincy desires me to ask you whether you have received a letter from him; he wrote you some time ago.

I like Dr. Franklin's device for a seal. It is such a one as will please most, at least it will be most agreeable to the spirit of New England.

We have not any news here—anxiously waiting the event, and in daily expectation of hearing tidings from New York. Heaven grant they may be glorious for our country and countrymen. Then will I glory in being an American.

Ever, Ever yours,   PORTIA

P.S. We are in such want of lead as to be obliged to take down the leads from the windows in this town.

135. ABIGAIL ADAMS

Boston, 29 August 1776

I have spent the three days past almost entirely with you. The weather has been stormy. I have had little company, and I have amused myself in my closet, reading over the letters I have received from you since I have been here.

I have possession of my aunt's chamber, in which, you know, is a very convenient, pretty closet, with a window which looks into her flower garden. In this closet are a number of book-shelves, which are but poorly furnished. However I have a pretty little desk or cabinet here, where I write all my letters and keep my papers, unmolested by any one. I do not covet my neighbor's goods, but I should like to be the owner of such conveniences. I always had a fancy for a closet with a window, which I could more particularly call my own.

Here I say I have amused myself in reading and thinking of my absent friend, sometimes with a mixture of pain, sometimes with pleasure, sometimes anticipating a joyful and happy meeting, whilst my heart would bound and palpitate with the pleasing idea, and with the purest affection I have held you to my bosom till my whole soul has dissolved in tenderness and my pen fallen from my hand. How often do I reflect with pleasure that I hold in possession a heart equally warm with my own, and full as sus-ceptable of the tenderest impressions, and who even now whilst he is reading here, feels all I describe. Forgive this reverie, this delusion, and since I am debarred real, suffer me to enjoy and indulge in ideal pleasures—and tell me they are not inconsistent with the stern virtue of a senator and a patriot. I must leave my pen to recover myself and write in another strain.

I feel anxious for a post day, and am full as solicitous for two letters a week, and as uneasy if I do not get them, as I used to be when I got but one in a month or five weeks. Thus do I presume upon indulgence, and this is human nature. It brings to my mind a sentiment of one of your correspondents, to wit, that "man is the only animal who is hungry with his belly full."

Last evening Dr. Cooper came in and brought me your favor, from the post-office, of August 18 and Colonel Whipple arrived yesterday morning and delivered to me the two bundles you sent and a letter of the 12th of August. They have already afforded me much amusement, and I expect much more from them.

I am sorry to find from your last, as well as from some others of your letters, that you feel so dissatisfied with the office to which you are chosen. Though in your acceptance of it I know you were actuated by the purest motives, and I know of no person here so well qualified to discharge the important duties of it, yet I will not urge you to it. In accepting of it you must be excluded from all other employments. There never will be a salary adequate to the importance of the office or to support you and your family from penury. If you possessed a fortune I would urge you to it, in spite of all the fleers and gibes of minds which themselves are incapable of acting a disinterested part, and have no conception that others can. I have never heard any one speak about it, nor did I know that such insinuations had been thrown out.

Pure and disinterested virtue must ever be its own reward. Mankind are too selfish and too depraved to discern the pure gold from the baser metal.

I wish for peace and tranquillity. All my desire and all my ambition is to be esteemed and loved by my partner, to join with him in the education and instruction of our little ones, to sit under our own vines in peace, liberty, and safety.

Adieu, my dearest friend! Soon, soon return to your most affectionate   PORTIA

P.S. Charley is cleverly. A very odd report has been propagated in Braintree, namely, that you were poisoned upon your return, at New York.

136. JOHN ADAMS

Philadelphia, 5 September 1776

Mr. Bass arrived this day with the joyful news that you were all well. By this opportunity I shall send you a canister of green tea by Mr. Hare. Before Mr. Gerry went away from hence, I asked Mrs. Yard to send a pound of green tea to you. She readily agreed. When I came home at night I was told Mr. G. was gone. I asked Mrs. Y. if she had sent the canister. She said, yes, and that Mr. G. undertook to deliver it with a great deal of pleasure. From that time I flattered myself you would have the poor relief of a dish of good tea, under all your fatigues with the children, and under all the disagreeable circumstances attending the small-pox, and I never conceived a single doubt that you had received it, until Mr. Gerry's return. I asked him, accidentally, whether he delivered it, and he said, "Yes, to Mr. Samuel Adams's lady." I was astonished. He misunderstood Mrs. Yard entirely; for upon inquiry she affirms she told him it was for Mrs. J. A. I was so vexed at this that I have ordered another canister, and Mr. Hare has been kind enough to undertake to deliver it. How the dispute will be settled I don't know. You must send a card to Mrs. S. A., and let her know that the canister was intended for you, and she may send it you, if she chooses, as it was charged to me. It is amazingly dear; nothing less than forty shillings, lawful money, a pound.

I am rejoiced that my horses are come. I shall now be able to take a ride. But it is uncertain when I shall set off for home. I will not go at present. Affairs are too delicate and critical. The panic[1] may seize whom it will. It shall not seize me. I will stay here until the public countenance is better, or much worse. It must and will be better. I think it is not now bad. Lies by the million will be told you. Don't believe any of them. There is no danger of the communication being cut off between the northern and southern colonies. I can go home when I please, in spite of all the fleet and army of Great Britain.

137. JOHN ADAMS

Philadelphia, Friday, 6 September 1776

This day, I think, has been the most remarkable of all. Sullivan came here from Lord Howe, five days ago, with a message that his lordship desired a half an hour's conversation with some of the members of Congress in their private capacities. We have spent three or four days in debating whether we should take any notice of it. I have, to the utmost of my abilities, during the whole time, opposed our taking any notice of it. But at last it was determined by a majority, "that the Congress being the representatives of the free and independent States of America, it was improper to appoint any of their members to confer in their private characters with his lordship. But they would appoint a committee of their body to wait on him, to know whether he had power to treat with Congress upon terms of peace, and to hear any propositions that his lordship may think proper to make."

When the committee came to be balloted for, Dr. Franklin and your humble servant were unanimously chosen. Colonel R. H. Lee and Mr. Rutledge[1] and an equal number; but, upon a second vote, Mr. Rutledge was chosen. I requested to be excused, but was desired to consider of it until to-morrow. My friends here advise me to go. All the stanch and intrepid are very earnest with me to go, and the timid and wavering, if any such there are, agree in the request. So I believe I shall undertake the journey. I doubt whether his lordship will see us, but the same committee will be directed to inquire into the state of the army at New York, so that there will be business enough, if his lordship makes none. It would fill this letter-book to give you all the arguments for and against this measure, if I had liberty to attempt it. His lordship seems to have been playing off a number of Machiavelian manoeuvres, in order to throw upon us the odium of continuing this war. Those who have been advocates for the appointment of this committee are for opposing manoeuvre to manoeuvre, and are confident that the consequence will be that the odium will fall upon him. However this may be, my lesson is plain, to ask a few questions and take his answers.

I can think of but one reason for their putting me upon this embassy, and that is this. An idea has crept into many minds here that his lordship is such another as Mr. Hutchinson, and they may possibly think that a man who has been accustomed to penetrate into the mazy windings of Hutchinson's heart, and the serpentine wiles of his head, may be tolerably qualified to converse with his lordship.

Sunday, 8 September

Yesterday's post brought me yours of August 29. The report you mention, "that I was poisoned upon my return home, at New York," I suppose will be thought to be a prophecy delivered by the oracle, in mystic language, and meant that I should be politically or morally poisoned by Lord Howe. But the prophecy shall be false.

138. ABIGAIL ADAMS

Braintree, 7 September 1776

Last Monday I left the town of Boston, underwent the operation of a smoking at the lines, and arrived at my brother Cranch's, where we go for purification;[1] there I tarried till Wednesday, and then came home, which seemed greatly endeared to me by my long absence. I think I never felt greater pleasure at coming home after an absence in my life. Yet I felt a vacuum in my breast and sent a sigh to Philadelphia. I longed for a dear friend to rejoice with me. Charley is banished yet. I keep him at his aunt Cranch's, out of the way of those who have not had the distemper; his arm has many scabs upon it, which are yet very sore. He is very weak and sweats a-nights prodigiously. I am now giving him the bark. He recovered very fast considering how ill he was. I pity your anxiety and feel sorry that I wrote you when he was so bad, but I knew not how it might turn with him; had it been otherwise than well, it might have proved a greater shock than to have known that he was ill.

This night our good uncle came from town and brought yours of August 20, 21, 25, 27, and 28, for all of which I most sincerely thank you. I have felt uneasy to hear from you. The report of your being dead has no doubt reached you by Bass, who heard enough of it before he came away. It took its rise among the Tories, who, as Swift said of himself, "By their fears betray their hopes." How they should ever take it into their heads that you was poisoned at New York, a fortnight before that we heard anything of that villain Zedtwitz's plan[2] of poisoning the waters of the city, I cannot tell. I am sometimes ready to suspect that there is a communication between the Tories of every State; for they seem to know all news that is passing before it is known by the Whigs.

We have had many stories concerning engagements upon Long Island this week; of our lines being forced and of our troops returning to New York. Particulars we have not yet obtained. All we can learn is that we have been unsuccessful there; having lost many men as prisoners, among whom are Lord Stirling and General Sullivan.

But if we should be defeated, I think we shall not be conquered. A people fired like the Romans with love of their country and of liberty, a zeal for the public good, and a noble emulation of glory, will not be disheartened or dispirited by a succession of unfortunate events. But like them may we learn by defeat the power of becoming invincible!

I hope to hear from you by every post till you return. The herbs[3] you mention I never received. I was upon a visit to Mrs. S. Adams about a week after Mr. Gerry returned, when she entertained me with a very fine dish of green tea. The scarcity of the article made me ask her where she got it. She replied that her *sweetheart* sent it to her by Mr. Gerry. I said nothing, but thought my sweetheart might have been equally kind, considering the disease I was visited with, and that was recommended a bracer. A little after, you mentioned a couple of bundles sent. I supposed one of them might contain the article, but found they were letters. How Mr. Gerry should make such a mistake I know not. I shall take the liberty of sending for what is left of it, though I suppose it is half gone, as it was very freely used. If you had mentioned a single word of it in your letter, I should have immediately found out the mistake.

It is said that the efforts of our enemies will be to stop the communication between the Colonies by taking possession of Hudson's Bay. Can it be effected? The *Milford* frigate rides triumphant in our bay, taking vessels every day, and no colony or Continental vessel has yet attempted to hinder her. She mounts but twenty-eight guns, but is one of the finest sailers in the British navy. They complain we have not weighty metal enough, and I suppose truly. The rage for privateering is as great here as anywhere, and I believe the success has been as great.

It will not be in my power to write you so regularly as when I was in town. I shall not fail doing it once a week. If you come home by the post road you must inquire for letters wherever the post set out from. 'Tis here a very general time of health. I think 'tis near a twelvemonth since the pestilence raged here. I fear your being seized with a fever; 'tis very prevalent I hear where you are. I pray God preserve you and return you in health. The Court will not accept your resignation; they will appoint Mr. Dalton and Mr. Dana to relieve you. I am most affectionately yours.

139. JOHN ADAMS

Philadelphia, Saturday, 14 September 1776

Yesterday morning I returned with Dr. Franklin and Mr. Rutledge from Staten Island, where we met Lord Howe and had about three hours' conversation with him. The result of this interview will do no disservice to us. It is now plain that his lordship has no power but what is given him in the act of Parliament. His commission authorizes him to grant pardons upon submission, and to converse, confer, consult, and advise with such persons as he may think proper, upon American grievances, upon the instructions to Governors and the acts of Parliament, and if any errors should be found to have crept in, his Majesty and the ministry were willing they should be rectified.

I found yours of 31st of August and 2d of September. I now congratulate you on your return home with the children. I am sorry to find you anxious on account of idle reports. Don't regard them. I think our friends are to blame to mention such silly stories. What good do they expect to do by it?

My ride has been of service to me. We were absent but four days. It was an agreeable excursion. His lordship is about fifty years of age. He is a well-bred man, but his address is not so irresistible as it has been represented. I could name you many Americans, in your own neighborhood, whose art, address, and abilities are greatly superior. His head is rather confused, I think.

When I shall return I can't say. I expect now every day fresh hands from Watertown.

140. ABIGAIL ADAMS

15 September 1776

I have been so much engaged with company this week, that though I never cease to think of you I have not had leisure to write. It has been High Court week with us. Judge Cushing and lady kept here. The judges all dined with me one day and the bar another day. The Court sit till Saturday night and then are obliged to continue many causes. The people seem to be pleased and gratified at seeing justice returning into its old regular channel again.

I this week received two letters, one dated 27th and one 29th July. Where they have been these two months I cannot conceive. I hear of another by the express, but have not yet been able to find it. I write now not knowing where to direct to you; whether you are in the American Senate or on board the British fleet, is a matter of uncertainty. I hear to-day that you are one of a committee sent by Congress to hold a conference with Lord Howe. Some say to negotiate an exchange of General Sullivan. Others say you are charged with other matters.

May you be as wise as serpents. I wish to hear from you. The 28th of August was the last date. I may have letters at the post-office. The town is not yet clear of the small-pox, which makes it difficult for me to get a conveyance from there unless I send on purpose.

I only write now to let you know we are all well, anxiously longing for your return.

As this is a child of chance I do not choose to say anything more than that I am   Sincerely Yours.

141. ABIGAIL ADAMS

Braintree, 20 September 1776

I sit down this evening to write you, but I hardly know what to think about your going to New York. The story has been told so many times, and with circumstances so particular, that I with others have given some heed to it, though my not hearing anything of it from you leaves me at a loss.

Yours of September 4 came to hand last night. Our worthy uncle is a constant attendant upon the post-office for me, and brought it me. Yours of September 5 came to-night to Braintree, and was left as directed with the canister. I am sorry you gave yourself so much trouble about it. I got about half you sent me by Mr. Gerry. Am much obliged to you, and hope to have the pleasure of making the greater part of it for you. Your letter damped my spirits. When I had no expectation of your return till December, I endeavored to bring my mind to acquiesce in the too painful situation. I have reckoned the days since Bass went away a hundred times over, and every letter expected to find the day set for your return.

But now I fear it is far distant. I have frequently been told that the communication would be cut off, and that you would not be able ever to return. Sometimes I have been told so by those who really wished it might be so, with malicious pleasure. Sometimes your timid folks have apprehended that it would be so. I wish anything would bring you nearer. If there is really any danger I should think you would remove. It is a plan your enemies would rejoice to see accomplished, and will effect if it lies in their power. I am not apt to be intimidated, you know. I have given as little heed to that, and a thousand other bugbear reports, as possible. I have slept as soundly since my return, notwithstanding all the ghosts and hobgoblins, as ever I did in my life. It is true I never close my eyes at night till I have been to Philadelphia, and my first visit in the morning is there.

How unfeeling are the world! They tell me they heard you was dead with as little sensibility as a stock or a stone; and I have now got to be provoked at it, and can hardly help snubbing the person who tells me so.

The story of your being upon this conference at New York came in a letter, as I am told, from R. T. P. to his brother-in-law G——fe.[1] Many, very many have been the conjectures of the multitude upon it. Some have supposed the war concluded, the nation settled. Others an exchange of prisoners. Others, a reconciliation with Britain, etc., etc.

I cannot consent to your tarrying much longer. I know your health must greatly suffer from so constant application to business, and so little exercise. Besides, I shall send you word by and by, as Regulus's steward[2] did, that whilst you are engaged in the Senate, your own domestic affairs require your presence at home; and that your wife and children are in danger of wanting bread. If the Senate of America will take care of us, as the Senate of Rome did of the family of Regulus, you may serve them again; but unless you return, what little property you possess will be lost. In the first place the house at Boston is going to ruin. When I was there, I hired a girl to clean it; it had a cart load of dirt in it. I speak within bounds. One of the chambers was used to keep poultry in, another sea coal, and another salt. You may conceive how it looked. The house is so exceedingly damp, being shut up, that the floors are mildewed, the ceiling falling down, and the paper mouldy and falling from the walls. I took care to have it opened and aired whilst I tarried in town. I put it into the best state I could.

In the next place, the lighter of which you are, or should be, part owner is lying rotting at the wharf. One year more without any care, and she is worth nothing. You have no bill of sale, no right to convey any part of her should any person appear to purchase her. The pew I let, after having paid a tax for the repairs of the meeting-house.

As to what is here under my more immediate inspection, I do the best I can with it. But it will not, at the high price labor is, pay its way. I know the weight of public cares lie so heavy upon you that I have been loath to mention your own private ones.

The best accounts we can collect from New York, assure us that our men fought valiantly. We are no wise dispirited here. We possess a spirit that will not be conquered. If our men are all drawn off and we should be attacked, you would find a race of Amazons in America. But I trust we shall yet tread down our enemies.

I must entreat you to remember me often. I never think your letters half long enough. I do not complain. I have no reason to. No one can boast of more letters than your   PORTIA

142. JOHN ADAMS

Philadelphia, 22 September 1776

We have at last agreed upon a plan for forming a regular army. We have offered twenty dollars and a hundred acres of land to every man who will enlist during the war. And a new set of articles of war are agreed on. I will send you, if I can, a copy of these resolutions and regulations.

I am at a loss what to write. News we have not. Congress seems to be forgotten by the armies. We are most unfaithfully served in the post-office, as well as many other offices, civil and military. Unfaithfulness in public stations is deeply criminal. But there is no encouragement to be faithful. Neither profit, nor honor, nor applause is acquired by faithfulness. But I know by what. There is too much corruption even in this infant age of our republic. Virtue is not in fashion. Vice is not infamous.

1 October 1776

Since I wrote the foregoing, I have not been able to find time to write you a line. Although I cannot write you so often as I wish, you are never out of my thoughts. I am repining at my hard lot in being torn from you much oftener than I ought. I have often mentioned to you the multiplicity of my engagements, and have been once exposed to the ridicule and censure of the world for mentioning the great importance of the business which lay upon me; and if this letter should ever see the light, it would be again imputed to vanity that I mention to you how busy I am. But I must repeat it by way of apology for not writing you oftener.

From four o'clock in the morning until ten at night, I have not a single moment which I can call my own. I will not say that I expect to run distracted, to grow melancholy, to drop in an apoplexy, or fall into a consumption; but I do say, it is little less than a miracle that one or other of these misfortunes has not befallen me before now.

Your favors of 15th, 20th, and 23d September are now before me. Every line from you gives me inexpressible pleasure, but it is a great grief to me that I can write no oftener to you. There is one thing which excites my utmost indignation and contempt. I mean the brutality with which people talk to you of my death. I beg you would openly affront every man, woman, or child, for the future, who mentions any such thing to you, except your relations and friends, whose affections you cannot doubt. I expect it of all my friends, that they resent, as affronts to me, every repetition of such reports.

I shall inclose to you Governor Livingston's speech;[1] the most elegant and masterly ever made in America. Depend upon it, the enemy cannot cut off the communication. I can come home when I will. They have New York, and this is their *ne plus ultra*.

143. ABIGAIL ADAMS

29 September 1776

Not since the 6th of September have I had one line from you, which makes me very uneasy. Are you all this time conferring with his Lordship? Is there no communication? or are the postriders all dismissed? Let the cause be what it will, not hearing from you has given me much uneasiness.

We seem to be kept in total ignorance of affairs at York. I hope you at Congress are more enlightened. Who fell, who are wounded, who prisoners, or their number, is as undetermined as it was the day after the battle. If our army is in ever so critical a state I wish to know it, and the worst of it. If all America is to be ruined and undone by a pack of cowards and knaves, I wish to know it. Pitiable is the lot of their commander. Caesar's tenth legion never was forgiven. We are told for truth that a regiment of Yorkers refused to quit the city, and that another regiment be-

haved like a pack of cowardly villains by quitting their posts. If
they are unjustly censured, it is for want of proper intelligence.

I am sorry to see a spirit so venal prevailing everywhere. When
our men were drawn out for Canada, a very large bounty was
given them; and now another call is made upon us; no one will
go without a large bounty, though only for two months, and
each town seems to think its honor engaged in outbidding one
another. The province pay is forty shillings. In addition to that,
this town voted to make it up six pounds. They then drew out the
persons most unlikely to go, and they are obliged to give three
pounds to hire a man. Some pay the whole fine, ten pounds.
Forty men are now drafted from this town. More than one half,
from sixteen to fifty, are now in the service. This method of conducting will create a general uneasiness in the Continental army.
I hardly think you can be sensible how much we are thinned in
this province.

The rage for privateering is as great here as anywhere. Vast
numbers are employed in that way. If it is necessary to make any
more drafts upon us, the women must reap the harvests. I am
willing to do my part. I believe I could gather corn, and husk it;
but I should make a poor figure at digging potatoes.

There has been a report that a fleet was seen in our bay yesterday. I cannot conceive from whence, nor do I believe the story.

'Tis said you have been upon Staten Island to hold your conference. 'Tis a little odd that I have never received the least intimation of it from you. Did you think I should be alarmed? Don't
you know me better than to think me a coward? I hope you will
write me everything concerning this affair. I have a great curiosity to know the result.

As to government, nothing is yet done about it. The Church[1]
is opened here every Sunday, and the King prayed for, as usual,
in open defiance of Congress. Parker of Boston is more discreet
and so is Serjeant.

You have wrote me once or twice to know whether your
brother inclined to go into the service. I think he wholly declines
it. As to mine I have not heard anything from him since his application to Court. Nathaniel Belcher goes as captain and Tertius
Bass as lieutenant from this town. They march tomorrow. Poor

Soper, we have lost him with a nervous fever; he died a Friday. A great loss to this town, a man so enterprising a temper, more especially when we are so destitute of them. I should be obliged to you if you would direct Bass to buy me a Barcelona handkerchief and two ounces of thread number eighteen. Mr. Gerry said goods were five percent dearer here than with you, and by the way I hope you are not charged equally dear for the last canister as for the first; the first is the best of Hyson, the other very good Souchong.

If the next post does not bring me a letter, I think I will leave off writing, for I shall not believe you get mine.

Adieu.   Yours,

P.S. Master John has become post-rider from Boston to Braintree.

144. JOHN ADAMS

Philadelphia, 4 October 1776

I am seated in a large library room with eight gentlemen round about me, all engaged in conversation. Amidst these interruptions, how shall I make it out to write a letter?

The first day of October, the day appointed by the charter of Pennsylvania for the annual election of Representatives, has passed away, and two counties only have chosen members, Bucks and Chester. The Assembly is therefore dead and the Convention is dissolved. A new Convention is to be chosen the beginning of November. The proceedings of the late Convention are not well liked by the best of the Whigs. Their Constitution is reprobated, and the oath with which they have endeavored to prop it, by obliging every man to swear that he will not add to, or diminish from, or any way alter that Constitution, before he can vote, is execrated.

We live in the age of political experiments. Among many that will fail, some, I hope, will succeed. But Pennsylvania will be divided and weakened, and rendered much less vigorous in the cause by the wretched ideas of government which prevail in the minds of many people in it.

145. JOHN ADAMS

Philadelphia, 8 October 1776

I ought to acknowledge with gratitude your constant kindness in writing to me by every post. Your favor of 29 September came by the last. I wish it had been in my power to have returned your civilities with the same punctuality, but it has not. Long before this, you have received letters from me, and newspapers containing a full account of the negotiation. The communication is still open, and the post-riders now do their duty, and will continue to do so.

I assure you, we are as much at a loss about affairs at New York as you are. In general, our Generals were outgeneraled on Long Island, and Sullivan and Stirling with a thousand men were made prisoners, in consequence of which and several other unfortunate circumstances a council of war thought it prudent to retreat from that island and Governor's Island, and then from New York. They are now posted at Haarlem, about ten or eleven miles from the city. They left behind them some provisions, some cannon, and some baggage. Wherever the men of war have approached, our militia have most manfully turned their backs and run away, officers and men, like sturdy fellows; and their panics have sometimes seized the regular regiments. One little skirmish on Montresor's Island ended with the loss of the brave Major Henley and the disgrace of the rest of the party. Another skirmish, which might indeed be called an action, ended in the defeat and shameful flight of the enemy, with the loss of the brave Colonel Knowlton on our part. The enemy have possession of Paulus Hook and Bergen Point, places on the Jersey side of North River. By this time their force is so divided between Staten Island, Long Island, New York, Paulus Hook, and Bergen Point, that I think they will do no great matter more this fall, unless the expiration of the term of enlistment of our army should disband it. If our new enlistment fill up for soldiers during the war, we shall do well enough. Everybody must encourage this.

You are told that a regiment of Yorkers behaved ill, and it may be true; but I can tell you that several regiments of Massachusetts men behaved ill too. The spirit of venality you mention is the most dreadful and alarming enemy America has to oppose. It is as rapacious and insatiable as the grave. We are in the *faece Romuli non republica Platonis*.[1] This predominant avarice will ruin America, if she is ever ruined. If God Almighty does not interfere by his grace to control this universal idolatry to the mammon of unrighteousness, we shall be given up to the chastisements of his judgments. I am ashamed of the age I live in.

You surprise me with your account of the prayers in public for an abdicated king, a pretender to the crown. Nothing of that kind is heard in this place, or any other part of the continent but New York and the place you mention. This practice is treason against the State, and cannot be long tolerated.

I lament the loss of Soper, as an honest and useful member of society.

Don't leave off writing to me. I write as often as I can. I am glad master John has an office so useful to his mamma and papa as that of post-rider.

146. JOHN ADAMS

Dedham, 9 January 1777

The irresistible hospitality of Dr. Sprague[1] and his lady has prevailed upon me and my worthy fellow-traveller to put up at his happy seat. We had an agreeable ride to this place, and to-morrow morning we set off for Providence, or some other route.

Present my affection in the tenderest manner to my little deserving daughter and my amiable sons. It was cruel parting this morning. My heart was most deeply affected, although I had the presence of mind to appear composed. May God Almighty's providence protect you, my dear, and all our little ones. My good genius, my guardian angel, whispers me that we shall see happier days, and that I shall live to enjoy the felicities of domestic life with her whom my heart esteems above all earthly blessings.

147. JOHN ADAMS

Hartford, 13 January 1777

The riding has been so hard and rough, and the weather so cold, that we have not been able to push farther than this place. My little colt has performed very well hitherto, and I think will carry me through this journey very pleasantly.

Our spirits have been cheered by two or three pieces of good news, which Commissary Trumbull,[1] who is now with me, tells us he saw yesterday in a letter from General Washington, who has gained another considerable advantage of the enemy at Stony Brook, in the Jerseys, as General Putnam has gained another at Burlington, and the Jersey militia a third. The particulars you will have, before this reaches you, in the public prints. The communication of intelligence begins to be more open, and we have no apprehensions of danger in the route we shall take. Howe has reason to repent of his rashness, and will have more.

My love to my dear little ones. They are all very good children, and I have no doubt will continue so. I will drop a line as often as I can. Adieu.

148. JOHN ADAMS

Hartford, 14 January 1777

It is now generally believed that General Washington has killed and taken at least two thousand of Mr. Howe's army since Christmas. Indeed, the evidence of it is from the General's own letters. You know I ever thought Mr. Howe's march through the Jerseys a rash step. It has proved so. But how much more so would it have been thought if the Americans could all have viewed it in that light and exerted themselves as they might and ought! The whole flock would infallibly have been taken in the net.

The little nest of hornets in Rhode Island! Is it to remain unmolested this winter? The honor of New England is concerned. If they are not ousted, I will never again glory in being a New

England man. There are now New England Generals, officers, and soldiers, and if something is not done, any man may, after that, call New England men poltroons, with all my heart.

149. JOHN ADAMS

Fishkill, 1777

After a march like that of Hannibal over the Alps, we arrived last night at this place, where we found the utmost difficulty to get forage for our horses and lodgings for ourselves, and at last were indebted to the hospitality of a private gentleman, Colonel Brinkhoff,[1] who very kindly cared for us.

We came from Hartford through Farmington, Southington, Waterbury, Woodbury, New Milford, New Fairfield, the oblong, etc., to Fishkill. Of all the mountains I ever passed these are the worst. We found one advantage, however, in the cheapness of travelling. I don't find one half of the discontent nor of the terror here that I left in the Massachusetts. People seem sanguine that they shall do something grand this winter.

I am well and in good spirits. My horse performs extremely well. He clambers over mountains that my old mare would have stumbled on. The weather has been dreadfully severe.

150. JOHN ADAMS

Poughkeepsie, 19 January 1777

There is too much ice in Hudson's River to cross it in ferry-boats, and too little to cross it without, in most places, which has given us the trouble of riding up the Albany road as far as this place, where we expect to go over on the ice; but if we should be disappointed here, we must go up as far as Esopus, about fifteen miles farther.

This, as well as Fishkill, is a pretty village. We are almost wholly among the Dutch, zealous against the Tories, who have not half the tranquillity here that they have in the town of Boston, after all the noise that has been made about New York

Tories. We are treated with the utmost respect wherever we go, and have met with nothing like an insult from any person whatever. I heard ten reflections and twenty sighs and groans among my constituents to one here.

I shall never have done hoping that my countrymen will contrive some *coup de main* for the wretches at Newport. The winter is the time. Our enemies have divided their force. Let us take advantage of it.

151. JOHN ADAMS

Bethlehem, Orange County,
State of New York, 20 January 1777

This morning we crossed the North River, at Poughkeepsie, on the ice, after having ridden many miles on the east side of it, to find a proper place. We landed in New Marlborough, and passed through that and Newborough, to New Windsor, where we dined. This place is nearly opposite to Fishkill, and but little above the Highlands, where Fort Constitution and Fort Montgomery stand. The Highlands are a grand sight, a range of vast mountains which seem to be rolling like a tumbling sea. From New Windsor we came to this place, where we put up, and now we have a free and uninterrupted passage in a good road to Pennsylvania.

General Washington, with his little army, is at Morristown. Cornwallis, with his larger one, at Brunswick. Oh, that the Continental army was full! Now is the time!

My little horse holds out finely, although we have lost much time, and travelled a great deal of unnecessary way, to get over the North River. We have reports of our people's taking Fort Washington again, and taking four hundred more prisoners and six more pieces of cannon. But as I know not the persons who bring these accounts, I pay no attention to them.

152. JOHN ADAMS

Easton, at the Forks of Delaware River, in the
State of Pennsylvania, 24 January 1777

We have at last crossed the Delaware and are agreeably lodged at Easton, a little town situated on a point of land formed by the Delaware on one side, and the river Lehigh on the other. There is an elegant stone Church here, built by the Dutch people,[1] by whom the town is chiefly inhabited, and what is remarkable, because uncommon, the Lutherans and Calvinists united to build this Church, and the Lutheran and Calvinist ministers alternately officiate in it. There is also a handsome Court House. The buildings, public and private, are all of limestone. Here are some Dutch Jews.

Yesterday we had the pleasure of seeing the Moravian mills in New Jersey. These mills belong to the society of Moravians in Bethlehem in Pennsylvania. They are a great curiosity. The building is of limestone, four stories high. It is not in my power to give a particular description of this piece of mechanism. A vast quantity of grain of all sorts is collected here.

We have passed through the famous county of Sussex in New Jersey, where the Sussex Court House stands, and where, we have so often been told, the Tories are so numerous and dangerous. We met with no molestation nor insult. We stopped at some of the most noted Tory houses, and were treated everywhere with the utmost respect. Upon the strictest inquiry I could make, I was assured that a great majority of the inhabitants are stanch Whigs. Sussex, they say, can take care of Sussex. And yet all agree that there are more Tories in that county than in any other. If the British army should get into that county in sufficient numbers to protect the Tories, there is no doubt to be made, they would be insolent enough, and malicious and revengeful. But there is no danger, at present, and will be none until that event takes place. The weather has been sometimes bitterly cold, sometimes warm, sometimes rainy, and sometimes snowy, and the roads abominably hard and rough, so that this journey has been the most tedious I ever attempted. Our accommodations have been often very bad, but much better and cheaper than they would have been if we had taken the road from Peekskill to Morristown, where the army lies.

153. JOHN ADAMS

Baltimore, 2 February 1777

Last evening we arrived safe in this town, after the longest journey and through the worst roads and the worst weather that I have ever experienced. My horses performed extremely well.

Baltimore is a very pretty town, situated on Patapsco River, which empties itself into the great bay of Chesapeake. The inhabitants are all good Whigs, having some time ago banished all the Tories from among them. The streets are very dirty and miry, but everything else is agreeable, except the monstrous prices of things. We cannot get a horse kept under a guinea a week. Our friends are well.

The Continental army is filling up fast, here and in Virginia. I pray that the Massachusetts may not fail of its quota in season. In this journey we have crossed four mighty rivers: Connecticut, Hudson, Delaware, and Susquehannah. The two first we crossed upon the ice, the two last in boats; the last we crossed a little above the place where it empties into Chesapeake Bay.

I think I have never been better pleased with any of our American States than with Maryland. We saw most excellent farms all along the road, and what was more striking to me, I saw more sheep and flax in Maryland than I ever saw in riding a like distance in any other State. We scarce passed a farm without seeing a fine flock of sheep, and scarce a house without seeing men or women dressing flax. Several times we saw women breaking and swingling this necessary article.

I have been to meeting and heard my old acquaintance, Mr. Allison, a worthy clergyman of this town, whom I have often seen in Philadelphia.

154. JOHN ADAMS

Baltimore, 3 February 1777

This day has been observed in this place with exemplary decency and solemnity, in consequence of an appointment of the government, in observance of a recommendation of Congress, as a day of fasting. I went to the Presbyterian meeting, and heard Mr. Allison deliver a most pathetic and animating as well as pious, patriotic, and elegant discourse. I have seldom been better pleased or more affected with a sermon. The Presbyterian meeting-house in Baltimore stands upon a hill just at the back of the town, from whence we have a very fair prospect of the town and of the water upon which it stands, and of the country round it. Behind this eminence, which is the Beacon Hill of Baltimore, lies a beautiful meadow, which is entirely encircled by a stream of water. This most beautiful scene must be partly natural and partly artificial. Beyond the meadow and canal, you have a charming view of the country. Besides the meeting-house, there is upon this height a large and elegant Court House, as yet unfinished within, and a small church of England, in which an old clergyman officiates, Mr. Chase,[1] father of Mr. Chase one of the delegates of Maryland, who, they say, is not so zealous a Whig as his son.

I shall take opportunities to describe this town and State more particularly to you hereafter. I shall inquire into their religion, their laws, their customs, their manners, their descent and education, their learning, their schools and colleges, and their morals. It was said of Ulysses, I think, that he saw the manners of many men and many cities; which is like to be my case, as far as American men and cities extend, provided Congress should continue in the rolling humor, which I hope they will not. I wish, however, that my mind was more at rest than it is, that I might be able to make more exact observation of men and things, as far as I go.

When I reflect upon the prospect before me, of so long an absence from all that I hold dear in this world, I mean, all that contributes to my private personal happiness, it makes me melancholy. When I think on your circumstances I am more so, and yet I rejoice at them in spite of all this melancholy. God Almighty's providence protect and bless you, and yours and mine.

155. JOHN ADAMS

Baltimore, 7 February 1777

I am at last, after a great deal of difficulty, settled in comfortable quarters, but at an infinite expense. The price I pay for my board is more moderate than any other gentlemen give, excepting my colleagues, who are all in the same quarters and at the same rates, except Mr. Hancock, who keeps a house by himself. The prices of things here are much more intolerable than at Boston. The attempt of New England to regulate prices is extremely popular in Congress, who will recommend an imitation of it to the other States. For my own part I expect only a partial and a temporary relief from it, and I fear that after a time the evils will break out with greater violence. The water will flow with greater rapidity for having been dammed up for a time. The only radical cure will be to stop the emission of more paper, and to draw in some that is already out and devise means effectually to support the credit of the rest. To this end we must begin forthwith to tax the people as largely as the distressed circumstances of the country will bear. We must raise the interest from four to six per cent. We must, if possible, borrow silver and gold from abroad. We must, above all things, endeavor this winter to gain further advantages of the enemy, that our power may be in somewhat higher reputation than it is, or rather than it has been.

156. JOHN ADAMS

Baltimore, 7 February 1777

I think in some letter I sent you since I left Bethlehem I promised you a more particular account of that curious and remarkable town. When we first came in sight of the town we found a country better cultivated and more agreeably diversified with prospects of orchards and fields, groves and meadows, hills and valleys, than any we had seen. When we came into the town, we were directed to a public-house kept by a Mr. Johnson, which I think was the best inn I ever saw. It belongs, it seems, to the society, is furnished at their expense, and is kept for their profit or at their loss. Here you might find every accommodation that you could wish for yourself, your servants, and horses, and at no extravagant rates neither.

The town is regularly laid out, the streets straight and at right angles, like those in Philadelphia. It stands upon an eminence, and has a fine large brook flowing on one end of it, and the Lehigh, a branch of the Delaware, on the other. Between the town and the Lehigh are beautiful public gardens. They have carried the mechanical arts to greater perfection here than in any place which I have seen. They have a set of pumps which go by water, which force the water up through leaden pipes from the river to the top of the hill, near a hundred feet, and to the top of a little building in the shape of a pyramid or obelisk, which stands upon the top of the hill, and is twenty or thirty feet high. From this fountain water is conveyed in pipes to every part of the town. Upon the river they have a fine set of mills; the best grist mills and bolting mills that are anywhere to be found; the best fulling mills, an oil mill, a mill to grind bark for the tanyard, a dyeing house where all colors are dyed, machines for shearing cloth, etc.

There are three public institutions[1] here of a very remarkable nature. One a society of the young men, another of the young women, and a third of the widows. There is a large building divided into many apartments, where the young men reside by themselves and carry on their several trades. They pay a rent to the society for their rooms and they pay for their board, and what they earn is their own. There is another large building appropriated in the same manner to the young women. There is a governess, a little like the lady abbess in some other institutions, who has the superintendence of the whole, and they have Elders. Each apartment has a number of young women who are vastly industrious, some spinning, some weaving, others employed in all the most curious works in linen, wool, cotton, silver and gold, silk and velvet. This institution displeased me much. Their dress was uniform and clean, but very inelegant. Their rooms were kept extremely warm with Dutch stoves, and the heat, the want of fresh air and exercise, relaxed the poor girls in such a manner as must, I think, destroy their health. Their countenances were languid and pale.

The society of widows is very similar. Industry and economy are remarkable in all these institutions. They showed us their Church, which is hung with pictures of our Saviour from his birth to his death, resurrection, and ascension. It is done with very strong colors and very violent passions, but not in a very elegant taste. The painter, who is still living in Bethlehem, but very old, has formerly been in Italy, the school of painting. They have a very good organ in their Church, of their own make. They have a public building on purpose for the reception of the dead, to which the corpse is carried as soon as it expires, where it lies until the time of sepulture.

Christian love is their professed object, but it is said they love money and make their public institutions subservient to the gratification of that passion. They suffer no lawsuits with one another, and as few as possible with other men. It is said that they now profess to be against war. They have a custom peculiar respecting courtship and marriage. The elders pick out pairs to be coupled together, who have no opportunity of conversing together more than once or twice before the knot is tied. The youth of the two sexes have very little conversation with one another before marriage.

Mr. Hassey, a very agreeable, sensible gentleman, who showed us the curiosities of the place, told me, upon inquiry, that they profess the Augsburg confession of faith, are Lutherans rather than Calvinists, distinguish between Bishops and Presbyters, but have no idea of the necessity of the uninterrupted succession, are very liberal and candid in their notions in opposition to bigotry, and live in charity with all denominations.

157. ABIGAIL ADAMS

8 February 1777

Before this time I fancy you at your journey's end. I have pitied you. The season has been a continued cold. I have heard oftener from you than I ever did in any of your former journeys. It has greatly relieved my mind under its anxiety. I have received six letters from you, and have the double pleasure of hearing you are well and that your thoughts are often turned this way.

I have wrote once, by Major Rice. Two gentlemen set off for Baltimore Monday or Tuesday, and have engaged to take this letter. I feel under so many restraints when I sit down to write, that I scarcely know what to say to you. The conveyance of letters is so precarious that I shall not trust anything of consequence to them, until we have more regular passes.

Indeed, very little of any consequence has taken place since you left us. We seem to be in a state of tranquillity—rather too much so. I wish there was a little more zeal to join the army.

Nothing new, but the regulating bill[1] engrosses their attention. The merchant scolds, the farmer growls, and every one seems wroth that he cannot grind his neighbor.

We have a report here, said to come in two private letters, that a considerable battle has taken place in Brunswick, in which we have taken fifteen thousand prisoners. I cannot credit so good news. The letters are said to be without date.

I beg you would write by every opportunity, and if you cannot send so often as you used to, write and let them lie by till you make a packet.

What has become of the Farmer.[2] Many reports are abroad to his disadvantage.

I feel as if you were gone to a foreign country. Philadelphia seemed close by; but now I hardly know how to reconcile myself to the thought that you are five hundred miles distant; but though distant, you are always near to   PORTIA

158. JOHN ADAMS

Baltimore, 10 February 1777

Fell's Point, which I mentioned in a letter this morning, has a considerable number of houses upon it. The shipping all lies now at this point. You have from it on one side a complete view of the harbor, and on the other a fine prospect of the town of Baltimore. You see the hill in full view, and the Court-house, the Church, and Meeting-house upon it. The Court-house makes a haughty appearance from this point. There is a fortification erected on this point, with a number of embrasures for cannon facing the Narrows which make the entrance into the harbor. At the Narrows they have a fort with a garrison in it.

It is now a month and a few days since I left you. I have heard nothing from you nor received a letter from the Massachusetts. I hope the post-office will perform better than it has done. I am anxious to hear how you do. I have in my mind a source of anxiety, which I never had before, since I became such a wanderer. You know what it is. Can't you convey to me in hieroglyphics, which no other person can comprehend, information which will relieve me? Tell me you are as well as can be expected.[1] My duty to your papa and my mother. Love to brothers and sisters. Tell Betsey I hope she is married, though I want to throw the stocking. My respects to Mr. Shaw.[2] Tell him he may be a Calvinist if he will, provided always that he preserves his candor, charity, and moderation. What shall I say of or to my children? What will they say to me for leaving them, their education, and fortune so much to the disposal of chance? May Almighty and all gracious Providence protect and bless them!

I have this day sent my resignation of a certain mighty office.[3] It has relieved me from a burden which has a long time oppressed me. But I am determined that while I am ruining my constitution of mind and body, and running daily risks of my life and fortune, in defense of the independence of my country, I will not knowingly resign my own.

159. ABIGAIL ADAMS

12 February 1777

Mr. Bromfield was so obliging as to write me word that he designed a journey to the Southern States and would take particular care of a letter to you. I rejoice in so good an opportunity of letting you know that I am well as usual, but that I have not yet got reconciled to the great distance between us. I have many melancholy hours, when the best company is tiresome to me and solitude the greatest happiness I can enjoy.

I wait most earnestly for a letter to bring me the welcome tidings of your safe arrival. I hope you will be very particular and let me know how you are, after your fatiguing journey; how you are accommodated; how you like Maryland; what state of mind you find the Congress in. You know how little intelligence we received during your stay here with regard to what was passing there or in the army. We know no better now. All communication seems to be embarrassed. I got more knowledge from a letter written to you from your namesake,[1] which I received since you left me, than I had before obtained since you left Philadelphia. I find by that letter that six Hessian officers, together with Colonel Campbell,[2] had been offered in exchange for General Lee. I fear he receives very ill treatment. The terms were not complied with, as poor Campbell finds. He was much surprised when the officers went to take him and begged to know what he had been guilty of. They told him it was no crime of his own, but they were obliged, though reluctantly, to commit him to Concord Jail, in consequence of the ill treatment of General Lee. He then begged to know how long his confinement was to last. They told him that was impossible for them to say, since it laid wholly in the power of General Howe to determine it.

By a vessel from Bilbao, we have accounts of the safe arrival of Dr. Franklin in France, ten days before she sailed. A French gentleman who came passenger says we may rely upon it that two hundred thousand Russians will be here in the spring.

A lethargy seems to have seized our countrymen. I hear no more of molesting or routing those troops at Newport than of attacking Great Britain. We just begin to talk of raising men for the standing army. I wish to know whether the reports may be credited of the Southern regiments being full.

You will write me by the bearer of this letter, to whose care you may venture to commit anything you have liberty to communicate. I have wrote to you twice before this; hope you have received them.

The children all desire to be remembered. So does your

PORTIA

160. JOHN ADAMS

Baltimore, 15 February 1777

Mr. Hall, by whom this letter will be sent, will carry several letters to you, which have been written and delivered to him several days. He has settled his business agreeably. I have not received a line from the Massachusetts since I left it. Whether we shall return to Philadelphia soon or not, I cannot say. I rather conjecture it will not be long. You may write to me in Congress, and the letter will be brought me wherever I shall be.

I am settled now, agreeably enough, in my lodgings. There is nothing in this respect that lies uneasily upon my mind, except the most extravagant price which I am obliged to give for everything. My constituents will think me extravagant, but I am not. I wish I could sell or send home my horses, but I cannot. I must have horses and a servant, for Congress will be likely to remove several times, in the course of the ensuing year. I am impatient to hear from you, and most tenderly anxious for your health and happiness. I am also most affectionately solicitous for my dear children, to whom remember   Yours.

We long to hear of the formation of a new army. We shall lose the most happy opportunity of destroying the enemy this spring if we do not exert ourselves instantly. We have from New Hampshire a Colonel Thornton,[1] a physician by profession, a man of humor. He has a large budget of droll stories with which he entertains company perpetually. I heard, about twenty or five-and-twenty years ago, a story of a physician in Londonderry, who accidentally met with one of our New England enthusiasts, called exhorters. The fanatic soon began to examine the Dr. concerning the articles of his faith and what he thought of original sin. "Why," says the Dr., "I satisfy myself about it in this manner. Either original sin is divisible or indivisible. If it is divisible, every descendant of Adam and Eve must have a part, and the share which falls to each individual at this day is so small a particle that I think it is not worth considering. If indivisible, then the whole quantity must have descended in a right line, and must now be possessed by one person only; and the chances are millions and millions and millions to one that that person is now in Asia or Africa, and that I have nothing to do with it." I told Thornton the story, and that I suspected him to be the man. He said he was. He belongs to Londonderry.

161. JOHN ADAMS

Baltimore, 17 February 1777

It was this day determined to adjourn, to-morrow week, to Philadelphia.

Howe, as you know my opinion always was, will repent his mad march through the Jerseys. The people of that Commonwealth begin to raise their spirits exceedingly and to be firmer than ever. They are actuated by resentment now, and resentment, coinciding with principle, is a very powerful motive.

I have got into the old routine of war office and Congress, which takes up my time in such a manner that I can scarce write a line. I have not time to think nor to speak. There is a United States Lottery abroad. I believe you had better buy a ticket and make a present of it to our four sweet ones, not forgetting the other sweet one. Let us try their luck. I hope they will be more lucky than their papa has ever been, or ever will be. I am as well as can be expected. How it happens I don't know, nor how long it will last. My disposition was naturally gay and cheerful, but the prospects I have ever had before me and these cruel times will make me melancholy. I, who would not hurt the hair of the head of any animal, I, who am always made miserable by the misery of every susceptible being that comes to my knowledge, am obliged to hear continual accounts of the barbarities, the cruel murders in cold blood even by the most tormenting ways of starving and freezing, committed by our enemies, and continued accounts of the deaths and diseases contracted by our people by their own imprudence. These accounts harrow me beyond description. These incarnate demons say in great composure, that "humanity is a Yankee virtue, but that they are governed by policy." Is there any policy on this side of hell that is inconsistent with humanity? I have no idea of it. I know of no policy, God is my witness, but this, piety, humanity, and honesty are the best policy. Blasphemy, cruelty, and villainy have prevailed and may again. But they won't prevail against America in this contest, because I find the more of them are employed the less they succeed.

162. JOHN ADAMS

Baltimore, 21 February 1777

Yesterday I had the pleasure of dining with Mr. Purviance. There are two gentlemen of this name in Baltimore, Samuel and Robert, eminent merchants and in partnership. We had a brilliant company, the two Mrs. Purviances, the two Lees, the ladies of the two Colonels, R. H. and F.,[1] Mrs. Hancock and Miss Katy, and a young lady that belongs to the family. If this letter, like some other wise ones, should be intercepted, I suppose I shall be called to account for not adjusting the rank of these ladies a little better. Mr. Hancock, the two Colonels Lee, Colonel Whipple, Colonel Page, Colonel Ewing, the two Mr. Purviances, and a young gentleman. I fancy I have named all the company. How happy would this entertainment have been to me if I could, by a single volition, have transported one lady about five hundred miles. But alas! this is a greater felicity than falls to my share. We have voted to go to Philadelphia next week.

We have made General Lincoln a Continental Major-general. We shall make Colonel Glover a Brigadier. I sincerely wish we could hear more from General Heath. Many persons are extremely dissatisfied with numbers of the General officers of the highest rank. I don't mean the Commander-in-chief, his character is justly very high, but Schuyler, Putnam, Spencer, Heath, are thought by very few to be capable of the great commands they hold. We hear of none of their heroic deeds of arms. I wish they would all resign. For my part, I will vote upon the genuine principles of a republic for a new election of General officers annually, and every man shall have my consent to be left out who does not give sufficient proof of his qualifications.

I wish my lads were old enough. I would send every one of them into the army in some capacity or other. Military abilities and experience are a great advantage to any character.

163. JOHN ADAMS

Philadelphia, 7 March 1777

The President, who is just arrived from Baltimore, came in a few minutes ago and delivered me yours of February 8, which he found at Susquehanna River, on its way to Baltimore. It gives me great pleasure to find that you have received so many letters from me, although I knew they contained nothing of importance. I feel a restraint in writing, like that which you complain of, and am determined to go on trifling. However, the post now comes regularly, and I believe you may trust it. I am anxious and impatient to hear of the march of the Massachusetts soldiers for the new army. They are much wanted.

This city is a dull place in comparison of what it was. More than one half the inhabitants have removed into the country, as it was their wisdom to do. The remainder are chiefly Quakers, as dull as beetles. From these neither good is to be expected nor evil to be apprehended. They are a kind of neutral tribe, or the race of the insipids. Howe may possibly attempt this town, and a pack of sordid scoundrels, male and female, seem to have prepared their minds and bodies, houses and cellars, for his reception; but these are few, and more despicable in character than number. America will lose nothing by Howe's gaining this town. No such panic will be spread by it now as was spread by the expectation of it in December. However, if we can get together twenty thousand men by the first of April Mr. Howe will scarcely cross Delaware River this year. New Jersey may yet be his tomb, where he will have a monument very different from his brother's in Westminster Abbey.[1]

I am very uneasy that no attempt is made at Rhode Island. There is but a handful left there, who might be made an easy prey. The few invalids who are left there are scattered over the whole island, which is eleven miles in length, and three or four wide. Are New England men such sons of sloth and fear as to lose this opportunity? We may possibly remove again from hence, perhaps to Lancaster or Reading. It is good to change place; it promotes health and spirits; it does good many ways; it does good to the place we remove from, as well as to that we remove to, and it does good to those who move. I long to be at home at the opening spring, but this is not my felicity. I am tenderly anxious for your health and for the welfare of the whole house.

164. JOHN ADAMS

Philadelphia, 16 March 1777

The spring advances very rapidly, and all nature will soon be clothed in her gayest robes. The green grass which begins to show itself here and there revives in my longing imagination my little farm and its dear inhabitants. What pleasure has not this vile war deprived me of? I want to wander in my meadows, to ramble over my mountains, and to sit, in solitude or with her who has all my heart, by the side of the brooks. These beautiful scenes would contribute more to my happiness than the sublime ones which surround me. I begin to suspect that I have not much of the grand in my composition. The pride and pomp of war, the continual sound of drums and fifes as well played as any in the world, the prancings and tramplings of the Light Horse, numbers of whom are paraded in the streets every day, have no charms for me. I long for rural and domestic scenes, for the warbling of birds and prattle of my children. Don't you think I am somewhat poetical this morning, for one of my years, and considering the gravity and insipidity of my employment? As much as I converse with sages and heroes, they have very little of my love or admiration. I should prefer the delights of a garden to the dominion of a world. I have nothing of Caesar's greatness in my soul. Power has not my wishes in her train. The Gods, by granting me health and peace and competence, the society of my family and friends, the perusal of my books, and the enjoyment of my farm and garden, would make me as happy as my nature and state will bear. Of that ambition which has power for its object, I don't believe I have a spark in my heart. There are other kinds of ambition of which I have a great deal.

I am now situated in a pleasant part of the town, in Walnut Street, on the south side of it, between Second and Third Streets, at the house of Mr. Duncan, a gentleman from Boston, who has a wife and three children. General Wolcot,[1] of Connecticut, and Colonel Whipple, of Portsmouth, are with me in the same house. Mr. Adams has removed to Mrs. Cheesman's, in Fourth Street, near the corner of Market Street, where he has a curious group of company, consisting of characters as opposite as north and south. Ingersoll, the stamp man and Judge of Admiralty; Sherman, an old Puritan, as honest as an angel and as firm in the cause of American independence as Mount Atlas; and Colonel Thornton, as droll and funny as Tristram Shandy. Between the fun of Thornton, the gravity of Sherman, and the formal Toryism of Ingersoll, Adams will have a curious life of it. The landlady, too, who has buried four husbands, one tailor, two shoemakers, and Gilbert Tennent,[2] and still is ready for a fifth, and well deserves him too, will add to the entertainment. Gerry and Lovell are yet at Miss Leonard's, under the auspices of Mrs. Yard. Mr. Hancock has taken a house in Chestnut Street, near the corner of Fourth Street, near the State House.

17 March

We this day received letters from Dr. Franklin and Mr. Deane. I am not at liberty to mention particulars, but in general, the intelligence is very agreeable. I am now convinced there will be a general war.

165. JOHN ADAMS

Philadelphia, 28 March 1777

"A plot, a plot! a horrid plot! Mr. A.," says my barber, this morning. "It must be a plot, first, because there is British gold in it; second, because there is a woman in it; third, because there is a Jew in it; fourth, because I don't know what to make of it."

The barber means that a villain was taken up and examined yesterday, who appears, by his own confession, to have been employed, by Lord Howe and Jo. Galloway, to procure pilots to conduct the fleet up Delaware River and through the chevaux de frise. His confidant was a woman, who is said to be kept by a Jew. The fellow and the woman will suffer for their wickedness.

166. JOHN ADAMS

Philadelphia, 31 March 1777

I know not the time when I have omitted to write you so long. I have received but three letters from you since we parted, and these were short ones. Do you write by the post? If you do, there must be some legerdemain. The post comes now constantly, once a week, and brings me newspapers, but no letters. I have ventured to write by the post, but whether my letters are received or not, I don't know. If you distrust the post, the Speaker or your uncle Smith will find frequent opportunities of conveying letters.

I never was more desirous of hearing from home, and never before heard so seldom. We have reports here not very favorable to the town of Boston. It is said that dissipation prevails, and that Toryism abounds and is openly avowed at the coffeehouses. I hope the reports are false. Apostasies in Boston are more abominable than in any other place. Toryism finds worse quarter here. A poor fellow detected here as a spy, employed, as he confesses, by Lord Howe and Mr. Galloway, to procure pilots for Delaware River and for other purposes, was this day at noon executed on the gallows, in the presence of an immense crowd of spectators. His name was James Molesworth. He has been Mayor's Clerk to three or four Mayors.

I believe you will think my letters very trifling; indeed, they are. I write in trammels. Accidents have thrown so many letters into the hands of the enemy, and they take such a malicious pleasure in exposing them, that I choose they should have nothing but trifles from me to expose. For this reason I never write anything of consequence from Europe, from Philadelphia, from camp, or anywhere else. If I could write freely, I would lay open to you the whole system of politics and war, and would delineate all the characters in either drama, as minutely, although I could not do it so elegantly, as Tully did in his letters to Atticus.

We have letters, however, from France by a vessel in at Portsmouth.[1] Of her important cargo you have heard. There is news of very great importance in the letters, but I am not at liberty. The news, however, is very agreeable.

167. ABIGAIL ADAMS

2 April 1777

I sit down to write, though I feel very languid. The approach of spring unstrings my nerves, and the south winds have the same effect upon me which Brydone[1] says the sirocco winds have upon the inhabitants of Sicily. It gives the vapors—blows away all their gayety and spirits, and gives a degree of lassitude both to the body and mind which renders them absolutely incapable of performing their usual functions.

He adds that "it is not surprising that it should produce these effects upon a phlegmatic English constitution; but that he had just had an instance that all the mercury of France must sink under the weight of this horrid leaden atmosphere. A smart Parisian Marquis came to Naples about ten days ago. He was so full of animal spirits that the people thought him mad. He never remained a moment in the same place, but at their grave conversations used to skip from room to room with such amazing elasticity that the Italians swore he had got springs in his shoes. I met him this morning walking with the step of a philosopher, a smelling bottle in his hand and all his vivacity extinguished. I asked what was the matter. 'Ah, mon ami,' said he, 'je m'ennuie á la mort—moi, qui n'ai jamais sçu l'ennui. Mais cet exécrable vent m'accable; et deux jours de plus, et je me pend.'"[2]

I think the author of "Common Sense" somewhere says that no persons make use of quotations but those who are destitute of ideas of their own. Though this may not at all times be true, yet I am willing to acknowledge it at present.

Yours of the 7th of March received by the post. 'Tis said here that Howe is meditating another visit to Philadelphia. If so, I would advise him to taking down all the doors, that the panels may not suffer for the future.

'Tis said here that General Washington has but eight thousand troops with him. Can it be true? That we have but twelve hundred at Ticonderoga? I know not who has the care of raising them here, but this I know, we are very dilatory about it. All the troops which were stationed upon Nantasket and at Boston are dismissed this week, so that we are now very fit to receive an enemy. I have heard some talk of routing the enemy at Newport; but if anything was designed against them, believe me 'tis wholly laid aside. Nobody seems to consider them as dangerous, or indeed to care anything about them. Where is General Gates? We hear nothing of him.

The Church-doors were shut up last Sunday in consequence of a presentiment; a farewell sermon preached and much weeping and wailing; persecuted, be sure, but not for righteousness' sake. The conscientious parson had taken an oath upon the Holy Evangelists to pray for his most gracious Majesty as his sovereign lord, and having no father confessor to absolve him, he could not omit it without breaking his oath.[3]

Who is to have the command at Ticonderoga? Where is General Lee? How is he treated? Is there a scarcity of grain in Philadelphia? How is flour sold there by the hundred? Are there any stocking weavers needles to be had? Hardwick has been with me to desire me to write to you, to send Turner to procure five hundred and to beg you to inclose to me fifty or a hundred at a time, as he is in great want of them. Says Turner knows what sort he wants, and if you will send word what the price is he will pay it, and make me a present of the best pair of brants he gets this year. He is full of work, but almost out of needles.

We are just beginning farming business. I wish most sincerely you was here to amuse yourself with it and to unbend your mind from the cares of State. I hope your associates are more to your mind than they have been in times past. Suppose you will be joined this month by two from this State.

Adieu.   Yours.

168. JOHN ADAMS

Philadelphia, 6 April 1777

You have had many rumors propagated among you which I suppose you know not how to account for. One was that Congress, the last summer, had tied the hands of General Washington, and would not let him fight, particularly on the White Plains. This report was totally groundless. Another was that at last Congress untied the General, and then he instantly fought and conquered at Trenton. This also was without foundation, for as his hands were never tied, so they were not untied. Indeed, within a few days past a question has been asked Congress, to the surprise, I believe, of every member there, whether the General was bound by the advice of a council of war? No member of Congress, that I know of, ever harbored or conceived such a thought. "Taking the advice of a council of war" are the words of the General's instructions, but this meant only that councils of war should be called and their opinions and reasons demanded, but the General, like all other commanders of armies, was to pursue his own judgment after all.

Another report, which has been industriously circulated, is that the General has been made by Congress dictator. But this is as false as the other stories. Congress, it is true, upon removing to Baltimore, gave the General power to raise fifteen battalions, in addition to those which were ordered to be raised before, and to appoint the officers, and also to raise three thousand horse, and to appoint their officers, and also to take necessaries for his army, at an appraised value. But no more. Congress never thought of making him dictator or of giving him a sovereignty. I wish I could find a correspondent who was idle enough to attend to every report, and write it to me. Such false news, uncontradicted, does more or less harm. Such a collection of lies would be a curiosity for posterity.

The report you mention in your last, that the British administration had proposed to Congress a Treaty and terms, is false, and without a color. On the contrary, it is now more than ever past a doubt that their fixed determination is conquest and unconditional subjugation. But there will be many words and blows too, before they will accomplish their wishes. Poor, abandoned, infatuated nation! Infatuation is one of the causes to which great historians ascribe many events, and if it ever produced any effect, it has produced this war against America.

Arnold, who carries this, was taken in his passage from Baltimore. He sailed with Harden[1] for Boston. They took fifteen vessels while he was on board the man-of-war. Your flour was highly favored with good luck.

169. JOHN ADAMS

Philadelphia, 8 April 1777

Yours of 26th March came by this day's post. I am happy to hear you have received so many letters from me. You need not fear writing in your cautious way, by the post, which is now well regulated. But if your letters should be intercepted, they would do no harm. The F. turns out to be the man that I have seen him to be these two years. He is in total neglect and disgrace here. I am sorry for it, because of the forward part he took in the beginning of the controversy. But there is certainly such a thing as falling away in polities, if there is none in grace.

Lee fares as well as a man in close prison can fare, I suppose, constantly guarded and watched. I fancy Howe will engage that he shall be treated as a prisoner of war, and in that case we shall all be easy. For my own part I don't think the cause depends upon him. I am sorry to see such wild panegyrics in your newspapers. I wish they would consider the wars against idolatry.

11 April

Congress is now full. Every one of the thirteen States has a representation in it, which has not happened before, a long time. Maryland has taken a step which will soon complete their quota. They have made it lawful for their officers to enlist servants and apprentices.

The fine new frigate, called the *Delaware,* Captain Alexander, has sailed down the river. I stood upon the wharf to see the fine figure and show she made. They are fitting away the *Washington,* Captain Reed, with all imaginable dispatch. We have at last finished the system of officers for the hospitals, which will be printed to-morrow. As soon as it is done, I will inclose it to you. A most ample, generous, liberal provision it is. The expense will be great, but humanity overcame avarice.

170. JOHN ADAMS

Philadelphia, Sunday, 13 April 1777

Inclosed with this you have a correspondence between the two Generals concerning the cartel for the exchange of prisoners. Washington is in the right, and has maintained his argument with a delicacy and dignity which do him much honor. He has hinted at the flagitious conduct of the two Howes towards their prisoners in so plain and clear a manner that he cannot be misunderstood, but yet a decency and a delicacy are preserved, which is the more to be applauded because the natural resentment of such atrocious cruelties renders it very difficult to avoid a more pointed language in describing them. They might indeed, without much impropriety, have been painted in crimson colors of a deeper die. If Mr. Howe's heart is not callous, what must be his feelings when he recollects the starvings, the freezings, the pestilential diseases, with which he coolly and deliberately destroyed the lives of so many unhappy men! If his conscience is not seared, how will he bear its lashes when he remembers his breach of honor, his breach of faith, his offense against humanity and divinity, his neighbor, and his God (if he thinks there is any such Supreme Being), in impairing health that he ought to have cherished, and in putting an end to lives that he ought to have preserved, and in choosing the most slow, lingering, and torturing death that he could have devised. I charitably suppose, however, that he would have chosen the shortest course and would have put every man to the sword or bayonet, and thereby have put an end to their sufferings at once, if he could have done it without detection. But this would have been easily proved upon him, both by friends and enemies, whereas, by hunger, frost, and disease he might commit the murders with equal certainty, and yet be able to deny that he had done it. He might lay it to hurry, to confusion, to the fault of commissaries and other officers; nay, might deny that they were starved, frozen, and infected. He was determined to put them out of the way and yet to deny it; to get rid of his enemies and yet save his reputation. But his reputation is ruined forever.

The two brothers will be ranked by posterity with Pizarro, with Borgia, with Alva, and with others in the annals of infamy, whose memories are entitled to the hisses and execrations of all virtuous men. These two unprincipled men are the more detestable because they were in the opposition at home, their connections, friendships, and interest lay with the opposition; to the opposition they owed their rise, promotion, and importance. Yet they have basely deserted their friends and party, and have made themselves the servile tools of the worst of men in the worst of causes. But what will not desperate circumstances tempt men to do, who are without principle and who have a strong, aspiring ambition, a towering pride, and a tormenting avarice? These two Howes were very poor, and they have spent the little fortunes they had in bribery at elections, and having obtained seats in Parliament, and having some reputation as brave men, they had nothing to do but to carry their votes and their valor to market, and, it is very true, they have sold them at a high price.

Are titles of honor the reward of infamy? Is gold a compensation for vice? Can the one or the other give that pleasure to the heart, that comfort to the mind, which it derives from doing good? from a consciousness of acting upon upright and generous principles, of promoting the cause of right, freedom, and the happiness of men? Can wealth or titles soften the pains of the mind upon reflecting that a man has done evil and endeavored to do evil to millions, that he has destroyed free governments and established tyrannies? I would not be a Howe for all the empires of the earth and all the riches and glories thereof. Who would not rather be brave even though unfortunate in the cause of liberty? Who would not rather be Sidney than Monk?[1]

However, if I am not deceived, misfortune as well as infamy awaits these men. They are doomed to defeat and destruction. It may take time to effect it, but it will certainly come. America is universally convinced of the necessity of meeting them in the field in firm battalion, and American fire is terrible.

171. JOHN ADAMS

Philadelphia, 13 April 1777

I have spent an hour this morning in the congregation of the dead. I took a walk into the Potter's Field, a burying ground between the new stone prison and the hospital, and I never in my whole life was affected with so much melancholy. The graves of the soldiers who have been buried in this ground from the hospital and bettering house during the course of the last summer, fall, and winter, dead of the small-pox and camp diseases, are enough to make the heart of stone to melt away. The sexton told me that upwards of two thousand soldiers had been buried there, and by the appearance of the graves and trenches it is most probable to me he speaks within bounds. To what causes this plague is to be attributed I don't know. It seems to me that the want of tents, clothes, soap, vegetables, vinegar, vaults, etc., cannot account for it all. Oatmeal and peas are a great preservative of our enemies. Our frying-pans and gridirons slay more than the sword. Discipline, discipline is the great thing wanted. There can be no order nor cleanliness in an army without discipline. We have at last determined on a plan for the sick, and have called into the service the best abilities in physic and chirurgery that the continent affords. I pray God it may have its desired effect, and that the lives and health of the soldiers may be saved by it. Disease has destroyed ten men for us where the sword of the enemy has killed one.

Upon my return from my pensive, melancholy walk, I heard a piece of disagreeable news; that the ship *Morris,* Captain Anderson, from Nantes, with cannon, arms, gun-locks, powder, etc., was chased into Delaware Bay by two or three men-of-war; that she defended herself manfully against their boats and barges, but finding no possibility of getting clear, she ran aground. The crew and two French gentlemen passengers got on shore, but the captain, determined to disappoint his enemy in part, laid a train and blew up the ship, and lost his own life, unfortunately, in the explosion. I regret the loss of so brave a man much more than that of the ship and cargo. The people are fishing in order to save what they can, and I hope they will save the cannon. The French gentlemen, it is said, have brought dispatches from France to the Congress. I hope this is true. If it is, I will let you know the substance of it if I may be permitted to disclose it.

172. JOHN ADAMS

Philadelphia, 19 April 1777

We have now an ample representation from New York. It consists of six delegates, and they are to all appearance as high, as decisive, and as determined as any men ever were or can be. There is a new hand, a Mr. Duer,[1] who is a very fine fellow, a man of sense, spirit, and activity, and is exceeded by no man in zeal. Mr. Duane and Mr. Philip Livingston are apparently as determined as any men in Congress. You will see, by the inclosed newspapers, that Duane and Jay have arrived at the honor of being ranked with the two Adamses. I hope they will be duly sensible of the illustrious distinction, and be sure to behave in a manner becoming it.[2]

This is the anniversary of the ever memorable 19th April, 1775. Two complete years we have maintained open war with Great Britain and her allies, and, after all our difficulties and misfortunes, are much abler to cope with them now than we were at the beginning.

173. ABIGAIL ADAMS

20 April 1777

The post is very regular, and faithfully brings me all your letters, I believe. If I do not write so often as you do, be assured that 'tis because I have nothing worth your acceptance to write. Whilst the army lay this way I had constantly something by way of intelligence to write. Of late there has been a general state of tranquillity, as if we had no contending armies.

There seems to be something preparing against Newport at last. If we are not wise too late, it will be well. Two thousand militia are ordered to be drafted for that place, and last week the independent company marched very generally; expect to tarry six weeks, till the militia are collected.

Your obliging favors of various dates came safe to hand last week, and contain a fine parcel of agreeable intelligence, for which I am much obliged, and I feel very important to have such a budget to communicate.

As to the town of Boston, I cannot give you any very agreeable account of it. It seems to be really destitute of the choice spirits which once inhabited it, though I have not heard any particular charges of Toryism against it. No doubt you had your intelligence from better authority than I can name. I have not been into town since your absence, nor do I desire to go till a better spirit prevails. If 'tis not Toryism it is a spirit of avarice and contempt of authority, an inordinate love of gain, that prevails not only in town but everywhere I look or hear from. As to dissipation, there was always enough of it in the town, but I believe not more now than when you left us.

There is a general cry against the merchants, against monopolizers, etc., who, 'tis said, have created a partial scarcity. That a scarcity prevails of every article, not only of luxury but even the necessaries of life, is a certain fact. Everything bears an exorbitant price. The Act, which for a while was in some measure regarded and stemmed the torrent of oppression, is now no more heeded than if it had never been made. Indian corn at five shillings; rye, eleven and twelve shillings, but none scarcely to be had even at that price; beef, eightpence; veal, sixpence and eightpence; butter, one and sixpence; mutton, none; lamb, none; pork, none; mean sugar, four pounds per hundred; molasses, none; cotton-wool, none; New England rum, eight shillings per gallon; coffee, two and sixpence per pound; chocolate, three shillings.

What can be done? Will gold and silver remedy this evil? By your accounts of board, horsekeeping, etc., I fancy you are not better off than we are here. I live in hopes that we see the most difficult time we have to experience. Why is Carolina so much better furnished than any other State, and at so-reasonable prices?

I hate to tell a story unless I am fully informed of every particular. As it happened yesterday, and to-day is Sunday, I have not been so fully informed as I could wish. About eleven o'clock yesterday William Jackson, Dick Green, Harry Perkins, and Sargent, of Cape Ann, and A. Carry, of Charlestown, were carted out of Boston under the direction of Joice junior,[1] who was mounted on horseback, with a red coat, a white wig, and a drawn sword, with drum and fife following. A concourse of people to the amount of five hundred followed. They proceeded as far as Roxbury, when he ordered the cart to be tipped up, then told them if they were ever caught in town again it should be at the expense of their lives. He then ordered his gang to return, which they did immediately without any disturbance.

Whether they had been guilty of any new offense I cannot learn. 'Tis said that a week or two ago there was a public auction at Salem, when these five Tories went down and bid up the articles to an enormous price, in consequence of which they were complained of by the Salem Committee. Two of them, I hear, took refuge in this town last night.

I believe we shall be the last State to assume government. Whilst we harbor such a number of designing Tories amongst us, we shall find government disregarded and every measure brought into contempt by secretly undermining and openly contemning them. We abound with designing Tories and ignorant, avaricious Whigs.

Monday 21st

Have now learned the crime of the carted Tories. It seems they have refused to take paper money, and offered their goods lower for silver than for paper; bought up articles at a dear rate, and then would not part with them for paper.

Yesterday arrived two French vessels—one a twenty, some say thirty-six gun frigate; dry goods, and four hundred stand of arms, 'tis said they contain. I believe I wrote you that Manly had sailed, but it was only as far as Cape Ann. He and MacNeal[2] both lie at anchor in the harbor.

174. JOHN ADAMS

Philadelphia, 23 April 1777

My barber has just left the chamber. The following curious dialogue was the amusement during the gay moments of shaving.

"Well, Burne, what is the lie of the day?"

"Sir, Mr. ——— told me that a privateer from Baltimore has taken two valuable prizes with sixteen guns each. I can scarcely believe it."

"Have you heard of the success of the *Rattlesnake,* of Philadelphia, and the *Sturdy Beggar,* of Maryland, Mr. Burne? These two privateers have taken eleven prizes, and sent them into the West India Islands; nine transports and two Guinea-men."

"Confound the ill luck, sir; I was going to sea myself on board the *Rattlesnake,* and my wife fell a-yelping. These wives are queer things. I told her I wondered she had no more ambition. 'Now,' says I, 'when you walk the streets and anybody asks who that is, the answer is, *"Burne the barber's wife."* Should you not be better pleased to hear it said, *"That is Captain Burne's lady,* the captain of marines on board the *Rattlesnake"*?' 'Oh,' says she, 'I would rather be called Burne the barber's wife, than Captain Burne's widow. I don't desire to live better than you maintain me, my dear.' So it is, sir, by this sweet, honey language, I am choused out of my prizes, and must go on with my soap and razors and pincers and combs. I wish she had my ambition."

If this letter should be intercepted by the Tories, they will get a booty. Let them enjoy it. If some of their wives had been as tender and discreet as the barber's, their husbands' ambition would not have led them into so many salt ponds. What an *ignis fatuus* this ambition is? How few of either sex have arrived at Mrs. Burne's pitch of moderation, and are able to say, "I don't desire to live better, and had rather be the Barber's wife than the Captain's widow!" Quite smart, I think, as well as philosophical.

175. JOHN ADAMS

Philadelphia, Saturday Evening, 26 April 1777

I have been lately more remiss than usual in writing to you. There has been a great dearth of news. Nothing from England, nothing from France, Spain, or any other part of Europe, nothing from the West Indies, nothing from Howe and his banditti, nothing from General Washington. There are various conjectures that Lord Howe is dead, sick, or gone to England, as the proclamations run in the name of Will. Howe only, and nobody from New York can tell anything of his lordship.

I am wearied out with expectations that the Massachusetts troops would have arrived, ere now, at headquarters. Do our people intend to leave the continent in the lurch? Do they mean to submit? or what fatality attends them? With the noblest prize in view that ever mortals contended for, and with the fairest prospect of obtaining it upon easy terms, the people of the Massachusetts Bay are dead. Does our State intend to send only half or a third of their quota? Do they wish to see another crippled, disastrous, and disgraceful campaign, for want of an army? I am more sick and more ashamed of my own countrymen than ever I was before. The spleen, the vapors, the dismals, the horrors seem to have seized our whole State. More wrath than terror has seized me. I am very mad. The gloomy cowardice of the times is intolerable in New England. Indeed, I feel not a little out of humor from indisposition of body. You know I cannot pass a spring or fall without an ill turn, and I have had one these four or five weeks; a cold, as usual. Warm weather and a little exercise, with a little medicine, I suppose, will cure me, as usual. I am not confined, but mope about and drudge, as usual, like a galley-slave. I am a fool, if ever there was one, to be such a slave. I won't be much longer. I will be more free in some world or other. Is it not intolerable, that the opening spring, which I should enjoy with my wife and children, upon my little farm, should pass away, and laugh at me for laboring, day after day and month after month, in a conclave where neither taste, nor fancy, nor reason, nor passion, nor appetite can be gratified?

Posterity! you will never know how much it cost the present

generation to preserve your freedom! I hope you will make a good use of it. If you do not, I shall repent it in heaven that I ever took half the pains to preserve it.

176. JOHN ADAMS

Philadelphia, 27 April 1777

Your favors of April 2d and 7th I have received. The inclosed "Evening Post" will give you some idea of the humanity of the present race of Britons.[1] My barber whom I quote as often as ever I did any authority, says "he has read histories of cruelty and he has read romances of cruelty, but the cruelty of the British exceeds all that he ever read." For my own part I think we cannot dwell too much on this part of their character and conduct. It is full of important lessons. If the facts only were known, in the utmost simplicity of narration, they would strike every pious and humane bosom in Great Britain with horror. Every conscience in that country is not callous, nor every heart hardened. The plainest relation of facts would interest the sympathy and compassion of all Europe in our favor. And it would convince every American that a nation, so great a part of which is thus deeply depraved, can never be again trusted with power over us. I think that not only history should perform her office, but painting, sculpture, statuary, and poetry ought to assist, in publishing to the world and perpetuating to posterity the horrid deeds of our enemies. It will show the persecution we suffer in defense of our rights; it will show the fortitude, patience, perseverance, and magnanimity of Americans, in as strong a light as the barbarity and impiety of Britons, in this persecuting war. Surely impiety consists in destroying with such hellish barbarity the rational works of the Deity, as much as in blaspheming and defying his majesty.

If there is a moral law, if there is a divine law,—and that there is, every intelligent creature is conscious,—to trample on these laws, to hold them in contempt and defiance, is the highest exertion of wickedness and impiety that mortals can be guilty of. The author of human nature, who can give it its rights, will not see it ruined, and suffer its destroyers to escape with impunity. Divine vengeance will, some time or other, overtake the Alberts, the Philips and Georges, the Alvas, the Geslers, and Howes, and vindicate the wrongs of oppressed human nature. I think that medals in gold, silver, and copper ought to be struck in commemoration of the shocking cruelties, the brutal barbarities, and the diabolical impieties of this war; and these should be contrasted with the kindness, tenderness, humanity, and philanthropy which have marked the conduct of Americans towards their prisoners. It is remarkable that the officers and soldiers of our enemies are so totally depraved, so completely destitute of the sentiments of philanthropy in their own hearts, that they cannot believe that such delicate feelings can exist in any other, and therefore have constantly ascribed that milk and honey with which we have treated them, to fear, cowardice, and conscious weakness. But in this they are mistaken, and will discover their mistake too late to answer any good purpose for them.

177. JOHN ADAMS

Philadelphia, 28 April 1777

There is a clock calm at this time in the political and military hemispheres. The surface is smooth and the air serene. Not a breath nor a wave, no news nor noise.

Nothing would promote our cause more than Howe's march to this town. Nothing quickens and determines people so much as a little smart. The Germans, who are numerous and wealthy in this State, and who have very imperfect ideas of freedom, have a violent attachment to property. They are passionate and vindictive, in a degree that is scarcely credible to persons who are unacquainted with them, and the least injury to their property excites a resentment beyond description. A few houses and plantations plundered (as many would be if Howe should come here) would set them all on fire. Nothing would unite and determine Pennsylvania so effectually. The passions of men must cooperate with their reason in the prosecution of a war. The public may be clearly convinced that a war is just, and yet, until their passions are excited, will carry it languidly on. The prejudices, the anger, the hatred of the English against the French contributes greatly to their valor and success. The British Court and their officers have studied to excite the same passions in the breasts of their soldiers against the Americans, well knowing their powerful effects. We, on the contrary, have treated their characters with too much tenderness. The Howes, their officers, and soldiers too, ought to be held up to the contempt, derision, hatred, and abhorrence of the populace in every State, and of the common soldiers in every army. It would give me no pain to see them burned or hanged in effigy in every town and village.

178. JOHN ADAMS

Philadelphia, 4 May 1777

Inclosed with this you will have an "Evening Post" containing some of the tender mercies of the barbarians to their prisoners. If there is a man, woman, or child in America who can read these depositions without resentment and horror, that person has no soul, or a very wicked one. Their treatment of prisoners last year, added to an act of Parliament which they have made, to enable them to send prisoners to England, to be there murdered with still more relentless cruelty in prisons, will bring our officers and soldiers to the universal resolution to *conquer or die*. This maxim, "CONQUER OR DIE," never failed to raise a people who adopted it to the head of mankind. An express from Portsmouth, last night, brought us news of the arrival of arms and ordnance enough to enable us to take vengeance of these foes of human nature.

179. ABIGAIL ADAMS

6 May 1777

'Tis ten days, I believe, since I wrote you a line, yet not ten minutes pass without thinking of you. 'Tis four months wanting three days since we parted. Every day of the time I have mourned the absence of my friend, and felt a vacancy in my heart which nothing, nothing can supply. In vain the spring blooms or the birds sing. Their music has not its former melody, nor the spring its usual pleasures. I look around with a melancholy delight and sigh for my absent partner. I fancy I see you worn down with cares, fatigued with business, and solitary amidst a multitude.

And I think it probable before this reaches you that you may be driven from the city by our barbarous and hostile foes, and the city sharing the fate of Charlestown and Falmouth, Norfolk and Danbury. So vague and uncertain are the accounts with regard to the latter, that I shall not pretend to mention them. 'Tis more than a week since the event, yet we have no accounts which can be depended upon. I wish it may serve the valuable purpose of arousing our degenerated countrymen from that state of security and torpitude into which they seem to be sunk.

9 May

I have been prevented writing for several days by company from town. Since I wrote you I have received several letters; two of the 13th of April, one of the 19th, and one of the 22d. Though some of them were very short, I will not complain. I rejoice to hear from you though you write but a line.

Since the above we have some account of the affair at Danbury, and of the loss of General Wooster.[1] That they had no more assistance, 'tis said, was owing to six expresses being stopped by the Tories. We shall never prosper till we fall upon some method to extirpate that blood-thirsty set of men. Too much lenity will prove our ruin. We have rumors too of an action at Brunswick much to our advantage, but little credit is yet given to the report. I wish we may be able to meet them in the field, to encounter and conquer so vile an enemy.

The two Continental frigates lie windbound, with three brigs of twenty guns and some others, which are all going out in company. The wind has been a long time at east and prevented the vessels from going out.

I was mistaken in my brother's going with MacNeal. He is going in the *Tartar,* a vessel which mounts twenty-four guns, is private property, but sails with the fleet.

I cannot write you half so much as I would. I have left company because I would not lose an opportunity of sending this. The children are well. I cannot say that I am so well as I have been. The disorder I had in my eyes has in some measure left them but communicated itself all over me and turned to the salt rhume, which worries me exceedingly, and is very hurtful in my present situation. However, I am doing what I dare to carry it off. Believe me, etc.

I must add a little more. A most horrid plot has been discovered of a band of villains counterfeiting the Hampshire currency to a great amount. No person scarcely but what has more or less of these bills. I am unlucky enough to have about five pounds L. M. of it, but this is not the worst of it. One Colonel Farrington, who has been concerned in the plot, was taken sick, and has confessed not only the counterfeiting, but says they had engaged and enlisted near two thousand men, who, upon the troops' coming to Boston, were to fall upon the people and make a general havoc.

How much more merciful God is than man, in thus providentially bringing to light these horrid plots and schemes. I doubt not Heaven will still continue to favor us unless our iniquities prevent. The Hampshire people have been stupid enough to let one of the principal plotters, Colonel Holland, out upon bail, and he has made his escape.

180. JOHN ADAMS

Philadelphia, 7 May 1777

We have no news here except what we get from your country. The privateers act with great spirit, and are blessed with remarkable success. Some merchant ships are arrived this week from Maryland. They were first chased by men-of-war in attempting to get into Chesapeake Bay. They ran from them and attempted Delaware Bay. There they were chased again, whereupon they again shifted their course for Chesapeake, and got in safe, in spite of all the men-of-war could do. Thus, you see, we can and will have trade in spite of them, and this trade will probably increase fast. It requires time for the stream of commerce to alter its channel. Time is necessary for our merchants and foreign merchants to think, plan, and correspond with each other. Time, also, is necessary for our masters of vessels and mariners

to become familiar with the coasts, forts, and harbors of foreign
countries, and a longer time still is needful for French, Spanish,
and Dutch masters and mariners to learn our coasts and harbors.

Yours ever, ever yours.

181. JOHN ADAMS

Philadelphia, 10 May 1777

The day before yesterday I took a walk with my friend Whipple
to Mrs. Wells's, the sister of the famous Mrs. Wright,[1] to see her
wax-work. She has two chambers filled with it. In one, the para-
ble of the prodigal son is represented. The prodigal is prostrate
on his knees before his father, whose joy and grief and compassion all appear in his eyes and face, struggling with each other. A
servant-maid, at the father's command, is pulling down from a
closet shelf the choicest robes to clothe the prodigal, who is all in
rags. At an outward door in a corner of the room stands the
brother, chagrined at this festivity, a servant coaxing him to
come in. A large number of guests are placed round the room. In
another chamber are the figures of Chatham, Franklin, Sawbridge, Mrs. Macauley, and several others.[2] At a corner is a miser,
sitting at his table weighing his gold, his bag upon one side of the
table and a thief behind him endeavoring to pilfer the bag.

There is genius as well as taste and art discovered in this exhi-
bition. But I must confess the whole scene was disagreeable to
me. The imitation of life was too faint, and I seemed to be walking among a group of corpses, standing, sitting, and walking,
laughing, singing, crying, and weeping. This art, I think, will
make but little progress in the world.

Another historical piece I forgot, which is Elisha restoring to
life the Shunamite's son. The joy of the mother upon discovering
the first symptoms of life in the child is pretty strongly expressed.
Dr. Chovet's wax-work,[3] in which all the various parts of the human body are represented for the benefit of young students in
anatomy, and of which I gave you a particular description a year
or two ago, was much more pleasing to me. Wax is much fitter
to represent dead bodies than living ones.

Upon a hint from one of our Commissioners abroad, we are looking about for American curiosities to send across the Atlantic as presents to the ladies. Mr. Rittenhouse's planetarium, Mr. Arnold's collection[4] of varieties in the virtuoso way, which I once saw at Norwalk in Connecticut, Narraganset pacing mares, mooses, wood-ducks, flying squirrels, red-winged blackbirds, cranberries, and rattlesnakes have all been thought of. Is not this a pretty employment for great statesmen as we think ourselves to be? Frivolous as it seems, it may be of some consequence. Little attentions have great influence. I think, however, we ought to consult the ladies upon this point. Pray what is your opinion?

182. JOHN ADAMS

Philadelphia, 15 May 1777

General Warren writes me that my farm never looked better than when he last saw it, and that Mrs. ——— was likely to outshine all the farmers. I wish I could see it. But I can make allowances. He knows the weakness of his friend's heart, and that nothing flatters it more than praises bestowed upon a certain lady. I am suffering every day for want of my farm to ramble in. I have been now for near ten weeks in a drooping, disagreeable way, constantly loaded with a cold. In the midst of infinite noise, hurry, and bustle, I lead a lonely, melancholy life, mourning the loss of all the charms of life, which are my family, and all the amusements that I ever had in life, which is my farm. If the warm weather, which is now coming on, should not cure my cold and make me better, I must come home. If it should, and I should get tolerably comfortable, I shall stay, and reconcile myself to the misery I here suffer as well as I can. I expect that I shall be chained to this oar until my constitution both of mind and body are totally destroyed and rendered wholly useless to myself and family for the remainder of my days.

However, now we have got over the dreary, dismal, torpid winter, when we had no army, not even three thousand men, to protect us against all our enemies, foreign and domestic, and now we have got together a pretty respectable army, which renders us tolerably secure against both, doubt not we shall be able to persuade some gentleman or other in the Massachusetts to vouchsafe to undertake the dangerous office of delegate to Congress. However, I will neither whine nor croak. The moment our affairs are in a prosperous way and a little more out of doubt, that moment I become a private gentleman, the respectful husband of the amiable Mrs. A., of B, and the affectionate father of her children, two characters which I have scarcely supported for these three years past, having done the duties of neither.

183. JOHN ADAMS

Philadelphia, 17 May 1777

I never fail to inclose to you the newspapers, which contain the most intelligence that comes to my knowledge. I am obliged to slacken my attention to business a little, and ride and walk for the sake of my health, which is but infirm. Oh, that I could wander upon Penn's Hill and in the meadows and mountains in its neighborhood, free from care! But this is a felicity too great for me.

Mr. Gorham and Mr. Russell are here with a petition from Charlestown.[1] It grieves me that they are to return without success. I feel, most exquisitely, for the unhappy people of that town. Their agents have done everything in their power or in the power of men to do, and the Massachusetts delegates have seconded their efforts to the utmost of their power, but all in vain. The distress of the States, arising from the quantity of money abroad, and the monstrous demands that would be made from Virginia, New Jersey, New York, and elsewhere, if a precedent should be once set, has determined the Congress, almost with tears in their eyes, to withstand this application at present. Every man expressed the utmost tenderness and humanity upon the occasion; but at the same time every man, except the Massachusetts delegates, expressed his full conviction of the ill policy of granting anything at present.

184. ABIGAIL ADAMS

Sunday, 18 May 1777

I think myself very happy that not a week passes but what I receive a letter or two, sometimes more, from you; and though they are longer in coming than formerly, owning, I suppose, to the post being obliged to travel farther round, yet I believe they all faithfully reach me; even the curious conversation between Mr. Burne and your honor arrived safe, and made me laugh very heartily.

I think before this time many of our troops must have arrived at headquarters, for though we have been dilatory in this and the neighboring towns, others, I hear, have done their duty better. Not an hour in the day but what we see soldiers marching. The sure way to prevent their distressing us here would be to have a strong army with the General. There are a number, not more than half, I believe though, of this town's proportion, enlisted. The rest were to be drawn at our May meeting, but as nothing was done in that way, they concluded to try a little longer to enlist them. The town send but one representative this year, and that is Mr. N——s,[1] of the middle parish. Give him his pipe and let him laugh, he will not trouble anybody.

Phileleutheros[2] I suppose will be chosen into the Council, since he finds that the plan for making them lackeys and tools to the House was not so acceptable as he expected.

> "Then let me have the highest post,
> Suppose it but an inch at most."

I should feel more unhappy and anxious than ever if I realized our being again invaded by the wickedness and cruelty of our enemies. The recital of the inhuman and brutal treatment of those poor creatures who have fallen into their hands freezes me with horror.

'Tis an observation of Bishop Butler's[3] at they who have lost all tenderness and fellow-feeling for others have withal contracted a certain callousness of heart which renders them insensible to all other satisfactions but those of the grossest kind. Our enemies have found the truth of the observation in every instance of their conduct. Is it not astonishing what men may at last bring themselves to by suppressing passions and affections of the best kind, and suffering the worst to rule over them in their full strength?

Infidelity has been a growing part of the British character for many years. It is not so much to be wondered at that those who pay no regard to a Supreme Being should throw off all regard to their fellow-creatures and to those precepts and doctrines which require peace and good will to men, and in a particular manner distinguish the followers of Him who hath said, "By this shall all men know that ye are my disciples, if ye have love one towards another."[4]

Let them reproach us ever so much for our kindness and tenderness to those who have fallen into our hands, I hope it will never provoke us to retaliate their cruelties. Let us put it as much as possible out of their power to injure us, but let us keep in mind the precepts of Him who hath commanded us to love our enemies and to exercise towards them acts of humanity, benevolence, and kindness, even when they despitefully use us.

And here suffer me to quote an authority which you greatly esteem, Dr. Tillotson:[5]—

"It is commonly said that revenge is sweet, but to a calm and considerate mind patience and forgiveness are sweeter, and do afford a much more rational and solid and durable pleasure than revenge. The monuments of our mercy and goodness are a far more pleasing and delightful spectacle than of our rage and cruelty, and no sort of thought does usually haunt men with more terror than the reflection upon what they have done in the way of revenge."

If our cause is just, it will be best supported by justice and righteousness. Though we have many other crimes to answer for, that of cruelty to our enemies is not chargeable upon Americans, and I hope never will be. If we have erred it is upon the side of mercy; and we have exercised so much lenity to our enemies as to endanger our friends. But their malice and wicked designs against us have and will oblige every State to proceed against them with more rigor. Justice and self-preservation are duties as much incumbent upon Christians as forgiveness and love of enemies.

Adieu. I have devoted an hour this day to you. I dare say you are not in debt.

Ever remember with the tenderest affection one whose greatest felicity consists in the belief of a love unabated either by years or absence.   PORTIA

185. JOHN ADAMS

Philadelphia, 22 May, 4 o'clock in the morning

After a series of the sourest rest and harshest weather that ever I felt in this climate, we are at last blessed with a bright sun and a soft air. The weather here has been like our old easterly winds to me and southerly winds to you. The charms of the morning at this hour are irresistible. The streaks of glory dawning in the east, the freshness and purity in the air, the bright blue of the sky, the sweet warblings of a great variety of birds intermingling with the martial clarions of a hundred cocks now within my hearing, all conspire to cheer the spirits.

This kind of puerile description is a very pretty employment for an old fellow whose brow is furrowed with the cares of politics and war. I shall be on horseback in a few minutes, and then I shall enjoy the morning in more perfection. I spent last evening at the war office with General Arnold. He has been basely slandered and libeled. The regulars say "he fought like Julius Caesar."[1] I am wearied to death with the wrangles between military officers, high and low. They quarrel like cats and dogs. They worry one another like mastiffs, scrambling for rank and pay like apes for nuts. I believe there is no one principle which predominates in human nature so much, in every stage of life from the cradle to the grave, in males and females, old and young, black and white, rich and poor, high and low, as this passion for superiority. Every human being compares itself in its imagination with every other round about it, and will find some superiority over every other, real or imaginary, or it will die of grief and vexation. I have seen it among boys and girls at school, among lads at college, among practitioners at the bar, among the clergy in their associations, among clubs of friends, among the people in town-meetings, among the members of a House of Representatives, among the grave councillors on the more solemn bench of justice, and in that awfully august body, the Congress, and on many of its committees, and among ladies everywhere; but I never saw it operate with such keenness, ferocity, and fury as among military officers. They will go terrible lengths in their emulation, their envy, and revenge in consequence of it.

So much for philosophy. I hope my five or six babes are all well. My duty to my mother and your father, and love to sisters and brothers, aunts and uncles. Pray how does your asparagus perform? etc. I would give three guineas for a barrel of your cider. Not one drop is to be had here for gold, and wine is not to be had under six or eight dollars a gallon, and that very bad. I would give a guinea for a barrel of your beer. The small beer here is wretchedly bad. In short, I can get nothing that I can drink, and I believe I shall be sick from this cause alone. Rum, at forty shillings a gallon, and bad water will never do in this hot climate in summer, when acid liquors are necessary against putrefaction.

186. JOHN ADAMS

Philadelphia, 25 May 1777

At half past four this morning I mounted my horse and took a ride in a road that was new to me. I went to Kensington and then to "Point-no-point" by land, the place where I went once before with a large company in the row-galleys by water. That frolic was almost two years ago. I gave you a relation of it in the time, I suppose. The road to Point-no-point lies along the river Delaware, in fair sight of it and its opposite shore. For near four miles the road is as straight as the streets of Philadelphia. On each side are beautiful rows of trees, buttonwoods, oaks, walnuts, cherries, and willows, especially down towards the banks of the river. The meadows, pastures, and grass-plats are as green as leeks. There are many fruit trees and fine orchards set with the nicest regularity. But the fields of grain, the rye and wheat, exceed all description. These fields are all sown in ridges, and the furrow between each couple of ridges is as plainly to be seen as if a swath had been mown along. Yet it is no wider than a plough-share, and it is as straight as an arrow. It looks as if the sower had gone along the furrow with his spectacles, to pick up every grain that should accidentally fall into it. The corn is just coming out of the ground. The furrows struck out for the hills to be planted in are each way as straight as mathematical right lines, and the squares between every four hills as exact as they could be done by plumb and line, or scale and compass.

I am ashamed of our farmers. They are a lazy, ignorant set; in husbandry, I mean; for they know infinitely more of everything else than these. But after all, the native face of our country, diversified as it is with hill and dale, sea and land, is to me more agreeable than this enchanting artificial scene.

27 May

The post brought me yours of May 6th and 9th. You express apprehensions that we may be driven from this city. We have no such apprehensions here. Howe is unable to do anything but by stealth. Washington is strong enough to keep Howe where he is.

How could it happen that you should have £5 counterfeit New Hampshire money? Can't you recollect who you had it of? Let me entreat you not to take a shilling of any but Continental money or Massachusetts, and be very careful of that. There is a counterfeit Continental bill abroad, sent out of New York, but it will deceive none but fools, for it is copper-plate, easily detected, miserably done.

187. JOHN ADAMS

Philadelphia, Monday, 2 June 1777

Artillery Election! I wish I was at it or near it. Yours of the 18th reached me this morning. The cause that letters are so long in travelling is that there is but one post in a week, who goes from hence to Peekskill, although there are two that go from thence to Boston. Riding every day has made me better than I was, although I am not yet quite well. I am determined to continue this practice, which is very necessary for me.

I rejoice to find that the town have had the wisdom to send but one Representative. The House last year was too numerous and unwieldy. The expense was too great. I suppose you will have a Constitution formed this year. Who will be the Moses, the Lycurgus, the Solon? or have you a score or two of such? Whoever they may be, and whatever form may be adopted, I am persuaded there is among the mass of our people a fund of wisdom, integrity, and humanity which will preserve their happiness in a tolerable measure.

If the enemy comes to Boston again, fly with your little ones, all of them, to Philadelphia. But they will scarcely get to Boston this campaign. I admire your sentiments concerning revenge. Revenge in ancient days (you will see it through the whole Roman history) was esteemed a generous and an heroic passion. Nothing was too good for a friend, or too bad for an enemy. Hatred and malice without limits against an enemy were indulged, were justified, and no cruelty was thought unwarrantable. Our Saviour taught the immorality of revenge, and the moral duty of forgiving injuries, and even the duty of loving enemies. Nothing can show the amiable, the moral, the divine excellency of these Christian doctrines in a stronger point of light than the characters and conduct of Marius and Sylla, Caesar, Pompey, Antony, and Augustus, among innumerable others. Retaliation we must practice in some instances, in order to make our barbarous foes respect, in some degree, the rights of humanity. But this will never be done without the most palpable necessity. The apprehension of retaliation alone will restrain them from cruelties which would disgrace savages. To omit it then would be cruelty to ourselves, our officers and men.

We are amused here with reports of troops removing from Rhode Island, New York, Staten Island, etc.; wagons, boats, bridges, etc., prepared; two old Indiamen cut down into floating batteries, mounting thirty-two guns, sent round into Delaware river, etc., etc.; but I heed it no more than the whistling of the zephyrs. In short, I had rather they should come to Philadelphia than not. It would purify this city of its dross. Either the furnace of affliction would refine it of its impurities, or it would be purged yet so as by fire. This town has been a dead weight upon us. It would be a dead weight upon the enemy. The mules here would plague them more than all their money.

188. JOHN ADAMS

Philadelphia, 4 June 1777

I wish I could know whether your season is cold or warm, wet or dry, fruitful or barren; whether you had late frosts, whether those frosts have hurt the fruit, the flax, the corn or vines, etc. We have a fine season here and a bright prospect of abundance.

You will see by the inclosed papers in a letter from my friend Parsons,[1] a very handsome narration of one of the prettiest exploits of this war, a fine retaliation of the Danbury mischief. Meigs, who was before esteemed a good officer, has acquired by this expedition a splendid reputation. You will see by the same papers, too, that the writers here in opposition to the Constitution of Pennsylvania are making factious use of my name and lucubrations; much against my will, I assure you, for although I am no admirer of the form of this government, yet I think it is agreeable to the body of the people, and if they please themselves they will please me. And I would not choose to lie impressed into the service of one party or the other, and I am determined I will not enlist. Besides, it is not very genteel in these writers to put my name to a letter from which I cautiously withheld it myself. However, let them take their own way; I shall not trouble myself about it.

I am growing better by exercise and air. I must write a letter, in behalf of Mr. Thaxter, to the bar and bench in Boston, in order to get him sworn, at July Court. Will my brother, when the time comes, officiate for his brother at a christening? If it is a young gentleman, call him William after your father—if a young lady, call her Elizabeth after your mother, and sister.

189. JOHN ADAMS

Philadelphia, 8 July 1777

Yours of 23d June I have received. I believe there is no danger of
an invasion your way, but the designs of the enemy are uncertain, and their motions a little mysterious. Before this letter is
sealed, which will not be till Sunday next, I hope I shall be able
to inform you better.

I rejoice at your fine season and at my brother Cranch's attention to husbandry. I am very glad he bought the farm and that be
likes it so well. I pant for domestic life and rural felicity like his.
I am better than I have been. But I dread the heats which are
coming on. This day completes six months since I left you. I am
wasted and exhausted in mind and body, with incessant application to business, but, if I can possibly endure it, will hold out the
year. It is nonsense to dance backwards and forwards. After this
year, I shall take my leave.

Our affairs are in a fine, prosperous train, and if they continue
so, I can leave this station with honor. Next month completes
three years that I have been devoted to the service of liberty. A
slavery it has been to me, whatever the world may think of it. To
a man whose attachments to his family are as strong as mine, absence alone from such a wife and such children would be a great
sacrifice. But in addition to this separation what have I not
done? What have I not suffered? What have I not hazarded?
These are questions that I may ask you, but I will ask such questions of none else. Let the cymbals of popularity tinkle still. Let
the butterflies of fame glitter with their wings. I shall envy neither their music nor their colors. The loss of property affects too
little. All other hard things I despise, but the loss of your company and that of my dear babes, for so long a time, I consider as
a loss of so much solid happiness. The tender social feelings of
my heart, which have distressed me beyond all utterance in my
most busy, active scenes, as well as in the numerous hours of
melancholy solitude, are known only to God and my own soul.

How often have I seen my dearest friend a widow, and her
charming prattlers orphans exposed to all the insolence of unfeeling, impious tyrants! Yet I can appeal to my final Judge, the

horrid vision has never for one moment shaken the resolution of my heart.

190. JOHN ADAMS

Philadelphia, 11 July 1777

This letter will go by the hand of the Honorable Joseph Hewes, Esquire, one of the delegates in Congress from North Carolina from the month of September, 1774, until 1777. I had the honor to serve with him upon the naval committee who laid the first foundations, the cornerstone, of an American navy, by fitting to sea the *Alfred, Columbus, Cabot, Andrew Doria, Providence,* and several others; an honor that I make it a rule to boast of upon all occasions and I hope my posterity will have reason to boast. Hewes has a sharp eye and keen, penetrating sense, but, what is of much more value, is a man of honor and integrity. If he should call upon you, and you should be about, I hope you will treat him with all the complaisance that is due to his character. I almost envy him his journey, although he travels for his health, which at present is infirm.

  I am, yours, yours, yours,   JOHN ADAMS

MY DEAREST FRIEND, — We have had no news from camp for three or four days. Mr. Howe, by the last advices, was manoeuvering his fleet and army in such a manner as to give us expectations of an expedition somewhere; but whether to Rhode Island, Halifax, up the North River, or the Delaware, is left to conjecture. I am much in doubt whether he knows his own intentions. A faculty of penetrating into the designs of an enemy is said to be the first quality of a General, but it is impossible to discover the designs of an enemy who has no design at all. An intention that has no existence, a plan that is not laid, cannot be divined. Be his intentions what they may, you have nothing to fear from him. He has not force to penetrate the country anywhere.

191. JOHN ADAMS

Philadelphia, 13 July 1777

MY DEAREST FRIEND, — We have a confused account from
the northward of something unlucky at Ticonderoga, but cannot
certainly tell what it is. I am much afraid we shall lose that post,
as we did Forts Washington and Lee; and indeed, I believe we
shall if the enemy surround it. But it will prove no benefit to him.
I begin to wish there was not a fort upon the continent. Discipline and disposition are our resources. It is our policy to draw
the enemy into the country, where we can avail ourselves of hills,
woods, rivers, defiles, etc., until our soldiers are more inured to
war. Howe and Burgoyne will not be able to meet this year, and
if they were met, it would only be better for us, for we should
draw all our forces to a point too. If they were met, they could
not cut off the communication between the northern and southern States. But if the communication was cut off for a time, it
would be no misfortune, for New England would defend itself,
and the southern States would defend themselves.

Colonel Miles is come out of New York on his parole. His account is, as I am informed, that Mr. Howe's projects are all de-
ranged. His army has gone round the circle, and is now
encamped in the very spot where he was a year ago. The spirits
of the Tories are sunk to a great degree, and those of the army
too. The Tories have been elated with prospects of coming to this
city and triumphing, but are miserably disappointed. The Hessians are disgusted, and their General De Heister gone home in a
miff.[1]

192. JOHN ADAMS TO JOHN Q. ADAMS

Philadelphia, 27 July 1777

If it should be the design of Providence that you should live to
grow up, you will naturally feel a curiosity to learn the history of
the causes which have produced the late Revolution of our Government. No study in which you can engage will be more worthy of you.

It will become you to make yourself master of all the considerable characters which have figured upon the stage of civil, political, or military life. This you ought to do with utmost candor, benevolence, and impartiality; and if you should now and then meet with an incident which shall throw some light upon your father's character, I charge you to consider it with an attention only to truth.

It will also be an entertaining and instructive amusement to compare our American Revolution with others that resemble it. The whole period of English history, from the accession of James the First to the accession of William the Third will deserve your most critical attention.

The History of the Revolutions in Portugal, Sweden, and Rome, by the Abbé de Vertot,[1] is well worth your reading.

The separation of the Helvetic Confederacy from the dominion of the House of Austria is also an illustrious event, that particularly resembles our American struggle with Great Britain.

But above all others I would recommend to your study the history of the Flemish Confederacy, by which the seven United Provinces of the Netherlands emancipated themselves from the domination of Spain.

There are several good histories of this great revolution. Sir William Temple's is short but elegant and entertaining. Another account of this period was written by Puffendorf, and another by Grotius.

But the most full and complete history that I have seen is one that I am now engaged in reading. It is entitled "The History of the Wars of Flanders," written in Italian by that learned and famous Cardinal Bentivoglio, Englished by the Right Honorable Henry, Earl of Monmouth. The whole work illustrated with a map of the seventeen Provinces and above twenty figures of the chief personages mentioned in the history.

Bentivoglio, like Clarendon, was a courtier, and on the side of monarchy and the hierarchy. But allowances must be made for that.[2]

There are three most memorable sieges described in this history, those of Haerlem, Leyden, and Antwerp.

You will wonder, my dear son, at my writing to you at your tender age such dry things as these; but if you keep this letter, you will in some future period thank your father for writing it. I am my dear son, with the utmost affection to your sister and brothers as well as to you, your father,   JOHN ADAMS

193. ABIGAIL ADAMS

30 July 1777

I dare say, before this time you have interpreted the Northern Storm.[1] If the presages chilled your blood, how must you be frozen and stiffened at the disgrace brought upon our arms! unless some warmer passion seize you, and anger and resentment fire your breast. How are all our vast magazines of cannon, powder, arms, clothing, provision, medicine, etc., to be restored to us? But, what is vastly more, how shall the disgrace be wiped away? How shall our lost honor be retrieved? The reports with regard to that fortress are very vague and uncertain. Some write from thence that there was not force sufficient to defend it. Others say it might have stood a long siege. Some there are who ought to know why and wherefore we have given away a place of such importance.

That the inquiry will be made, I make no doubt; and if cowardice, guilt, deceit, are found upon any one, howsoever high or exalted his station, may shame, reproach, infamy, hatred, and the execrations of the public be his portion.

I would not be so narrow-minded as to suppose that there are not many men of all nations, possessed of honor, virtue, and integrity; yet it is to be lamented that we have not men among ourselves sufficiently qualified for war to take upon them the most important command.

It was customary among the Carthaginians to have a military school, in which the flower of their nobility, and those whose talents and ambition prompted them to aspire to the first dignities, learned the art of war. From among these they selected all their general officers; for, though they employed mercenary soldiers, they were too jealous and suspicious to employ foreign generals. Will a foreigner, whose interest is not naturally connected with ours (any otherwise than as the cause of liberty is the cause of all mankind), will he act with the same zeal, or expose himself to equal dangers with the same resolution, for a republic of which he is not a member, as he would have done for his own native country? And can the people repose an equal confidence in them, even supposing them men of integrity and abilities, and that they meet with success equal to their abilities? How much envy and malice are employed against them! And how galling to pride, how mortifying to human nature, to see itself excelled.

31 July

I have nothing new to entertain you with, unless it be an account of a new set of mobility, which has lately taken the lead in Boston. You must know that there is a great scarcity of sugar and coffee, articles which the female part of the State is very loath to give up, especially whilst they consider the scarcity occasioned by the merchants having secreted a large quantity. There had been much rout and noise in the town for several weeks. Some stores had been opened by a number of people, and the coffee and sugar carried into the market and dealt out by pounds. It was rumored that an eminent, wealthy, stingy merchant[2] who is a bachelor) had a hogshead of coffee in his store, which he refused to sell to the committee under six shillings per pound. A number of females, some say a hundred, some say more, assembled with a cart and trucks, marched down to the warehouse, and demanded the keys, which he refused to deliver upon which one of them seized him by his neck, and tossed him into the cart. Upon his finding no quarter, he delivered the keys, when they tipped up the cart and discharged him; then opened the warehouse, hoisted out the coffee themselves, put it into the trucks and drove off.

It was reported that he had a spanking[3] among them; but this, I believe, was not true. A large concourse of men stood amazed, silent spectators of the whole transaction.

Your kind favor received, dated July 11, favored by the Honorable Mr. Hewes, left at my uncle's in Boston. 'Tis not likely he will make an excursion this way; if he should, shall treat him in the best manner I am able.

What day does your post arrive, and how long are letters traveling from me to you? I receive one from you every week, and I as regularly write one but you make no mention of receiving any, or very seldom. In your hurry do you forget it, or do they not reach you? I am very well for the time, not yet three weeks since my confinement, and yet I think I have wrote you a very long letter.

Adieu. Your good mother is just come; she desires to be remembered to you; so do my father and sister, who have just left me, and so does she whose greatest happiness consists in being tenderly beloved by her absent friend, and who subscribes herself ever his   PORTIA

194. ABIGAIL ADAMS

5 August 1777

If alarming half a dozen places at the same time is an act of generalship, Howe may boast of his late conduct. We have never, since the evacuation of Boston, been under apprehensions of an invasion equal to what we suffered last week. All Boston was in confusion packing up and carting out of town household furniture, military stores, goods, etc. Not less than a thousand teams were employed on Friday and Saturday; and, to their shame be it told, not a small trunk would they carry under eight dollars, and many of them, I am told, asked a hundred dollars a load; for carting a hogshead of molasses eight miles, thirty dollars. O human nature! or rather, O inhuman nature! what art thou? The report of the fleet's being seen off Cape Ann Friday night gave me the alarm, and, though pretty weak, I set about packing up my things, and on Saturday removed a load.

When I looked around me and beheld the bounties of Heaven so liberally bestowed, in fine fields of corn, grass, flax, and English grain, and thought it might soon become a prey to these merciless ravagers, our habitations laid waste, and if our flight preserved our lives, we must return to barren fields, empty barns, and desolate habitations, if any we find (perhaps not where to lay our heads), my heart was too full to bear the weight of affliction which I thought just ready to overtake us, and my body too weak almost to bear the shock, unsupported by my better half.

But, thanks be to Heaven, we are at present relieved from our fears respecting ourselves. I now feel anxious for your safety, but hope prudence will direct to a proper care and attention to yourselves. May this second attempt of Howe's prove his utter ruin. May destruction overtake him as a whirlwind.

We have a report of an engagement at the northward, in which our troops behaved well, drove the enemy into their lines, killed and took three hundred and fifty prisoners. The account came in last night. I have not particulars. We are under apprehensions that the *Hancock* is taken.

Your obliging letters of the 8th, 10th, and 13th came to hand last week. I hope before this time you are relieved from the anxiety you express for your bosom friend. I feel my sufferings amply rewarded, in the tenderness you express for me. But in one of your letters you have drawn a picture which drew a flood of tears from my eyes, and wrung my heart with anguish inexpressible. I pray Heaven I may not live to realize it.

It is almost thirteen years since we were united, but not more than half that time have we had the happiness of living together. The unfeeling world may consider it in what light they please. I consider it as a sacrifice to my country, and one of my greatest misfortunes, for you to be separated from my children, at a time of life when the joint instructions and admonition of parents sink deeper than in maturer years.

The hope of the smiles and approbation of my friend sweetens all my toils and labors.

> "Ye Powers, whom men and birds obey,
>   Great rulers of your creatures, say
>   Why mourning comes, by bliss conveyed,
>   And even the sweets of love allayed.
>   Where grows enjoyment tall and fair,
>   Around it twines entangling care;
>   While fear for what our souls possess
>   Enervates every power to bless.
>   Yet friendship forms the bliss above,
>   And, life! what art thou without love!"[1]

195. JOHN ADAMS

Philadelphia, 11 August 1777

Your kind favor of July 30th and 31st was handed me just now from the post-office. I have regularly received a letter from you every week, excepting one, for a long time past, and as regularly send a line to you, inclosing papers. My letters are scarcely worth sending. Indeed, I don't choose to indulge much speculation, lest a letter should miscarry, and free sentiments upon public affairs intercepted from me might do much hurt.

Where the scourge of God and the plague of mankind is gone, no one can guess. An express from Sinnepuxent, a place between the Capes of Delaware and the Capes of Chesapeake, informs that a fleet of one hundred sail was seen off that place last Thursday. But whether this is fishermen's news, like that from Cape Ann, I know not. The time spends and the campaign wears away, and Howe makes no great figure yet. How many men and horses will he cripple by this strange coasting voyage of five weeks?

We have given New England men what they will think a complete triumph in the removal of Generals from the northward and sending Gates there. I hope every part of New England will now exert itself to its utmost efforts. Never was a more glorious opportunity than Burgoyne has given us of destroying him by marching down so far towards Albany. Let New England turn out and cut off his retreat. Pray, continue to write me every week. You have made me merry with the female frolic with the miser. But I hope the females will leave off their attachment to coffee. I assure you the best families in this place have left off, in a great measure, the use of West India goods. We must bring ourselves to live upon the produce of our own country. What would I give for some of your cider? Milk has become the breakfast of many of the wealthiest and genteelest families here.

Fenno put me into a kind of frenzy to go home, by the description he gave me, last night, of the fertility of the season, the plenty of fish, etc., etc., etc., in Boston and about it. I am condemned to this place, a miserable exile from everything that is agreeable to me. God will my banishment shall not last long.

196. JOHN ADAMS

Same date

I think I have sometimes observed to you in conversation, that upon examining the biography of illustrious men, you will generally find some female about them, in the relation of mother or wife or sister, to whose instigation a great part of their merit is to be ascribed. You will find a curious example of this in the case of Aspasia, the wife of Pericles. She was a woman of the greatest beauty and the first genius. She taught him, it is said, his refined maxims of policy, his lofty imperial eloquence, nay, even composed the speeches on which so great a share of his reputation was founded. The best men in Athens frequented her house and brought their wives to receive lessons from her of economy and right deportment. Socrates himself was her pupil in eloquence, and gives her the honor of that funeral oration which he delivers in the "Menexenus" of Plato. Aristophanes, indeed, abuses this famous lady, but Socrates does her honor.

I wish some of our great men had such wives. By the account in your last letter, it seems the women in Boston begin to think themselves able to serve their country. What a pity it is that our Generals in the northern districts had not Aspasias to their wives!

I believe the two Howes have not very great women for wives. If they had, we should suffer more from their exertions than we do. This is our good fortune. A woman of good sense would not let her husband spend five weeks at sea in such a season of the year. A smart wife would have put Howe in possession of Philadelphia a long time ago.

197. JOHN ADAMS

Philadelphia, Tuesday, 19 August 1777

Your obliging favor of the 5th came by yesterday's post, and I intended to have answered it by this morning's post, but was delayed by many matters, until he gave me the slip.

I am sorry that you and the people of Boston were put to so

much trouble, but glad to hear that such numbers determined to fly. The prices for carting which were demanded were detestable. I wish your fatigue and anxiety may not have injured your health. Don't be anxious for my safety. If Howe comes here, I shall run away, I suppose, with the rest. We are too brittle ware, you know, to stand the dashing of balls and bombs. I wonder upon what principle the Roman senators refused to fly from the Gauls, and determined to sit with their ivory staves and hoary beards in the porticoes of their houses, until the enemy entered the city and, although they confessed they resembled the gods, put them to the sword. I should not choose to indulge this sort of dignity; but I confess I feel myself so much injured by these barbarian Britons that I have a strong inclination to meet them in the field. This is not revenge, I believe, but there is something sweet and delicious in the contemplation of it. There is in our hearts an indignation against wrong that is righteous and benevolent; and he who is destitute of it is defective in the balance of his affections and in his moral character.

As long as there is conscience in our breasts, a moral sense which distinguishes between right and wrong, approving, esteeming, loving the former, and undermining and detesting the other, we must feel a pleasure in the punishment of so eminent a contemner of all that is right and good and just, as Howe is. They are virtuous and pious passions that prompt us to desire his destruction, and to lament and deplore his success and prosperity. The desire of assisting towards his disgrace is an honest wish.

It is too late in life, my constitution is too much debilitated by speculation, and indeed it is too late a period in the war, for me to think of girding on a sword. But if I had the last four years to run over again, I certainly would.

198. JOHN ADAMS

Philadelphia, Tuesday, 19 August 1777

The weather still continues cloudy, and cool, and the wind easterly. Howe's fleet and army is still incognito. The gentlemen from South Carolina begin to tremble for Charleston. If Howe is under a judicial blindness, he may be gone there. But what will be the fate of a scorbutic army, cooped up in a fleet for six, seven, or eight weeks, in such intemperate weather as we have had? What will be their condition, landing on a burning shore abounding with agues and mosquitoes, in the most unwholesome season of the whole year? If he should get Charleston, or indeed the whole State, what progress will this make towards the conquest of America? He will stop the trade of rice and indigo, but what then? Besides, he will get some ugly knocks. They are honest, sincere, and brave, and will make his life uncomfortable.

I feel a strong affection for South Carolina for several reasons.

1. I think them as stanch patriots as any in America.

2. I think them as brave.

3. They are the only people in America who have maintained a post and defended a fort.

4. They have sent us a new delegate whom I greatly admire, Mr. Laurens,[1] their Lieutenant-governor, a gentleman of great fortune, great abilities, modesty and integrity, and great experience too. If all the States would send us such men, it would be a pleasure to be here.

In the northern department they begin to fight. The family of Johnson, the black part of it as well as the white, are pretty well thinned.[2] Rascals! They deserve extermination. I presume Gates will be so supported that Burgoyne will be obliged to retreat. He will stop at Ticonderoga, I suppose, for they can maintain posts although we cannot. I think we shall never defend a post until we shoot a General. After that we shall defend posts, and this event, in my opinion, is not far off. No other fort will ever be evacuated without an inquiry, nor any officer come off without a court martial. We must trifle no more. We have suffered too many disgraces to pass unexpiated. Every disgrace must be wiped off.

We have been several days hammering upon money. We are contriving every way we can to redress the evils we feel and fear from too great a quantity of paper. Taxation as deep as possible is the only radical cure. I hope you will pay every tax that is brought you, if you sell my books or clothes or oxen, or your cows, to pay it.

199. JOHN ADAMS

Philadelphia, Wednesday, 20 August 1777

This day completes three years since I stepped into the coach at Mr. Cushing's door, in Boston, to go to Philadelphia in quest of adventures. And adventures I have found. I feel an inclination sometimes to write the history of the last three years, in imitation of Thucydides. There is a striking resemblance in several particulars between the Peloponnesian and the American war. The real motive to the former was a jealousy of the growing power of Athens by sea and land. The genuine motive to the latter was a similar jealousy of the growing power of America. The true causes which incite to war are seldom professed or acknowledged.

We are now upon a full sea; when we shall arrive at a safe harbor, no mariner has skill and experience enough to foretell. But by the favor of Heaven we shall make a prosperous voyage, after all the storms and shoals are passed.

5 o'clock, Afternoon

It is now fair sunshine again, and very warm. Not a word yet from Howe's fleet. The most general suspicion now is that it is gone to Charleston, South Carolina. But it is a wild supposition. It may be right, however, for he is a wild General.

We have been hammering to-day upon a mode of trial for the general officers at Ti. Whether an inquiry will precede the court martial, and whether the inquiry shall be made by a committee of Congress or by a council of general officers, is not determined, but inquiry and trial both, I conjecture, there will be.

If Howe is gone to Charleston, you will have a little quiet, and enjoy your corn, and rye, and flax, and hay, and other good things, until another summer. But what shall we do for sugar and wine and rum? Why, truly, I believe we must leave them off. Loaf sugar is only four dollars a pound here, and brown only a dollar for the meanest sort, and ten shillings for that a little better. Everybody here is leaving off loaf sugar, and most are laying aside brown. As to rum and wine, give me cider and I would compound. New England rum is but forty shillings a gallon. But if wine was ten dollars a bottle I would have one glass a day in water while the hot weather continues, unless I could get cider.

200. JOHN ADAMS

Philadelphia, Thursday, 21 August 1777

This morning we have heard again from the fleet. At nine o'clock at night on the 14th instant, upwards of a hundred sail were seen standing in between the Capes of Chesapeake Bay. They had been seen from the eastern shore of Virginia, standing off and on, for two days before. This method of coasting along the shore, and standing off and on, is very curious. First, seen off Egg Harbor, then several times off the Capes of Delaware, standing in and out, then off Sinnepuxent, then off the eastern shore of Virginia, then standing in to Chesapeake Bay. How many men and horses will he lose in this sea ramble in the heat of dog-days? Whether he is going to Virginia to steal tobacco, to North Carolina to pilfer pitch and tar, or to South Carolina to plunder rice and indigo, who can tell? He will seduce a few negroes from their masters, let him go to which he will. But is this conquering America?

From the northward we learn that Arnold has marched with about two thousand men to the relief of Fort Schuyler. Our people have given Sir John Johnson, and his regulars, Tories, and Indians, a very fine drubbing. The Indians scarcely ever had such a mauling. The devils are so frightened that they are all run away to howl and mourn. The papers inclosed with this will give you more particular information. Can nothing be done at Rhode Island at this critical time? Opprobrium Novangliae! What is become of all the Massachusetts Continental troops? Every regiment and every man of them is at the northward under Gates, and yet we are told they have not four thousand men fit for duty, officers included. And there are three regiments there from New Hampshire, too.

10 o'clock at night

Just come in from Congress. We have within this hour received letters of General Schuyler and Lincoln, giving an account of the battle of Bennington, wherein General Stark[1] has acquired great glory, and so have his militia. The particulars are to be out in a hand-bill to-morrow morning. I will inclose you one.

201. JOHN ADAMS

Philadelphia, 23 August 1777

It is now no longer a secret where Mr. Howe's fleet is. We have authentic intelligence that it is arrived at the head of Chesapeake Bay, above the river Patapsco, upon which the town of Baltimore stands. I wish I could describe to you the geography of this country, so as to give you an adequate idea of the situation of the two great bays of Chesapeake and Delaware, because it would enable you to form a conjecture concerning the object he aims at. The distance across land from the heads of these bays is but small, and forms an isthmus, below which is a large peninsula, comprehending the counties of Accomac and Northampton in Virginia, the counties of Somerset and Worcester in Maryland, and the counties of Kent and Sussex in Delaware. His march by land to Philadelphia may be about sixty or seventy miles. I think there can be no doubt that he aims at this place, and he has taken this voyage of six weeks, long enough to have gone to London, merely to avoid an army in his rear. He found he could not march this way from Somerset Court House without leaving General Washington in his rear. We have called out the militia of Virginia, Maryland, Delaware, and Pennsylvania to oppose him, and General Washington is handy enough to meet him; and as General Washington saved Philadelphia last winter by crossing the Delaware and marching to Morristown and so getting in the rear of Howe, so, I conjecture, he will still find means to get in his rear between him and Chesapeake Bay. You may now sit under your own vine and have none to make you afraid. I sent off my man and horse at an unlucky time, but if we should be obliged to remove from hence, we shall not go far.

If Congress had deliberated and debated a month, they could not have concerted a plan for Mr. Howe more to our advantage than that which he has adopted. He gives us an opportunity of exerting the strength of all the middle States against him, while

New York and New England are destroying Burgoyne. Now is the time! Never was so good an opportunity for my countrymen to turn out and crush that vaporing, blustering bully to atoms.

202. JOHN ADAMS

Philadelphia, Saturday, 23 August 1777, 4 o'clock

We have an express to-day from Governor Johnson, Captain Nicholson,[1] and several other gentlemen, with an account that the fleet, to the number of two hundred and sixty-three sail, have gone up towards the head of Chesapeake Bay. They lie over against the shore between the river Sassafras and the river Elk. We have also a letter from General Washington, acquainting us that to-morrow morning at seven o'clock he shall march his army through the city of Philadelphia, along Front Street, and then turn up Chestnut Street in his way to cross over the bridge at Schuylkill River; so that General Howe will have a grand Continental army to oppose him, in very good season, aided by a formidable collection of militia. I like this movement of the General through the city. Such a show of artillery, wagons, light horse, and infantry, which takes up a line of nine or ten miles upon their march, and will not be less than five or six hours passing through the town, will make a good impression upon the minds of the timorous Whigs for their confirmation; upon the cunning Quakers for their restraint; and upon the rascally Tories for their confusion.

I think there is a reasonable ground for confidence, with the favor of Heaven, that Howe will not be able to reach this city. Yet I really doubt whether it would not be more for our interest that he should come here, and get possession of the town.

1. Because there are impurities here which will never be so soon or so fully purged away as by that fire of affliction which Howe enkindles wherever he goes.

2. Because it would employ nearly the whole of his force to keep possession of this town, and the rest of the continent would be more at liberty.

3. We could counteract him here, better than in many other places.

4. He would leave New England and New York at leisure to kill or catch Burgoyne.

In all events you may rejoice and sing, for the season is so far gone that he cannot remove to you.

203. JOHN ADAMS

Philadelphia, 24 August 1777

MY DEAREST FRIEND,—We had, last evening, a thunder-gust very sharp and violent, attended with a plentiful rain. The lightning struck in several places. It struck the Quaker alms-house in Walnut Street, between Third and Fourth Streets, not far from Captain Duncan's, where I lodge. They had been wise enough to place an iron rod upon the top of the steeple, for a vane to turn on, and had provided no conductor to the ground. It also struck in Fourth Street, near Mrs. Cheesman's. No person was hurt.

This morning was fair, but now it is overcast and rains very hard, which will spoil our show and wet the army.

12 o'clock

The rain ceased, and the army marched through the town between seven and ten o'clock. The wagons went another road. Four regiments of light horse, Bland's, Baylor's, Sheldon's, and Moylan's. Four grand divisions of the army, and the artillery with the matrosses. They marched twelve deep, and yet took up above two hours in passing by. General Washington and the other general officers with their aides on horseback. The Colonels and other field-officers on horseback. We have now an army well appointed between us and Mr. Howe, and this army will be im-mediately joined by ten thousand militia, so that I feel as secure here as if I was at Braintree, but not so happy. My happiness is nowhere to be found but there.

After viewing this fine spectacle and firm defense, I went to Mr. Duffield's meeting to hear him pray, as he did most fervently, and I believe he was most sincerely joined by all present, for its success.

The army, upon an accurate inspection of it, I find to be ex-

tremely well armed, pretty well clothed, and tolerably disciplined. Gill and Town,[1] by the motto to their newspapers, will
bring discipline into vogue in time. There is such a mixture of the
sublime and the beautiful together with the useful in military discipline, that I wonder every officer we have is not charmed with
it. Much remains yet to be done. Our soldiers have not yet quite
the air of soldiers. They don't step exactly in time. They don't
hold up their heads quite erect, nor turn out their toes so exactly
as they ought. They don't all of them cock their hats; and such
as do, don't all wear them the same way.

A disciplinarian has affixed to him commonly the ideas of cruelty, severity, tyranny, etc., but if I were an officer, I am convinced I should be the most decisive disciplinarian in the army. I
am convinced there is no other effective way of indulging benevolence, humanity, and the tender social passions in an army.
There is no other way of preserving the health and spirits of the
men. There is no other way of making them active and skillful in
war; no other way of guarding an army against destruction by
surprises, and no other method of giving them confidence in one
another, of making them stand by one another in the hour of
battle. Discipline in an army is like the laws in civil society.
There can be no liberty, in a commonwealth where the laws are
not revered and most sacredly observed, nor can there be happiness or safety in an army for a single hour where the discipline is
not observed.

Obedience is the only thing wanting now for our salvation.
Obedience to the laws in the States, and obedience to officers in
the army.

12 o'clock

No express nor accidental news from Maryland to-day, as yet.

204. JOHN ADAMS

Philadelphia, 25 August 1777

Yours of August 12th and 13th came by this morning's post. A
letter from Chesapeake Bay, dated yesterday morning, informs
that the enemy had not then landed. This morning, General

Nash,[1] with his brigade of North Carolina forces, marched
through the town with their band of music, their train of artillery, and their baggage wagons, their bread wagons, travelling
forges, etc. General Washington's army encamped last night at
Derby. Sullivan's division is expected along in two days. Our intelligence of the fleet has been as good as could be expected.
They have been six weeks at sea.

If our people do not now turn out and destroy Burgoyne's
gang, root and branch, they may justly be reproached as lost to
honor and to virtue. He is completely in our power. Gates writes
to Congress that Burgoyne is lessened twelve hundred men by
the Bennington action.

205. JOHN ADAMS

Philadelphia, Tuesday, 26 August 1777

Howe's army, at least about five thousand of them, besides his
light horse, are landed upon the banks of the Elk River, and the
disposition he has made of his forces indicates a design to rest
and refresh both men and horses. General Washington was at
Wilmington last night, and his army is there to-day. The militia
are turning out with great alacrity both in Maryland and Pennsylvania. They are distressed for want of arms. Many have none,
others have only little fowling-pieces. However, we shall rake and
scrape enough to do Howe's business, by the favor of Heaven.

Howe must have intended that Washington should have sent
his army up to fight Burgoyne. But he is disappointed. The kindness of Heaven towards us has in nothing appeared more conspicuous than in this motion of Howe. If the infatuation is not so
universal as to seize Americans as well as him, it will prove the
certain destruction of Burgoyne's army. The New England troops
and New York troops are every man of them at Peekskill and
with Gates. The Massachusetts men are all with Gates. General
Washington has none but southern troops with him, and he has
much the largest army to encounter.

If my countrymen do not now turn out and do something, I
shall be disappointed indeed. One fifth part of Burgoyne's army

has been totally destroyed by Stark and Herkimer. The remainder must be shocked and terrified at the stroke. Now is the time to strike. New England men, strike home!

206. JOHN ADAMS

Philadelphia, Friday, 29 August 1777

The newspapers inclosed will give you all the intelligence of any consequence. General Washington, with a very numerous army, is between Wilmington and the Head of Elk. Howe will make but a pitiful figure. The militia of four States are turning out with much alacrity and cheerful spirits. The Continental army under Washington, Sullivan, and Nash, besides, is in my opinion more numerous by several thousands than Howe's whole force. I am afraid that he will be frightened, and run on board his ships, and go away plundering to some other place. I almost wish he had Philadelphia, for then he could not get away. I really think it would be the best policy to retreat before him, and let him into this snare, where his army must be ruined. However, this policy will not be adopted.

In a letter from good authority, Mr. Paca,[1] we are informed that many dead horses have been driven on the eastern shore of Maryland; horses thrown overboard from the fleet, no doubt.

Prices current. Four pounds a week for board, besides finding your own washing, shaving, candles, liquors, pipes, tobacco, wood, etc. Thirty shillings a week for a servant. It ought to be thirty shillings for a gentleman and four pounds for the servant, because he generally eats twice as much and makes twice as much trouble. Shoes, five dollars a pair. Salt, twenty-seven dollars a bushel. Butter, ten shillings a pound. Punch, twenty shillings a bowl. All the old women and young children are gone down to the Jersey shore to make salt. Salt water is boiling all round the coast, and I hope it will increase. For it is nothing but heedlessness and shiftlessness that prevents us from making salt enough for a supply. But necessity will bring us to it. As to sugar, molasses, rum, etc., we must leave them off. Whiskey is used here instead of rum, and I don't see but it is just as good. Of this the wheat and rye countries can easily distill enough for the use of the country. If I could get cider I would be content.

The business of the country has been in so critical and dangerous a situation for the last twelve months that it was necessary the Massachusetts should have a full representation, but the expenses of living are grown so enormous that I believe it will be necessary to reduce the number of delegates to three, after the campaign is over.

207. JOHN ADAMS

Philadelphia, Saturday, 30 August 1777

A letter from General Washington was received last night by the President, which I read. It is dated the 29th, yesterday.

The enemy are in possession of the Head of Elk, a little town at the head of the river Elk, in which they found a quantity of corn and oats belonging to the States. Wagons were so universally taken up in conveying away the valuable effects of the inhabitants, that none could be proccured to transport this grain. Part of their army has advanced to Gray's Hill, about two miles from the Head of Elk, but whether to take post there, or only to cover while they remove their plunder from the Head of Elk, is uncertain.

Our army is at Wilmington. We have many officers out reconnoitering the country and the enemy. Our scouting parties have taken between thirty and forty prisoners, and twelve deserters are come in from the fleet and eight from the army. They say the men are generally healthy, but their horses have suffered much from the voyage. These prisoners and deserters are unable to give any other intelligence. The enemy give out that they are eighteen thousand strong. But these are like Burgoyne's "make believes" and "insinuations." We know better, and that they have not ten thousand. The militia from four States are joining General Washington in large numbers. The plan of their military operations this campaign is well calculated for our advantage. I hope we shall have heads and hearts to improve it.

For my own part I feel a secret wish that they might get into this city, because I think it more for our interest that they should be cooped up here than that they should run away again to New York. But according to present appearances they will not be able to get here. By going into the Chesapeake Bay they have betrayed a dread of the fire-works in the river Delaware, which indeed are formidable. They must make the most of their time, for they cannot rationally depend upon so fine a season late in the fall and early in winter as they had the last year. September, October, and November are all that remain.

We expect, hourly, advices from Gates and Arnold. We have rumors of an expedition to Long Island under Parsons, and another to Staten Island under Sullivan, but no regular accounts. I suppose it certain that such expeditions have been made, but know not the success.

208. JOHN ADAMS

Philadelphia, Monday, 1 September 1777

We have now run through the summer, and although the weather is still warm, the fiercest of the heat is over. And although the extreme intemperance of the late season has weakened and exhausted me much, yet I think, upon the whole, I have got through it as well as upon any former occasion.

A letter from General Washington, dated Saturday, informs that our light parties have brought in four-and-twenty prisoners more. So that the prisoners and deserters since Mr. Howe landed are near a hundred. The question now is, whether there will be a general engagement. In the first place, I think after all that has passed, it is not good policy for us to attack them, unless we can get a favorable advantage of them in the situation of the ground, or an opportunity to attack a detachment of their army with superior numbers. It would be imprudent, perhaps, for us with our whole force to attack them with all theirs.

But another question arises, whether Mr. Howe will not be able to compel us to a general engagement. Perhaps he may; but I make a question of it. Washington will manoeuvre it with him a good deal to avoid it. A general engagement, in which Howe should be defeated, would be ruin to him. If we should be defeated, his army would be crippled, and perhaps we might suddenly reinforce our army, which he could not. However, all that he could gain by a victory would be the possession of this town, which would be the worst situation he could be in, because it would employ his whole force by sea and land to keep it and the command of the river.

Their principal dependence is not upon their arms, I believe, so much as upon the failure of our revenue. They think they have taken such measures by circulating counterfeit bills, to depreciate the currency, that it cannot hold its credit longer than this campaign. But they are mistaken.

We, however, must disappoint them by renouncing all luxuries, and by a severe economy. General Washington sets a fine example. He has banished wine from his table, and entertains his friends with rum and water. This is much to the honor of his wisdom, his policy, and his patriotism. And the example must be followed by banishing sugar and all imported articles from our families. If necessity should reduce us to a simplicity of dress and diet becoming republicans, it would be a happy and glorious necessity.

Yours, yours, yours.

209. JOHN ADAMS

Philadelphia, Tuesday, 2 September 1777

I had, yesterday, the pleasure of yours of ———, from Boston, and am happy to find that you have been able to do so well amidst all your difficulties. There is but one course for us to take, and that is to renounce the use of all foreign commodities. For my own part, I never lived in my whole life so meanly and poorly as I do now, and yet my constituents will growl at my extravagance. Happy should I be indeed, if I could share with you in the produce of your little farm. Milk, and apples, and pork, and beef, and the fruits of the garden would be luxury to me.

We had nothing yesterday from the General. Howe's army are in a very unwholesome situation. Their water is very bad and brackish. There are frequent morning and evening fogs, which produce intermittent fevers in abundance. Washington has a great body of militia assembled and assembling, in addition to a grand Continental army. Whether he will strike or not, I can't say. He is very prudent, you know, and will not unnecessarily hazard his army. By my own inward feelings, I judge, I should put more to risk if I were in his shoes, but perhaps he is right. Gansevoort has proved that it is possible to hold a post. Herkimer has shown that it is possible to fight Indians, and Stark has proved that it is practicable even to attack lines and posts with militia. I wish the Continental army would prove that anything can be done. But this is sedition at least. I am weary, however, I own, with so much insipidity.

St. Leger[1] and his party have run away. So will Burgoyne. I wish Stark had the supreme command in the northern department. I am sick of Fabian[2] systems in all quarters. The officers drink, A long and moderate war. My toast is, A short and violent war. They would call me mad and rash, etc., but I know better. I am as cool as any of them, and cooler too, for my mind is not inflamed with fear nor anger, whereas I believe theirs are with both. If this letter should be intercepted and published, it would do as much good as another did two years ago.

210. JOHN ADAMS

Philadelphia, Monday, 8 September 1777

There has been a very general apprehension during the last week, that a general action would happen as on yesterday, but we hear of none. Our army is encamped between Newport and White Clay Creek, on advantageous ground. The General has harangued his army, and published in general orders, in order to prepare their minds for something great, and has held up the example of Stark, Herkimer, Gansevoort, and their troops to animate his officers and men with emulation. Whether he expects to be attacked, or whether he designs to offend, I can't say.

A general action which should terminate in a defeat of Howe would be complete and final ruin to him. If it should terminate only in a drawn battle, it would be the same thing. If he should gain a victory and maintain possession of the field, he would lose so many men killed and wounded that he would scarcely have enough left to march to Philadelphia, surrounded as he would be with militia and the broken remains of the Continental army. But if there should be no general battle, and the two armies should lounge away the remainder of the campaign in silent inactivity, gazing at each other, Howe's reputation would be ruined in his own country and in all Europe, and the dread of him would cease in all America. The American mind, which, I think, has more firmness now than it ever had before, since this war began, would acquire a confidence and strength that all the efforts of Great Britain afterwards would not be able to relax.

You will see by the papers inclosed that we have been obliged to attempt to humble the pride of some Jesuits who call themselves Quakers,[1] but who love money and land better than liberty and religion. The hypocrites are endeavoring to raise the cry of persecution, and to give this matter a religious turn, but they can't succeed. The world knows them and their communications. Actuated by a land-jobbing spirit like that of William Penn, they have been soliciting grants of immense regions of land on the Ohio. American independence has disappointed them, which makes them hate it. Yet the dastards dare not avow their hatred to it, it seems.

The moments are critical here. We know not but the next will bring us an account of a general engagement begun, and when once begun, we know not how it will end, for the battle is not always to the strong. The events of war are uncertain. All that we can do is to pray, as I do most devoutly, that we may be victorious; at least, that we may not be vanquished. But if it should be the will of Heaven that our army should be defeated, our artillery lost, our best generals killed, and Philadelphia fall into Mr. Howe's hands, still America is not conquered. America would yet be possessed of great resources, and, capable of great exertions, as mankind would see. It may for what I know, be the design of Providence that this should be the case. Because it would only lay the foundations of American independence deeper, and cement them stronger. It would cure Americans of their vicious and luxurious and effeminate appetites, passions, and habits, a more dangerous army to American liberty than Mr. Howe's.

However, without the loss of Philadelphia we must be brought to an entire renunciation of foreign commodities, at least of West India produce. People are coming to this resolution very fast here. Loaf sugar at four dollars a pound, wine at three dollars a bottle, etc., will soon introduce economy in the use of these articles. This spirit of economy would be more terrible to Great Britain than anything else, and it would make us more respectable in the eyes of all Europe. Instead of acrimonious altercations between town and country, and between farmer and merchant, I wish that my dear countrymen would agree in this virtuous resolution of depending on themselves alone. Let them make salt and live without sugar and rum.

I am grieved to hear of the angry contentions among you. That improvident act for limiting prices has done great injury, and in my sincere opinion, if not repealed, will ruin the State and introduce a civil war. I know not how unpopular this sentiment may be, but it is sincerely mine. There are rascally upstarts in trade, I doubt not, who have made great fortunes in a small period, who are monopolizing and oppressing. But how this can be avoided entirely, I know not, but by disusing their goods and letting them perish in their hands.

211. JOHN ADAMS

Philadelphia, 14 September 1777

You will learn from the newspapers, before this reaches you, the situation of things here. Mr. Howe's army is at Chester,[1] about fifteen miles from this town. General Washington's is over the Schuylkill, awaiting the flank of Mr. Howe's army.

How much longer Congress will stay is uncertain. I hope we shall not move until the last necessity, that is, until it shall be rendered certain that Mr. Howe will get the city. If we should move, it will be to Reading, Lancaster, York, Easton, or Bethlehem, some town in this State. It is the determination not to leave this State. Don't be anxious about me, nor about our great and sacred cause. It is the cause of truth and will prevail. If Howe gets the city, it will cost him all his force to keep it, and so he can get nothing else.

My love to all friends.

212. ABIGAIL ADAMS

17 September 1777

I have to acknowledge a feast of letters from you since I wrote last; their dates from August 19th to September 1st. It is a very great satisfaction to me to know from day to day the movement of Howe and his banditti. We live in hourly expectation of important intelligence from both armies. Heaven grant us victory and peace; two blessings, I fear, we are very undeserving of.

Inclosed you will find a letter to Mr. Lovell, who was so obliging as to send me a plan of that part of the country which is like to be the present seat of war. He accompanied it with a very polite letter, and I esteem myself much obliged to him; but there is no reward this side the grave that would be a temptation to me to undergo the agitation and distress I was thrown into by receiving a letter in his handwriting, franked by him. It seems almost impossible that the human mind could take in, in so small a space of time, so many ideas as rushed upon mine in the space of a moment. I cannot describe to you what I felt.

The sickness or death of the dearest of friends, with ten thousand horrors, seized my imagination. I took up the letter, then laid it down, then gave it out of my hand unable to open it, then collected resolution enough to unseal it but dared not read it; began at the bottom,—read a line,—then attempted to begin it, but could not. A paper was inclosed; I ventured upon that, and finding it a plan, recovered enough to read the letter; but I pray Heaven I may never realize such another moment of distress.

I designed to have written you a long letter, for really I owe you one, but have been prevented by our worthy Plymouth friends, who are here upon a visit, in their way home; and it is now so late at night, just struck twelve, that I will defer anything further till the next post. Good night, friend of my heart, companion of my youth, husband, and lover. Angels watch thy repose!

213. ABIGAIL ADAMS

21 September

I imagine before this reaches you some very important event must take place between the two armies. Affairs on all sides seem to be worked up to a crisis. Howe is putting his whole force in action, and seems determined to drive or be driven.

I feel in a most painful situation between hope and fear. There must be fighting, and very bloody battles too, I apprehend. How my heart recoils at the idea. Why is man called *humane,* when he delights so much in blood, slaughter, and devastation. Even those who are styled civilized nations think this little spot worth contending for even to blood.

23 September

We have confused accounts of a battle at the northward,[1] last Friday, in which the enemy were put to flight. God grant it may prove true. Vigorous exertions now on all sides may prove of the most happy consequence and terminate this cruel war. I long for a decisive battle and for peace, an honorable peace. I hope the enemy are as much in our power as you fancy them.

24 September

Have just read a handbill giving a particular account of the engagement at the northward. You will have it long before this reaches you. The loss of Ticonderoga has awakened the sleeping genius of America, and called forth all her martial fire. May it never again be lulled to rest till crowned with victory and peace. Good officers will make good soldiers. Xanthippus, the Lacedaemonian General, who had been educated in the discipline of Sparta and had learned the art of war in that renowned and excellent school, when he was called to assist the Carthaginians, who had been defeated in several battles against the Romans, declared publicly, and repeated it often in the hearing of their officers, that the misfortunes of the Carthaginians were owing entirely to the incapacity of their Generals; and he proved clearly to the council that by a conduct opposite to the former, they would not only secure their dominions, but drive the enemy out of them. Upon his accepting the command of the Carthaginians, the gloomy consternation (says Rollin) which had before seized the whole army was succeeded by joy and alacrity. The soldiers were urgent to be led against the enemy, in the firm assurance of being victorious under their new leader and of obliterating the disgrace of former defeats. Xanthippus did not suffer their ardor to cool, but led them on to battle, and entirely routed and defeated the Romans, making Regulus their prisoner. That General, who a few days before was insolent with victory, inexorable to the conquered, and deaf to all their remonstrances, in a few days experienced by the fate of war a sad reverse of fortune.

This is a case, I think, very similar to our own. May it prove so in the end! "There are two ways," says Rollin, "of acquiring improvement and instruction: first, by one's own experience, and secondly, by that of other men. It is much more wise and useful to improve by other men's miscarriages than by our own."

We have not yet received any intelligence from the southern army since the account of the engagement on the 11th, which must have been very severe upon both sides. You now experience what we suffered when the army lay this way. I feel very anxious for their success. The suspense which the distance occasions is painful, but still I find very different sensations between having the enemy at such a distance and having them in my own neighborhood. I hope you will all look to your own safety. As you are not called to action, kidnapping would be rather disagreeable, but were you in the army I should despise myself for such a sentiment,—as much as I did a certain gentleman who was in the horrors a few days ago upon hearing that General Washington had retreated to within six miles of Philadelphia. If Howe should get possession of that city, it would immediately negotiate a peace. I could not help warmly replying that I did not believe it, even though that should be the case, and the General with his whole army should be cut off. I hoped then that an army of women would oppose him. Was it not the Saracens who turned their backs upon the enemy, and were slain by their women, who were placed behind them for that purpose?

Your favors of the 2d and 8th reached me upon the 20th. Your observations with regard to luxury are just, but trade and commerce will always support it. The necessity of the time will be a temporary restraint upon it, and put us upon seeking resources among ourselves. An instance of that may be seen in the progress which is made in grinding cornstalks and boiling the liquor into molasses. Scarcely a town or parish within forty miles of us but what has several mills at work; and had the experiment been made a month sooner, many thousand barrels would have been made. No less than eighty have been made in the small town of Manchester. It answers very well to distill, and may be boiled down to sugar. There are two mills fitting up in this parish. They have three rollers, one with cogs and two smooth. The stalks are stripped of the leaves and tops, so that it is no robbery upon the cattle, and the juice ground out. 'Tis said four barrels of juice will make one of molasses, but in this, people differ widely. They have a method of refining it so that it looks as well as the best imported molasses.

Thus you see we go from step to step in our improvements. We can live much better than we deserve within ourselves. Why should we borrow foreign luxuries? Why should we wish to bring ruin upon ourselves? I feel as contented when I have break-fasted upon milk as ever I did with Hyson or Souchong. Coffee and sugar I use only as a rarity. There are none of these things but I could totally renounce. My dear friend knows that I could always conform to times and circumstances. As yet I know nothing of hardships. My children have never cried for bread nor been destitute of clothing. Nor have the poor and needy gone empty from my door, whenever it was in my power to assist them.

Heaven grant that I may continue to receive its blessings. One of its greatest is that I can subscribe myself wholly yours.

214. JOHN ADAMS

Yorktown, Pennsylvania, Tuesday, 30 September 1777

It is now a long time since I had an opportunity of writing to you, and I fear you have suffered unnecessary anxiety on my account. In the morning of the 19th instant, the Congress were alarmed in their beds by a letter from Mr. Hamilton, one of General Washington's family, that the enemy was in possession of the ford over the Schuylkill and the boats, so that they had it in their power to be in Philadelphia before morning. The papers of Congress belonging to the Secretary's office, the War office, the Treasury office, etc., were before sent to Bristol. The President and all the other gentlemen were gone that road, so I followed with my friend Mr. Marchant,[1] of Rhode Island, to Trenton, in the Jerseys. We stayed at Trenton until the 21st, when we set off to Easton, upon the forks of Delaware. From Easton we went to Bethlehem, from thence to Reading, from thence to Lancaster, and from thence to this town, which is about a dozen miles over the Susquehanna River. Here Congress is to sit. In order to convey the papers with safety, which are of more importance than all the members, we were induced to take this circuit, which is near a hundred and eighty miles, whereas this town, by the direct road, is not more than eighty-eight miles from Philadelphia. This tour has given me an opportunity of seeing many parts of this country which I never saw before.

This morning Major Troup[2] arrived here with a large packet from General Gates, containing very agreeable intelligence, which I need not repeat, as you have much earlier intelligence from that part than we have. I wish affairs here wore as pleasing an aspect. But alas, they do not.

I shall avoid everything like history, and make no reflections. However, General Washington is in a condition tolerably respectable, and the militia are now turning out from Virginia, Maryland, and Pennsylvania, in small numbers. All the apology that can be made for this part of the world is that Mr. Howe's march from Elk to Philadelphia was through the very regions of passive obedience. The whole country through which he passed is inhabited by Quakers. There is not such another body of Quakers in all America, perhaps not in all the world.

I am still of opinion that Philadelphia will be no loss to us. I am very comfortably situated here in the house of General Roberdeau,[3] whose hospitality has taken in Mr. S. Adams, Mr. Gerry, and me. My health is as good as common, and I assure you my spirits not the worse for the loss of Philadelphia. Biddle in the Continental frigate,[4] at South Carolina, has made a noble cruise and taken four very valuable prizes.

215. ABIGAIL ADAMS

Sunday, 6 October 1777

I know not where to direct to you, but hope you are secure; 'tis said in some part of the Jerseys, but I know this only from report. I sent to town yesterday, but the post did not get in before the person whom I sent came out of town. I could not rest, but sent again this morning. The post came but brought no letters for me, and but two for any person that I could learn, and no late intelligence.

To the removal of the Congress I attribute my not hearing, but I never was more anxious to hear. I want to know every movement of the armies. Mr. Niles, by whom I send this, sets off tomorrow and promises to find you and deliver this into your hand. I doubt not you will let me hear from you by the first conveyance. Tell me where you are, how you are situated, and how you do. Whether your spirits are good, and what you think of the present state of our arms. Will Mr. Howe get possession of the city? 'Tis a day of doubtful expectation. Heaven only knows our destiny. I observe often in the account of actions that our men are obliged to retreat for want of ammunition. Their cartridges are spent. How is this? Is it good generalship? We never hear of that complaint in the regular army.

There is a private expedition,[1] 'tis said. The troops have all marched last Monday. I own I have no great faith in it. I wish it may succeed better than I apprehend.

No news of any importance from the northward. I long for spirited exertions everywhere. I want some grand, important actions to take place. We have both armies from their shipping. 'Tis what we have long sought for. Now is the important day. Heaven seems to have granted us our desire. May it also direct us to improve it aright.

We are all well. I write nothing of any importance till I know where you are and how to convey to you.

Believe me at all times unalterably   Yours, yours.

216. JOHN ADAMS

Yorktown, 7 October 1777

I have no time nor accommodation to write of late; besides, I seldom know what to write, and when I do, I don't love to write it. One thing is now becoming more and more certain every day, that is, that our people will and do fight. And although they make a clumsy hand of it, yet they do better and better.

I am lodged in the house of General Roberdeau, an Israelite indeed, I believe, who with his sisters and children and servants does everything to make us happy. We are highly favored. No other delegates are so well off. I am as well as usual. Your dream will never come to pass. You never can be coolly received by me while my heart beats and my senses remain.

I had no letter from you by the last post.

Yours, yours, yours,   JOHN ADAMS

217. JOHN ADAMS

Yorktown, 15 October 1777

I have not been able of late to keep up my correspondence with you so constantly as my heart inclined me to do. But I hope now to write you oftener; but I don't incline to write very particularly, lest my letters should be intercepted. I am in tolerable health, but oppressed with a load of public cares. I have long foreseen that we should be brought down to a great degree of depression before the people of America would be convinced of their real danger, of the true causes of it, and be stimulated to take the necessary steps for a reformation. Government and law in the States, large taxation, and strict discipline in our armies are the only things wanting as human means. These with the blessing of Heaven will certainly produce glory, triumph, liberty and safety, and peace, and nothing but these will do.

I long with the utmost impatience to come home. Don't send a servant for me. The expense is so enormous that I cannot bear the thought of it. I will crawl home upon my little pony, and wait upon myself as well as I can. I think you had better sell my horse.

The people are universally calling for fighting and for blood. Washington is getting into the humor of fighting, and Howe begins to dread it. And well he may. Fighting will certainly answer the end, although we may be beaten every time for a great while. We have been heretofore greatly deceived concerning the numbers of militia. But there are numbers enough, if they knew how to fight, which as soon as their Generals will let them, they will learn.

218. ABIGAIL ADAMS

20 October 1777

'Tis true, my dearest friend, that I have spent an anxious three weeks, and the sight of a letter from you gave me joy beyond expression. I had sent every post day, and every post was disappointed. I could not learn one word with certainty. Nor can I now determine whether you are eighty-eight miles nearer to me, or farther off than you were before.

I was greatly surprised when I heard that the enemy was in possession of Philadelphia, without any engagement on our part. If men will not fight and defend their own particular spot, if they will not drive the enemy from their doors, they deserve the slavery and subjection which awaits them. There is much, I think, comprised in that short sentence, "I shall avoid all history and make no reflections." I think I can construe a volume from it. I will follow the example, lest a miscarriage of this should give triumph to an enemy.

Our affairs at the northward wear a more pleasing aspect. The sunshine from the north gilds the dark clouds of the south, or the storm would look dismal indeed.

It is a New England observation that in some late general orders, when many motives and stimulatives were set before the men to excite them to action, they were assured of conquest without once acknowledging the superintendence of Divine Providence.

Our favorite Dr. Tillotson observes that "in all our concernments we ought to have a particular regard to the Supreme Disposer of all things, and earnestly to seek his favor and blessing upon all our undertakings, but more especially in the affairs of war, in which the providence of God is pleased many times in a very peculiar manner to interpose and interest itself, because all war is as it were an appeal to God, and a reference of those causes to the decision of His providence which through pride and injustice and perverse passions of men can receive no other determination."

'Tis not more than three weeks since I thought our affairs looked in a more prosperous train than they had done since the commencement of the war. Though they have not taken the turn I hoped for, yet I doubt not they will finally terminate in our favor. Providence for wise purpose has oftentimes since the commencement of this war brought about our deliverance by ways and means which have appeared to us the most improbable and unlikely; has given into our hands those things which we were destitute of, and in the greatest necessity for. So true it is, Acknowledge Him in all thy ways and He shall direct thy paths.

To you, my dear friend, I need not excuse these moral reflections. I have ever considered it as a happiness to be united to one whose sentiments in religion were not only agreeable to my own, but to what I have ever esteemed the truth.

22 October

I believe I may venture to congratulate my love upon the completion of his wishes with regard to Burgoyne. 'Tis reported today from many ways that he has with his whole army fallen into our hands, and 'tis said the post brings the same intelligence. If true, as I most sincerely hope, let us with gratitude acknowledge the interposition of Heaven in our favor.

We have, too, accounts of an engagement at the southward. I am glad to hear of fighting, even though we come off second-best; not because, Heaven is my witness, that I delight in the effusion of human blood, but because I believe by delay we should lose more lives than by the sword. It sinks our spirits, disheartens our soldiers, makes them both idle and wicked. How great would be my joy could I see peace and quietness once more restored to this distressed land,—

> "Peace o'er this land her olive branch extend,
> And white rob'd innocence from heaven descend."[1]

It gave me great pleasure to hear of your health and spirits. Did you save your clothes, or have they fallen into the hands of the enemy? We are all very well in the family. The whooping cough prevails much and is just coming into the family. I long for the month of your return to come. I wrote you with regard to Brackett but received no answer. You will let me know, and when to send. Dr. Tufts desires to know if you have received a letter from him within these two months; he fears that it did not reach you, as it was about the time of your removal. The spirit of barter and exchange predominates so much here that people dispose of their own bodies. Matrimony prevails among all orders and ages; the scarcity of the commodity enhances the value. Men are a very scarce article to be sure. Among the late marriages which have taken place, and are likely to, Miss Betsey Smith to Mr. Shaw last Thursday, old Deacon Webb of this town to a maiden sister of John Ruggles's wife, who has lived to the age of sixty-six unmarried, our friend Mrs. Lincoln of this town to Deacon Storer of Boston, an exceeding good match and much approved of. Numbers of others in the lower class not worth mentioning, but I ask my cousin Polly Smith's pardon for omitting her. She marries in about two months to a Mr. Gray, a brother of Mr. Ellis Gray's of Boston.

'Tis very cold for the season. We had snow yesterday and ice in the streets this morning. When shall I see my friend? 'Tis more than nine long months since we parted. Shall I send the beginning of December? Heaven grant us a joyful meeting.

Ever yours.

219. JOHN ADAMS

Yorktown, 24 October 1777

It is with shame that I recollect that I have not written you more than two or three letters these five weeks, and those very short. News I am afraid to write, because I never know, until it is too late, what is true. From last Sunday to this moment, Friday afternoon, four o'clock, we have been in a state of tormenting uncertainty concerning our affairs at the northward. On Sunday we had news from the committee of Albany, through Governor

Clinton and General Washington, of a capitulation of Burgoyne and his whole army. To this moment we have no express from Gates nor any authentic confirmation.

Howe has drawn his army into the city, and Washington is at Germantown. Supplies will be cut off from the British army in a great measure.

I am, etc., yours forever.

We shall finish a plan of Confederation in a few days.

220. JOHN ADAMS

Yorktown, 25 October 1777

This town is a small one, not larger than Plymouth. There are in it two German Churches, the one Lutheran, the other Calvinistical. The congregations are pretty numerous and their attendance upon public worship is decent. It is remarkable that the Germans, wherever they are found, are careful to maintain the public worship, which is more than can be said of the other denominations of Christians, this way. There is one Church here, erected by the joint contributions of Episcopalians and Presbyterians, but the minister, who is a missionary, is confined for Toryism, so that they have had for a long time no public worship. Congress have appointed two chaplains, Mr. White and Mr. Duffield, the former of whom, an Episcopalian, is arrived, and opens Congress with prayers every day. The latter is expected every hour. Mr. Duché, I am sorry to inform you, has turned out an apostate and a traitor. Poor man! I pity his weakness and detest his wickedness.

As to news, we are yet in a painful suspense about affairs at the northward, but from Philadelphia we have accounts that are very pleasing. Commodore Hazelwood with his galleys and Lieutenant-colonel Smith[1] in the garrison of Fort Mifflin have behaved in a manner the most gallant and glorious. They have defended the river and the fort with a firmness and perseverance which does honor to human nature. If the news from the northward is true, Mr. Howe will scarcely venture upon winter-quarters in Philadelphia. We are waiting for news from Rhode Island.

I am wearied with the life I lead, and long for the joys of my family. God grant I may enjoy it in peace. Peace is my dear delight. War has no charms for me. If I live much longer in banishment I shall scarcely know my own children. Tell my little ones that if they will be very good, papa will come home.

221. ABIGAIL ADAMS

Boston, 25 October 1777

The joyful news of the surrender of General Burgoyne and all his army, to our victorious troops, prompted me to take a ride this afternoon with my daughter to town, to join, to-morrow, with my friends in thanksgiving and praise to the Supreme Being who hath so remarkably delivered our enemies into our hands. And, hearing that an express is to go off to-morrow morning, I have retired to write you a few lines. I have received no letters from you since you left Philadelphia, by the post, and but one by any private hand. I have written you once before this. Do not fail of writing by the return of this express, and direct your letters to the care of my uncle, who has been a kind and faithful hand to me through the whole season, and a constant attendant upon the post-office.

Burgoyne is expected in by the middle of the week. I have read many articles of capitulation, but none which ever contained so generous terms before. Many people find fault with them, but perhaps do not consider sufficiently the circumstances of General Gates, who, by delaying and exacting more, might have lost all. This must be said of him, that he has followed the Golden Rule, and done as he would wish himself, in like circumstances, to be dealt with. Must not the vaporing Burgoyne, who, it is said, possesses great sensibility, be humbled to the dust? He may now write the "Blockade of Saratoga."[1] I have heard it proposed that he should take up his quarters in the Old South,[2] but believe he will not be permitted to come to this town. Heaven grant us success at the southward. That saying of Poor Richard often occurs to my mind, "God helps them who help themselves"; but if men turn their backs and run from an enemy, they cannot surely expect to conquer him.

This day, dearest of friends, completes thirteen years since we were solemnly united in wedlock. Three years of this time we have been cruelly separated. I have, patiently as I could, endured it, with the belief that you were serving your country and rendering your fellow-creatures essential benefits. May future generations rise up and call you blessed, and the present behave worthy of the blessings you are laboring to secure to them, and I shall have less reason to regret the deprivation of my own particular felicity. Adieu, dearest of friends, adieu.

222. JOHN ADAMS

Yorktown, 26 October 1777

Mr. Colman goes off for Boston to-morrow. I have seized a moment to congratulate you on the great and glorious success of our arms at the northward and in Delaware River. The forts at Province Island and Redbank have been defended with a magnanimity which will give our country a reputation in Europe. Colonel Greene[1] repulsed the enemy from Redbank and took Count Donop and his aide prisoners. Colonel Smith repulsed a bold attack upon Fort Mifflin, and our galleys disabled two men-of-war, a sixty-four and a twenty gun ship, in such a manner that the enemy blew them up. This comes confirmed this evening, in letters from General Washington, inclosing original letters from officers in the forts.

Congress will appoint a thanksgiving; and one cause of it ought to be that the glory of turning the tide of arms is not immediately due to the Commander-in-chief nor to southern troops. If it had been, idolatry and adulation would have been unbounded; so excessive as to endanger our liberties, for what I know. Now, we can allow a certain citizen[2] to be wise, virtuous, and good, without thinking him a deity or a savior.

223. JOHN ADAMS

Yorktown, 28 October 1777

We have been three days soaking and poaching in the heaviest rain that has been known for several years, and what adds to the gloom is the uncertainty in which we remain to this moment concerning the fate of Gates and Burgoyne. We are out of patience. It is impossible to bear this suspense with any temper.

I am in comfortable lodgings, which is a felicity that has fallen to the lot of a very few of our members. Yet the house where I am is so thronged that I cannot enjoy such accommodations as I wish. I cannot have a room as I used, and therefore cannot find opportunities to write as I once did.

The people of this country are chiefly Germans, who have schools in their own language, as well as prayers, psalms, and sermons, so that multitudes are born, grow up, and die here, without ever learning the English. In politics they are a breed of mongrels or neutrals, and benumbed with a general torpor. If the people in Pennsylvania, Maryland, Delaware, and Jersey had the feelings and the spirit of some people that I know, Howe would be soon ensnared in a trap more fatal than that in which, as it is said, Burgoyne was taken. Howe is completely in our power, and if he is not totally ruined it will be entirely owing to the awkwardness and indolence of this country. Fighting, however, begins to become fashionable. Colonel Greene has exhibited a glorious example in the defense of Red Bank. But this must be done by a New England man at the head of two New England regiments, Rhode Islanders. Colonel Smith, however, is a Marylander from Baltimore. He has shown another example of magnanimity which gives me the most agreeable hopes. Commodore Hazelwood, too, has behaved in a manner that exceeds all praise. This spirit will be caught by other officers, for bravery is epidemical and contagious as the plague. This army suffers much for want of blankets and shoes.

I celebrated the 25th of this month in my own mind and heart much more than I shall the 30th,[1] because I think the first a more fortunate day than the last. My duty to your father and my mother, to uncles and aunts. Love to brothers and sisters; but above all, present all the affection that words can express to our dear babes.

224. ABIGAIL ADAMS

16 November 1777

In a letter which came to me to-night you chide yourself for
neglecting to write so frequently as you had done. 'Tis true a
very long space of near a fortnight passed without hearing one
word from you. I cannot help feeling anxious when such a space
elapses without receiving a line, but I have no reason to complain. You have, considering your avocations, been more attentive than I had reason to expect.

> "Heaven sure taught letters for some wretch's aid,
> Some banished lover or some captive maid."[1]

I have been more fearful than formerly of writing by the post,
as I have never received a letter from you by that conveyance
since you left Philadelphia. Mr. Colman brought me yours of 25
and 26 October. You have before this time received from me one
of the same date, since which I have not written. I have been too
much mortified with a late expedition to write you any particulars concerning it. Indeed, it was from the beginning a subject of
burlesque, owing, I believe, to the small opinion most people
had of the heroic talents of the commanders. It was called a secret expedition to Newport. A fortnight before the troops
marched, there were by all accounts as fine a set collected as any
spirited commander could have wished for, and 'tis said for
twenty days the island might have been successfully (to all appearance) attacked. The public are very angry, as well they may
be, and demand an inquiry. I know you will be mortified, because it has been a favorite object with you, but if you want your
arms crowned with victory, you should not appoint what General Gates calls dreaming Deacons[2] to conduct them.

General Burgoyne and his troops arrived last week in Cambridge. All seems to be quietness at present. From the southward
we get no very authentic accounts. To-day Howe and his whole
army are captives! To-morrow they have got possession of our
forts and weighed the chevaux de frise.

No news at all. Our mountebank story of captivating Howe and his army is come to nothing. The southern troops must have some assistance from the northern before anything very brilliant will take place. Providence overrules things for the best, and will work out our salvation for us in the wisest and best manner, provided we perform our duty.

My brother has had the misfortune to be taken upon his return from a cruise up the Baltic. They had a valuable prize with them loaded with duck and cordage. He was captain of marines on board the *Tartar,* Captain Grimes, master, and was carried into Newfoundland, since which we have not heard from him.

Now, my dear friend, shall I ask you when you will return, a question I have not asked for these ten months? Knowing your determination when you left me, I have summoned patience and endeavored to submit to my destiny. By the time this reaches you eleven months will be elapsed, and you, I hope, preparing for your journey. It will be a tedious one, I fear, in the depth of winter but let the thought of the cordial reception you will be assured of meeting warm the cold wintry blasts and make your return joyful. You make no mention of receiving any letters from me for a long time. I hope none have miscarried. I must beg you would write whilst you continue absent. We have had very great rains this fall, and severe cold weather for the season. A flight of snow yesterday and to-day as cold as January.

Adieu.   Yours.

225. JOHN ADAMS

Portsmouth (N.H.), 15 December 1777

I arrived here last evening, in good health. This morning General Whipple made me a visit at the tavern, Tilton's, and insisted upon my taking a bed at his house, in so very affectionate and urgent a manner that I believe I shall go.

The cause comes on to-morrow[1] before my old friend Dr. Joshua Brackett, as Judge of Admiralty. How it will go, I know not. The captors are a numerous company, and are said to be very tenacious, and have many connections; so that we have prejudice and influence to fear. Justice, policy, and law are, I am sure, on our side.

I have had many opportunities, in the course of this journey, to observe how deeply rooted our righteous cause is in the minds of the people; and could write you many anecdotes in proof of it. But I will reserve them for private conversation.

On second thoughts, why should I? One evening, as I sat in one room, I overheard a company of the common sort of people in another, conversing upon serious subjects. One of them, whom I afterwards found upon inquiry to be a reputable, religious man, was more eloquent than the rest. He was upon the danger of despising and neglecting serious things, and said "whatever person or people made light of them would soon find themselves terribly mistaken." At length I heard these words: "It appears to me the eternal Son of God is operating powerfully against the British nation for their treating lightly serious things."

One morning I asked my landlady what I had to pay? "Nothing," she said, "I was welcome, and she hoped I would always make her house my home. And she should be happy to entertain all those gentlemen who had been raised up by Providence to be the saviors of their country." This was flattering enough to my vain heart. But it made a greater impression on me as a proof how deeply this cause had sunk into the minds and hearts of the people.

In short, everything I see and hear indicates the same thing.

226. JOHN ADAMS

Uncle Quincy's, half after 11 o'clock,
13 February 1778

DEAREST OF FRIENDS,—I had not been twenty minutes in this house before I had the happiness to see Captain Tucker[1] and a midshipman coming for me. We shall be soon on board, and may God prosper our voyage in every stage of it as much as at the beginning, and send to you, my dear children, and all my friends, the choicest of blessings! So wishes and prays, with an ardor that neither absence nor any other event can abate, yours.

JOHN ADAMS

P.S. Johnny sends his duty to his mamma and his love to his sister and brothers. He behaves like a man.

227. ABIGAIL ADAMS

8 March 1778

'Tis a little more than three weeks since the dearest of friends and tenderest of husbands left his solitary partner, and quitted all the fond endearments of domestic felicity for the dangers of the sea, exposed, perhaps, to the attack of a hostile foe, and, O good Heaven! can I add, to the dark assassin, to the secret murderer, and the bloody emissary of as cruel a tyrant as God, in his righteous judgments, ever suffered to disgrace the throne of Britain.

I have travelled with you over the wide Atlantic, and could have landed you safe, with humble confidence, at your desired haven, and then have set myself down to enjoy a negative kind of happiness in the painful part which it has pleased Heaven to allot me; but the intelligence with regard to that great philosopher, able statesman, and unshaken friend of his country, has planted a dagger in my breast, and I feel, with a double edge, the weapon that pierced the bosom of a Franklin.[1]

> "For nought avail the virtues of the heart,
>   Nor towering genius claims its due reward;
>   From Britain's fury, as from death's keen dart,
>   No worth can save us, and no fame can guard"

The more distinguished the person, the greater the inveteracy of these foes of human nature. The argument of my friends to alleviate my anxiety, by persuading me that this shocking attempt will put you more upon your guard and render your person more secure than if it had never taken place, is kind in them, and has some weight, but my greatest comfort and consolation arise from the belief of a superintending Providence, to whom I can with confidence commit you, since not a sparrow falls to the ground without his notice. Were it not for this, I should be miserable and overwhelmed by my fears and apprehensions.

Freedom of sentiment, the life and soul of friendship, is in a great measure cut off by the danger of miscarriage and the apprehension of letters falling into the hands of our enemies. Should this meet with that fate, may they blush for their connection with a nation who have rendered themselves infamous and abhorred by a long list of crimes, which not their high achievements, nor the lustre of former deeds, nor the tender appellation of parent, nor the fond connection which once subsisted, can ever blot from our remembrance, nor wipe out those indelible stains of their cruelty and baseness. They have engraven them with a pen of iron and lead on a rock forever.

To my dear son remember me in the most affectionate terms. I would have written to him, but my notice is so short that I have not time. Enjoin it upon him never to disgrace his mother, and to behave worthily of his father. Tender as maternal affection is, it was swallowed up in what I found a stronger, or so intermixed that I felt it not in its full force till after he had left me. I console myself with the hopes of his reaping advantages, under the careful eye of a tender parent, which it was not in my power to bestow upon him.

There has nothing material taken place in the political world since you left us. This letter will go by a vessel for Bilbao, from whence you may perhaps get better opportunities of conveyance than from any other place. The letter you delivered to the pilot came safe to hand. All the little folks are anxious for the safety of their papa and brother, to whom they desire to be remembered; to which are added the tenderest sentiments of affection, and the fervent prayers for your happiness and safety, of your

PORTIA

228. JOHN ADAMS

Passy, in France, 12 April 1778

I am so sensible of the difficulty of conveying letters safe to you, that I am afraid to write anything more than to tell you that after all the fatigues and dangers of my voyage and journey I am here in health.

The reception I have met in this kingdom has been as friendly, as polite, and as respectful as was possible. It is the universal opinion of the people here, of all ranks, that a friendship between France and America is the interest of both countries, and the late alliance, so happily formed, is universally popular; so much so, that I have been told by persons of good judgment that the government here would have been under a sort of necessity of agreeing to it, even if it had not been agreeable to themselves. The delights of France are innumerable. The politeness, the elegance, the softness, the delicacy, are extreme. In short, stern and haughty republican as I am, I cannot help loving these people for their earnest desire and assiduity to please.

It would be futile to attempt descriptions of this country, especially of Paris and Versailles. The public buildings and gardens, the paintings, sculpture, architecture, music, etc., of these cities have already filled many volumes. The richness, the magnificence and splendor are beyond all description. This magnificence is not confined to public buildings, such as Churches, hospitals, schools, etc., but extends to private houses, to furniture, equipage, dress, and especially to entertainments. But what is all this to me? I receive but little pleasure in beholding all these things, because I cannot but consider them as bagatelles, introduced by time and luxury in exchange for the great qualities and hardy, manly virtues of the human heart. I cannot help suspecting that the more elegance, the less virtue, in all times and countries. Yet I fear that even my own dear country wants the power and opportunity more than the inclination to be elegant, soft, and luxurious.

All the luxury I desire in this world is the company of my dearest friend, and my children, and such friends as they delight in, which I have sanguine hopes I shall, after a few years, enjoy in peace. I am, with inexpressible affection,

Yours, yours,   JOHN ADAMS

229. JOHN ADAMS

Passy, 25 April 1778

Monsieur Chaumont[1] has just informed me of a vessel bound to Boston, but I am reduced to such a moment of time that I can only inform you, that I am well, and inclose a few lines from Johnny to let you know that he is so. I have ordered the things you desired to be sent you, but I will not yet say by what conveyance, for fear of accidents.

If human nature could be made happy by anything that can please the eye, the ear, the taste, or any other sense, or passion, or fancy, this country would be the region for happiness. But if my country were at peace, I should be happier among the rocks and shades of Penn's Hill; and would cheerfully exchange all the elegance, magnificence, and sublimity of Europe for the simplicity of Braintree and Weymouth.

To tell you the truth, I admire the ladies here. Don't be jealous. They are handsome and very well educated. Their accomplishments are exceedingly brilliant, and their knowledge of letters and arts exceeds that of the English ladies, I believe.

Tell Mrs. Warren that I shall write her a letter, as she desired, and let her know some of my reflections in this country. My venerable colleague enjoys a privilege here that is much to be envied. Being seventy years of age, the ladies not only allow him to embrace them as often as he pleases, but they are perpetually embracing him. I told him yesterday I would write this to America.

230. ABIGAIL ADAMS

18 May 1778

I have waited with great patience, restraining, as much as possible, every anxious idea for three months. But now every vessel which arrives sets my expectation upon the wing, and I pray my guardian genius to waft me the happy tidings of your safety and welfare. Hitherto my wandering ideas have roved, like the son of Ulysses, from sea to sea, and from shore to shore, not knowing where to find you; sometimes I fancied you upon the mighty wa-

ters, sometimes at your desired haven, sometimes upon the ungrateful and hostile shore of Britain, but at all times, and in all
places, under the protecting care and guardianship of that Being
who not only clothes the lilies of the field, and hears the young
ravens when they cry, but hath said, "Of how much more worth
are ye than many sparrows"; and this confidence, which the
world cannot deprive me of, is my food by day and my rest by
night, and was all my consolation under the horrid ideas of assassination,—the only event of which I had not thought, and in
some measure prepared my mind.

When my imagination sets you down upon the Gallic shore, a
land to which Americans are now bound to transfer their affections, and to eradicate all those national prejudices which the
proud and haughty nation whom we once revered craftily instilled into us, whom they once styled their children, I anticipate
the pleasure you must feel, and, though so many leagues distant,
share in the joy of finding the great interest of our country so
generously espoused and nobly aided by so powerful a monarch.
Your prospects must be much brightened; for when you left your
native land they were rather gloomy. If an unwearied zeal and
persevering attachment to the cause of truth and justice, regard-
less of the allurements of ambition on the one hand or the
threats of calamity on the other, can entitle any one to the reward of peace, liberty, and safety, a large portion of those blessings are reserved for my friend in his native land.

> "Oh, wouldst thou keep thy country's loud applause,
>   Loved as her father, as her God adored,
>   Be still the bold asserter of her cause,
>   Her voice in council; (in the fight her sword;)
>   In peace, in war, pursue thy country's good:
>   For her, bare thy bold breast and pour thy generous blood."[1]

Difficult as the day is, cruel as this war has been, separated as
I am, on account of it, from the dearest connection in life, I
would not exchange my country for the wealth of the Indies, or
be any other than an American, though I might be queen or em-
press of any nation upon the globe. My soul is unambitious of
pomp or power. Beneath my humble roof, blessed with the soci-

ety and tenderest affection of my dear partner, I have enjoyed as much felicity and as exquisite happiness as falls to the share of mortals. And, though I have been called to sacrifice to my country, I can glory in my sacrifice and derive pleasure from my intimate connection with one who is esteemed worthy of the important trust devolved upon him.

Britain, as usual, has added insult to injustice and cruelty, by what she calls a conciliatory plan. From my soul I despise her meanness; but she has long ago lost that treasure which, a great authority tells us, exalteth a nation, and is receiving the reproaches due to her crimes. I have been much gratified with the perusal of the Duke of Richmond's speech.[2] Were there ten such men to be found, I should still have some hopes that a revolution would take place in favor of the virtuous few, "and the laws, the rights, the generous plan of power delivered down from age to age by our renowned forefathers" be again restored to that unhappy island.

I hope by the close of this month to receive from you a large packet. I have written twice before this. Some opportunities I may miss by my distance from the capital. I have enjoyed a good share of health since you left me. I have not mentioned my dear son, though I have often thought of him since I began this letter, because I propose writing to him by this opportunity. I omit many domestic matters because I will not risk their coming to the public eye. I shall have a small bill to draw upon you in the month of June. I think to send it to Mr. McCreery,[3] who, by a letter received since you went away, is, I find, settled in Bordeaux in the mercantile way, and I dare say will procure for me anything I may have occasion for. I wish you would be so good as to write him a line requesting the favor of him to procure me such things, and, in addition to the bills which may be drawn, let him add ten pounds sterling at a time, if I desire it. The bills will be at three different times in a year. If they should arrive safe they would render me essential service.

Our public finances are upon no better footing than they were when you left us. Five hundred dollars is now offered by this town, per man, for nine months, to recruit the army. Twelve pounds a month for farming labor is the price, and it is not to be procured under. Our friends are all well and desire to be remembered to you. So many tender sentiments rush upon my mind, when about to close this letter to you, that I can only ask you to measure them by those which you find in your own bosom for

    Your affectionate   PORTIA

231. JOHN ADAMS

Passy, 3 June 1778

On the 13th of February I left you. It is now the 3d of June, and I have not received a line nor heard a word, directly nor indirectly, concerning you, since my departure. This is a situation of mind in which I never was before, and I assure you I feel a great deal of anxiety at it; yet I do not wonder at it, because I suppose few vessels have sailed from Boston since ours. I have shipped for you the articles you requested, and the black cloth for your father, to whom present my most affectionate and dutiful respects. Captain Tucker, if he should not be unlucky, will give you an account of your things.

It would be endless to attempt a description of this country. It is one great garden. Nature and art have conspired to render everything here delightful. Religion and government, you will say, ought to be excepted. With all my heart. But these are no afflictions to me, because I have well fixed it in my mind as a principle, that every nation has a right to that religion and government which it chooses, and as long as any people please themselves in these great points, I am determined they shall not displease me.

There is so much danger that my letter may fall into malicious hands, that I should not choose to be too free in my observations upon the customs and manners of this people. But thus much I may say with truth and without offense, that there is no people in the world who take so much pains to please, nor any whose endeavors in this way have more success. Their arts and manners, taste and language, are more respected in Europe than those of any other nation. Luxury, dissipation, and effeminacy are pretty nearly of the same degree of excess here and in every other part of Europe. The great cardinal virtue of temperance, however, I believe flourishes here more than in any other part of Europe.

My dear countrymen! how shall I persuade you to avoid the

plague of Europe! Luxury has as many and as bewitching charms on your side of the ocean as on this; and luxury, wherever she goes, effaces from human nature the image of the Divinity. If I had power I would forever banish and exclude from America all gold, silver, precious stones, alabaster, marble, silk, velvet, and lace.

Oh, the tyrant! the American ladies would say. What! Aye, my dear girls, these passions of yours which are so easily alarmed, and others of my own sex which are exactly like them, have done and will do the work of tyrants in all ages. Tyrants different from me, whose power has banished, not gold indeed, but other things of greater value, wisdom, virtue, and liberty. My son and servant are well. I am, with an ardor that words have not power to express,

Yours.

232. ABIGAIL ADAMS TO
JOHN QUINCY ADAMS

10 June 1778

MY DEAR SON, — 'Tis almost four months since you left your native land, and embarked upon the mighty waters, in quest of a foreign country. Although I have not particularly written to you since, yet you may be assured you have constantly been upon my heart and mind.

It is a very difficult task, my dear son, for a tender parent, to bring her mind to part with a child of your years, going to a distant land; nor could I have acquiesced in such a separation under any other care than that of the most excellent parent and guardian who accompanied you. You have arrived at years capable of improving under the advantages you will be likely to have, if you do but properly attend to them. They are talents put into your hands, of which an account will be required of you hereafter; and being possessed of one, two, or four, see to it that you double your numbers.

The most amiable and most useful disposition in a young mind is diffidence of itself; and this should lead you to seek advice and instruction from him who is your natural guardian and will always counsel and direct you in the best manner, both for your present and future happiness. You are in possession of a natural good understanding, and of spirits unbroken by adversity and untamed with care. Improve your understanding by acquiring useful knowledge and virtue, such as will render you an ornament to society, an honor to your country, and a blessing to your parents. Great learning and superior abilities, should you ever possess them, will be of little value and small estimation, unless virtue, honor, truth, and integrity are added to them. Adhere to those religious sentiments and principles which were early instilled into your mind, and remember that you are accountable to your Maker for all your words and actions.

Let me enjoin it upon you to attend constantly and steadfastly to the precepts and instructions of your father, as you value the happiness of your mother and your own welfare. His care and attention to you render many things unnecessary for me to write, which I might otherwise do; but the inadvertency and heedlessness of youth require line upon line and precept upon precept, and, when enforced by the joint efforts of both parents, these will, I hope, have a due influence upon your conduct; for, dear as you are to me, I would much rather you should have found your grave in the ocean you have crossed, or that any untimely death should crop you in your infant years, than see you an immoral, profligate, or graceless child.

You have entered early in life upon the great theatre of the world, which is full of temptations and vice of every kind. You are not wholly unacquainted with history, in which you have read of crimes which your inexperienced mind could scarcely believe credible. You have been taught to think of them with horror, and to view vice as

> "a monster of so frightful mien
> That, to be hated, needs but to be seen."[1]

Yet you must keep a strict guard upon yourself, or the odious monster will soon lose its terror by becoming familiar to you. The modern history of our own times furnishes as black a list of crimes as can be paralleled in ancient times, even if we go back to Nero, Caligula, or Caesar Borgia. Young as you are, the cruel war into which we have been compelled by the haughty tyrant of Britain and the bloody emissaries of his vengeance may stamp upon your mind this certain truth, that the welfare and prosperity of all countries, communities, and, I may add, individuals, depend upon their morals. That nation to which we were once united, as it has departed from justice, eluded and subverted the wise laws which formerly governed it, and suffered the worst of crimes to go unpunished, has lost its valor, wisdom, and humanity, and, from being the dread and terror of Europe, has sunk into derision and infamy.

But, to quit political subjects, I have been greatly anxious for your safety, having never heard of the frigate since she sailed, till, about a week ago, a New York paper informed that she was taken and carried into Plymouth. I did not fully credit this report, though it gave me much uneasiness. I yesterday heard that a French vessel was arrived at Portsmouth, which brought news of the safe arrival of the *Boston;* but this wants confirmation. I hope it will not be long before I shall be assured of your safety. You must write me an account of your voyage, of your situation, and of everything entertaining you can recollect.

Be assured I am most affectionately yours,   ————.

Mr. Hardwick desires if such a thing as stocking weavers needles are to be had that Stevens or you would procure two thousand number six and convey with anything your papa may have to send me.

233. JOHN ADAMS

Passy, 16 June 1778

Since my last, I have had the inexpressible pleasure of yours of the 25th of March by the way of Holland, which is the first and the last letter as yet received from you. This will be delivered to you by a young gentleman of the name of Archer, who is going to America to serve in our army as a volunteer. He is a promising youth, and will tell you all the news both in England and

France. Germany seems at the eve of war. The Emperor and King of Prussia are at the head of armies, and on tiptoe to strike the blow. England seems to be lost in a stupor. Byron's fleet is not yet sailed. D'Estaing's[1] passed the straits of Gibraltar the 16th of May.

We long to hear from America the ratification of the Treaty with France, the captivity of General Clinton's army,[2] and of Lord Howe's fleet. John is very well at school.

I want a few pamphlets here, "The Thoughts on Government," "The New York Constitution," "An Essay of a Constitution of Government for Pennsylvania," said to have been written by Mr. Dickinson. Look them up and send them.

I cannot learn that any reinforcement is to be sent to America this summer. They can spare none. They are in a panic from an apprehension of an invasion. Ireland is grown tumultuous, is concerting a non-importation agreement, and gives symptoms of an insurrection.

234. ABIGAIL ADAMS

30 June 1778

DEAREST OF FRIENDS,—Shall I tell my dearest that tears of joy filled my eyes this morning at the sight of his well-known hand?—the first line which has blessed my sight since his four months' absence, during which time I have never been able to learn a word from him or my dear son, till, about ten days ago, an English paper, taken in a prize and brought into Salem, contained an account, under the Paris news, of your arrival at the abode of Dr. Franklin; and last week a cartel from Halifax brought Captain Welch, of the *Boston*,[1] who informed that he left you well the 11th of March, and that he had letters for me, but destroyed them when he was taken; and this is all the information I have ever been able to obtain. Our enemies have told us the vessel was taken, and named the frigate which took her, and that she was carried into Plymouth. I have lived a life of fear and anxiety ever since you left me. Not more than a week after your absence the horrid story of Dr. Franklin's assassination was received from France, and sent by Mr. Purviance, of Baltimore, to Congress and to Boston. Near two months before that was contradicted. Then we could not hear a word from the *Boston,* and most people gave her up as taken or lost. Thus has my mind been agitated like a troubled sea.

You will easily conceive how grateful your favor of April 25th, and those of our son, were to me and mine; though I regret your short warning, and the little time you had to write, by which means I know not how you fared upon your voyage, what reception you have met with (not even from the ladies, though you profess yourself an admirer of them), and a thousand circumstances which I wish to know, and which are always particularly interesting to near connections. I must request you always to be minute and to write me by every conveyance. Some, perhaps, which may appear unlikely to reach me, will be the first to arrive. I own I was mortified at so short a letter, but I quiet my heart with thinking there are many more upon their passage to me. I have written several before this, and some of them very long.

Now I know you are safe, I wish myself with you. Whenever you entertain such a wish, recollect that I would have willingly hazarded all dangers to have been your companion; but, as that was not permitted, you must console me in your absence by a recital of all your adventures; though, methinks, I would not have them in all respects too similar to those related of your venerable colleague,[2] whose Mentor-like appearance, age, and philosophy most certainly lead the politico-scientific ladies of France to suppose they are embracing the god of wisdom in a human form; but I, who own that I never yet wished an angel, whom I loved a man, shall be full as content if those divine honors are omitted. The whole heart of my friend is in the bosom of his partner. More than half a score of years have so riveted it there that the fabric which contains it must crumble into dust ere the particles can be separated. I can hear of the brilliant accomplishments of any of my sex with pleasure, and rejoice in that liberality of sentiment which acknowledges them. At the same time, I regret the trifling, narrow, contracted education of the females of my own country. I have entertained a superior opinion of the accomplishments of the French ladies, ever since I read the letters of Dr. Shebbeare,[3] who professes that he had rather take the opinion of an accomplished lady, in matters of polite writing, than the first wits of Italy; and should think himself safer with her approbation than with that of a long list of literati; and he gives this reason for it, that women have, in general, more delicate sensations than men; what touches them is for the most part true in nature, whereas men, warped by education, judge amiss from previous prejudice, and, referring all things to the mode of the ancients, condemn that by comparison, where no true similitude ought to be expected.

But, in this country, you need not be told how much female education is neglected, nor how fashionable it has been to ridicule female learning; though I acknowledge it my happiness to be connected with a person of a more generous mind and liberal sentiments. I cannot forbear transcribing a few generous sentiments which I lately met with upon this subject.

"If women," says the writer, "are to be esteemed our enemies, methinks it is an ignoble cowardice, thus to disarm them, and not allow them the same weapons we use ourselves; but if they deserve the title of our friends, 'tis an inhuman tyranny to debar them of the privileges of ingenious education, which would also render their friendship so much the more delightful to themselves and us. Nature is seldom observed to be niggardly of her choicest gifts to the sex. Their senses are generally as quick as ours, their reason as nervous, their judgment as mature and solid. To these natural perfections add but the advantages of acquired learning, what polite and charming creatures would they prove; whilst their external beauty does the office of a crystal to the lamp, not shrouding, but disclosing, their brighter intellects. Nor need we fear to lose our empire over them by thus improving their native abilities; since, where there is most learning, sense, and knowledge, there is always observed to be the most modesty and rectitude of manners."

235. JOHN ADAMS

Passy, 23 September 1778

A very idle, vain conversation at a dinner has produced you this letter from a venerable old lady in this neighborhood, the wife of Monsieur Grand,[1] the banker. As the subject was introduced, and according to the turn the conversation really took, there was not so much vanity and ostentation on my part as you will suspect from her account of it. But as I speak French very imperfectly, and she understands not a syllable of English, I suppose she did not fully understand me. All that I maintained was that it was the duty of a good citizen to sacrifice all to his country in some circumstances. God grant I may never be called to do this again so often as I have done already, for I have hazarded all, very often, and done as much as sacrifice all, sometimes. You will have a delicate task to answer her. Write to her in English. She has a son about five-and-twenty, who is a master of English and will interpret. It is a virtuous family, and very civil to me and my dear Johnny, of whom the whole family is very fond.

We are in deep concern for America; the last accounts having left D'Estaing going to Rhode Island and Lord Howe after him.

It is high time for me to write to my children, but hitherto I have not had time. I hope you have received twenty letters from me, in which I have desired you to draw upon me for what money you want.

236. ABIGAIL ADAMS

The morning after I received your very short letter, I determined to devote the day to writing to my friend; but I had only just breakfasted when I had a visit from Monsieur Rivière,[1] an officer on board the *Languedoc*, who speaks English well, the captain of the *Zara*, and six or eight other officers, from on board another ship. The first gentleman dined with me, and spent the day, so that I had no opportunity of writing that day. The gentlemen officers made me several visits, and I have dined twice on board, at very elegant entertainments. Count d'Estaing has been exceedingly polite to me. Soon after he arrived here, I received a message from him requesting that I would meet him at Colonel Quincy's, as it was inconvenient leaving his ship for any long time. I waited upon him, and was very politely received. Upon parting, he requested that the family would accompany me on board his ship and dine with him the next Thursday, with any friends we chose to bring; and his barge should come for us. We went, according to the invitation, and were sumptuously entertained, with every delicacy that this country produces, and the addition of every foreign article that could render our feast splendid. Music and dancing for the young folks closed the day.

The temperance of these gentlemen, the peaceable, quiet disposition both of officers and men, joined to many other virtues which they have exhibited during their continuance with us, are sufficient to make Europeans, and Americans too, blush at their own degeneracy of manners. Not one officer has been seen the least disguised with liquor since their arrival. Most that I have seen appear to be gentlemen of family and education. I have been the more desirous to take notice of them, as I cannot help saying that they have been neglected in the town of Boston. Generals Heath and Hancock have done their part, but very few, if any, private families have any acquaintance with them. Perhaps I feel more anxious to have them distinguished, on account of the near and dear connections I have among them. It would gratify me much, if I had it in my power, to entertain every officer in the fleet.

In the very few lines I have received from you, not the least mention is made that you have ever received a line from me. I have not been so parsimonious as my friend,—perhaps I am not so prudent; but I cannot take my pen, with my heart overflowing, and not give utterance to some of the abundance which is in it. Could you, after a thousand fears and anxieties, long expectation, and painful suspense, be satisfied with my telling you that I was well, that I wished you were with me, that my daughter sent her duty, that I had ordered some articles for you, which I hoped would arrive, etc., etc.? By Heaven, if you could, you have changed hearts with some frozen Laplander, or made a voyage to a region that has chilled every drop of your blood; but I will restrain a pen already, I fear, too rash, nor shall it tell you how much I have suffered from this appearance of—inattention.

The articles sent by Captain Tucker have arrived safe, and will be of great service to me. Our money is very little better than blank paper. It takes forty dollars to purchase a barrel of cider; fifty pounds lawful for a hundred of sugar, and fifty dollars for a hundred of flour; four dollars per day for a laborer, and find him, which will amount to four more. You will see, by bills drawn before the date of this, that I had taken the method which I was happy in finding you had directed me to. I shall draw for the rest as I find my situation requires. No article that can be named, foreign or domestic, but what costs more than double in hard money what it once sold for. In one letter I have given you an account of our local situation, and of *everything* I thought you might wish to know. Four or five sheets of paper, written to you by the last mail, were destroyed when the vessel was taken. Duplicates are my aversion, though I believe I should set a value upon them, if I were to receive them from a certain friend, a friend who never was deficient in testifying his regard and affection to his   PORTIA

237. JOHN ADAMS

Passy, 6 November 1778

We have received information that so many of our letters have been thrown overboard that I fear you will not have heard so often from me as both of us wish. I have written often, but my letters have not been worth so much as other things which I have sent you. I sent you a small present by Captain Niles, but he is taken by a Jersey privateer. I sent you also some other things by Captain Barnes;[1] and what affects me quite as much, I sent the things that my dear brother Cranch requested me to send, by these same vessels. These vessels were chosen because they were fast sailers, and so small as to be able to see danger before they could be seen; but all is taken and sent into Guernsey and Jersey. By Captain Tucker I sent you the whole of the list you gave me of articles for the family. These, I hope, have arrived safe, but I have been so unlucky that I feel averse to meddling in this way. The whole loss is a trifle, it is true. But to you in the convenience of the family, and to Mr. Cranch in his business, it would have been of value. If the *Boston* arrives, the little chest she carries to you will be of service.

My anxiety for you and for the public is not diminished by time or distance. The great number of accidental disappointments in the course of the last summer are afflicting. But we hope for better luck another year. It seems to be the intention of Heaven that we should be taught the full value of our liberty by the dearness of the purchase, and the importance of public virtue by the necessity of it. There seems to be also a further design, that of eradicating forever from the heart of every American every tender sentiment towards Great Britain, that we may, some time or other, know how to make the full advantage of our independence by more extensive connections with other countries. Whatever siren songs of peace may be sung in your ears, you may depend upon it from me (who unhappily have been seldom mistaken in my guesses of the intentions of the British government for fourteen years) that every malevolent passion and every insidious art will predominate in the British cabinet against us. Their threats of Russians and of great reinforcements are false and impracticable, and they know them to be so; but their threats of doing mischief with the forces they have will be verified as far as their power.

It is by no means pleasant to me to be forever imputing malicious policy to a nation that I have ever wished and still wish I could esteem. But truth must be attended to; and almost all Europe, the Dutch especially, are at this day talking of Great Britain in the style of American sons of liberty. I hope the unfortunate events at Rhode Island will produce no heart-burnings between our countrymen and the Comte d'Estaing, who is allowed by all Europe to be a great and worthy officer, and by all who know him to be a zealous friend of America.

I have enjoyed uncommon health since my arrival in this country, and, if it was peace, and my family here, I could be happy. But never, never shall I enjoy happy days without either. My little son gives me great pleasure both by his assiduity to his books and his discreet behavior. The lessons of his mamma are a constant lesson to him, and the reflection that they are so to his sister and brothers is a never-failing consolation to me at times when I feel more tenderness for them than words can express, or than I should choose to express if I had power. Remember me in the most affectionate manner to our parents, brothers, sisters, uncles, aunts, and—what shall I say—children.

My respects where they are due, which is in so many places that I cannot name them. With regard to my connections with the public business here, which you will be naturally inquisitive to know something of, I can only say that we have many disagreeable circumstances here, many difficulties to accomplish the wishes of our constituents, and to give satisfaction to certain half-anglified Americans, and, what is more serious and affecting, to real and deserving Americans, who are suffering in England, and escaping from thence. But from this Court, this city and nation, I have experienced nothing but uninterrupted politeness. It is not possible for me to express more tenderness and affection to you than will be suggested by the name of

JOHN ADAMS

238. JOHN ADAMS

Passy, 27 November 1778

Mr. Brown is here, and I cannot miss the opportunity by him to write you a line. I know not how often you receive letters from me, so many are taken or sunk; but I write as often as I can.

I have received some letters from you, which will occasion your name to be classed with Mrs. Macaulay and Madame Dacier,[1] for aught I know. Johnny is very well. Stevens[2] had a fall yesterday, which hurt him a little, but not very badly. He is in a good way this morning. The things inclosed, which were a present to me, you will do as you please with.

Europe is the dullest place in the world. No news but the lies which the emissaries of England are making and spreading in every part. We get no news from Congress, or any part of America. By hints in some letters which I have heard of, I expect the first vessel will bring us news of some new regulations of Congress concerning foreign affairs. It is said that Congress has determined to have but one commissioner at this Court. If this is true, as I suppose it is, as it comes from Mr. Deane, I am uncertain what is to be done with me. It is said that I am to be sent to some other Court, and that the Dr. is to be here alone. If this should be the case, I should be puzzled what to do. The motives of Congress are very good to save expenses, but this motive will not have its effect if I am to be maintained here in idleness, or sent upon my travels to other countries, where I shall not be received, which will be the most painful situation imaginable to me. In this case I should be at a loss whether to return home immediately or wait until I could write to Congress and obtain leave. Some of my friends here are of opinion that I ought not to return without leave. I would not take any step that should give any just cause of offense to Congress or the people. But I cannot eat pensions and sinecures. They would stick in my throat. I wish some honest vessel would arrive and resolve my doubts.

239. JOHN ADAMS

Passy, 2 December 1778

MY DEAREST FRIEND, — Last night an express from M. de Sartine,[1] whose politeness upon this occasion was very obliging, brought me your letters of September 29th and October 10th. The joy which the receipt of these packets afforded me was damped by the disagreeable articles of intelligence; but still more so by the symptoms of grief and complaint which appeared in the letters. For Heaven's sake, my dear, don't indulge a thought that it is possible for me to neglect or forget all that is dear to me in this world. It is impossible for me to write as I did in America. What should I write? It is not safe to write anything that one is not willing should go into all the newspapers of the world. I know not by whom to write. I never know what conveyance is safe. Vessels may have arrived without letters from me. I am five hundred miles from Bordeaux, and not much less distant from Nantes. I know nothing of many vessels that go from the seaports, and if I knew of all, there are some that I should not trust. Notwithstanding this, I have written to you not much less than fifty letters. I am astonished that you have received no more. But almost every vessel has been taken. Two vessels by which I sent goods to you for the use of your family, and one by which I sent Mr. Cranch's things, we know have been taken. In every one of these I sent large packets of letters and papers for Congress, for you, and for many friends. God knows I don't spend my time in idleness, or in gazing at curiosities. I never wrote more letters, however empty they may have been. But by what I hear, they have been all, or nearly all, taken or sunk. My friends complain that they have not received letters from me. I may as well complain. I have received scarcely any letters from America. I have written three where I have received one. From my friend Mr. Adams I have received only one short card; from Mr. Gerry, not a syllable; from Mr. Lovell, only two or three, very short. What shall I say? I doubt not they have written oftener, but letters miscarry. Drs. Cooper and Gordon write to Dr. Franklin, not to me. My friend Warren has been good as usual. I have received several fine, long letters, full of sound sense, useful intelligence, and reflections as virtuous, as wise as usual, from him. I have answered them and written more, but whether they arrive, I know not.

I approve very much of your draught upon me in favor of your cousin. The moment it arrives, it shall be paid. Draw for more as you may have occasion. But make them give you gold and silver for your bills. Your son is the joy of my heart, without abating in the least degree of my affection for the young rogue that did not seem as if he had a father, or his brother or sister. Tell Nabby her papa likes her the better for what she tells her brother, viz., "that she don't talk much," because I know she thinks and feels the more. I hope the *Boston* has arrived. She carried many things for you.

Last night a friend from England brought me the King's speech. Their delirium continues, and they go on with the war, but the speech betrays a manifest expectation that Spain will join against them, and the debates betray a dread of Holland. They have reason for both. They have not and cannot get an ally. They cannot send any considerable reinforcement to America.

Your reflections upon the rewards of the virtuous friends of the public are very just. But if virtue was to be rewarded with wealth, it would not be virtue. If virtue was to be rewarded with fame, it would not be virtue of the sublimest kind. Who would not rather be Fabricius[2] than Caesar? Who would not rather be Aristides than even William the Third? Who! Nobody would be of this mind but Aristides and Fabricius. These characters are very rare, but the more precious. Nature has made more insects than birds, more butterflies than eagles, more foxes than lions, more pebbles than diamonds. The most excellent of her productions, both in the physical, intellectual, and moral world, are the most rare. I would not be a butterfly because children run after them, nor because dull philosophers boast of them in their cabinets.

Have you ever read J. J. Rousseau? If not, read him. Your cousin Smith has him. What a difference between him and Chesterfield and even Voltaire. But he was too virtuous for the age and for Europe. I wish I could not say for another country.

I am much disappointed in not receiving dispatches from Congress by this opportunity. We expect alterations in the plan here. What will be done with me I can't conjecture. If I am recalled, I will endeavor to get a safe opportunity home. I will watch the proper season, and look out for a good vessel; and if I can get safe to Penn's Hill, shall never repent of my voyage to Europe, because I have gained an insight into several things that I never should have understood without it.

I pray you to remember me with every sentiment of tenderness, duty, and affection to your father and my mother, your and my brothers and sisters, uncles, aunts, cousins, and everybody else that you know deserves it. What shall I say, too, of my dear young friends by your fireside? May God Almighty bless them and make them wise!

240. JOHN ADAMS

Passy, 27 December 1778

Mr. Greenleaf is about to set off towards Nantes, and from thence to Boston.

Last night I walked to Paris and saw the illumination for the birth of the princess Maria Theresa Charlotte, Fille du Roi. Splendid indeed! My little friend, who was with me, will write you a description of it. The military schools, the hospital of invalids, and the palace of Bourbon were beautiful and sublime indeed; as much so as an illumination can be. I could scarcely have conceived that an illumination could have such an effect. I suppose the expense of this is a million of livres. As much as I respect this country, particularly the King and royal family, I could not help reflecting how many families in another country would this tallow make happy for life; how many privateers would this tallow fit out for chasing away the Jersey-men[1] and making reprisals on Messieurs les Anglais. But taste will have its way in this country.

The Queen and her illustrious infant are very well, and this nation is very happy to have discovered a way[2] by which a dauphin may come to them next year or the year after. The King and Queen are greatly beloved here. Every day shows fresh proofs of it. On the other side the channel there is a King who is in a fair way to be the object of opposite sentiments to a nation, if he is not at present. If Keppel[3] should be destroyed in life or reputation, I shall expect to hear that all restraints are taken off, and passions allowed to sport themselves without reserve. Keppel told the King he would not fight against America; an unpardonable offense. He will be ruined if possible. However, I think that Keppel was wrong even to accept a command against the French. If Britain is wrong in this war against America, she is wrong in that against the French, for France and America have the same object in view, and no other. France is right if America is right, because France only assisted the American cause, for which John Bull abused and fought her. But John will come off wretchedly. He will be beaten. He has been beaten. There have been more British men-of-war already taken and destroyed than they lost in two former wars, and more sailors prisoners.

241. ABIGAIL ADAMS

Sunday Evening, 27 December 1778

How lonely are my days! how solitary are my nights! secluded from all society but my two little boys and my domestics. By the mountains of snow which surround me, I could almost fancy myself in Greenland. We have had four of the coldest days I ever knew, and they were followed by the severest snow-storm I ever remember. The wind, blowing like a hurricane for fifteen or twenty hours, rendered it impossible for man or beast to live abroad, and has blocked up the roads so that they are impassable. A week ago I parted with my daughter, at the request of our Plymouth friends, to spend a month with them; so that I am solitary indeed.

Can the best of friends recollect that, for fourteen years past I have not spent a whole winter alone? Some part of the dismal season has heretofore been mitigated and softened by the social converse and participation of the friend of my youth.

How insupportable the idea that three thousand leagues and the vast ocean now divide us! but divide only our persons, for the heart of my friend is in the bosom of his partner. More than half a score of years has so riveted it there, that the fabric which contains it must crumble into dust ere the particles can be separated; for

> "In one fate, our hearts, our fortunes,
> And our beings blend."[1]

I cannot describe to you how much I was affected the other day with a Scotch song, which was sung to me by a young lady in order to divert a melancholy hour; but it had quite a different effect, and the native simplicity of it had all the power of a well-wrought tragedy. When I could conquer my sensibility I begged the song, and Master Charles has learned it, and consoles his mamma by singing it to her. I will inclose it to you. It has beauties in it to me which an indifferent person would not feel, perhaps.

> "His very foot has music in 't,
> As he comes up the stairs."

How oft has my heart danced to the sound of that music!

> "And shall I see his face again?
> And shall I hear him speak?"[2]

Gracious Heaven! hear and answer my daily petition, by banishing all my grief.

I am sometimes quite discouraged from writing. So many vessels are taken that there is little chance of a letter's reaching your hands. That I meet with so few returns is a circumstance that lies heavy at my heart. If this finds its way to you, it will go by the *Alliance*. By her I have written before. She has not yet sailed, and I love to amuse myself with my pen, and pour out some of the tender sentiments of a heart overflowing with affection, not for the eye of a cruel enemy, who, no doubt, would ridicule every humane and social sentiment, long ago grown callous to the finer sensibilities, but for the sympathetic heart that beats in unison with   PORTIA'S

242. JOHN ADAMS

Passy, 30 December 1778

We wait, and wait, and wait forever, without any news from America. We get nothing but what comes from England and to other people here, and they make it as they please. We have had nothing from Congress an immense while. Every merchant and every merchant's apprentice has letters and news when I have none. In truth, I have been so long from Boston that everybody there, almost, has forgotten me. I have expected, every moment for almost two months, my recall.

Carlisle, Cornwallis, and Eden[1] are arrived in England, but bring no good news for the English, or we should have had it in the "Gazette." The two houses of Parliament join ministry and commissioners, in threatening fire and sword. They seem to think it necessary to threaten most when they can do least. They, however, show their disposition, which they will indulge and gratify if they can. But be not dismayed. They can do no great things. Patience, perseverance, and firmness will overcome all our difficulties. Where the Comte d'Estaing is, is a great mystery. The greater, the better. The English fancy he is returning to Europe. But we believe he is gone where he will do something. The English reproach the French with gasconade, but they never gasconaded as the English do now. I suppose they will say as Burgoyne did, "Speak daggers but use none." But I believe, however that they and he would use them if they could. Of all the wrong heads Johnstone is the most consummate. The Tories at New York and Philadelphia have filled his head with a million lies. He seems to have taken a New York newspaper for holy writ. Parliament is adjourned to the 14th January. Of this you may be assured, that England can get no allies. The new secretary at war makes a vast parade of the number of men in their service by sea and land. But it is a mere delusion. They intend to Byngify[2] Keppel to all appearances; but killing him will not mend rotten ships nor make sailors.

I dined to-day at the Duchess d'Enville's.[3] When I saw the companies of militia on their march to fight her husband, I did not expect this. Did you?

Passy, 1 January 1779

I wish you a happy new year and many happy years, and all the blessings of life. Who knows but this year may be more prosperous for our country than any we have seen? For my own part, I have hopes that it will. Great blessings are in store for it, and they may come this year as well as another. You and I, however, must prepare our minds to enjoy the prosperity of others, not our own. In poverty and simplicity we shall be happy, whenever our country is so. Johnny sends duty. Mr. Williams[4] waits. I knew of his going but this moment. I think I shall see you this year in spite of British men-of-war. If it should be otherwise ordered, however, we must submit.

243. JOHN ADAMS

Passy, 9 February 1779

It is now a year, within a day or two, of my departure from home. It is in vain for me to think of writing of what is passed. The character and situation in which I am here, and the situation of public affairs, absolutely forbid my writing freely. I must be excused. So many vessels are taken, and there are so many persons indiscreet and so many others inquisitive, that I may not write. God knows how much I suffer for want of writing to you. It used to be a cordial to my spirits.

Thus much I can say with perfect sincerity, that I have found nothing to disgust me, or in any manner disturb me, in the French nation. My evils here arise altogether from Americans. If I would have enlisted myself under the banner of either party,[1] I might have filled America, I doubt not, with panegyrics of me from one party and curses and slanders from another. I have endeavored to be hitherto impartial, to search for nothing but the truth, and to love nobody and nothing but the public good, at least not more than the public good. I have hoped that animosities might be softened, and the still small voice of reason heard more and the boisterous roar of passions and prejudices less. But the publication of a certain address to the people has destroyed all such hopes. Nothing remains now but the fearful looking for of the fiery indignation of the monster party, here.

My consolation is that the partisans are no more than

> "Bubbles on the sea of matter borne;
> They rise, they break, and to that sea return."[2]

The people of America, I know, stand like Mount Atlas; but these altercations occasion a great deal of unhappiness for the present, and they prolong the war. Those must answer for it who are guilty. I am not.

244. JOHN ADAMS

Passy, 13 February 1779

Yours of 15th December was sent me yesterday by the Marquis,[1] whose praises are celebrated in all the letters from America. You must be content to receive a short letter, because I have not time now to write a long one. I have lost many of your letters, which are invaluable to me, and you have lost a vast number of mine. Barnes, Niles, and many other vessels are lost.

I have received intelligence much more agreeable than that of a removal to Holland; I mean that of being reduced to a private citizen, which gives me more pleasure than you can imagine. I shall therefore soon present before you your own good man. Happy, happy indeed shall I be, once more to see our fireside. I have written before to Mrs. Warren, and shall write again now. Dr. J.[2] is transcribing your Scotch song, which is a charming one. Oh, my leaping heart!

I must not write a word to you about politics, because you are a woman.

What an offense have I committed? A woman!

I shall soon make it up. I think women better than men, in general, and I know that you can keep a secret as well as any man whatever. But the world don't know this. Therefore if I were to write my sentiments to you, and the letter should be caught and hitched into a newspaper, the world would say I was not to be trusted with a secret.

I never had so much trouble in my life as here, and yet I grow fat. The climate and soil agree with me. So do the cookery and even the manners of the people, of those of them at least that I converse with, churlish republican as some of you on your side the water call me. The English have got at me in their newspapers. They make fine work of me—fanatic, bigot, perfect cipher, not one word of the language, awkward figure, uncouth dress, no address, no character, cunning, hard-hearted attorney. But the falsest of it all is, that I am disgusted with the Parisians; whereas I admire the Parisians prodigiously. They are the happiest people in the world, I believe, and have the best disposition to make others so. If I had your ladyship and our little folks here, and no politics to plague me, and a hundred thousand livres a year rent, I should be the happiest being on earth. Nay, I believe I could make it do with twenty thousand.

One word of politics. The English reproach the French with gasconade, but I don't believe their whole history could produce so much of it as the English have practiced this war. The commissioners' proclamation, with its sanction from the ministry and ratification by both houses, I suppose is hereafter to be interpreted like Burgoyne's "Speaking daggers but using none." They cannot send any considerable reinforcement, nor get an ally in Europe. This I think you may depend upon. Their artifice in throwing out such extravagant threats was so gross that I presume it has not imposed on any. Yet a nation that regarded its character never could have threatened in that manner.

Adieu.

245. JOHN ADAMS

Passy, 20 February 1779

A new commission has arrived by which the Dr. is sole minister. Mr. Lee continues commissioner for Spain, but I am reduced to the condition of a private citizen. The Congress have not taken the least notice of me. On the 11th of September they resolved to have one minister only in France. On the 14th they chose the Dr. In October they made out his Commission, the *Alliance* sailed on the 14th January, and in all that interval they never so much as bid me come home, bid me stay, or told me I had done well or done ill. Considering the accusation against Mr. Lee,[1] how unexpected it was and how groundless it is, I should not be at all surprised if I should see an accusation against me for something or other, I know not what, but I see that all things are possible.

Of all the scenes I ever passed through, this is the most extraordinary. The delirium among Americans here is the most extravagant. All the infernal arts of stock-jobbers, all the voracious avarice of merchants, have mingled themselves with American politics here, disturbed their operations, distracted our counsels, and turned our heads.

The Congress, I presume, expect that I should come home, and I shall come accordingly. As they have no business for me in Europe, I must contrive to get some for myself at home. Prepare yourself for removing to Boston, into the old house, for there you shall go, and there I will draw writs and deeds, and harangue juries, and be happy.

246. JOHN ADAMS

Passy, 20 February 1779

In the margin are the dates of all the letters I have received from you. I have written you several times that number. They are almost all lost, I suppose by yours. But you should consider it is a different thing to have five hundred correspondents and but one. It is a different thing to be under an absolute restraint and under none. It would be an easy thing for me to ruin you and your children by an indiscreet letter, and what is more, it would be easy to throw our country into convulsions. For God's sake never reproach me again with not writing or with writing scrips. Your wounds are too deep. You know not, you feel not, the dangers that surround me nor those that may be brought upon our country. Millions would not tempt me to write you as I used. I have no security that every letter I write you will not be broken open, and copied, and transmitted to Congress and to English newspapers. They would find no treason nor deceit in them, it is true, but they would find weakness and indiscretion, which they would make as ill a use of.

There are spies upon every word I utter, and every syllable I write. Spies planted by the English, spies planted by stock-jobbers, spies planted by selfish merchants, and spies planted by envious and malicious politicians. I have been all along aware of this, more or less, but more so now than ever. My life has been often in danger, but I never considered my reputation and character so much in danger as now. I can pass for a fool, but I will not pass for a dishonest or mercenary man. Be upon your guard, therefore. I must be upon mine, and I will.

247. JOHN ADAMS

Passy, 21 February 1779

Yours by Mr. Williams I have received. The little bill must be paid, but I confess it alarms me a little. The expense of my son here is greater than I ever imagined. Although his company is almost all the pleasure I have in life, yet I should not have brought him if I had known the expense. His expenses, together with what you have drawn for, and a little collection of books I have bought, will amount to more than will ever be allowed me. My accounts must not be drawn into intricacy or obscurity. I must not be involved in suspicions of meddling in trade or anything else but my proper business.

You complain that I don't write often enough, and that when I do, my letters are too short. If I were to tell you all the tenderness of my heart, I should do nothing but write to you. I beg of you not to be uneasy. I write you as often and as much as I ought. If I had a heart at ease, and leisure enough, I could write you several sheets a day, of the curiosities of this country. But it is as much impossible for me to think of such subjects as to work miracles. Let me entreat you to consider, if some of your letters had by any accident been taken, what a figure would they have made in a newspaper, to be read by the whole world? Some of them, it is true, would have done honor to the most virtuous and most accomplished Roman matron; but others of them would have made you and me very ridiculous. In one of yours you hint that I am to go to Holland. But I think you must be misinformed. By all that I can learn, some gentlemen intend to vote for me to Holland vs. Mr. Deane; others to Spain vs. Mr. Lee. Neither, I think, will succeed; and therefore I think I have but one course to steer, and that is, homewards. But I can determine nothing absolutely. I must govern myself according to the intelligence which may hereafter arise, the orders of Congress, and the best judgment I can form of my own duty and the public good.

I am advised to take a ride to Geneva, or to Amsterdam; and I have been so confined from exercise, having never been farther from Paris than Versailles since my arrival here, that some such excursion seems necessary for my health, yet I cannot well bear the thought of putting the public to an expense merely for the sake of my pleasure, health, or convenience. Yet my situation here is painful. I never was in such a situation before as I am now, and my present feelings are new to me. If I should return, and in my absence any orders should arrive here for me to execute, in that case nobody would be here to execute them, and they might possibly fail of success for want of somebody with power to perform them; at least, this may be suspected and said and believed. However, upon the whole, as Congress have said nothing to me, good or bad, I have no right to presume that they mean to say anything, and therefore, on the whole, it is my duty to return by the first opportunity, unless I should receive counter orders before that occurs. If ever the time should arrive when I could have a little leisure and a quiet mind, I could entertain you with accounts of things which would amuse you and your children. There are an infinity of curiosities here, but so far from having leisure to describe them, I have found none even to see them, except a very few.

The climate here is charming. The weather is every day pleasant as the month of May; soft, mild air; some foggy days, and about ten or twelve days in January were cold and icy. But we have had scarce three inches of snow the whole winter. The climate is more favorable to my constitution than ours. The cookery and manner of living here, which you know Americans were taught by their former absurd masters to dislike, is more agreeable to me than you can imagine. The manners of the people have an affection in them that is very amiable. There is such a choice of elegant entertainments in the theatric way, of good company, and excellent books, that nothing would be wanting to me in this country but my family and peace to my country, to make me one of the happiest of men. John Bull would growl and bellow at this description. Let him bellow if he will, for he is but a brute.

248. JOHN ADAMS

Passy, 27 February 1779

The weather continuing fine, I went to Saint Denis, a little village about eight miles from this place, where are the tombs of all the kings and queens. The statues of all lie in state in marble. The church is called the royal Church of Saint Denis, is magnificent, and there is an apartment in a chamber, where the crowns and many other curiosities are preserved. It is curious to see such a collection of gold, ivory, and precious stones, as there is every species, I suppose, that is mentioned in the Revelation. The diamonds and rubies glitter. But I confess I have so much of the savage sachem in me that these things make no great impression upon me. There are several little crucifixes here, which the ecclesiastic who showed them told us were made of bits of the true cross. This may be, for anything that I know.

In my return, I took a circuit round by Montmartre, and dined at home with the Dr., who has a fit of the gout, but is getting better.

The situation in which my masters have left me puzzles me very much. They have said nothing to me. But one set of gentlemen write that I am to go to Spain, another to Holland, a third to Vienna; upon the whole, I believe they don't intend to send me to either, but leave me to stay here in a ridiculous situation, or return home if I can get there. I shall return unless I should receive, before the time arrives for the vessel to sail, orders which I can execute with honor and with a prospect of rendering some service to the public. But of these two last points I will judge for myself.

249. ABIGAIL ADAMS

20 March 1779

MY DEAREST FRIEND, — Your favor of December 9th came to hand this evening from Philadelphia. By the same post I received a letter from Mr. Lovell, transcribing some passages from one of the same date to him, and the only one, he says, which he has received since your absence, and his pocket-book proves that he has written eighteen different times; yet possibly you may have received as few from him. The watery world alone can boast of large packets received,—a discouraging thought when I take my pen. Yet I will not be discouraged. I will persist in writing, though but one in ten should reach you. I have been impatient for an opportunity, none having offered since January, when the *Alliance* sailed, which, my presaging mind assures me, will arrive safe in France, and I hope will return as safely.

Accept my thanks for the care you take of me, in so kindly providing for me the articles you mention. Should they arrive safe, they will be a great assistance to me. The safest way, you tell me, of supplying my wants is by drafts; but I cannot get hard money for bills. You had as good tell me to procure diamonds for them; and, when bills will fetch but five for one, hard money will exchange ten, which I think is very provoking; and I must give at the rate of ten, and sometimes twenty, for one, for every article I purchase. I blush whilst I give you a price current: all butcher's meat from a dollar to eight shillings per pound; corn twenty-five dollars, rye thirty, per bushel; flour fifty pounds per hundred; potatoes ten dollars per bushel; butter twelve shillings a pound, cheese eight; sugar twelve shillings a pound; molasses twelve dollars per gallon; labor six and eight dollars a day; a common cow from sixty to seventy pounds; and all English goods in proportion. This is our present situation. It is a risk to send me anything across the water, I know; yet if one in three arrives, I should be a gainer. I have studied, and do study, every method of economy in my power; otherwise a mint of money would not support a family. I could not board our two sons under forty dollars per week apiece at a school. I therefore thought it most prudent to request Mr. Thaxter to look after them, giving him his board and the use of the office, which he readily accepted, and, having passed the winter with me, will continue through the summer, as I see no probability of the times speedily growing better.

We have had much talk of peace through the mediation of Spain, and great news from Spain, and a thousand reports, as various as the persons who tell them. Yet I believe slowly, and rely more upon the information of my friend than on all the whole legion of stories which rise with the sun, and set as soon. Respecting Georgia, other friends have written you. I shall add nothing of my own, but that I believe it will finally be a fortunate event to us.

Our vessels have been fortunate in making prizes, though many were taken in the fall of the year. We have been greatly distressed for [want of] grain. I scarcely know the looks or taste of biscuit or flour for this four months; yet thousands have been much worse off, having no grain of any sort.

The great commotion raised here by Mr. Deane has sunk into contempt for his character; and it would be better for him to leave a country which is now supposed to have been injured by him. His friends are silent, not knowing how to extricate him. It would be happy for him if he had the art himself. He most certainly had art enough, in the beginning, to blow up a flame, and to set the whole continent in agitation.

More than a month has passed away since writing the above, and no opportunity has yet offered of conveying you a line; next to the pain of not receiving is that of not being able to send a token of remembrance and affection. (You must excuse my not copying, as paper is ten dollars per quire.) Last week a packet arrived from Brest with dispatches for Congress, but no private letters. I was disappointed, but did not complain. You would have written, I know, had you supposed she was coming to Boston. By her we heard of the safe arrival of the *Alliance* in France, which gave me much pleasure. May she have as safe a return to us again. Last week, arrived here the frigate *Warren,* after a successful cruise. She had been out about six weeks, in company with the *Queen of France,* and the *Ranger,* Captain Jones.[1] They fell in with and captured a fleet bound from New York to Georgia, consisting of ship *Jason,* twenty guns and one hundred and fifty men; ship *Maria,* sixteen guns, eighty-four men, having on board eighteen hundred barrels of flour; privateer schooner *Hibernian,* eight guns and forty-five men; brigs *Patriot, Prince Frederick, Bachelor John,* and schooner *Chance;* all of which are safe arrived, to the universal joy and satisfaction of every well-wisher of his country. The officers who were captured acknowledge that this loss will be severely felt by the enemy, and it is hoped that it will give General Lincoln important advantages over him in Georgia.

Respecting domestic affairs, I shall do tolerably whilst my credit is well supported abroad; and my demands there shall be as small as possible, considering the state of things here; but I, cannot purchase a bushel of grain under three hard dollars, though the scarcity of that article makes it dearer than other things. Our friends here all desire to be remembered to you. I remind your daughter to write and she promises to, but she does not love it. Charley is very busy gardening, sends his duty, and hopes to write soon. My pen is very bad, but you are so used to the hand you can pick it out, and if it goes into the sea, it is no matter. I should be very glad of some woolens by the *Alliance,* for winter gowns; nothing will be amiss, unless it be men's white

silk stockings, which I have no occasion for. I suppose the pair
sent among the letters which came in the *Mifflin,* an accident.

My pen is really so bad that I cannot add any further than that
I am wholly   Yours.

250. JOHN ADAMS

L'Orient, 14 May 1779

When I left Paris, the 8th of March, I expected to have been at
home before this day, and have done my utmost to get to sea, but
the embarrassments and disappointments I have met with have
been many, very many. I have, however, in the course of them,
had a fine opportunity of seeing Nantes, L'Orient, and Brest, as
well as the intermediate country.

By the gracious invitation of the King, I am now to take passage in his frigate, the *Sensible,* with his new Ambassador to
America, the Chevalier de la Luzerne. I hope to see you in six or
seven weeks. Never was any man in such a state of uncertainty
and suspense as I have been from last October, entirely unin-
formed of the intentions of Congress concerning me. This would
not have been very painful to me if I could have got home. Your
conversation is a compensation to me for all other things.

My son has had a great opportunity to see this country; but
this has unavoidably retarded his education in some other things.
He has enjoyed perfect health, from first to last, and is respected
wherever he goes, for his vigor and vivacity both of mind and
body, for his constant good humor, and for his rapid progress in
French as well as his general knowledge, which, for his age, is
uncommon. I long to see his sister and brothers. I need not add—

251. ABIGAIL ADAMS

8 June 1779

Six months have already elapsed since I heard a syllable from
you or my dear son, and five since I have had one single opportunity of conveying a line to you. Letters of various dates have

lain months at the Navy Board, and a packet and frigate, both ready to sail at an hour's warning, have been months waiting the orders of Congress. They no doubt have their reasons, or ought to have, for detaining them. I must patiently wait their motions, however painful it is; and that it is so, your own feelings will testify. Yet I know not but you are less a sufferer than you would be to hear from us, to know our distresses, and yet be unable to relieve them. The universal cry for bread, to a humane heart, is painful beyond description, and the great price demanded and given for it verifies that pathetic passage of Sacred Writ, "All that a man hath will he give for his life."[1] Yet He who miraculously fed a multitude with five loaves and two fishes has graciously interposed in our favor, and delivered many of the enemy's supplies into our hands, so that our distresses have been mitigated. I have been able as yet to supply my own family, sparingly, but at a price that would astonish you. Corn is gold at four dollars, hard money, per bushel, which is equal to eighty at the rate of exchange.

Labor is at eight dollars per day, and in three weeks it will be at twelve, it is probable, or it will be more stable than anything else. Goods of all kinds are at such a price that I hardly dare mention it. Linens are sold at twenty dollars per yard; the most ordinary sort of calicoes at thirty and forty; broadcloths at forty pounds per yard; West India goods full as high; molasses at twenty dollars per gallon; sugar four dollars per pound; bohea tea at forty dollars; and our own produce in proportion; butcher's meat at six and eight shillings per pound; board at fifty and sixty dollars per week; rates high. That, I suppose, you will rejoice at; so would I, did it remedy the evil. I pay five hundred dollars, and a new Continental rate has just appeared, my proportion of which will be two hundred more. I have come to this determination, to sell no more bills, unless I can procure hard money for them, although I shall be obliged to allow a discount. If I sell for paper, I throw away more than half, so rapid is the depreciation; nor do I know that it will be received long. I sold a bill to Blodget at five for one, which was looked upon as high at that time. The week after I received it, two emissions were taken out of circulation, and the greater part of what I had proved to be of that sort; so that those to whom I was indebted are obliged to wait, and before it becomes due, or is exchanged, it will be good for—as much as it will fetch, which will be nothing, if it goes on as it has done for this three months past. I will not tire your patience any longer. I have not drawn any further upon you. I mean to wait the return of the *Alliance,* which with longing eyes I look for. God grant it may bring me comfortable tidings from my dear, dear friend, whose welfare is so essential to my happiness that it is entwined around my heart and cannot be impaired or separated from it without rending it asunder.

In contemplation of my situation, I am sometimes thrown into an agony of distress. Distance, dangers, and oh, I cannot name all the fears which sometimes oppress me, and harrow up my soul. Yet must the common lot of man one day take place, whether we dwell in our own native land or are far distant from it. That we rest under the shadow of the Almighty is the consolation to which I resort, and find that comfort which the world cannot give. If He sees best to give me back my friend, or to preserve my life to him, it will be so.

Our worthy friend, Dr. Winthrop, is numbered with the great congregation, to the inexpressible loss of Harvard College.

> "Let no weak drop
> Be shed for him. The virgin, in her bloom
> Cut off, the joyous youth, and darling child,
> These are the tombs that claim the tender tear
> And elegiac song. But Winthrop calls
> For other notes of gratulation high,
> That now he wanders through those endless worlds
> He here so well descried, and wondering talks,
> And hymns their Author with his glad compeers."[2]

The testimony he gave with his dying breath, in favor of revealed religion, does honor to his memory and will endear it to every lover of virtue. I know not who will be found worthy to succeed him.

Congress have not yet made any appointment of you to any other Court. There appears a dilatoriness, an indecision, in their proceedings. I have in Mr. Lovell an attentive friend, who kindly informs me of everything which passes relative to you and your situation, and gives me extracts of your letters both to himself and others. I know you will be unhappy whenever it is not in your power to serve your country, and wish yourself at home, where at least you might serve your family. I cannot say that I think our affairs go very well here. Our currency seems to be the source of all our evils. We cannot fill up our Continental army by means of it. No bounty will prevail with them. What can be done with it? It will sink in less than a year. The advantage the enemy daily gains over us is owing to this. Most truly did you prophesy when you said that they would do all the mischief in their power with the forces they had here.

Many letters are lying in Boston for you, which have been written months. My good uncle Smith yesterday let me know that a letter of marque, bound for Nantes, would sail in a day or two. I eagerly seized the opportunity, and beg you to give my blessing to my son, to whom I have not time now to write. I dare not trust myself with the idea, nor can express how ardently I long to see both parent and son. Our whole family has enjoyed great health in your absence; daughter and sons, who delight in talking of papa and brother, present their duty and love. Your worthy mamma, who is now here, requests me to add her tenderest affection to you, who next to the writer is anxious to hear from you. Your brother requests me to desire you to procure for him two pieces of linen to the amount of twenty-four dollars, which he will pay to me, and to send them whenever you have an opportunity of sending to me. I shall not write for anything until the *Alliance* returns, and I find what success she has had.

My tenderest regards ever attend you. In all places and situations, know me to be ever, ever yours.

252. JOHN ADAMS

Boston, 13 November 1779

MY DEAREST FRIEND, — I have just sent Mr. Thaxter, Johnny, and Stevens, with the things, on board. I shall go with Charles at four o'clock. It is now three. I have seen the captain and the navy board, etc. It is proposed to sail to-morrow; perhaps, however, it may not be till next day. Mr. Dana[1] will come on board at nine to-morrow. Mr. Hancock has sent me a card to invite me to go on board with him in the castle barge. Don't make many words of this. Your aunt has given me a barrel of cranberries. I shall make a good use of them, I hope.

Let me entreat you to keep up your spirits and throw off cares as much as possible. Love to Nabby and Tommy. We shall yet be happy, I hope and pray, and I don't doubt it. I shall have vexations enough, as usual. You will have anxiety and tenderness enough, as usual. Pray strive not to have too much. I will write by every opportunity I can get.

Yours ever, ever yours,   JOHN ADAMS

253. ABIGAIL ADAMS

14 November 1779

DEAREST OF FRIENDS, — My habitation, how disconsolate it looks! my table, I sit down to it, but cannot swallow my food! Oh, why was I born with so much sensibility, and why, possessing it, have I so often been called to struggle with it? I wish to see you again. Were I sure you would not be gone, I could not withstand the temptation of coming to town, though my heart would suffer over again the cruel torture of separation.

What a cordial to my dejected spirits were the few lines last night received! And does your heart forebode that we shall again be happy? My hopes and fears rise alternately. I cannot resign more than I do, unless life itself were called for. My dear sons, I cannot think of them without a tear. Little do they know the feelings of a mother's heart. May they be good and useful as their father! Then will they in some measure reward the anxiety of a mother. My tenderest love to them. Remember me also to Mr. Thaxter, whose civilities and kindness I shall miss.

God Almighty bless and protect my dearest friend, and, in his own time, restore him to the affectionate bosom of

PORTIA

254. JOHN ADAMS

*At Sea, not far from the Grand
Bank of N. F. L., 29 November 1779*

MY DEAREST FRIEND, — A brave fellow from Boston, Captain Carr,[1] gives me an opportunity of writing one line, to let you know that we are all very well thus far. Charles behaves quite as well as John, and lies in my room anights. Mr. Dana has been very sick, but is now pretty well. We are now out of danger of the *Romulus* and *Virginia,* and I hope have little to fear from the enemy. We have had one storm, which made us all sea-sick, but brought us on well in our course. I wish I could write to you these two hours, but time fails. Ships cannot wait for each other at sea.

My love to Nabby and Tommy. Tell them to mind their studies. Tell Nabby though she has lost her French master for some time, I hope she will persevere, and perhaps a French mistress in her mamma may do better. Duty to your father, my mother, brothers, sister, etc., etc. Don't fail to let me know how the Constitution[2] goes on.

I write this on my knees, and the ship rolls so that I write worse than common.

255. ABIGAIL ADAMS

10 December 1779

I will not omit any opportunity of writing, though ever so great an uncertainty whether it will reach your hand. My uncle Smith has a vessel bound to Calais. He advises me to write, and I most willingly comply, though my faith in the conveyance is but poor. Indeed, I have lost my faith with my spirits.

My friends assure me from their observations that you must have had a good passage. God grant it, I say, but my fears and anxieties are many, very many. I had a faith and reliance that supported me before, but now my heart so misgives me that I cannot find that confidence which I wish for. Your letter from Cape Ann arrived and cheered my drooping spirits. Could I hear of your safe arrival, I would try to compose my agitated mind, which has horrors both day and night.

My dear sons! Little do they know how many veins of their mother's heart bled when she parted from them. My delicate Charles, how has he endured the fatigue of his voyage? John is a hardy sailor, seasoned before. I do not feel so much for him. Your fellow-travellers, too, I do not forget to think of them. I will not wish myself with you, because you say a lady cannot help being an odious creature at sea; and I will not wish myself in any situation that should make me so to you.

Nothing new in the political way but the raising the siege of Savannah and being unfortunate. You will have particulars, no doubt. Our friends are all well. Mr. Laurens is appointed to Holland—has not yet given his answer. Adieu.

Ever, ever yours,   PORTIA

256. JOHN ADAMS

Ferrol, 11 December 1779

MY DEAREST FRIEND, — We have had an escape again, but are arrived safely in Spain. As the frigate will probably not get from this place these two months, I must go by land to Paris, which I suppose is a journey of between three and four hundred leagues. That part of it which is in Spain is very mountainous. No post, bad roads, bad taverns, and very dear. We must ride mules, horses not being to be had. I must get some kind of carriage for the children, if possible. They are very well. Charles has sustained the voyage and behaves as well as ever his brother did. He is much pleased with what he sees. Sammy Cooper[1] too, is very well. These young gentlemen give me a vast deal of trouble in this unexpected journey. I have bought a dictionary and grammar, and they are learning the Spanish language as fast as possible. What could we do, if you and all the family were with me?

Ferrol is a magnificent port and harbor. It is fortified by nature by rows of lofty rocky mountains on each side the narrow entrance of it, and the public works, the fortifications, barracks, arsenals, etc., which are of stone very like Braintree stone, exceed anything I have seen. I dined the day before yesterday with

Don Joseph Saint Vincent, the Lieutenant-general of the Marine, who is the commandant of this port, with four-and-twenty French and Spanish officers. The difference between gravity and gayety was an amusing speculation. Yesterday I dined on board the *Triomphant,* an eighty-gun French ship, commanded by the Chef d'Escadre, M. Sade, and have engagements for every day for a much longer time than I shall stay. The French consul and vice-consul have been particularly polite and obliging to me. In short, I never was better pleased with a reception at any place.

There is no news. Nothing has been done in Europe. England is as insolent in language as ever; but this is only ridiculous, as it is apparently impotent.

257. JOHN ADAMS

Ferrol, 12 December 1779

The French consul had agreed to carry me, Mr. Dana, Mr. Allen, and my three children and our three servants, this day to Corunna, which is about five leagues from this place, by water, in a barge of fourteen oars, but the weather proved so boisterous that it was impossible to go.

To give you some idea of the place where we are, Cape Finisterre and Cape Ortagal are two long arms of land stretched out into the sea, which embrace a large body of water. Within this bay are two other points of land, within one of which is Ferrol, where we now are, and within the other is Corunna, where we intended to have gone this day, if the weather had permitted; but we hope to go to-morrow. We can get neither horses nor mules nor carriages, in this place, for ourselves or our baggage, which I am much surprised at, as it is so grand a port. Living and conveniences for conveyance are very dear in this place, which will run my expenses very high. There is nothing remarkable here but the natural strength of the place and the artificial fortifications, together with the arsenals, dry docks, barracks, and military matters by sea and land. The city is small, not very well built nor accommodated. Very little commerce or manufactures, industry or diversions. There are two or three elegant Churches, and there is an Italian opera. There is the appearance of much devotion, and there are many ecclesiastics.

It is dull enough to be in a country, so wholly ignorant of the language and usages; but we have furnished ourselves with a dictionary and grammar, and are learning every hour. Charles is much pleased with what he sees and hears, and behaves very discreetly. John is writing to you and his sister and brother. I excused myself from dining to-day on board the *Souverain* and on board the *Jason,* two French men-of-war. Yesterday I dined on board the *Triomphant,* and the children on board the *Jason.* The French officers appear to-day with cockades in honor of the triple alliance—a large white ribbon for the French, a smaller red one for the Spaniards, and a black one for the Americans, which makes a pretty appearance.

Upon looking a little into the Spanish language, I find it so very nearly like the Latin that I am persuaded we shall learn more of it in a month than we did of French in half a year. The manners of the Spaniards and French are as opposite as grave and gay. The dress of the Spanish officers is much like the French. That of the people a little different. Men and women, gentlemen and ladies, are very fond of long hair, which often reaches, braided in a queue or bound round with a black ribbon, almost to their hams. The ladies wear cloaks, black or white, which come over their heads and shoulders and reach down to their waists. They have fine black eyes, and consequently dark but yet lively complexions.

When, oh when shall I see you again, and live in peace?

The Russian ambassador lately appointed to relieve the one lately in London, passed through France and was a fortnight or three weeks at Paris, from whence the shrewd politicians have conjectured that peace was about to be mediated by that power. But it is said that England is as reluctant to acknowledge the independence of America as to cede Gibraltar, the last of which is insisted upon as well as the first. But this is only bruit. Adieu.

258. JOHN ADAMS

Corunna, 16 December 1779

MY DEAREST FRIEND, — Last night we all arrived in this place from Ferrol. The distance is about twenty miles by land, over high mountains and bad roads. You would have been diverted to have seen us all mounted upon our mules and marching in train. From the mountains we had all along the prospect of a rich, fertile country, cultivated up to the tops of the highest hills and down to the very edge of water, all along the shore.

I made my visit last night to the Governor of the province, who resides here, and to the Governor of the town, and was politely received by both. I have a long journey before me of a thousand miles, I suppose, at least, to Paris. Through this kingdom we shall have bad roads and worse accommodations. I don't expect to be able to get to Paris in less than thirty days. I shall have an opportunity of seeing Spain, but it will be at a great expense. I am advised by everybody to go by land. The frigate, the *Sensible,* is in so bad condition as to make it probable she will not be fit to put to sea in less than three or four weeks, perhaps five or six; and then we should have the storms and enemies of the Bay of Biscay to escape or encounter. After this wandering way of life is passed, I hope to return to my best friend and pass the remainder of our days in quiet.

I cannot learn that Great Britain is yet in temper to listen to propositions of peace, and I don't expect before another winter to have much to do in my present capacity. My tenderest affection to our dear children, and believe me

Ever yours.

259. JOHN ADAMS

Bilbao, 16 January 1780

MY DEAREST FRIEND, — We arrived here last night, all alive, but all very near sick with violent colds taken on the road for want of comfortable accommodations. I was advised on all hands to come by land rather than wait an uncertain time for a passage by sea. But if I had known the difficulties of travelling in that part of Spain which I have passed through, I think I should not have ventured upon the journey. It is vain to attempt a description of our passage. Through the province of Gallicia, and again when we came to that of Biscay, we had an uninterrupted succession of mountains; through that of Leon and the old Castile, constant plains. A country tolerably good by nature, but not well cultivated. Through the whole of the journey the taverns were inconvenient to us, because there are no chimneys in their houses, and we had cold weather. A great part of the way, the wretchedness of our accommodation exceeds all description.

At Bilbao we fare very well, and have received much civility from Messrs. Gardoqui and Sons, as we did at Ferrol and Corunna from M. de Tournelle and M. Lagoanere.[1] I wish I could send you some few things for the use of the family from hence, but the risk is such that I believe I had better wait until we get to France. I have undergone the greatest anxiety for the children through a tedious journey and voyage. I hope their travels will be of service to them, but those at home are best off. My love to them. Adieu, adieu.

260. JOHN ADAMS

Paris, Hotel de Valois, 16 February 1780

My dearest Friend, — I have the honor to be lodged here with no less a personage than the Prince of Hesse Cassel, who is here upon a visit. We occupy different apartments in the same house, and have no intercourse with each other, to be sure; but some wags are of opinion that if I were authorized to open a negotiation with him, I might obtain from him as many troops to fight on our side of the question as he has already hired out to the English against us.

I have found everything agreeable here as yet. The children are happy in their academy, of which I send you the plan inclosed.

The English bounce a great deal about obtaining seven thousand troops from the petty German princes and ten thousand from Ireland, to send to America, but this is only a repetition of their annual gasconade. We are in pain for Charleston, S.C., being apprehensive that they have made or will make an effort to obtain that; which will be a terrible misfortune to that people, and a great loss to the United States, but will be no lasting advantage to our enemies.

The channel of correspondence you propose, by way of Bilbao and Cadiz, will bring many letters, no doubt, and I have received one of the 10th of December, but the postage is so expensive, being obliged to pay forty-four livres for the packet that came with yours, that I would not advise you to send anything that way, unless it be a single letter or anything material in the journals of Congress, or letters from my friends in Congress or elsewhere, that contain anything particularly interesting. The house of Joseph Gardoqui and Sons have sent to you, by Captain Babson, of Newburyport, belonging to Mr. Tracy,[1] some necessaries for the family, and you may write to Mr. Gardoqui for anything you want by any vessel belonging to your uncle, to Mr. Jackson, or Mr. Tracy, provided you don't exceed one hundred dollars by any one vessel. Mr. Gardoqui will readily send them and draw upon me for the money.

I had a great deal of pleasure in the acquaintance of this family of Guardoquis, and was treated by them with the magnificence of a prince. They will be very glad to be useful to you in anything they can do. You will remember, however, that we have many children, and that our duty to them requires that we should manage all our affairs with the strictest economy. My journey through Spain has been infinitely expensive to me, and exceeded far my income. It is very expensive here, and I fear that I shall find it difficult to make both ends meet; but I must and will send you something for necessary use by every opportunity. If Mr. Lovell does not procure me the resolution of Congress I mentioned to him, that of drawing on a certain gentleman or his banker,[2] I shall soon be starved out. Pray mention it to him. If you should have an inclination to write to Cadiz for anything by any vessel going there, Mr. Robert Montgomery, who is settled there, I fancy would cheerfully send it to you, and draw upon me in Paris for his pay. If any vessel should go to Corunna, Mr. Michael Lagoanere would do the same, but this is not a likely way.

I shall write as often as possible, but conveyances will be very rare, I fear.

I am, as I ever was and ever shall be,

Yours, your, yours.

261. JOHN ADAMS

Paris, Hotel de Valois,
Rue de Richelieu, 23 February 1780

MY DEAREST FRIEND, — The children made me a visit to-day, and went with me to dine with my old friends, the two Abbés, whom you have often heard me mention, Chalut and Arnoux, who desire me to mention them to you in my letters as devoted friends of America, and particular friends to me and to you, notwithstanding the difference of religion. The children are still in good health and spirits, and well pleased with their academy. Ah! how much pain have these young gentlemen cost me within these three months! The mountains, the cold, the mules, the houses without chimneys or windows, the—I will not add. I wish for a painter to draw me and my company mounted on muleback, or riding in the calèches, or walking, for we walked one third of the way. Yet by the help of constant care and expense, I have been able to get them all safe to Paris. The other moiety of the family is quite as near my heart, and therefore I hope they will never be ramblers. I am sick of rambling. If I could transport the other moiety across the Atlantic with a wish, and be sure of returning them, when it should become necessary, in the same manner, how happy should I be!

I have been received here with much cordiality, and am daily visited by characters who do me much honor. Some day or other you will know, I believe, but I had better not say at present. Your friend the Comte d'Estaing, however, I ought to mention, because you have been acquainted with him. I have dined with him, and he has visited me and I him, and I hope to have many more conversations with him, for public reasons, not private, for on a private account great men and little are much alike to me.

Mr. Lee and Mr. Izard are going home in the *Alliance* and, I hope, will make you a visit. How many vicissitudes they are to

experience, as well as I and all the rest of our countrymen, I
know not. The events of politics are not less uncertain than those
of war. Whatever they may be, I shall be content. Of one thing I
am pretty sure, that if I return again safe to America, I shall be
happy the remainder of my days, because I shall stay at home,
and at home I must be to be happy. There is no improbability
that I may be obliged to come home again soon, for want of
means to stay here. I hope, however, care will be taken that
something may be done to supply us. My tenderest affection to
Nabby and Tommy. They are better off than their brothers, after
all. I have been taking measures to send home your things, my
brother's, Mrs. Cranch's, Mr. W[ibird's], and Mr. S[hute's]. I
hope to succeed by the *Alliance*. It shall not be my fault, if I do
not. If I cannot send by her, I will wait for another frigate, if it is
a year, for I have no confidence in other vessels.

Yours, forever yours.

262. ABIGAIL ADAMS

28 February 1780

MY DEAREST FRIEND,—This day I am happy in the news of
your safe arrival at Corunna by a vessel arrived at Newburyport
in sixty days from thence. I cannot be sufficiently thankful for
this agreeable intelligence or for the short and I hope comfortable passage with which you were favored. I suppose you will
proceed from thence by land, and flatter myself that a few weeks
will bring me the tidings of your arrival in France.

Captain Sampson has at last arrived after a tedious passage of
eighty-nine days. By him came three letters for you, two from
Arthur Lee and one from Mr. Gellée.[1] Both these gentlemen are
pleased to make mention of me. You will therefore return my respectful compliments to them and tell them that I esteem myself
honored by their notice.

I wrote you by Mr. Austin,[2] who I hope is safely arrived. He
went from here in the height of the sublimest winter I ever saw.
In the latter part of December and beginning of January there
fell the highest snow known since the year 1740; and from that
time to this day the Bay has been frozen so hard that people have

walked, rode, and sledded over it to Boston. It was frozen across Nantasket Road so that no vessel could come in or go out for a month after the storms. We had neither snow, rain, nor the least thaw. It has been remarkably healthy, and we have lived along very comfortable, though many people have suffered greatly for fuel. The winter has been so severe that very little has been attempted and less performed by our army. The enemy have been more active and mischievous, but have failed in their grand attempt of sending large successors to Georgia, by a severe storm which dispersed and wrecked many of their fleet.

We have hopes that, as the combined fleets are again at sea, they will facilitate a negotiation for peace,—a task arduous and important, beset with many dangers.

In one of these letters received by Captain Sampson, Mr. Gellée mentions a report which was raised and circulated concerning you after you left France.

The best reply that could possibly be made to so groundless an accusation is the unsolicited testimony of your country in so speedily returning you there in a more honorable and important mission than that which you had before sustained.

Pride, vanity, envy, ambition, and malice are the ungrateful foes that combat merit and integrity; though for a while they may triumph, to the injury of the just and good, the steady, unwearied perseverance of virtue and honor will finally prevail over them. He who can retire from a public life to a private station with a self-approving conscience, unambitious of pomp or power, has little to dread from the machinations of envy, the snares of treachery, the malice of dissimulation, or the clandestine stabs of calumny. In time they will work their own ruin.

You will be solicitous to know how our Constitution prospers. The Convention are still sitting. I am not at present able to give you an accurate account of their proceedings, but shall endeavor to procure a satisfactory one against a more direct conveyance.

I earnestly long to receive from your own hand assurance of your safety and that of my dear sons. I send the journals and papers I have received. All our friends are well, and desire to be remembered. Enclosed is a list of taxes, since December. In April a much larger is to be collected to pay Penobscot score.[3] Compliments to Mr. Dana. His uncle is recovered from a pleurisy, which threatened his life, but Mrs. Dana will no doubt write by this conveyance, which renders it unnecessary for me to be particular.

Success attend all your endeavors for the public weal; and that happiness and approbation of your country be the reward of your labors is the ardent wish of your affectionate

PORTIA

263. JOHN ADAMS

Without date, 1780

MY DEAR PORTIA, — Yesterday we went to see the garden of the King, *Jardin du Roi,* and his cabinet of natural history, *cabinet d'histoire naturelle.* The cabinet of natural history is a great collection of metals, minerals, shells, insects, birds, beasts, fishes, and precious stones. They are arranged in good order and preserved in good condition, with the name of everything, beautifully written on a piece of paper, annexed to it. There is also a collection of woods and marbles. The garden is large and airy, affording fine walks between rows of trees. Here is a collection, from all parts of the world, of all the plants, roots, and vegetables that are used in medicine, and indeed of all the plants and trees in the world. A fine scene for the studious youths in physic and philosophy. It was a public day. There was a great deal of company, and I had opportunity only to take a cursory view. The whole is very curious. There is a handsome statue of M. Buffon, the great natural historian, whose works you have,[1] whose labors have given fame to this cabinet and garden. When shall we have in America such collections? The collection of American curiosities that I saw in Norwalk, in Connecticut, made by Mr. Arnold, which he afterwards, to my great mortification, sold to Governor Tryon, convinces me that our country affords as ample materials for collections of this nature as any part of the world.

Five midshipmen of the *Alliance* came here last night, Marston, Hogan, Fitzgerald, and two others, from Norway, where they were sent with prizes, which the court of Denmark were absurd and unjust enough to restore to the English. They, however, treated the officers and people well, and defrayed their expenses. They say the Norwegians were very angry with the court of Copenhagen for delivering up these vessels. It was the blunder of ignorance, I believe, rather than any ill will.

Every day, when I ride out without any particular business to do or visit to make, I order my servant to carry me to some place where I never was before, so that, at last, I believe, I have seen all Paris and all the fields and scenes about it that are near it. It is very pleasant. Charles is as well beloved here as at home. Wherever he goes everybody loves him. Mr. Dana is as fond of him, I think, as I am. He learns very well.

There is a volume in folio just published here, which I yesterday ran over at a bookseller's shop. It is a description and a copperplate of all the engravings upon precious stones in the collection of the Duke of Orleans. The stamps are extremely beautiful, and are representations of the gods and heroes of antiquity, with most of the fables of their mythology. Such a book would be very useful to the children in studying the classics, but it is too dear; three guineas, unbound. There is everything here that can inform the understanding or refine the taste, and indeed, one would think, that could purify the heart. Yet it must be remembered there is everything here, too, which can seduce, betray, deceive, deprave, corrupt, and debauch it. Hercules marches here in full view of the steeps of virtue on one hand and the flowery paths of pleasure on the other, and there are few who make the choice of Hercules. That my children may follow his example is my earnest prayer; but I sometimes tremble when I hear the siren song of sloth, lest they should be captivated with her bewitching charms and her soft, insinuating music.

264. JOHN ADAMS

Without date, 1780

MY DEAR PORTIA, — The inclosed "Dialogue in the Shades" was written by Mr. Edmund Jenings,[1] now residing at Brussels, a native of Maryland. I will send you the rest when I can get it. How I lament the loss of my packets by Austin! There were, I suppose, letters from Congress of great importance to me. I know not what I shall do without them. I suppose there was authority to draw, etc. Mr. T[haxter]'s letter from his father hints that Mr. L[aurens?] is coming here. This will be excellent.

Since my arrival this time, I have driven about Paris more than I did before. The rural scenes around this town are charming. The public walks, gardens, etc., are extremely beautiful. The gardens of the Palais Royal and the gardens of the Tuileries are very fine. The Place de Louis XV, the Place Vendôme or Place de Louis XIV, the Place Victoire, the Place Royale, are fine squares, ornamented with very magnificent statues. I wish I had time to describe these objects to you, in a manner that I should have done twenty-five years ago; but my head is too full of schemes, and my heart of anxiety, to use expressions borrowed from you know whom. To take a walk in the gardens of the palace of the Tuileries, and describe the statues there, all in marble, in which the ancient divinities and heroes are represented with exquisite art, would be a very pleasant amusement and instructive entertainment, improving in history, mythology, poetry, as well as in statuary. Another walk in the gardens of Versailles would be useful and agreeable. But to observe these objects with taste, and describe them so as to be understood, would require more time and thought than I can possibly spare. It is not indeed the fine arts which our country requires; the useful, the mechanic arts are those which we have occasion for in a young country as yet simple and not far advanced in luxury, although perhaps much too far for her age and character. I could fill volumes with descriptions of temples and palaces, paintings, sculptures, tapestry, porcelain, etc., etc., etc., if I could have time; but I could not do this without neglecting my duty. The science of government it is my duty to study, more than all other sciences; the arts of legislation and administration and negotiation ought to take place of, indeed to exclude, in a manner, all other arts. I must study politics and war, that my sons may have liberty to study mathematics and philosophy. My sons ought to study mathematics and philosophy, geography, natural history and naval architecture, navigation, commerce, and agriculture, in order to give their children a right to study painting, poetry, music, architecture, statuary, tapestry, and porcelain. Adieu.

265. JOHN ADAMS

Paris, 17 June 1780

MY DEAR PORTIA, — I yesterday received a letter of the 26th of April from brother Cranch, for which I thank him, and will answer as soon as possible. He tells me you have drawn a little bill upon me. I am sorry for it, because I have sent and should continue to send you small presents, by which you would be enabled to do better than by drawing bills. I would not have you draw any more. I will send you things which will defray your expenses better. The machine is horribly dear. Mr. C. desires to know if he may draw on me. I wish it was in my power to oblige him, but it is not. I have no remittances, nor anything to depend on. Not a line from Congress, nor any member, since I left you. My expenses through Spain were beyond all imagination, and my expenses here are so exorbitant that I can't answer any bill from anybody, not even from you, excepting the one you have drawn. I must beg you to be as prudent as possible. Depend upon it, your children will have occasion for all your economy. Mr. Johonnot must send me some bills. Every farthing is expended, and more. You can have no idea of my unavoidable expenses. I know not what to do. Your little affairs and those of all our friends, Mr. Wibird, etc., are on board the *Alliance,* and have been, so these four months, or ready to be. Pray write me by way of Spain and Holland, as well as France. We are all well. My duty to your father, my mother, and affection and respects where due. My affections, I fear, got the better of my judgment in bringing my boys. They behave very well, however.

London is in the horrors.[1] Governor Hutchinson fell down dead at the first appearance of mobs. They have been terrible. A spirit of bigotry and fanaticism, mixing with the universal discontents of the nation, has broken out into violences of the most dreadful nature, burned Lord Mansfield's house, books, manuscripts; burned the King's Bench prison and all the other prisons, let loose all the debtors and criminals, tore to pieces Sir George Saville's house, insulted all the lords of Parliament, etc., etc. Many have been killed, martial law proclaimed, many hanged.

Lord George Gordon committed to the Tower for high treason, and where it will end, God only knows. The mobs all cried, Peace with America and war with France. Poor wretches! as if this were possible!

In the English papers they have inserted the death of Mr. Hutchinson with severity, in these words: "Governor Hutchinson is no more. On Saturday last he dropped down dead. It is charity to hope that his sins will be buried with him in the tomb, but they must be recorded in his epitaph. His misrepresentations have contributed to the continuance of the war with America. Examples are necessary. It is to be hoped that all will not escape into the grave without a previous appearance either on a gibbet or a scaffold."

Governor Bernard, I am told, died last fall.[2] I wish that, with these primary instruments of the calamities that now distress almost all the world, the evils themselves may come to an end. For although they will undoubtedly end in the welfare of mankind, and accomplish the benevolent designs of Providence towards the two worlds, yet for the present they are not joyous but grievous. May Heaven permit you and me to enjoy the cool evening of life in tranquillity, undisturbed by the cares of politics or war, and above all, with the sweetest of all reflections, that neither ambition nor vanity nor avarice nor malice nor envy nor revenge nor fear nor any base motive or sordid passion, through the whole course of this mighty revolution, and the rapid, impetuous course of great and terrible events that have attended it, have drawn us aside from the line of our duty and the dictates of our consciences. Let us have ambition enough to keep our simplicity or frugality, and our integrity, and transmit these virtues as the fairest of inheritances to our children.

266. ABIGAIL ADAMS

Sunday Evening, 16 July 1780

MY DEAREST FRIEND, — I had just returned to my chamber and taken up my pen to congratulate you upon the arrival of the fleet of our allies at Newport, when I was called down to receive

the most agreeable of presents,—letters from my dearest friend.
One bearing date March 28th, by Mr. Izard, and one of May 3d,
taken out of the post-office; but to what port they arrived first I
know not. They could not be those by the fleet, as in these you
make mention of letters which I have not yet received, nor by the
Alliance, since Mr. Williams sailed twenty-five days after the
fleet, and she was then in France. A pity, I think, that she should
stay there when here we are *almost destitute.* Our navy has been
unfortunate indeed. I am sorry to find that only a few lines have
reached you from me. I have written by way of Spain, Holland,
and Sweden, but not one single direct conveyance have I had to
France since you left me. I determine to open a communication
by way of Gardoqui, and wish you would make use of the same
conveyance. This with some others will go direct to you, by the
Mars, Captain Sampson commander, a state vessel. She will return in the fall; by her should be glad you would order all the articles I have written for by Mr. Guild[1] or any other way. So few
opportunities offer that my list will contain more articles than I
should otherwise mention.

What shall I say of our political affairs? Shall I exclaim at
measures now impossible to remedy? No. I will hope *all* from
the generous aid of our allies, in concert with our own exertions.
I am not suddenly elated or depressed. I know America capable
of anything she undertakes with spirit and vigor. "Brave in distress, serene in conquest, drowsy when at rest," is her true char-
acteristic. Yet I deprecate a failure in our present effort. The
efforts are great, and we give, this campaign, more than half our
property to defend the other. He who tarries from the field cannot possibly earn sufficient at home to reward him who takes it.
Yet, should Heaven bless our endeavors, and crown this year
with the blessings of peace, no exertion will be thought too
great, no price of property too dear. My whole soul is absorbed
in the idea. The honor of my dearest friend, the welfare and happiness of this wide-extended country, ages yet unborn, depend
for their happiness and security upon the able and skillful, the
honest and upright, discharge of the important trust committed
to him. It would not become me to write the full flow of my
heart upon this occasion. My constant petition for him is that he

may so discharge the trust reposed in him as to merit the approving eye of Heaven, and peace, liberty, and safety crown his latest years in his own native land.

The Marchioness, at the Abbé Raynal's,[2] is not the only lady who joins an approving voice to that of her country, though at the expense of her present domestic happiness. It is easier to admire virtue than to practice it; especially the great virtue of self-denial. I find but few sympathizing souls. Why should I look for them? since few have any souls, but of the sensitive kind. That nearest allied to my own they have taken from me, and tell me honor and fame are a compensation.

> "Fame, wealth, or honor,—what are ye to love?"[3]

But hushed be my pen. Let me cast my eye upon the letters before me. What is the example? I follow it in silence. I have repeated to you in former letters that I had received all your letters from Spain, unless you wrote by Captain Trask, who brought me some articles, but no letters. My father desires to be remembered to you, but will, I fear, never again see you. He declines daily; has a slow fever banging about him, which wastes his flesh and spirits. These are tender ties, and how far soever advanced in life, the affectionate child feels loath to part with the guide of youth, the kind adviser of riper years. Yet the pillars must moulder with time, and the fabric fall to the dust.

Present my compliments to Mr. Dana. Tell him I have called upon his lady, and we enjoyed an afternoon of sweet communion. I find she would not be averse to taking a voyage, should he be continued abroad. She groans most bitterly, and is irreconcilable to his absence. I am a mere philosopher to her. I am *inured*, but not hardened, to the painful portion. Shall I live to see it otherwise?

Your letters are always valuable to me, but more particularly so when they close with an affectionate assurance of regard, which, though I do not doubt, is never repeated without exciting the tenderest sentiments; and never omitted without pain to the affectionate bosom of your   PORTIA

267. ABIGAIL ADAMS

23 August 1780

I could not omit so favorable an opportunity as the present of writing you a line by Mr. Warren,[1] who is upon his travel and probably may take France in his way. The welfare of your family is so essential to your happiness that I would improve every means of assuring you of it and of communicating to you the pleasure I have had in receiving every letter you have written since you first left the harbor of Boston. Mine to you have not been equally successful. Several packets have been sent to Neptune, though improperly directed, and I query whether, having found his mistake, he has had complaisance enough to forward them. So that you must not charge to me any failure, in point of punctuality or attention, but to the avidity of the watery god who I really believe has destroyed them. But enough of romance.

You see me in good spirits. I can tell you the cause. The *Alliance* arrived last week and brought me the feast of reason and the flow of soul; assurances too of the health of my dear absent friends. Those only who know what a separation is of the tenderest connections can form adequate ideas of the happiness which even a literary communication affords.

I have written to you and my dear sons by Captain Sampson. If Mr. Warren should be bearer of this to you, I need not ask you to love him. His merit will insure him that, and every attention he may stand in need of, from one who never suffers the promising youth to pass unnoticed by. He has a double claim to your friendship, not only on account of his own worth but the long and intimate friendship which has ever subsisted between his worthy parents and the friend I address, who will accept of the tenderest sentiments for his health and happiness from his ever affectionate   A. ADAMS

268. JOHN ADAMS

Amsterdam, 15 September 1780

MY DEAR PORTIA, — I wish you to write me by every opportunity to this place as well as to France. It seems as if I never
should get any more letters from America. I have sent you some
things by Captain Davis, but he has no arms, and I fear they will
be lost by capture. I sent things by the *Alliance*.

The country where I am is the greatest curiosity in the world.
This nation is not known anywhere, not even by its neighbors.
The Dutch language is spoken by none but themselves. Therefore they converse with nobody, and nobody converses with
them. The English are a great nation, and they despise the Dutch
because they are smaller. The French are a greater nation still,
and therefore they despise the Dutch because they are still
smaller in comparison to them. But I doubt much whether there
is any nation of Europe more estimable than the Dutch in proportion. Their industry and economy ought to be examples to
the world. They have less ambition, I mean that of conquest and
military glory, than their neighbors, but I don't perceive that
they have more avarice. And they carry learning and arts, I
think, to greater extent. The collections of curiosities, public and
private, are innumerable.

I am told that Mr. Searle[1] is arrived at Brest; but I have learned
nothing from him as yet, nor do I know his destination. The
French and Spanish fleets have made a sweep of sixty upon the
English East India and West India fleets. This must have great effects. We are all well. Don't expect peace. The English have not
yet forgotten the acquisition of Charleston, for which they are
making the most childish exaltations. The new Parliament will
give ministry a run. Mark my words, you will have no peace but
what you give yourselves by destroying, root and branch, all the
British force in America. The English cannot bear the thought
that France should dictate the terms of peace, as they call it. They
say they must make a dishonorable peace now, a shameful peace,
a degrading peace. This is worse than death to them, and thus
they will go on, until they are forced to sue for a peace still more
shameful and humiliating.

269. ABIGAIL ADAMS

15 October 1780

MY DEAREST FRIEND, — I closed a long letter to you only two days ago, and sent it to Cadiz, but as no opportunity is omitted by me, I embrace this, as Colonel Fleury[1] was kind enough to write me on purpose, from Newport, to inform me of it, and to promise a careful attention to it. Yet I feel doubtful of its safety. The enemy seems to be collecting a prodigious force into these seas, and is bent upon the destruction of our allies. We are not a little anxious for them, and cannot but wonder that they are not yet reinforced. Graves's fleet, Arbuthnot's, and Rodney's, all here; with such a superiority, can it be matter of surprise if M. de Ternay[2] should fall a sacrifice? My own mind, I own, is full of apprehension; yet I trust we shall not be delivered over to the vengeance of a nation more wicked and perverse than our own. We daily experience the correcting and the defending arm. The inclosed papers will give you the particulars of an infernal plot,[3] and the providential discovery of it. For, however the belief of a particular Providence may be exploded by the modern wits, and the infidelity of too many of the rising generation deride the idea, yet the virtuous mind will look up and acknowledge the great First Cause, without whose notice not even a sparrow falls to the ground.

I am anxious to hear from you. Your last letter, which I have received, was dated June 17th. I have written you repeatedly, that my trunk was not put on board the *Alliance;* that poor vessel was the sport of more than winds and waves. The conduct with regard to her is considered as very extraordinary. She came to Boston, as you have no doubt heard. Landais is suspended.[4] The man must be new-made before he can be entitled to command. I hope Captain Sampson arrived safe. He carried the resolve of Congress which you wanted.

As to our domestic affairs, Mr. Hall is dead, and your mother went to your brother, he having lost his wife in the spring, and was there taken ill. I sent for her home, and have nursed the old lady through a severe turn of a fever in which I feared for her life. She is, however, upon the recovery and desires her tenderest regards to you, though she fears she shall not live to see your return. I am myself just recovering from a slow fever, weak and feeble yet. If you have an opportunity by way of Holland by Mr. Austin to send me some paint and oil, stone color, I wish you would.

You tell me to send you prices current. I will aim at it. Corn is now thirty pounds, rye twenty-seven, per bushel. Flour from a hundred and forty to a hundred and thirty per hundred. Beef, eight dollars per pound; mutton, nine; lamb, six, seven, and eight. Butter, twelve dollars per pound; cheese, ten. Sheep's wool, thirty dollars per pound; flax, twenty. West India articles: sugar, from a hundred and seventy to two hundred pounds per hundred; molasses, forty-eight dollars per gallon; tea, ninety; coffee, twelve; cotton-wool, thirty per pound. Exchange from seventy to seventy-five for hard money. Bills at fifty. Money scarce; plenty of goods; *enormous* taxes. Our State affairs are thus. Hancock will be Governor, by a *very great* majority; the Senate will have to choose the Lieutenant-governor. Our constitution is read with great admiration in New York, and pronounced by the Royal Governor the best republican form he ever saw, but with sincere hopes that it might not be accepted. How will it be administered? is now the important question.

I request you would write to me by the way of Bilbao and Holland. I have sent you a set of bills for four hundred dollars. I have one more for a hundred which I have not yet inclosed. I did not know but I had best send it to Holland or Bilbao, but am not determined. Enclosed is a letter for Mr. Thaxter. Shall write again to Amsterdam; a vessel will soon sail. Let Mr. Dana know that I heard last night from Mrs. Dana that she, the judge, and family were all well.

The report of the day is that three thousand troops are arrived at New York from England.

Adieu!   Most affectionately yours.

270. JOHN ADAMS

Amsterdam, 18 December 1780

MY DEAREST PORTIA, — I have this morning sent Mr. Thaxter with my two sons to Leyden, there to take up their residence for some time, and there to pursue their studies of Latin and Greek under the excellent masters, and there to attend lectures of the celebrated professors in that university. It is much cheaper there than here. The air is infinitely purer, and the company and conversation are better. It is perhaps as learned a University as any in Europe.

I should not wish to have children educated in the common schools in this country, where a littleness of soul is notorious. The masters are mean-spirited wretches, pinching, kicking, and boxing the children upon every turn. There is besides a general littleness arising from the incessant contemplation of stivers and doits,[1] which pervades the whole people. Frugality and industry are virtues everywhere, but avarice and stinginess are not frugality. The Dutch say that without a habit of thinking of every doit before you spend it, no man can be a good merchant, or conduct trade with success. This I believe is a just maxim in general, but I would never wish to see a son of mine govern himself by it. It is the sure and certain way for an industrious man to be rich. It is the only possible way for a merchant to become the first merchant or the richest man in the place. But this is an object that I hope none of my children will ever aim at. It is indeed true, everywhere, that those who attend to small expenses are always rich.

I would have my children attend to doits and farthings as devoutly as the merest Dutchman upon earth, if such attention was necessary to support their independence. A man who discovers a disposition and a design to be independent seldom succeeds. A jealousy arises against him. The tyrants are alarmed on one side lest he should oppose them. The slaves are alarmed on the other lest he should expose their servility. The cry from all quarters is, "He is the proudest man in the world. He cannot bear to be under obligation." I never in my life observed any one endeavoring to lay me under particular obligations to him, but I suspected he had a design to make me his dependent, and to have claims upon my gratitude. This I should have no objection to, because gratitude is always in one's power. But the danger is that men will expect and require more of us than honor and innocence and rectitude will permit us to perform.

In our country, however, any man, with common industry and

prudence, may be independent. But to put an end to this stuff, adieu—most affectionately adieu.

271. ABIGAIL ADAMS

28 January 1781

MY DEAREST FRIEND,—Last evening General Lincoln called here, introducing to me a gentleman by the name of Colonel Laurens,[1] the son, as I suppose, of your much esteemed friend, the late President of Congress, who informed me that he expected to sail for France in a few days, and would take dispatches from me. Although I closed letters to you, by way of Holland, a few days ago, I would not omit so good an opportunity as the present. 'Tis a long time since the date of your last letters, the 25th of September. I wait with much anxiety, listening to the sound of every gun, but none announce the arrival of the *Fame,* from Holland, which we greatly fear is taken or lost, nor the *Mars,* from France. I wish you had been fortunate enough to have sent letters by Updike to Providence, who sailed the day after the *Fame,* but suppose you wrote by her, and sailing so near together, did not think it worth your while to write by him. Colonel Laurens is enabled, I suppose, to give you every kind of intelligence respecting the army, which you may wish to learn. Mr. Cranch has written you upon the same subject by way of Holland. Your friends here complain that you do not write to them. I suppose Davis threw over half a hundred letters. If you are unfortunate in that way, it is not to be helped.

I have the pleasure to inform you that a repeal of the obnoxious tender act[2] has passed the House and Senate. The Governor, as has been heretofore predicted, when anything not quite popular is in agitation, has the gout, and is confined to his bed. A false weight and a false balance are an abomination, and in that light this tender act must be viewed by every impartial person. Who, but an idiot, would believe that forty was equal to seventy-five? But the repeal gives us reason to hope that justice and righteousness will again exalt our nation; that public faith will be restored; that individuals will lend to the public; and that the heavy taxes, which now distress all orders, will be lessened.

A late committee, who have been sitting upon ways and means for raising money, tell us that a tax for two years more, equal to what we have paid in the last, would clear this State of debt. You may judge of the weight of them; yet our State taxes are but as a grain of mustard seed, when compared with our town taxes. Clinton, I hear, has sent out a proclamation upon Germain's plan, inviting the people to make a separate peace, which will only be a new proof of the ignorance and folly of our enemies, without making a single proselyte. Even the revolted Pennsylvania troops gave up to justice the spies whom Clinton sent to them offering them clothing and pay, letting him know that it was justice from their State, not favors from their enemies, which they wanted.

It is reported that Arnold, with a body of troops,[3] is gone to Virginia, where it is hoped he and his Myrmidons will meet their fate. Had Clinton been a generous enemy, or known human nature, he would, like Aurelian, upon a like occasion, have given up the traitor to the hands of justice;[4] knowing that it was in vain to expect fidelity in a man who had betrayed his own country, which, from his defection, may learn to place a higher value upon integrity and virtue than upon a savage ferocity, so often mistaken for courage. He who, as an individual, is cruel, unjust, and immoral, will not be likely to possess the virtues necessary in a general or statesman. Yet in our infant country, infidelity and debauchery are so fashionably prevalent that less attention is paid to the characters of those who fill important offices, than a love of virtue and zeal for public liberty can warrant; which, we are told by wise legislators of old, are the surest preservatives of public happiness.

You observe in a late letter that your absence from your native State will deprive you of an opportunity of being a man of importance in it. I hope you are doing your country more extensive service abroad than you could have done had you been confined to one State only; and whilst you continue in the same estimation among your fellow-citizens in which you are now held, you will not fail of being of importance to them at home or abroad.

Heaven preserve the life and health of my dear absent friend, and, in its own time, return him to his country and to the arms of his ever affectionate   PORTIA

P.S. Love to my dear boys. I have sent you a present by Colonel Laurens.

272. ABIGAIL ADAMS

25 May 1781

In this beautiful month, when nature wears her gayest garb, and animal and vegetable life is diffused on every side, when the cheerful hand of industry is laying a foundation for a plentiful harvest, who can forbear to rejoice in the season, or refrain from looking "through nature up to nature's God";[1]

> "To feel the present Deity, and taste
> The joy of God, to see a happy world."

While my heart expands, it, sighing, seeks its associate, and joins its first parent in that beautiful description of Milton:—

> "Sweet is the breath of Morn, her rising sweet,
>   With charm of earliest birds; pleasant the sun,
>   When first on this delightful land he spreads
>   His orient beams on herb, tree, fruit, and flower,
>   Glistering with dew, fragrant the fertile earth
>   After soft showers; and sweet the coming on
>   Of grateful Evening mild; then silent Night
>   With this her solemn bird, and this fair moon,
>   And these the gems of heaven, her starry train:
>   But neither breath of morn when she ascends
>   With charm of earliest birds; nor rising sun
>   On this delightful land; nor herb, fruit, flower,
>   Glistering with dew; nor fragrance after showers;
>   Not grateful Evening mild; nor silent Night
>   With this her solemn bird, nor walk by moon,
>   Or glittering starlight, *without thee is sweet.*"

This passage has double charms for me, painted by the hand of truth; and for the same reason that a dear friend of mine, after having viewed a profusion of beautiful pictures, pronounced that which represented the parting of Hector and Andromache[2] to be worth them all. The journal in which this is mentioned does not add any reason why it was so; but Portia felt its full force, and paid a grateful tear to the acknowledgment.

This day, my dear friend, completes eight months since the date of your last letter, and five since it was received. You may judge of my anxiety. I doubt not but you have written many times since, but Mars, Bellona, and Old Neptune are in league against me. I think you must still be in Holland, from whence no vessels have arrived since the declaration of war.[3] There are some late arrivals from France, but no private letters. I have had the pleasure of hearing of the safety of several vessels which went from hence, by which I wrote to you, so that I have reason to think I have communicated pleasure, though I have not been a partaker in the same way.

This will be delivered to you by Mr. Storer,[4] who is going first to Denmark, and who designs to tarry abroad some time. If you had been a resident in your own country, it would have been needless for me to have told you that Mr. Storer is a gentleman of fair character, I need not add, of amiable manners, as these are so discoverable in him upon the slightest acquaintance.

We are anxiously waiting for intelligence from abroad. We shall have in the field a more respectable army than has appeared there since the commencement of the war; and all raised for three years or during the war, most of them men who have served before. The towns have exerted themselves upon this occasion with a spirit becoming patriots.

We wish for a naval force, superior to what we have yet had, to act in concert with our army. We have been flattered from day to day, yet none has arrived. The enemy exults in the delay, and is improving the time to ravage Carolina and Virginia.

We hardly know what to expect from the United Provinces, because we are not fully informed of their disposition. Britain has struck a blow, by the capture of Eustatia, sufficient to arouse and unite them against her, if there still exists that spirit of liberty which shone so conspicuous in their ancestors, and which, under much greater difficulties, led their hardy forefathers to reject the tyranny of Philip. I wish your powers may extend to an alliance with them, and that you may be as successful against the artifices of Britain as a former ambassador was against those of another nation, when he negotiated a triple alliance in the course of five days, with an address which has ever done honor to his memory. If I was not so nearly connected, I should add that there is no small similarity in the character of my friend and the gentleman, whose memoirs[5] I have read with great pleasure.

Our State affairs I will write you, if the vessel does not sail till after election. Our friend Mr. Cranch goes from here representative, by a unanimous vote. Dr. Tufts, of Weymouth, is chosen senator. Our Governor and Lieutenant-governor, as at the beginning. Our poor old currency is breathing its last gasp. It received a most fatal wound from a collection of near the whole body's entering here from the southward; having been informed that it was treated here with more respect, and that it could purchase a solid and durable dress here for seventy-five paper dollars, but half the expense it must be at there, it travelled here with its whole train; and, being much debauched in its manners, communicated the contagion all of a sudden, and is universally rejected. It has given us a great shock. Mr. Storer can give you more information.

I have by two or three opportunities acquainted you that I received the calicoes you ordered for me, by Sampson, though many of them were much injured by being wet. I have not got my things yet from Philadelphia. I have acquainted you with my misfortune there, owing to the bad package. I have no invoice or letter from Mr. Moylan, though I have reason to think many things have been stolen, as all Dr. Tufts's are missing, and several of mine, according to Mr. Lovell's invoice, who was obliged to unpack what remained and dry them by a fire, most of them much damaged.

Our friends in general are well, your mother in a declining way. I rather think the good lady will not continue many years, unless her health mends. I fear not the present. She is anxious to hear from you whilst she lives, but bids me tell you not to expect to see her again. To my dear sons I shall write by this opportunity. I have not received a line from them for this twelvemonth.

I hope they continue to behave worthy the esteem of everybody, which will never fail to communicate the greatest pleasure to their affectionate parents. I inclosed an invoice of a few articles by Captain Brown. I will repeat it here. Everything in the goods way will be an acceptable remittance to

Your ever affectionate   PORTIA

273. ABIGAIL ADAMS TO
JOHN QUINCY ADAMS

Braintree, 26 May 1781

MY DEAR JOHN, — I hope this letter will be more fortunate than yours have been of late. I know you must have written many times since I had the pleasure of receiving a line from you, for this month completes a year since the date of your last letter. Not a line from you or my dear Charles since you arrived in Holland, where I suppose you still are. I never was more anxious to hear, yet not a single vessel arrives from that port, though several are looked for. I hope my dear boy that the universal neatness and cleanliness, of the people where you reside, will cure you of all your slovenly tricks, and you will learn from them industry, economy, and frugality.

I would recommend it to you to become acquainted with the history of that country, as in many respects it is similar to the Revolution of your own. Tyranny and oppression were the original causes of the revolt of both countries. It is from a wide and extensive view of mankind that a just and true estimate can be formed of the powers of human nature. She appears ennobled or deformed, as religion, government, laws, and custom guide or direct her. Fierce, rude, and savage in the uncultivated desert; gloomy, bigoted, and superstitious where truth is veiled in obscurity and mystery; ductile, pliant, elegant, and refined, you have seen her in that dress, as well as in the active, bold, hardy, and intrepid garb of your own country.

Inquire of the historic page, and let your own observations second the inquiry, Whence arises the difference? and when compared, learn to cultivate those dispositions, and to practice those virtues, which, tend most to the benefit and happiness of mankind.

The great Author of our religion frequently inculcates universal benevolence, and taught us both by precept and example, when He promulgated peace and good-will to man, a doctrine very different from that which actuates the hostile invaders and the cruel ravagers of mighty kingdoms and nations.

I hope you will be very particular, when you write, and let me know how you have passed your time in the course of the year past.

Your favorable account of your brother gave me great pleasure, not only as it convinced me that he continues to cultivate that agreeable disposition of mind and heart which so greatly endeared him to his friends here, but as it was a proof of the brotherly love and affection of a son not less dear to his parents.

Your brother Tommy has been very sick with the rheumatism, taken by going too early into the water, by which means he lost the use of his limbs and a fever ensued. He has, however, happily recovered, and learnt wisdom I hope by his sufferings. He hopes soon to write you a letter. He has a good school and is attentive to his books. I shall write to your brother, so shall only add the sincere wishes for your improvement and happiness of

Your ever affectionate   MOTHER

274. JOHN ADAMS

Amsterdam, 2 December 1781

MY DEAREST FRIEND, — Your favors of September 29 and October 21 are before me. I avoided saying anything about Charles to save you the anxiety which I fear you will now feel in its greatest severity a long time. I thought he would go directly home in a short passage in the best opportunity which would probably ever present. But I am disappointed. Charles is at Bilbao with Major Jackson and Colonel Trumbull,[1] who take the best care of his education, as well as his health and behavior. They are to go hence with Captain Hill[2] in a good vessel of twenty guns. Charles's health was so much affected by this tainted atmosphere, and he had set his heart so much upon go-

ing home with Gillon,[3] that it would have broken it to have refused him. I desire I may never again have the weakness to bring
a child to Europe. They are infinitely better at home. We have all
been sick here, myself, Mr. Thaxter, Stevens, and another servant, but are all better. Mr. Thaxter's indisposition has been
slight and short, mine and Stevens's long and severe.

I beg you would not flatter yourself with hopes of peace. There
will be no such thing for several years. Don't distress yourself
neither about any malicious attempts to injure me in the estimation of my countrymen. Let them take their course and go the
length of their tether. They will never hurt your husband, whose
character is fortified with a shield of innocence and honor ten
thousand fold stronger than brass or iron. The contemptable essays made by you know who[4] will only tend to his own confusion. My letters have shown them their own ignorance, a sight
they could not bear. Say as little about it as I do. It has already
brought them into the true system, and that system is triumphant. I laugh and will laugh before all posterity at their impotent rage and envy. They could not help blushing, themselves,
if they were to review their conduct.

Dear Tom, thy letter does thee much honor. Thy brother
Charles shall teach thee French and Dutch at home. I wish I
could get time to correspond with thee and thy sister more regularly, but I cannot. I must trust Providence and thine excellent
mamma for the education of my children. Mr. Dana and our son
are well at Petersburg.[5] Hayden has some things for you. I hope
he is arrived. I am sorry to learn you have a sum of paper. How
could you be so imprudent? You must be frugal, I assure you.
Your children will be poorly off. I can but barely live in the manner that is indispensably demanded of me by everybody. Living
is dear indeed here. My children will not be so well left by their
father as he was by his. They will be infected with the examples
and habits and tastes for expensive living without the means. He
was not. My children shall never have the smallest soil of dishonor or disgrace brought upon them by their father, no, not to
please ministers, kings, or nations. At the expense of a little of
this, my children might perhaps ride at their ease through life,
but dearly as I love them, they shall live in the service of their
country, in her navy, her army, or even out of either in the ex-

tremest degree of poverty, before I will depart in the smallest iota from my sentiments of honor and delicacy; for I, even I, have sentiments of delicacy as exquisite as the proudest minister that ever served a monarch. They may not be exactly like those of some ministers.

I beg you would excuse me to my dear friends, to whom I cannot write so often as I wish. I have indispensable duties which take up all my time, and require more than I have.

General Washington has done me great honor and much public service by sending me authentic accounts of his own and General Greene's last great actions.[6] They are in the way to negotiate peace. It lies wholly with them. No other ministers but they and their colleague in the army can accomplish the great event.

I am keeping house, but I want a housekeeper. What a fine affair it would be, if we could flit across the Atlantic as they say the angels do from planet to planet! I would dart to Penn's Hill and bring you over on my wings; but, alas, we must keep house separately for some time. But one thing I am determined on. If God should please to restore me once more to your fireside, I will never again leave it without your ladyship's company—no, not even to Congress to Philadelphia, and there I am determined to go, if I can make interest enough to get chosen, whenever I return. I would give a million sterling that you were here; and I could afford it as well as Great Britain can the thirty millions she must spend, the ensuing year, to complete her own ruin. Farewell, farewell.

275. ABIGAIL ADAMS

9 December 1781

MY DEAREST FRIEND, — I hear the *Alliance* is again going to France, with the Marquis de la Fayette and the Count de Noailles.[1] I will not envy the Marquis the pleasure of annually visiting his family, considering the risk he runs in doing it; besides, he deserves the good wishes of every American, and a large portion of the honors and applause of his own country. He returns with the additional merit of laurels won at Yorktown by the capture of a whole British army. America may boast that she has accomplished what no power before her ever did, contending with Britain,—captured two of their celebrated generals, and each with an army of thousands of veteran troops to support them. This event, whilst it must fill Britain with despondency, will draw the Union already framed still closer and give us additional allies; and, if properly improved, will render a negotiation easier and more advantageous to America.

But I cannot reflect much upon public affairs until I have unburdened the load of my own heart. Where shall I begin my list of grievances? Not by accusations, but lamentations. My first is that I do not hear from you; a few lines only, dated in April and May, have come to hand for fifteen months. You do not mention receiving any from me except by Captain Casneau, though I wrote by Colonel Laurens, by Captain Brown, by Mr. Storer, Dexter, and many others; to Bilbao by Babson, by Trask, and several times by way of France. You will refer me to Gillon, I suppose. Gillon has acted a base part, of which, no doubt, you are long ere now apprised. You had great reason to suppose that he would reach America as soon or sooner than the merchant vessels, and placed much confidence in him by the treasure you permitted to go on board of him. Ah, how great has my anxiety been! What have I not suffered since I heard my dear Charles was on board, and no intelligence to be procured of the vessel for four months after he sailed. Most people concluded that she was foundered at sea, as she sailed before a violent storm. Only three weeks ago did I hear the contrary. My uncle dispatched a messenger, the moment a vessel from Bilbao arrived with the happy tidings that she was safe at Corunna; that the passengers had all left the ship in consequence of Gillon's conduct, and were arrived at Bilbao. The vessel sailed the day that the passengers arrived at Bilbao, so that no letters came by Captain Lovett; but a Dr. Sands reports that he saw a child, who they told him was yours, and that he was well. This was a cordial to my dejected spirits. I know not what to wish for. Should he attempt to come at this season upon the coast, it has more horrors than I have fortitude. I am still distressed; I must resign him to the kind, protecting hand of that Being who hath hitherto preserved him, and submit to whatever dispensation is allotted me.

What is the matter with Mr. Thaxter? Has he forgotten all his

American friends, that, out of four vessels which have arrived, not a line is to be found on board of one of them from him? I could quarrel with the climate, but surely, if it is subject to the ague, there is a fever fit as well as a cold one. Mr. Guild tells me he was charged with letters, but left them, with his other things, on board the frigate. She gave him the slip and he stepped on board of Captain Brown's ship, and happily arrived safe. From him I have learned many things respecting my dear connections; but still I long for that free communication which I see but little prospect of obtaining. Let me again entreat you to write by way of Gardoqui. Bilbao is as safe a conveyance as I know of. Ah, my dear John! where are you? In so remote a part of the globe, that I fear I shall not hear a syllable from you. Pray write me all the intelligence you get from him; send me his letters to you. Do you know I have not had a line from him for a year and a half? Alas! my dear, I am much afflicted with a disorder called the *heartache*, nor can any remedy be found in America. It must be collected from Holland, Petersburg, and Bilbao.

And now, having recited my griefs and complaints, the next in place are those of my neighbors. I have been applied to by the parents of several Braintree youth to write to you in their behalf, requesting your aid and assistance, if it is in your power to afford it. Captain Cathcart, in the privateer *Essex*, from Salem, went out on a cruise last April in the Channel of England, and was, on the 10th of June, so unfortunate as to be taken and carried into Ireland. The officers were confined there, but the sailors were sent prisoners to Plymouth jail, twelve of whom are from this town, a list of whom I inclose. The friends of these people have received intelligence by way of an officer who belonged to the *Protector*, and who escaped from the jail, that in August last they were all alive, several of them very destitute of clothing, having taken but a few with them and those for the summer, particularly Ned Savil and Job Field. Their request is, that, if you can, you would render them some assistance; if not by procuring an exchange, that you would get them supplied with necessary clothing. I have told them that you would do all in your power for them, but what that would be, I could not say. Their friends here are all well, many of them greatly distressed for their children, and in a particular manner the mother of Jeriah Bass. I wish you to be very particular in letting me know, by various opportunities and ways after the receipt of this, whether you have been able to do anything for them, that I may relieve the minds of these distressed parents. The Captain got home about three months ago by escaping to France, but could give no account of his men after they were taken.

Two years, my dearest friend, have passed away since you left your native land. Will you not return ere the close of another year? I will purchase you a retreat in the woods of Vermont, and retire with you from the vexations, toils, and hazards of public life. Do you not sometimes sigh for such a seclusion? Public peace and domestic happiness;—

> "An elegant sufficiency, content,
> Retirement, rural quiet; friendship, books,
> Ease and alternate labor; useful life,
> Progressive virtue, and approving Heaven."[2]

May the time, the happy time, soon arrive when we may realize these blessings, so elegantly described by Thomson; for, though many of our countrymen talk in a different style with regard to their intentions, and express their wishes to see you in a conspicuous point of view in your own State, I feel no ambition for a share of it. I know the voice of fame to be a mere weathercock, unstable as water and fleeting as a shadow. Yet I have pride; I know I have a large portion of it.

I very fortunately received, by the *Apollo*, by the *Juno*, and by the *Minerva*, the things you sent me, all in good order. They will enable me to do, I hope, without drawing upon you, provided I can part with them; but money is so scarce and taxes so high that few purchasers are found. Goods will not double, yet they are better than drawing bills, as these cannot be sold but with a large discount. I could not get more than ninety for a hundred dollars, should I attempt it.

I shall inclose an invoice to the house of Ingraham and Bromfield, and one to De Neufville.[3] There is nothing from Bilbao that can be imported to advantage. Handkerchiefs are sold here at seven dollars and a half per dozen. There are some articles which would be advantageous from Holland, but goods there run high, and the retailing vendues, which are tolerated here, ruin the shop-keepers. The articles put up by the American house were better in quality for the price than those by the house of De Neufville. Small articles have the best profit; gauze, ribbons, feathers, and flowers, to make the ladies gay, have the best advance. There are some articles, which come from India, I should suppose would be lower-priced than many others,—Bengals, nankeens, Persian silk, and bandanna handkerchiefs; but the house of Bromfield know best what articles will suit here. I have been fortunate and unfortunate. The things which came with Jones remain at Philadelphia yet.

Our friends here are all well. Your mother is in rather better health, and my father is yet sprightly. Believe me, with more affection than words can express, ever, ever yours,

PORTIA

276. JOHN ADAMS

Amsterdam, 18 December 1781

MY DEAREST FRIEND, — I have letters from Mr. Dana and his young attendant at St. Petersburg. Both well and in good spirits. Letters to Mrs. Dana and to you go by Captain Trowbridge and by Dr. Dexter. I have no certain news as yet of Charles's sailing from Bilbao, but I presume he is sailed. You will have suffered great anxiety on his account, but I pray he may arrive safe. I acted for the best when I consented he should go with Gillon, lit-tle expecting that he would be landed in Spain again. Keep him to his studies, and send him to college, where I wish his brother John was.

My health is feeble, but better than it was. I am busy enough, yet not to much perceptible purpose as yet. There is no prospect at all of peace. Let our people take care of their trade and priva-teers next year. They have not much of a land war to fear. Gen-eral Washington has struck the most sublime stroke of all in that article of the capitulation which reserves the Tories for trial by their peers. This has struck Toryism dumb and dead. I expect that all the rancor of the refugees will be poured out upon Cornwallis for it. Our enemies now really stand in a ridiculous light. They feel it, but cannot take the resolution to be wise. The Romans never saw but one Caudine Forks[1] in their whole history. Americans have shown the Britons two in one war. But they must do more. Remember, you never will have peace while the Britons have a company of soldiers at liberty within the United States. New York must be taken, or you will never have peace. All in good time.

The British army estimates are the same as last year. The navy less by several ships of the line. What can these people hope for? I fancy the southern States will hold their heads very high. They have a right. They will scarcely be overrun again, I believe, even in the hasty manner of Cornwallis. Burgoyne don't seem to be affronted that his nose is out of joint. He is in good spirits. Experience has convinced him, so I hope it has Cornwallis, that the American war is impracticable. The flower, the choice of the British army was with him. The King of England consoles his people under all their disgraces, disasters, and dismal prospects, by telling them that they are brave and free. It is a pity for him that he did not allow the Americans to be so seven years ago. But the great designs of Providence must be accomplished. Great indeed! The progress of society will be accelerated by centuries by this Revolution. The Emperor of Germany is adopting, as fast as he can, American ideas of toleration and religious liberty, and it will become the fashionable system of all Europe very soon. Light spreads from the dayspring in the west, and may it shine more and more until the perfect day! Duty to parents. Love to brothers, sisters, and children. It is not in the power of words to express the tenderness with which I bid you farewell.

277. JOHN ADAMS

Hague, 31 August 1782

All well; you will send these papers to some printer when you have done with them.

We have found that the only way of guarding against fevers is to ride. We accordingly mount our horses every day. But the weather through the whole spring and most of the summer has been very dull, damp, cold, very disagreeable and dangerous. But shaking on horseback guards pretty well against it.

I am going to dinner with a Duke and a Duchess and a number of Ambassadors and Senators in all the luxury of this luxurious world; but how much more luxurious it would be to me to dine upon roast beef with Parson Smith, Dr. Tufts, or Norton Quincy! or upon rusticoat potatoes with Portia! Ah! Oh! hi, ho, hum, and her daughter and sons!

278. JOHN ADAMS

Hague, 17 September 1782

MY DEAREST FRIEND, — I have transmitted money to the young men whom you mentioned to me, and have expected, every day for a long time, to hear of their sailing in a cartel for America. They have been better treated since the change of ministers. My respects to their parents.

It is now five months since my public reception here,[1] but we have not yet learned that any news of it has arrived in America. The refugees in England are at their old game again. Andrew Sparhawk has published, in the "Morning Post," that his brother has received a letter from New York, that Massachusetts and several other States were upon the point of overturning the new government, throwing off the authority of Congress, and returning to the government of Great Britain. Their blood-thirsty souls are not yet satiated. They are laboring to bring on again an offensive war. But I think they can't succeed. I suppose the unhappy affair of the county of Hampshire[2] is the thing that gave occasion to this representation. Our countrymen must be very unreasonable if they can't be easy and happy under the government they have. I don't know where they will find a better, or how they will make one. I dread the consequences of the differences between chiefs. If Massachusetts gets into parties, they will worry one another very rudely. But I rely on the honesty and sobriety as well as good sense of the people. These qualities will overawe the passions of individuals and preserve a steady administration of the laws.

My duty to my mother and to your father. I hope to see them

again. Love to the children and all friends. What shall I say of my brother Cranch? I long, and yet I dread, to hear from him.

I hope to sign the Treaty[3] this week or next, or the week after. All points are agreed on and nothing remains but to transcribe the copies fair. This government is so complicated that months are consumed in doing what might be done in another in an hour.

I don't know what to do with the list of articles you send me. It would be better for you to write to Ingraham and Bromfield. I will pay.

279. ABIGAIL ADAMS

25 October 1782

MY DEAREST FRIEND, — The family are all retired to rest; the busy scenes of the day are over; a day which I wished to have devoted in a particular manner to my dearest friend; but company falling in prevented it, nor could I claim a moment until this silent watch of the night.

Look (is there a dearer name than *friend?* Think of it for me), look to the date of this letter, and tell me what are the thoughts which arise in your mind. Do you not recollect that eighteen years have run their circuit since we pledged our mutual faith to each other, and the hymeneal torch was lighted at the altar of Love? Yet, yet it burns with unabating fervor. Old Ocean has not quenched it, nor old Time smothered it in this bosom. It cheers me in the lonely hour; it comforts me even in the gloom which sometimes possesses my mind.

It is, my friend, from the remembrance of the joys I have lost, that the arrow of affliction is pointed. I recollect the untitled man to whom I gave my heart, and in the agony of recollection, when time and distance present themselves together, wish he had never been any other. Who shall give me back time? Who shall compensate to me those years I cannot recall? How dearly have I paid for a titled husband! Should I wish you less wise, that I might enjoy more happiness? I cannot find that in my heart. Yet Providence has wisely placed the real blessings of life within the reach of moderate abilities; and he who is wiser than his neighbor sees so much more to pity and lament, that I doubt whether the balance of happiness is in his scale.

I feel a disposition to quarrel with a race of beings who have cut me off, in the midst of my days, from the only society I delighted in. "Yet no man liveth for himself," says an authority[1] I will not dispute. Let me draw satisfaction from this source, and, instead of murmuring and repining at my lot, consider it in a more pleasing view. Let me suppose that the same gracious Being who first smiled upon our union, and blessed us in each other, endowed my friend with powers and talents for the benefit of mankind, and gave him a willing mind to improve them for the service of his country. You have obtained honor and reputation at home and abroad. Oh, may not an inglorious peace wither the laurels you have won!

I wrote you by Captain Grinnell. The *Firebrand* is in great haste to return, and I fear will not give me time to say half I wish. I want you to say many more things to me than you do; but you write so wise, so like a minister of state. I know your embarrassments. Thus again I pay for titles. Life takes its complexion from inferior things. It is little attentions and assiduities that sweeten the bitter draught and smooth the rugged road.

I have repeatedly expressed my desire to make a part of your family. But "Will you come and see me?" cannot be taken in that serious light I should choose to consider an invitation from those I love. I do not doubt but that you would be glad to see me, but I know you are apprehensive of dangers and fatigues. I know your situation may be unsettled, and it may be more permanent than I wish it. Only think how the words, "three, four, and five years' absence," sound! They sink into my heart with a weight I cannot express. Do you look like the miniature you sent? I cannot think so. But you have a better likeness, I am told. Is that designed for me? Gracious Heaven! restore to me the original, and I care not who has the shadow.

We are hoping for the fall of Gibraltar,[2] because we imagine that will facilitate the peace; and who is not weary of the war? The French fleet still remain with us, and the British cruisers insult them. More American vessels have been captured since they have lain here than for a year before; the *General Greene* is taken and carried into Halifax, by which, I suppose, I have lost some small bundles or packages. Beale told me that you gave him seven small packages, which he delivered to Captain Bacon for me. The prisoners have all arrived, except Savil, who is yet in France. I mentioned to you before, that some of them had been with me, and offered to repay the money with which you supplied them. I could only tell them that I had never received a line from you concerning the matter, and that I chose first to hear from you. I would not receive a farthing, unless I had your express direction, and your handwriting to prove, that what you had done was from your private purse, which I was confident was the case, or you would have been as ready to have relieved others, if you had any public funds for that purpose, as those which belonged to this town. I found a story prevailing that what you had done was at the public expense. This took its rise either from ignorance or ingratitude; but it fully determined me to receive your direction. The persons who have been with me are the two Clarks, the two Beales, and Job Field.

Adieu, my dear friend.

Ever ever yours,   PORTIA

280. ABIGAIL ADAMS

13 November 1782

MY DEAREST FRIEND, — I have lived to see the close of the third year of our separation. This is a melancholy anniversary to me, and many tender scenes arise in my mind upon the recollection. I feel unable to sustain even the idea that it will be half that period ere we meet again. Life is too short to have the dearest of its enjoyments curtailed; the social feelings grow callous by disuse, and lose that pliancy of affection which sweetens the cup of life as we drink it. The rational pleasures of friendship and society, and the still more refined sensations of which delicate minds only are susceptible, like the tender blossoms, when the rude northern blasts assail them, shrink within and collect themselves together, deprived of the all-cheering and beamy influence of the sun. The blossom falls and the fruit withers and decays; but here the similitude fails, for, though lost for the present, the season returns, the tree vegetates anew, and the blossom again puts forth.

But, alas! with me, those days which are past are gone forever, and time is hastening on that period when I must fall to rise no more until mortality shall put on immortality, and we shall meet again, pure and disembodied spirits. Could we live to the age of the antediluvians, we might better support this separation; but, when threescore years and ten circumscribe the life of man, how painful is the idea that, of that short space, only a few years of social happiness are our allotted portion.

Perhaps I make you unhappy. No. You will enter with a soothing tenderness into my feelings. I see in your eyes the emotions of your heart, and hear the sigh that is wafted across the Atlantic to the bosom of Portia. But the philosopher and the statesman stifles these emotions, and regains a firmness which arrests my pen in my hand.

25 November

I last evening received a line from Boston to hasten my letter down or I should again lose an opportunity of conveyance. I was most unfortunate by the *Firebrand*'s sailing and leaving all my letters behind. A storm prevented my sending on the day appointed, and she sailed by sunrise the next morning. Though my letters were in town by nine o'clock, they missed. I know, if she arrive, how disappointed you will feel.

I received from France by the *Alexander* yours, bearing no date, but, by the contents, written about the same time with those I received by Mr. Guild. Shall I return the compliment, and tell you in a poetical style,—

> "Should at my feet the world's great master fall,
>   Himself, his world, his throne, I'd scorn them all"?[1]

No. Give me the man I love; you are neither of an age or temper to be allured by the splendor of a Court or the smiles of princesses. I never suffered an uneasy sensation on that account. I know I have a right to your whole heart, because my own never knew another lord; and such is my confidence in you, that if you were not withheld by the strongest of all obligations, those of a moral nature, your honor would not suffer you to abuse my confidence.

But whither am I rambling? We have not anything in the political way worth noticing. The fleet of our allies still remains with us.

Who is there left that will sacrifice as others have done; Portia, I think, stands alone, alas, in more senses than one. This vessel will convey to you the packets designed for the *Firebrand.* I hope, unimportant as they are, they will not be lost.

Shall I close here, without a word of my voyage? I believe it is best to wait a reply, before I say anything further. Our friends desire me to remember them to you. Your daughter, your image, your superscription, desires to be affectionately remembered to you. Oh, how many of the sweet domestic joys do you lose by this separation from your family. I have the satisfaction of seeing my children thus far in life behaving with credit and honor. God grant the pleasing prospect may never meet with an alloy, and return to me the dear partner of my early years, rewarded for his past sacrifices by the consciousness of having been extensively useful, not having lived to himself alone; and may the approving voice of his country crown his later days in peaceful retirement, in the affectionate bosom of   PORTIA

281. JOHN ADAMS

Paris, 4 December 1782

MY DEAREST FRIEND, — Your proposal of coming to Europe has long and tenderly affected me. The dangers and inconveniences are such, and a European life would be so disagreeable to you, that I have suffered a great deal of anxiety in reflecting upon it. And upon the whole, I think it will be most for the happiness of my family, and most for the honor of our country, that I should come home. I have, therefore, this day written to Congress a resignation of all my employments, and as soon as I shall receive their acceptance of it, I will embark for America, which will be in the spring or beginning of summer. Our son is now on his journey from Petersburg, through Sweden, Denmark, and Germany, and if it please God he come safe, he shall come with me, and I pray we may all meet once more, you and I never to separate again.

Yours most tenderly,   J. ADAMS

282. ABIGAIL ADAMS

23 December 1782

MY DEAREST FRIEND, — I have omitted writing by the last opportunity to Holland, because I had but small faith in the designs of the owners or passengers. The vessel sails from Nantucket, Dr. Winship is a passenger, a Mr. Gray and some others, and I had just written you so largely, by a vessel bound to France, the *General Galvaye,* that I had nothing new to say. There are few occurrences in this northern climate, at this season of the year, to divert or entertain you; and, in the domestic way, should I draw you the picture of my heart, it would be what I hope you still would love, though it contained nothing new. The early possession you obtained there, and the absolute power you have ever maintained over it, leave not the smallest space unoccupied. I look back to the early days of our acquaintance and friendship, as to the days of love and innocence, and with an indescribable pleasure I have seen near a score of years roll over our heads, with an affection heightened and improved by time; nor have the dreary years of absence in the smallest degree effaced from my mind the image of the dear, untitled man to whom I gave my heart. I cannot sometimes refrain considering the honors with which he is invested as badges of my unhappiness. The unbounded confidence I have in your attachment to me and the dear pledges of our affection has soothed the solitary hour, and rendered your absence more supportable; for, had I [not] loved you with the same affection, it must have been misery to have doubted. Yet a cruel world too often injures my feelings by wondering how a person possessed of domestic attachments can sacrifice them by absenting himself *for years.*

"If you had known," said a person to me the other day, "that Mr. Adams would have remained so long abroad, would you have consented that he should have gone?" I recollected myself a moment, and then spoke the real dictates of my heart: "If I had known, sir, that Mr. Adams could have effected what he has done, I would not only have submitted to the absence I have endured, painful as it has been, but I would not have opposed it, even though three years more should be added to the number (which Heaven avert!). I feel a pleasure in being able to sacrifice my selfish passions to the general good, and in imitating the example which has taught me to consider myself and family but as the small dust of the balance, when compared with the great community."

Your Daughter[1] most sincerely regrets your absence; she sees me support it, yet thinks she could not imitate either parent in the disinterested motives which actuate them. She has had a strong desire to encounter the dangers of the sea to visit you. I, however, am not without a suspicion that she may lose her relish for a voyage by spring. The tranquillity of mine and my dear sister's family is in a great measure restored to us since the recovery of our worthy friend and brother. We had a most melancholy summer. The young folks of the two families together with those of Colonel Quincy's and General Warren preserve a great intimacy, and as they wish for but few connections in the beau monde, is it not to be wondered at that they are fond of each other's company. We have an agreeable young gentleman by the name of Robbins, who keeps our little school, son to the Reverend Mr. Robbins of Plymouth, and we have in the little circle another gentleman who has opened an office in town, for about nine months past, and boarded in Mr. Cranch's family. His father you knew. His name is Tyler, he studied law upon his coming out of college with Mr. Dana, but when Mr. Dana went to Congress he finished his studies with Mr. Angier. Losing his father young and having a very pretty patrimony left him possessing a sprightly fancy, a warm imagination, and an agreeable person; he was rather negligent in pursuing his business in the way of his profession, and dissipated two or three years of his life and too much of his fortune for to reflect upon with pleasure, all of which he now laments but cannot recall. At twenty-three, the time when he took the resolution of coming to Boston and withdrawing from a too numerous acquaintance, he resolved to pursue his studies and his business and save his remaining fortune, which suffered much more from the paper currency than any other cause; so that out of seventeen thousand pounds which fell to his share, he cannot now realize more than half that sum, as he told me a few days past. His mamma is in possession of a large estate and he is a very favorite child. When he proposed coming to settle here he met with but little encouragement, but he was determined upon the trial. He has succeeded beyond expectation, he has popular talents, and as his behavior has been unexceptionable since his residence in town, in consequence of which his business daily increases, he cannot fail making a distinguished figure in his profession if he steadily pursues it. I am not acquainted with any young gentleman whose attainments in literature are equal to his, who judges with greater accuracy or discovers a more delicate and refined taste. I have frequently looked upon him with the idea that you would have taken much pleasure in such a pupil. I wish I was as well assured that you would be equally pleased with him in another character, for such I apprehend are his distant hopes. I early saw that he was possessed with powerful attractions, and as he obtained and deserved, I believe, the character of a gay, though not a criminal, youth, I thought it prudent to keep as great a reserve as possible. In this I was seconded by the discreet conduct of a daughter who is happy in not possessing all her mother's sensibility. Yet I see a growing attachment in him stimulated by that very reserve. I feel the want of your presence and advice. I think I know your sentiments so well that the merit of a gentleman will be your first consideration, and I have made every inquiry which I could with decency, and without disclosing my motives. Even in his most dissipated state he always applied his mornings to study, by which means he has stored his mind with a fund of useful knowledge, I know not a young fellow upon the stage whose language is so pure, or whose natural disposition is more agreeable. His days are devoted to his office, his evenings of late to my fireside. His attachment is too obvious to escape notice. I do not think the lady wholly indifferent; yet her reserve and apparent coldness is such that I know he is in miserable doubt. Some conversation one evening of late took place which led me to write him a billet and tell him that at least it admitted a possibility that I might quit this country in the spring, that I never would go abroad without my daughter, and if I did go, I wished to carry her with a mind unattached; besides I could have but one voice, and for that I held myself accountable to you, that he was not yet established in business sufficient to think of a connection with any one;—to which I received this answer—

Madam

I have made an exertion to answer your billet. I can only say that the second impulse in my breast is my love and respect for you; and it is the foible of my nature to be the machine of those I love and venerate. Do with me as seemeth good unto thee. I can safely trust my dearest fondest wishes and pursuits in the hands of a friend that can feel, that knows my situation and her designs. If reason pleads against me, you will do well to hesitate. If friendship and reason unite I shall be happy. Only say I shall be happy when I *deserve;* and it shall be my every exertion to augment my merit, and this you may be assured of, whether I am blessed in my wishes or not, I will endeavor to be a character that you shall not blush once to have entertained an esteem for. Yours respectfully, etc.

What ought I to say? I feel too powerful a pleader within my own heart and too well recollect the love I bore to the object of my early affections to forbid him to hope. I feel a regard for him upon an account you will smile at; I fancy I see in him sentiments, opinions, and actions which endeared to me the best of friends. Suffer me to draw you from the depths of politics to endearing family scenes. I know you cannot fail being peculiarly interested in the present. I inclose you a little paper which though trifling in itself, may serve to show you the truth of my observations. The other day the gentleman I have been speaking of had a difficult writ to draw. He requested the favor of looking into your book of forms, which I readily granted; in the evening when he returned me the key he put into my hands a paper which I could not tell what to make of, until he exclaimed, "O! Madam Madam, I have now hopes that I shall one day become worthy your regard. What a picture have I caught of my own heart, my resolutions, my designs! I could not refrain breaking out into a rhapsody. I found this copy of a letter in a pamphlet with observations upon the study of the law and many excellent remarks; you will I hope forgive the theft, when I deliver the paper to you, and you find how much benefit I shall derive from it."

I daily see that he will win the affections of a fine majestic girl who has as much dignity as a princess. She is handsome, but not beautiful. No air of levity ever accompanies either her words or actions. Should she be caught by a tender passion, sufficient to remove a little of her natural reserve and soften her form and manners, she will be a still more pleasing character. Her mind is daily improving, and she gathers new taste for literature perhaps for its appearing in a more pleasing form to her. If I can procure a little ode which accompanied an ice heart I will inclose it to you.

It is now, my dear friend, a long, long time since I had a line from you. The fate of Gibraltar leads me to fear that a peace is far distant, and that I shall not see you,—God only knows when. I shall say little about my former request; not that my desire is less, but, before this can reach you, 'tis probable I may receive your opinion; if in favor of my coming to you, I shall have no occasion to urge it further; if against it, I would not embarrass you by again requesting it. I will endeavor to sit down and consider it as the portion allotted me. My dear sons are well. Their application and improvement go hand in hand. Our friends all desire to be remembered. The fleet of our allies expects to sail daily, but where destined we know not. A great harmony has subsisted between them and the Americans ever since their residence here. I wish to write to Mr. Thaxter but fear I shall not have time. Mrs. Dana and children are well. The judge has been very sick of a fever but I believe is better. This letter is to go by the *Iris,* which sails with the fleet. I hope it will reach you in safety. If it should fall into the hands of an enemy, I hope they will be kind enough to destroy it, as I could not wish to see such a family picture in print.

· Adieu, my dear friend. Why is it that I hear so seldom from my dear John? But one letter have I ever received from him since he arrived in Petersburg. I wrote him by the last opportunity. Ever remember me, as I do you, with all the tenderness which it is possible for one object to feel for another, which no time can obliterate, no distance alter, but which is always the same in the bosom of   PORTIA

283. JOHN ADAMS

Paris, 28 December 1782

I dare say there is not a lady in America treated with a more curious dish of politics than is contained in the inclosed papers. You may show them to discreet friends, but by no means let them go out of your hands or be copied. Preserve them in safety against accidents.

I am afraid we shall have another campaign; but do not despair, however, of a peace this winter. America has nothing to do but to be temperate, patient, avid faithful to her ally. This is as clearly her duty as it is her interest. She could not trust England if her honor was not engaged to France, which it is most certainly; and when this is said, all is said. Whether there should be peace or war, I shall come home in the summer. As soon as I shall receive from Congress their acceptance of the resignation of all my employments, which I have transmitted many ways, I shall embark, and you may depend upon a good domestic husband for the remainder of my life, if it is the will of Heaven that I should once more meet you. My promises are not lightly made with anybody. I have never broken one made to you, and I will not begin at this time of life.

My children, I hope, will once at length discover that they have a father who is not unmindful of their welfare. They have had too much reason to think themselves forgotten, although I know that an anxiety for their happiness has corroded me every day of my life.

With a tenderness which words cannot express, I am theirs and yours forever.

284. JOHN ADAMS

Paris, 18 February 1783

MY DEAREST FRIEND, — The peace,[1] which sets the rest of the world at ease, increases, I think, my perplexities and anxiety. I have written to Congress a resignation, but I foresee there will not be a speedy decision upon it, and I shall be left in a state of suspense that will be intolerable. Foreseeing this, I am determined not to wait for an acceptance of my resignation, but to come home without it, provided it does not arrive in a reasonable time. Don't think, therefore of coming to Europe. If you do, we shall cross each other, and I shall arrive in America about the same time that you may arrive in Europe.

I shall certainly return home in the spring. With or without leave, resignation accepted or not, home I will come, so you have nothing to do but wait to receive your old friend

J. ADAMS

Explanatory Notes

ABBREVIATIONS

AA = Abigail Adams
CFA = Charles Francis Adams
JA = John Adams
JQA = John Quincy Adams
AFC = *Adams Family Correspondence,* ed. L. H. Butterfield, et al. 6 vols. Cambridge: Harvard University Press, 1963–93.

LETTER 1. JOHN ADAMS

1. *the public news:* News had just arrived of the British Parliament's Boston Port Bill, which ordered the closing of the port effective June 1, 1744, in response to the destruction of the tea in the Boston Tea Party of the previous December.
2. *Lord North's despair:* Frederick Lord North, chancellor of the exchequer and effectively the prime minister, was responsible for repealing all the taxes protested by the American colonists except that for tea, and he was responsible for steering the coercive acts of 1774, including the Boston Port Bill, through Parliament.

LETTER 2. JOHN ADAMS

1. *David Sewall, . . . Theophilus Bradbury:* JA was in York, Maine, a part of Massachusetts until 1820, in order to do business at the circuit court held there. The comments on the local lawyers are mostly self-explanatory. The Sullivans would both support the Revolution; John (1740–95) became one of the Continental Army's first brigadier generals and eventually governor of New Hampshire, while James (1744–1808) became a prominent legislator and jurist in Massachu-

setts. David Wyer (1741–76) was a college friend of JA and became a successful lawyer at Falmouth; JA characterizes him in letter 9. David Sewall (1735–1825) was a Harvard classmate of JA's. Theophilus Bradbury (1739–1803) later served in the U.S. Congress and on the Massachusetts Superior Court.

2. *Governor Wentworth:* John Wentworth (1737–1820), JA's Harvard classmate, succeeded his uncle, Benning Wentworth, as royal governor of New Hampshire from 1767 to 1775.

3. *quaere:* I.e., inquire about this.

4. *the impeachment of the Judges:* JA had drawn up an impeachment of Chief Justice Peter Oliver because he would not renounce a salary grant from the crown. Adams and other Whigs feared that if judges were paid by the royal government and not the elected assembly, they would lose their independence. See *Massachusetts Historical Society Collections,* 5th series, 4 (1878), 345–65, and JA, *Diary and Autobiography of John Adams,* ed. L. H. Butterfield, et al. (Cambridge: Harvard University Press, 1962), 3:297–302.

5. *John Lowell:* Lowell (1743–1802) later served in the Continental Congress and became one of JA's Federalist friends.

LETTER 3. JOHN ADAMS

1. *gentlemen . . . bound with me to Philadelphia:* On June 17 JA had been chosen as a delegate to the First Continental Congress, scheduled to meet in Philadelphia; also chosen were Samuel Adams, James Bowdoin, Thomas Cushing, and Robert Treat Paine.

2. *Mr. Moody. Dr. Sayward:* CFA note: "Samuel Moody, born in 1675, graduated at Cambridge in 1697, and died in 1747; one of a class peculiar to colonial times, the like of whom are no longer to be found in the rural districts." Jonathan Sayward (1713–97) was a prominent citizen of York County, a loyalist by sympathy who retained his property and social position during and after the Revolution.

3. *their present parson:* CFA deleted JA's identification of the pastor as Isaac Lyman. In another letter to AA of this same date JA reports the result of his inquiries into "Parson Lyman's Affection to the Tories," describing how, at an earlier time, Thomas Hutchinson "that Arch Corrupter and Deceiver lodged at the house of Dr. Lyman the parson's Brother, and professed great Friendship for him as well as the Parson." *AFC,* 1:116.

LETTER 4. JOHN ADAMS

1. *Dr. Gardiner:* Dr. Silvester Gardiner, a Tory sympathizer with extensive land dealings in Maine, was JA's client. On June 27 and 28 a town meeting held in Faneuil Hall and later moved to Old South Church debated a Tory proposal for a public reading of all letters written and received by the Boston Committee of Correspondence. After protracted debate, this motion was defeated by a large majority, and a motion commending the committee passed by a similar margin.

LETTER 5. JOHN ADAMS

1. *Hemmenway:* Moses Hemmenway (1735–1811), another of JA's Harvard classmates, had been the minister at Wells, Maine, since 1759.

2. *Mr. Winthrop:* Samuel Winthrop was clerk of the Superior Court of Judicature.

3. *the late Governor Hutchinson:* Thomas Hutchinson (1711–80) had just been replaced as the royally appointed governor of Massachusetts; long unpopular, he had become the focus for Whig resentment of British ministerial policies.

4. *Judge Trowbridge:* Edmund Trowbridge (1709–93), a Superior Court judge, was regarded by fellow lawyers for his thoroughness and diligence as a lawyer.

5. *Kent . . . to Judge Lynde:* Benjamin Kent was a legal colleague of JA's. Benjamin Lynde Jr. (1700–1782) had been appointed chief justice of the Massachusetts Superior Court in March 1771, but he resigned the position a year later and was replaced by Peter Oliver.

LETTER 6. JOHN ADAMS

1. *Mr. Quincy:* Samuel Quincy (1735–89), older brother of the patriot Josiah Quincy Jr., was cultivated by Hutchinson and the Olivers; in 1770 he had been appointed solicitor general of Massachusetts. He left the country as the Revolution broke out and died in Antigua.

2. *Williams:* Jonathan Williams (d. 1780) was one of JA's law clerks.

3. *pistareens:* A pistareen was a small Spanish coin current in the West Indies and the American colonies; the term was used colloquially in the sense of "small change."

4. *Josiah Quincy:* Josiah Quincy Jr. (1744–75) had earlier joined JA in defending the soldiers tried for their role in the Boston Massacre. His important *Observations on the Act of Parliament Commonly Called the Boston Port Bill* appeared later in 1774.

5. *the Farmer's fourth letter:* One of the *Letters from a Farmer in Pennsylvania to the Inhabitants of the British Colonies,* written by John Dickinson in 1767–68 in protest of the Stamp Act. Widely reprinted, these letters constituted one of the most important American critiques of British power in the years before the Revolution.

6. *My brother Neg Freeman:* Enoch Freeman (1706–88) practiced law in Falmouth, Maine, now known as Portland, and thus was JA's "brother" as a fellow lawyer, but he was also a brother because, as with JA, his election in May to the Massachusetts Council, in effect the upper house of the legislature, had been negatived, i.e., rejected, by Governor Thomas Gage.

LETTER 7. JOHN ADAMS

1. *Will Gardiner and a Captain Pote:* William Gardiner was the son of Dr. Silvester Gardiner. Jeremiah Pote, merchant in Falmouth, was a loyalist who fled to New Brunswick in 1775.

2. *The non-consumption agreement:* Nonconsumption of British imports had been a strategy of protest in Massachusetts and the other colonies since the 1760s, and had been periodically renewed. Joseph Warren's "Solemn League and Covenant" of Massachusetts merchants to boycott British goods had just been published on June 8 and is undoubtedly referred to here.

3. *tarring Malcom:* The tarring and feathering of John Malcom, a customs collector in Boston, in January 1775 received considerable notice on both sides of the Atlantic. The incident was a possible inspiration for Nathaniel Hawthorne's story "My Kinsman, Major Molyneux."

4. *brother Porter:* Samuel Porter was a lawyer in Salem. The Massachusetts legislative body, the General Court, called to meet in Boston in May 1774, was adjourned to Salem for a session beginning June 7 in order to escape Boston political unrest. Salem was thought to be a Tory stronghold.

5. *Judge Cushing:* William Cushing (1732–1810), an associate justice for the Superior Court.

6. *Mr. Smith . . . Mr. Gilman:* Rev. Thomas Smith and Rev. Tristram Gilman of Falmouth.

7. *Oliver:* Peter Oliver (1713–91) was chief justice of the Massachusetts Superior Court, but JA may be referring to Lieutenant Governor

Andrew Oliver (1703–74), who along with his brother-in-law Thomas Hutchinson was a frequent target of JA's resentment. However, Andrew Oliver had died on March 3, 1774.

LETTER 8. JOHN ADAMS

1. *the killing of a child by R:* Ebenezer Richardson, a customs officer, shot and killed eleven-year-old Christopher Snider when an anti-British mob tried to break into his house on February 22, 1770. The boy's funeral became a political event, and his shooting was a prelude to the Boston Massacre, also referred to here. The incident was the subject of Phillis Wheatley's poem "On the Death of Mr. Snider Murder'd by Richardson." An earlier mob had destroyed Thomas Hutchinson's house on August 26, 1765.
2. *Fleet's paper, "Mein's Chronicle":* Thomas and John Fleet's *Boston Evening Post* and John Mein and John Fleeming's *Boston Chronicle* supported British policies to various degrees.

LETTER 9. JOHN ADAMS

1. *Justice Hutchinson:* Foster Hutchinson (1724–99), an associate justice of the Superior Court, was brother to Thomas Hutchinson.

LETTER 10. JOHN ADAMS

1. *a list of the addressers of the late Governor:* When Thomas Hutchinson was replaced as governor by General Thomas Gage in the spring of 1774, friends and supporters undersigned a testimonial of support, dated May 28 and issued as an "Address from the Merchants and Traders of the Town of Boston, and others." Patriot printers quickly circulated two broadsides listing the names of the addressers, their occupations, addresses, and contemptuous descriptions of their character or aspirations. JA and AA in subsequent letters use "addressers" as a shorthand term for Boston Tories in general.
2. *King, of Scarborough:* Richard King supported the Stamp Act but was also the largest creditor in Scarborough and the treasurer of the parish, which produced considerable resentment among many of his neighbors, some of whom were in his debt. They ransacked his house on March 19, 1766. For more details on this case see the extended note in *AFC*, 1:132–34.

3. *Mr. Collector Francis Waldo, Esquire:* Francis Waldo was the first customs collector for the port of Falmouth, although he no longer held the office at this time.

4. *a publication of Mr. Burke's . . . paragraphs from Junius Americanus:* Edmund Burke's 1766 "A Short Account of a Late Short Administration"; Arthur Lee's collection of pro-American propaganda pieces, *The Political Detection: or, The Treachery and Tyranny of Administration Both at Home and Abroad; Displayed in a Series of Letters, Signed Junius Americanus,* published in London in 1770.

LETTER 11. JOHN ADAMS

1. *"Bear me, some god! . . .":* Alexander Pope, "The Fourth Satire of Dr. John Donne Versified," lines 184–87. CFA corrected JA's misquotation of the first word; JA remembered Pope's "Bear" as "Snatch."

2. *Codman:* Richard Codman, a merchant of Falmouth.

3. *Brigadier Preble, Major Freeman:* Jedediah Preble had served under General James Wolfe in Canada and as a representative to the Massachusetts General Court. Enoch Freeman, noted in letter 6, note 6, was a major in the militia.

4. *Bill Tyng:* William Tyng (1737–1807), sheriff of Cumberland County, had recently been commissioned as a colonel by Governor Thomas Gage.

5. *Captain MacCarty:* Captain MacCarty, unidentified, was possibly a slave trader.

6. *Colonel Barré's speeches, . . . Robinson:* Isaac Barré (1726–1802) had been speaking out in the House of Commons during the previous decade for the rights of Americans; his 1765 speech against the Stamp Act featured one of the earliest references to American patriots as "sons of liberty." James Otis Jr. had been assaulted by John Robinson, a crown officer, on September 5, 1769. JA represented him in his suit for damages in which he was awarded £2000, but Otis, after receiving an apology, refused any damages beyond court costs, lawyer's fees, and medical expenses.

7. *Colonel Otis's phrase:* Colonel James Otis (1702–78) was the father of James Otis Jr., the orator and propagandist against parliamentary rule.

LETTER 12. ABIGAIL ADAMS

1. *friends from Watertown:* Before setting out to Philadelphia for the First Continental Congress, JA and the other delegates dined in Watertown, Massachusetts, with a large number of "Gentlemen from Boston" who had ridden out to see them off.

2. *Mr. A——r, of B——r:* Oakes Angier (1745–86), a former law student of JA's, practiced law at Bridgewater in Plymouth County, Massachusetts.

3. *C——l W——n, of P——h:* Colonel James Warren (1726–1808) of Plymouth was the husband of the poet and historian Mercy Otis Warren. The Warrens were longtime close friends of the Adamses, and they are often referred to in these letters as "our Plymouth friends."

4. *young Morton:* Perez Morton (1750–1837) would later deliver the funeral oration at the reburial of Dr. Joseph Warren in April 1776 (see letter 92, AA's letter of 7 April). He would go on to a distinguished political career in Massachusetts.

5. *Mr. Rice . . . Mr. Crosby:* Nathan Rice (1754–1834) and John Thaxter Jr. (1755–91), recent Harvard graduates, were law clerks in JA's office. Joseph Crosby (1751–83), another young Harvard graduate, kept school in Braintree in 1773–74. Thaxter later went to Europe with JA as his private secretary.

6. *Mr. Cunningham:* Possibly JA's uncle James Cunningham, husband of his mother's sister Elizabeth Boylston.

LETTER 13. ABIGAIL ADAMS

1. *Polybius:* Greek historian (c. 205–c. 123 BCE) whose discussion of government was widely read by eighteenth-century republicans.

2. *letter from . . . Mrs. Warren:* Mercy Otis Warren's letter is printed in AFC, 1:138–39.

3. *the Locrians:* Philip II of Macedon used the pretext of the Locrians' resistance to the Amphictyonic Council in 338 BCE to assert his power over the Greek city states, including Athens. In the letter referred to here, Mercy Otis Warren notes that "Mr. Adams has justly Compared [the Continental Congress] to the Amphyctiones of Greece." AFC, 1:138. AA quotes word for word Warren's caution against erecting a monarchic government.

4. *Rollin's Ancient History:* The historical works of French writer Charles Rollin (1661–1741) were widely popular in the eighteenth-

century, particularly among readers with Whiggish sentiments. JA's copy of Rollin's *The Antient History* (London, 1768) in ten volumes is now housed in the Boston Public Library.

LETTER 14. JOHN ADAMS

1. *Nassau Hall College:* A former name for Princeton University.
2. *his accidence:* Seven-year-old John Quincy Adams was learning Latin; accidence refers to the changing forms of words as demanded by grammatical usage.
3. *uncle Quincy . . . Dr. Tufts:* JA sends his regards to Norton Quincy (1716–1801), AA's uncle, and to Dr. Cotton Tufts (1732–1815), AA's uncle and a distinguished physician.
4. *Tudor, Trumbull, and Hill:* William Tudor (1750–1819), John Trumbull (1750–1831), who had recently published his satiric poem *The Progress of Dulness,* and Edward Hill (1755–75) were, like John Thaxter Jr., law clerks for Adams.
5. *Mr. Wibird:* Anthony Wibird (1729–1800) was minister of the First Church in Braintree and a friend of the Adams family.
6. *by way of journal:* For JA's diary account of his time at the First Continental Congress, see *The Adams Papers: Diary and Autobiography of John Adams,* 2:97–157.

LETTER 15. ABIGAIL ADAMS

1. *Mr. Adams . . . the Speaker:* Samuel Adams (1722–1803), the famous Boston patriot and JA's cousin; Thomas Cushing (1725–88), Speaker of the Massachusetts House of Representatives.
2. *a traitorous plot of Colonel Brattle's:* Brigadier General William Brattle informed Governor Thomas Gage (1720–87) on August 27 of plans by local militias to "meet at one Minutes Warning" in case of need. Gage ordered the powder stored in the nearby provincial arsenal to be seized and removed to Castle Island. Brattle's letter was discovered before Gage had an opportunity to remove the officers from the militias.
3. *Mr. Vinton . . . Messrs. Goldthwait and Price:* Vinton was the undersheriff for Braintree. The Massachusetts Government Act, which arrived with General Gage, provided that juries would be selected by the sheriffs instead of being elected by the voters. Ezekiel Goldthwait and Ezekiel Price, two of the addressers, were joint clerks of the Suffolk Court of Sessions who unsuccessfully tried to carry out this pol-

icy. See also letter 18, where AA notes that people prevented the courts from sitting.

4. *Stoughtonham:* Now Sharon, Massachusetts.

5. *the Quebec bill:* The Quebec Act granted religious liberty to Quebec Catholics, which alarmed New Englanders as an attempt to promote Roman Catholicism. It also extended the frontier of Quebec to the Ohio and Mississippi Rivers, thus confirming limitations on the ability of the other colonies to expand westward.

LETTER 16. JOHN ADAMS

1. *a dreadful catastrophe:* Exaggerated rumors concerning Gage's seizure on September 1 of the powder held in the Quarry Hill arsenal had reached Philadelphia. Boston was not bombarded.

2. *the new councillors:* These were members of the Massachusetts Council appointed by mandamus under the new act for the regulation of the province charter. Popular protest forced most of them to resign their appointments.

LETTER 18. ABIGAIL ADAMS

1. *a letter by the post:* JA and AA were sending their letters with acquaintances who were traveling between Boston and Philadelphia; using the regular postal service would have incurred a charge and would expose their letters to being opened by others.

2. *The County Congress:* On September 9 the delegates from Suffolk County passed the Suffolk Resolves that urged Massachusetts to form a popular government to withhold taxes from the crown until the Intolerable Acts were repealed, and to advise the people to arm. The Continental Congress endorsed the Resolves on September 17.

3. *Cleverly's and Etter's, . . . Major Miller's:* The Cleverly, Etter, and Miller families of Braintree all belonged to the Church of England and were suspected of Tory sympathies.

4. *Colonel Quincy's. . . . Mr. Sumner, Mr. Josiah and wife:* Colonel Josiah Quincy (1710–84) was the father of Samuel and Josiah Jr. noted above. Among those dining at Colonel Quincy's with AA were her daughter Abigail (Nabby) and sister Elizabeth Smith (Betsey). Increase Sumner (1746–99) of Roxbury had studied law with Samuel Quincy. For the political differences between Samuel Quincy and his brother Josiah Jr., see letter 6, notes 1 and 4.

5. *Bishop of St. Asaph:* Jonathan Shipley (1714–88), friend of Ben-

jamin Franklin and the American colonists, whose *A Speech Intended to Have Been Spoken on the Bill for Altering the Charters of the Colony of Massachusetts Bay* was reprinted at least eight times in the colonies in 1774, including twice in Boston and twice in Philadelphia.

6. *my two neighbors:* I.e., John Thaxter Jr. and Nathan Rice, JA's clerks.

7. *wisdom will flow down . . . the cities of our God:* A complex scriptural allusion. See Amos 5:24, "But let judgment run down as waters, and righteousness as a mighty stream," and 1 Chronicles 19:13, "Be of good courage, and let us behave ourselves valiantly for our people, and for the cities of our God." Also 2 Samuel 10:12.

8. *Miss Eunice:* CFA note: "Miss Eunice Paine, a sister of Robert Treat Paine, and for many years an intimate friend of the writer."

LETTER 19. JOHN ADAMS

1. *Mr. Jay . . . Mr. Rutledge:* John Jay (1745–1829) and Edward Rutledge (1749–1800).

2. *Mr. Duché:* Jacob Duché (1737–98), assistant rector of Christ Church and St. Peters, at this time supported the patriot cause, but in 1777 after the British occupied Philadelphia, he urged Washington to rescind the Declaration of Independence and fled to England.

3. *Dr. Cooper:* Rev. Samuel Cooper (1737–98) was minister of the Brattle Street Church in Boston, which the Adamses attended, and a famous orator.

4. *faith in the . . . Sortes Biblicae:* Sortes Virgilianae referred to the practice of randomly turning to a verse in Virgil's *Aeneid* in order to find a prognostication or advice. The works of Homer might be similarly used. Many people used the Bible in the same way, thus "Sortes Biblicae."

LETTER 20. JOHN ADAMS

1. *Camden, Chatham, Richmond, and St. Asaph:* The earl of Camden; William Pitt, earl of Chatham; and the duke of Richmond along with the bishop of St. Asaph were understood to be opponents of Lord North's policies toward the American colonies.

LETTER 21. JOHN ADAMS

1. *esteem . . . expressed yesterday:* These were resolutions supporting the Suffolk Resolves and calling for all the colonies to contribute toward alleviating "the distresses of our brethren at Boston."

LETTER 22. JOHN ADAMS

1. *to Mr. Cranch's:* Richard Cranch (1726–1811), JA's brother-in-law, had a watchmaking business on Hanover Street in Boston and passed on correspondence for his relatives.
2. *Brackett:* Mr. Brackett worked on JA's farm in Braintree.

LETTER 23. ABIGAIL ADAMS

1. *my brother:* AA's brother William Smith had taken up residence in Lincoln, Massachusetts.
2. *Scott:* Scott was captain of the ship *Hayley,* which had arrived in Salem from London (i.e., "home") on September 19.
3. *Justice Quincy:* Edmund Quincy (1703–88) was Colonel Josiah Quincy Sr.'s brother.
4. *Percy:* Hugh, Earl Percy (1742–1817), commanded the British camp at Boston.

LETTER 25. JOHN ADAMS

1. *Deacon Palmer:* Joseph Palmer (1716–88) was married to Richard Cranch's sister and resided in Braintree. He was the father of AA's friend Elizabeth Palmer. He is later referred to as Colonel Palmer and General Palmer because of his military service in the patriot forces.

LETTER 26. JOHN ADAMS

1. *Mr. Revere:* Paul Revere, mentioned earlier in letter 23, brought the Suffolk Resolves to Philadelphia and carried JA's letter back to Boston on his return.
2. *Edes and Gill's:* Benjamin Edes (1732–1803) and John Gill (1732–85)

were printers and publishers of the *Boston Gazette*, a newspaper favorable to the patriots.

3. *broad-brims:* I.e., conservative Quakers.

4. *Mr. Mifflin . . . Mr. Galloway:* Thomas Mifflin, here reelected to the Pennsylvania Assembly, was later a major general in the Revolution and eventually governor of Pennsylvania. Charles Thomson (1729–1824) continued as secretary of Congress until 1789. Joseph Galloway (1731–1803) was Speaker of the Pennsylvania Assembly. A delegate to the First Continental Congress, he believed in the possibility of reconciliation with Britain, but when Congress declared independence, he became a loyalist and eventually an exile.

LETTER 27. JOHN ADAMS

1. *Dr. Allison's meeting:* Francis Allison (1703–79) was the minister of the First Presbyterian Church in Philadelphia. When JA refers below to going to "Church," he means the Church of England service.

LETTER 28. ABIGAIL ADAMS

1. *the 10th of August:* JA left for Philadelphia on August 10.

2. *Mr. Quincy's so secret departure:* Josiah Quincy Jr. had, amid some secrecy, sailed for England on September 28 in order to present the views of patriot leaders to the British ministry and to the friends of America in England. In the following April, Quincy was supposedly returning with important information that he could only communicate orally, but he died on board ship of consumption just before arriving in America.

3. *the bearer:* This letter was sent with JA's clerk William Tudor.

LETTER 29. JOHN ADAMS

1. *Governor Martin:* Governor Josiah Martin (1737–86), the last royal governor of North Carolina.

LETTER 30. JOHN ADAMS

1. *Dr. Warren:* Dr. Joseph Warren (1741–75), a Boston physician and political leader who was later killed at the battle of Bunker Hill.

2. *Dr. Cooper:* Myles Cooper (1737–85), a Church of England clergyman, president of Kings College in New York, and outspoken loyalist, did not in fact flee the city until eight days later.

LETTER 31. JOHN ADAMS

1. *Mr. Eliot, of Fairfield:* Andrew Eliot was minister at Fairfield, Connecticut, and was the son of Dr. Andrew Eliot (1718–88), minister of
the New North Church in Boston, who remained at his post during
the siege.

LETTER 32. ABIGAIL ADAMS

1. *Hutchinson's letters . . . Bowers:* A trunk full of Thomas Hutchinson's papers was accidentally discovered in the attic of his country
house in Milton, Massachusetts. Jerathmael Bowers had been elected
to the Council in 1772, but then Governor Hutchinson negatived his
election. JA and William Phillips (Deacon Phillips) were elected the
next year and also negatived.
2. *the fate of Mordecai be his:* AA seems to have confused her biblical
reference here, if by "his" she means Hutchinson, who had negatived
Jerathmael Bowers's election to the Council in 1772. Mordecai was
the father of Esther, unjustly accused by Haman, but exonerated
when the latter's treachery was exposed.

LETTER 33. ABIGAIL ADAMS

1. *Nor doth the eye . . . :* AA uses a pastiche of scriptural quotations in
this letter. The sentence here is from 1 Corinthians 12:21, the next,
beginning "The Lord will not cast off his people," is from Psalm
94:14, and further down the paragraph the references to Pharaoh's
hardened heart are adapted from Exodus 7:13–14.

LETTER 34. JOHN ADAMS

1. *Jose Bass:* Joseph Bass, a young Braintree neighbor, accompanied JA
to the Second Continental Congress as his servant.
2. *I must pay . . . for his sulky:* CFA omitted this sentence. JA charged
Massachusetts £12 for the sulky.

3. *Mr. Livingston . . . and Mr. Rogers:* Rev. John Henry Livingston (1746–1825) and Rev. John Rodgers (1727–1811) were ministers in New York.

LETTER 35. ABIGAIL ADAMS

1. *The Dr:* I.e., Cotton Tufts, a resident of Weymouth, uncle of AA. Tufts is usually referred to as "the Dr." in these letters.
2. *The bad conduct of General Gage:* CFA note: "He had taken the [fire-fighting] engines under guard, in consequence of a report that the liberty party intended to fire the town."
3. *"To the houseless child . . .":* Oliver Goldsmith, "Edwin and Angelina," lines 13–16.
4. *Mr. Dilly:* Edward Dilly was a London bookseller and publisher who sympathized with the American Revolution. He had recently sent JA a parcel of books and pamphlets; see AA's letter to him in *AFC*, 1:200–202.

LETTER 36. JOHN ADAMS

1. *two young gentleman from Maryland:* Aquila and Josias Carvill Hall.

LETTER 37. JOHN ADAMS

1. *our president:* John Hancock had just been elected president of the Continental Congress. See letter 55, note 9.
2. *Dr. Young:* Thomas Young (1732–77) had practiced medicine in Boston and taken part in radical politics there. In 1775 he had moved to Philadelphia, where he continued his political and medical careers, ending up as the senior surgeon to the Continental Army hospital in Philadelphia before his death.
3. *quantum sufficit:* I.e., the necessary amount.
4. *Mr. Reed:* Joseph Reed (1741–85) was president of Pennsylvania's Second Provincial Congress; he later became George Washington's secretary, then adjutant general of the army.

LETTER 38. JOHN ADAMS

1. *Dr. Church:* Dr. Benjamin Church (1734–78), a member of the Massachusetts Provincial Congress and the Committee of Safety, was in fact a double agent, also supplying information to General Gage. His treachery will be mentioned in several letters, beginning with AA's letter 66.

2. *my brother:* JA's younger brother Elihu had applied for a commission in the army; AA had written a recommendation to Joseph Warren on his behalf on May 13, 1775. See *AFC,* 1:196.

LETTER 39. JOHN ADAMS

1. *Colonel Dyer and Mr. Deane:* Eliphalet Dyer (1721–1807) was a delegate to the Continental Congress from Connecticut; Silas Deane (1737–89) was also a delegate from Connecticut and later served on the mission to France with Benjamin Franklin and Arthur Lee.

2. *from prison:* I.e., from within British-occupied Boston.

LETTER 40. JOHN ADAMS

1. *Major Skene, . . . Arnold and Allen:* Major Philip Skene (1725–1810) was the commander at Ticonderoga and Crown Point, which Benedict Arnold (1741–1801) and Ethan Allen (1738–89) took on May 10, 1775.

LETTER 41. JOHN ADAMS

1. *Fenno:* Possibly John Fenno (1751–98), who subsequently founded and edited the *Gazette of the United States.*

LETTER 42. ABIGAIL ADAMS

1. *15 June 1775:* CFA probably placed AA's letter out of apparent chronological order because she discusses the disorder in the army besieging British-held Boston; JA's letter that follows, although begun four days earlier, was completed a day after AA's letter and an-

nounces the appointment of George Washington as the general of the American army.

2. *Mr. Bowdoin . . . Mrs. Borland:* James Bowdoin (1726–90), a patriot leader, had been named with JA as a delegate to Congress in 1774 but declined to serve; Anna Vassal Borland, the widow of a recently deceased Boston loyalist, owned the house in Quincy that JA and AA later purchased from her son for their own residence. It is now maintained by the National Park Service as a historic site.

3. *the best proclamation he could have issued:* Gage's proclamation was printed as a broadside and promised pardon to "the infatuated multitudes" who would cease their resistance, except for Samuel Adams and John Hancock.

LETTER 43. JOHN ADAMS

1. *Mr. Duffield:* George Duffield (1732–90) was minister of the Third Presbyterian Church in Philadelphia.

2. *a pastoral letter:* A Pastoral Letter from the Synod of New-York and Philadelphia (New York, 1775) was written by John Witherspoon (1723–94), president of the College of New Jersey (now Princeton University), who chaired the committee appointed to draft it. A year later he became a delegate to the Continental Congress from New Jersey and a signer of the Declaration.

3. *Swift:* Samuel Swift (Harvard, 1735) was one of JA's legal "brothers"; see AA in letter 48. The others mentioned here have been identified.

LETTER 44. JOHN ADAMS

1. *Ward, Lee, Gates, Gridley:* Artemas Ward (1727–1800) commanded the forces besieging Boston until Washington arrived. Charles Lee (1731–82) was third in line of command in the Continental Army after Washington and Ward as of his appointment to major general on this day, and Horatio Gates (1727–1806) was commissioned as adjutant general of the army. Richard Gridley (1711–96), military engineer and artillery officer, had laid out the defensive lines at Bunker Hill, where he was subsequently wounded, news that had not yet reached JA.

LETTER 45. ABIGAIL ADAMS

1. *"The race is not to the swift, . . . a refuge for us."*: The first part of the first sentence is from Ecclesiastes 9:11; the latter part is from Psalm 68:35. The second sentence is from Psalm 62:8.
2. *the Dr.'s death*: Dr. Joseph Warren (1741–75), patriot leader and president of the Massachusetts Provincial Assembly, was killed at the battle of Bunker Hill.
3. *"How sleep the brave . . ."*: AA quotes here from William Collins's "Ode Written in the Beginning of the Year 1746," which commemorates British troops who died in the battles of Prestonpans and Falkirk.

LETTER 46. ABIGAIL ADAMS

1. *Colonel Putnam . . . Captain Vinton*: Israel Putnam (1718–90) had recently been promoted to major general and given command of the center line of the besieging army. Captain Seth Turner and Captain John Vinton were members of the Braintree militia. See AA's account in letter 51 of Captain Vinton's company's attempt to vote. The Germantown referred to here was a neighborhood in Braintree.

LETTER 47. JOHN ADAMS

1. *Schuyler*: Philip Schuyler (1733–1804) was one of four major generals under Washington and in charge of the Northern Department.
2. *Gardner mortally*: Colonel Thomas Gardner of the First Middlesex Regiment died in July 1775 of his wounds.

LETTER 48. ABIGAIL ADAMS

1. *"Extremity is the trier of spirits; . . ."*: AA quotes here from Shakespeare, *Coriolanus*, act 4, scene 1.
2. *Mr. Taft*: Rev. Moses Taft (1722–91) was minister of the South Church in Braintree.
3. *"in his duty prompt, . . ."*: Oliver Goldsmith, "The Deserted Village," lines 165–66.
4. *General Heath's regiment*: William Heath (1737–1814) of Massachusetts had been appointed a brigadier general on June 22.

5. *Mr. Boylston . . . Mr. Mather:* Among the actual or potential refugees from Boston noted by AA are her first cousin Thomas Boylston (1721–98) and Rev. Samuel Mather (1706–85), pastor of the Tenth Congregational Society in Boston, son of Cotton Mather, grandson of Increase Mather; Joseph Gill is noted above.

LETTER 49. ABIGAIL ADAMS

1. *Master Lovell:* James Lovell (1737–1814), a Boston schoolmaster and flamboyant patriot, was imprisoned after letters from him were found on the body of Joseph Warren after the battle of Bunker Hill.
2. *your Judas:* The editors of *AFC* surmise that AA refers to Joseph Galloway, who after serving in the First Continental Congress refused to return because he opposed the measures adopted there tending toward independence. *AFC,* 1:240. See also letters 165 and 166.

LETTER 50. JOHN ADAMS

1. *Betsey Smith:* AA's younger sister, Elizabeth Smith.
2. *Mr. William Barrell:* Barell (d. 1776) had moved to Philadelphia from Boston.

LETTER 51. ABIGAIL ADAMS

1. *"Mark his majestic fabric; . . .":* AA quotes from John Dryden's play *Don Sebastian,* but interestingly enough changes the gender of the pronouns. Dryden's version reads:

> What honor is there in a Woman's death!
> Wrong'd as she says, but helpless to revenge;
> Strong in her Passion, impotent of Reason,
> Too weak to hurt, too fair to be destroy'd.
> Mark her Majestick Fabrick; She's a Temple
> Sacred by birth, and built by Hands Divine;
> Her Soul's the Deity, that lodges there:
> Nor is the Pile unworthy of the God. (act 2, scene 1, lines 383–90)

2. *men who were in jail:* American prisoners captured after the battle of Bunker Hill were held in the Boston jail.

3. *a little expedition:* The military action AA describes here occurred on Long Island and Moon Island in Boston harbor. Captain Benjamin Tupper led the American troops.

4. *(Simple Sapling):* Mercy Otis Warren in her play *The Group* had satirized the Tory Nathaniel R. Thomas as "Simple Sapling."

5. *Colonel Palmer ... Newcomb:* When Colonel Joseph Palmer, referred to in earlier letters as "the Deacon," was later elected by the House of Representatives to the Council, Colonel Ebenezer Thayer, the loser here, was elected in his place. Newcomb is perhaps Thomas Newcomb, a Braintree resident.

6. *General Thomas:* When on June 22, 1775, Congress appointed eight brigadier generals in the Continental Army, it placed William Heath above John Thomas, his senior in the Massachusetts military. See AA's comments in letter 55. When Seth Pomeroy, the first in rank of the brigadiers, declined his appointment, Thomas was elevated in his place on July 19.

7. *calamanco:* Woolen cloth with a shiny surface.

8. *Mr. Trott:* George Trott and family were refugees from Boston staying with AA in a crowded household. Mrs. Trott was JA's cousin.

9. *"This day be bread ...":* The first quotation here is from Alexander Pope, "The Universal Prayer," lines 45–48. The second quotation is unidentified.

LETTER 52. JOHN ADAMS

1. *one, whose abilities and virtues ... have been found wanting:* JA's reference is to John Dickinson, who resisted calls for independence.

2. *from Pennsylvania, ... two overgrown fortunes:* At this time the Pennsylvania delegation to Congress included among others Franklin, Dickinson, the lawyer James Wilson (1742–98), Edward Biddle (1739–79), Thomas Mifflin (1744–1800), and John Morton (1725–77). Also in the delegation was the wealthy and conservative merchant Thomas Willing (1731–1821). He and Dickinson were the "two overgrown fortunes"; they both opposed independence.

LETTER 54. JOHN ADAMS

1. *24 July 1775:* This letter, along with one to James Warren in which he referred to Dickinson as "A certain great Fortune and piddling Genius," was intercepted and published by the British. This led to a

distinct coolness between JA and Dickinson. The original manuscript of the letter disappeared, and CFA used a transcription.

LETTER 55. ABIGAIL ADAMS

1. *Deacon Newall, . . . John Cotton:* The diary of Deacon Timothy
   Newell of the Brattle Street Church is in *Massachusetts Historical
   Society Collections,* 4th series, 1 (1852), 261–76. John Cotton
   (1728–75) was deputy secretary of the Province of Massachusetts
   and related by marriage to Thomas Hutchinson.

2. *General Burgoyne:* John Burgoyne (1722–92) was in Boston at this
   time but without a command. He would eventually lead the British
   forces that were defeated at Saratoga in 1777.

3. *General Lee's letter:* Charles Lee responded to Burgoyne's *The
   Speech of a General Officer in the House of Commons, February
   20th, 1775* (London, 1775).

4. *"As to Burgoyne, . . . Lord Bute.":* The editors of *AFC* note that the
   "character" of Burgoyne seems to be taken from a letter to AA
   from Mercy Otis Warren, who purports to have received it from
   London. *AFC,* 1:264. John Stuart, earl of Bute (1713–92), the extremely unpopular prime minister in 1762–63, was seen as a chief
   upholder of royal prerogative. Privy seal and close political ally
   during Bute's ministry was John Russell, fourth duke of Bedford
   (1710–71).

5. *Clinton:* Sir Henry Clinton (1730–95) at this time was third in command of British forces in North America, after Generals Gage and
   Howe.

6. *Derby's arrival:* Captain John Derby of Salem was the first to carry
   the news of the April 19 fight at Concord to London. He had just
   returned with a report of the British response, sampled here by AA.

7. *"Ill fares the land, . . .":* Oliver Goldsmith, "The Deserted Village,"
   lines 51–56.

8. *Your address:* The Continental Congress had approved the "Address to the Inhabitants of Great Britain" on July 8 as well as a second petition to the king, the so-called Olive Branch petition that
   explained the necessity of armed defense and called upon the king
   to end the conflict.

9. *your President:* President Peyton Randolph (1721–75) was suddenly called home to Virginia on May 24, 1775, and John Hancock
   was subsequently chosen as the president of Congress.

10. *our inanimate old bachelor:* I.e., Anthony Wibird, the Braintree
    minister, apparently not a lively preacher.

11. *Mr. Haven, of Dedham:* Jason Haven (1733–1803) was the minister of Dedham.

LETTER 57. ABIGAIL ADAMS

1. *our evervalued friend Warren, . . . with many bodies over it:* Although Joseph Warren did not receive a dignified burial by the British, the rumors of mutilation were untrue. Warren's remains were exhumed and reburied in April 1776, after the British left Boston; see AA's description in letter 92.
2. *"Nor writ his name, . . .":* Edward Young, *Night Thoughts,* Night III, lines 179, 187–93.
3. *Admiral Montague:* John Montagu (1719–95) commanded the naval forces on the North American station from 1771 to 1774, when he was replaced by Admiral Samuel Graves.
4. *a talked-of appointment:* JA would be appointed chief justice of the Massachusetts Superior Court in October 1775.
5. *when they return:* I.e., from visiting Mifflin at the army encampment in Cambridge.

LETTER 59. ABIGAIL ADAMS

1. *Isaac:* Isaac Copeland was a boy employed on the Adams farm. Susy and Patty mentioned later in the paragraph were also servants in the family. Susy recovered, but Patty died in early October; see letter 66.

LETTER 60. ABIGAIL ADAMS

1. *Mr. Mason:* Jonathan Mason (1756–1831) was another of JA's law clerks.
2. *a most infamous versification:* Not found, but see AA's description of the title in letter 71, her letter to JA of 22 October 1775.
3. *Mr. Winslow:* Isaac Winslow (1743–93) was a Boston distiller and loyalist.
4. *Remonstrance, Address, and Petition:* The *Massachusetts Spy* printed "An Address, Petition, and Remonstrance in favor of the Americans presented by the City of London to the King on 5 July" in the issue of September 13, 1775.

LETTER 61. JOHN ADAMS

1. *Doctor Zubly:* John Joachim Zubly (1724–81).
2. *Mr. Bullock . . . Mr. Jones and Doctor Hall:* The other Georgia delegates who had arrived were Archibald Bulloch (1730–77) and John Houstoun (1750–96); Noble Wimberly Jones (1723–1805) and Dr. Lyman Hall (1724–90) were the Georgia delegates still expected.
3. *Mr. Henry . . . Messrs. Nelson, Wythe, and Lee:* Thomas Nelson (1738–1807), George Wythe (1726–1806), and Francis Lightfoot Lee (1734–97) were the new Virginia delegates, replacing Patrick Henry, Edmund Pendleton, and Richard Bland.

LETTER 62. JOHN ADAMS

1. *These letters:* I.e., the intercepted letters mentioned in letter 54, note 1.

LETTER 63. ABIGAIL ADAMS

1. *Havy pity upon me, . . . for the hand of God presseth me sore.:* AA paraphrases Job 19:21.

LETTER 64. JOHN ADAMS

1. *Major Bayard:* John Bayard (1738–1807) of New York.

LETTER 66. ABIGAIL ADAMS

1. *"Rare are solitary woes, . . .":* Cf. Edward Young, *Night Thoughts*, Night III, lines 163–64:

> Woes cluster, rare are solitary woes;
> They leave a train; they tread each other's heel.

2. *How long, O Lord, shall the whole land say, I am sick!:* Cf. Isaiah 33:24: "And the inhabitants shall not say, I am sick; the people that dwell therein shall be forgiven their iniquity."
3. *Your aunt Simpson:* Mary Boylston Simpson (1714–75) was the sister of JA's mother.

4. *"The sweet remembrance . . . bids it break."*: In the first of the two quotations here AA seems to misremember lines from Isaac Watts's "Psalm 112. As the 113th Psalm. Blessings of the liberal Man." In the second she quotes from *Macbeth*, act 4, scene 3, a passage she also quotes in letter 71.

5. *a patriot*: Dr. Benjamin Church's treachery was exposed when a letter turned up that he had written in cipher to British authorities. At this time, Church was director of the hospital for the Continental Army at Cambridge; he had also left his wife and was living with a mistress (who was unintentionally responsible for the discovery of his incriminating letter). AA and JA refer in letters 67, 68, 70, and 72 to Church in regard to these facts.

LETTER 67. JOHN ADAMS

1. *whose care has hitherto been successful*: AA's most recent letters had been most often sent to the care of James Warren, who as Speaker of the Massachusetts House of Representatives and also as paymaster general of the Continental Army was in communication with Congress in Philadelphia and had access to more secure military sources to send correspondence.

LETTER 69. JOHN ADAMS

1. *have the small-pox*: I.e., receive inoculation with smallpox.

LETTER 70. ABIGAIL ADAMS

1. *"There's not a day . . ."*: Edward Young, *Night Thoughts*, Night VIII, lines 78–80.

2. *"A foe to God . . ."*: Ibid., lines 704–5.

3. *a committee here*: Congress sent Benjamin Franklin along with Thomas Lynch of South Carolina and Benjamin Harrison of Virginia to meet with Washington in Cambridge on how to support the army.

4. *"Each friend . . ."*: Edward Young, *Night Thoughts*, Night III, lines 285–86.

LETTER 71. ABIGAIL ADAMS

1. *Mr. Lothrop:* The editors of *AFC* suggest that this is Isaac Lothrop of Plymouth, a colleague of James Warren's. 1:311.
2. *his communion day:* I.e., the Sunday appointed for administering the sacrament of communion in the Weymouth church of William Smith, AA's father.
3. *Hichborne:* Benjamin Hichborn had escaped from Admiral Graves's ship, *Preston,* on October 19. He had been captured in Rhode Island while carrying two letters from John Adams. See letter 54, note 1.
4. *the Paraphrase:* I.e., the parodies of JA's intercepted letters.

LETTER 72. JOHN ADAMS

1. *occasioned a fall:* Dr. Benjamin Church had just been publicly exposed as a British spy.

LETTER 76. JOHN ADAMS

1. *Chambly:* Near Montreal. In the autumn of 1775 the Americans launched an invasion of Canada, with one prong of the attack moving up Lake Champlain and the Richelieu River toward Montreal, with Quebec being the ultimate objective.

LETTER 77. ABIGAIL ADAMS

1. *a late appointment:* To the position of chief justice of the Superior Court, although JA never served in that office.

LETTER 78. ABIGAIL ADAMS

1. *The General sent his thanks:* Washington thanked Colonel William Thompson for his part in the skirmish at Lechmere Point in East Cambridge in his general orders of November 10.

LETTER 79. ABIGAIL ADAMS

1. *the Court:* I.e., the Massachusetts House of Representatives, formerly the General Court.

LETTER 80. JOHN ADAMS

1. *not I alone:* CFA note: "During his term of service in Congress, he was a member of ninety, and chairman of twenty-five committees."
2. *a long conversation with* ———: JA left this blank in his letter, but he is probably referring to his colleague Robert Treat Paine, whom he had described in an earlier letter to AA as having "taken an odd Turn in his Head of late, and is so peevish, passionate and violent that he will make the Place disagreeable, if he does not think better of it." *AFC,* 1:328. The reference to "another" later in the paragraph is possibly Thomas Cushing, who was more moderate than JA on the question of independence.

LETTER 81. ABIGAIL ADAMS

1. *Mrs. Morgan:* The wife of Dr. John Morgan (1735–89), professor of medicine at the College of Philadelphia (now the University of Pennsylvania), who had been recently appointed as director and surgeon general of the military hospital.
2. *Captain Sears; . . . Dr. M'Henry:* Isaac Sears (1730–86), ex-seaman, was a populist and radical leader in New York, and later an organizer of privateers in Boston; Dr. James McHenry (1753–1816), of Baltimore, entered into the medical service of the army and later became secretary of war in the administrations of Washington and JA. The Smiths and Mr. Elwyn, who are also mentioned in the paragraph, have not been identified.
3. *Mr. Spada:* This is Charles Lee's dog, which figured in one of JA's captured and subsequently published letters. JA referred to Lee's "Oddity" and noted, "You must love his Dogs if you love him." *AFC,* 1:338.
4. *military stores:* Captain John Manley (1732–93) of Marblehead had captured the British ordnance ship *Nancy* on November 29, the first important victory by American naval forces. Among the prizes was a large brass mortar that was removed to the besieging army in Cambridge and named "The Congress."

5. *their instructions:* When the New Hampshire Provincial Convention sought advice on erecting a new government, the Congress, not yet ready for a final break, advised them to establish a government "during the present dispute between Great Britain and the colonies."

LETTER 82. JOHN ADAMS

1. *Williams:* This was probably Thomas Thorawanken Williams, grandson of Eunice Williams, formerly of Deerfield, Massachusetts. For her captivity, her marriage, her life and that of her children among the Caughnawagas, see John Demos, *The Unredeemed Captive* (New York: Knopf, 1994). Her children were all born in Canada, however, and not in Massachusetts.

LETTER 83. JOHN ADAMS

1. *My companion:* Elbridge Gerry (1744–1814) had replaced Thomas Cushing in the Massachusetts delegation.
2. *Vandeput:* George Vandeput commanded the HMS *Asia*, then stationed in New York harbor.
3. *Dr. Smith . . . the brave Montgomery:* General Richard Montgomery was killed on December 31, 1775, leading the American attack on Quebec. The oration by Rev. William Smith (1727–1803), provost of the College of Philadelphia, was poorly received because of its loyalist sentiments.

LETTER 84. JOHN ADAMS

1. *at York:* I.e., at New York.
2. *Lord Stirling:* William Alexander (1726–83) was a brigadier general in the American army.
3. *"Non tali auxilio . . .":* "Not such aid nor such defenders does the time require." Virgil, *Aeneid,* book 2, lines 521–22.

LETTER 85. JOHN ADAMS

1. *"Common Sense,":* The famous and influential pamphlet by Thomas Paine that urged independence from Britain was published on January 10, 1776.

2. *Mr. Chase:* Samuel Chase (1741–1811) was a representative to Congress from Maryland.

LETTER 86. ABIGAIL ADAMS

1. *your President:* I.e., John Hancock, president of Congress.
2. *Mr. Ned Church's employ:* Edward Church was a sometime neighbor of the Adamses and would later carry letters between them.
3. *the sentiments of our cousin:* See the letter of Isaac Smith Jr. written from England, presumably to his uncle, AA's father. *AFC,* 1:333.
4. *"There is a tide . . .":* Shakespeare, *Julius Caesar,* act 4, scene 3.
5. *"domestic fury . . . pity choked,":* Shakespeare, *Julius Caesar,* act 3, scene 1.
6. *"Man wants but little . . .":* Oliver Goldsmith, "Edwin and Angelina," lines 31–32.

LETTER 87. ABIGAIL ADAMS

1. *Lord Chesterfield's Letters:* Philip Dormer Stanhope, earl of Chesterfield (1694–1773); his *Letters to His Son* were intended as in effect a conduct book for a young man aspiring to rise in society, but they were vigorously condemned by many readers like JA as a handbook of libertinism and corruption. JA's response is in letter 93.
2. *harmony with* ———: Undoubtedly a reference to Robert Treat Paine, JA's fellow Massachusetts representative, who had been difficult.
3. *the speech from the rostrum:* The funeral oration on General Montgomery by Rev. William Smith of Philadelphia.

LETTER 88. JOHN ADAMS

1. *Frank Dana:* Francis Dana (1743–1811) went to England in 1775 in order to seek a reconciliation between the ministry and Massachusetts, but he returned with the conviction that this was impossible.
2. *Wrixon:* Elias Wrixon, a German officer, was offered a colonel's commission as a military engineer but did not accept; his pamphlet seems not to have been published.
3. *The Baron de Woedtke:* Frederick William, Baron de Woedtke, was appointed a brigadier general but turned out to be a drunkard. He would die at Ticonderoga in the coming summer.

4. *Mr. Temple, . . . Mr. Sewall:* William Temple of New Hampshire had returned from London, claiming to have gone on a self-initiated diplomatic mission; his "news" was not entirely trusted. Jonathan Sewall (1728–96), a loyalist but an old friend of JA's, had been the colonial-era attorney general of Massachusetts and accompanied ex-Governor Hutchinson into exile.

5. *Mons. Dubourg:* Jacques Barbeau Dubourg (1709–79) was a noted botanist and a friend of Franklin's and the American cause.

LETTER 89. JOHN ADAMS

1. *certain letters:* CFA note: "The intercepted letters. Mrs. Adams's cousin, who lamented them, had caught the feelings of those about him. The spirit of independence which the letters showed was disapproved by many in England who sympathized with America, and still wished to keep open the avenues of reconciliation."

LETTER 90. JOHN ADAMS

1. *Governor Ward, . . . by the small-pox:* Samuel Ward (1725–76); on the smallpox epidemic that swept through the colonies in 1775–76, see Elizabeth Fenn, *Pox Americana* (New York: Hill & Wang, 2001).

2. *Mr. Randolph's. Mr. Stillman:* Peyton Randolph of Virginia, the first president of the Continental Congress, had died on October 22, 1775. Samuel Stillman (1737–87) was the pastor of the First Baptist Church (i.e., "Anabaptist") in Boston but fled to Philadelphia during the British occupation.

LETTER 91. ABIGAIL ADAMS

1. *Dunmore:* John Murray, fourth earl of Dunmore (1730–1809), royal governor of Virginia, had removed the seat of government to a warship after failing to persuade the assembly to consider Lord North's conciliatory propositions of 1775. He then offered freedom to slaves who would desert from their Virginia owners to the British side.

2. *your President . . . the Solicitor General:* John Hancock, president of the Congress; the loyalist solicitor general, Samuel Quincy.

3. *saltpetre:* Saltpeter, potassium nitrate, was an essential element of gunpowder and difficult to acquire for the American armies at this time.

LETTER 92. ABIGAIL ADAMS

1. *Johnstone's speech:* George Johnstone (1730–87), a former governor of West Florida and a member of Parliament, spoke against expectations of reducing the rebellious colonies by force.

2. *an oration by Mr. Morton:* Perez Morton's *An Oration; Delivered . . . April 8, 1776, on the Re-interment of the Remains of . . . Joseph Warren* was printed in Boston in 1776 and reprinted in New York and Philadelphia.

3. *"Like dumb mouths, . . .":* Shakespeare, *Julius Caesar,* act 3, scene 1. AA substituted "Britton" for "Italy."

4. *"Meanly poor in solitude to hide . . .":* AA either misremembers or reshapes poetry here. The first and the last four lines are from Mary Wortley Montagu, "An Epistle to Lord B . . . ," lines 26, 27–30, and the second line is adapted from James Thomson's "Spring," line 929, where it reads "And honest zeal, . . ."

5. *your Prussian General:* I.e., Baron de Woedtke.

6. *Admiral Hopkins:* Esek Hopkins (1718–1802) first commanded the Continental fleet but was removed from office in March 1777.

LETTER 95. ABIGAIL ADAMS

1. *the 17th of March:* The British forces left Boston on this day and went on board transport ships standing by in the harbor.

2. *Dr. Gardiner . . . Mr. Goldthwait:* JA's former client Silvester Gardiner, James Lloyd Sr., and Miles Whitworth Sr. were all loyalists; like Gardner, the latter two eventually left Boston with the British. Ezekiel Goldthwait (1710–82) was the clerk of the Suffolk Inferior Court of Common Pleas.

3. *a prologue of Burgoyne's:* General John Burgoyne, in Boston during the siege, wrote a play, *The Blockade of Boston,* parodied as *The Blockheads, or the Affrighted Officers.*

4. *Who is the writer of . . . "Cassandra"?:* Thomas Paine wrote *Common Sense* as well as *The Forester's Letters,* to which AA refers in her letter of April 21 (letter 99). In his reply on April 28 (letter 101), JA ascribes the letters of "Cassandra" to James Cannon and "Cato" to Rev. William Smith of Philadelphia.

LETTER 96. JOHN ADAMS

1. *Commissioners:* The Howe brothers were sent as a so-called conciliatory commission to the American insurgents, but they could not
act on American grievances and could offer only limited amnesty.
2. *my sagacious friend W.:* James Warren.
3. *have written about ten sheets of paper:* JA's *Thoughts on Government: Applicable to the Present State of the American Colonies* was
first published anonymously in Philadelphia in this month.

LETTER 98. ABIGAIL ADAMS

1. *a western number:* Joseph Hawley of Northampton (1723–88), political leader in western Massachusetts, suffered a "nervous col-
lapse" in 1776.

LETTER 99. ABIGAIL ADAMS

1. *Messrs. Foster and Sullivan:* Jedediah Foster and James Sullivan (see
letter 2, note 1). The excluded "certain person" was JA.
2. *"O thou whose wisdom, . . .":* AA here quotes lines 656–77 from the
"Winter" section of James Thomson's *The Seasons.*
3. *"Oh! are ye not those patriots . . .":* This quotation is also from James
Thomson's *The Seasons,* from the "Autumn" section, lines 910–26.
AA adapted Thomson's language to suit her own purposes; Thomson's passage here begins "Oh! is there not some patriot in whose
power," and AA has substituted "Britannia's" for "Batavian" in the
twelfth line.

LETTER 100. JOHN ADAMS

1. *the Bunch of Grapes, Israel Jacobs's:* Jacobs was a Quaker conservative who withdrew from the assembly election of 1775 when its
radical direction became clear. The Bunch of Grapes, a tavern on
Third Street in Philadelphia, catered to merchants and the more genteel. See Peter Thompson, *Rum Punch and Revolution: Taverngoing
and Public Life in Eighteenth-Century Philadelphia* (Philadelphia:
University of Pennsylvania Press, 1999).

2. *my barber, . . . one of the Philadelphia Associators:* The barber was John Byrne; JA noted in his diary that on May 30 he "Paid John Burn the Barber £3. Pen. Cur." *Diary and Autobiography of John Adams,* 2:254. "Associators" had signed up in support of Congress's 1774 Association of Nonimportation, Nonexportation, and Nonconsumption, which was "the most confident and ambitious prescription of republican values during the revolutionary era" (Peter Thompson, *Rum Punch and Revolution,* p. 163).

3. *pro aris et focis:* Literally, "for altars and hearths," from a phrase used by Livy and Cicero, *pro aris et focis pugnare,* in the sense of altars to the gods of the state, the Penates, and hearths dedicated to the household protectors, the Lares.

LETTER 101. JOHN ADAMS

1. *The oration:* Rev. William Smith's funeral oration for General Richard Montgomery.

2. *The late act of Parliament:* The American Prohibitory Act of December 22, 1775, subjected all American ships and goods to seizure.

LETTER 102. ABIGAIL ADAMS

1. *"'Tis a maxim . . . they are destructive.":* The fourth maxim in "Maxims of State" by George Savile, marquess of Halifax, *Miscellanies* (London, 1700).

2. *"engaged in a corrupted state, . . .":* Joseph Addison, *Cato,* act 4, scene 4.

LETTER 103. ABIGAIL ADAMS

1. *"Essays on . . . Pope.":* Joseph Warton's *An Essay on the Genius and Writings of Pope.*

2. *Mr. Gordon, Mr. Skilman, and Mr. Lothrop:* William Gordon, Isaac Skillman, and John Lothrop were ministers of churches in Roxbury and Boston.

3. *your friend:* I.e., James Warren.

4. *Mr. Lowell:* John Lowell (1743–1802), a Newburyport lawyer, had signed a friendly address to Thomas Hutchinson in 1774, but had since recanted and aligned himself with the patriot party.

LETTER 104. JOHN ADAMS

1. *headquarters:* The headquarters of the Continental Army.
2. *my office:* Of chief justice of the Massachusetts Superior Court. See the previous letter by AA.
3. *"the fifty or sixty men.":* The Continental Congress.

LETTER 105. JOHN ADAMS

1. *the resolve of the 15th:* CFA note: "Or rather of the preamble, which was adopted on that day, as an amendment to the resolution passed on the 10th. On the 6th, Mr. Adams had offered, in committee of the whole, a resolve that the colonies should form governments independent of the crown. The shape in which this proposition was adopted on the 10th was a recommendation to the respective assemblies and conventions of the united colonies, where no government sufficient to the exigencies of their affairs had been yet established, to adopt such government as might in their opinion best conduce to the safety and happiness of their constituents in particular, and America in general. This resolution was passed on the 10th of May, accompanied by another appointing Mr. Adams, Mr. Rutledge, and Mr. R. H. Lee a committee to prepare a preamble. This committee accordingly reported the draught of a preamble [with stronger language than the original resolve], which was agreed to on the 15th, the date named in this letter."

LETTER 107. JOHN ADAMS

1. *a letter under a marble cover:* JA refers to the copy of his *Thoughts on Government* that he had earlier sent to AA.
2. *Dr. Winthrop:* John Winthrop (1714–79), Hollis Professor of Mathematics and Natural Philosophy at Harvard.

LETTER 108. ABIGAIL ADAMS

1. *an uncle of ours:* Norton Quincy.
2. *Sully:* Maximilien de Béthune, duc de Sully (1560–1641), financial minister to Henri IV. JA owned two editions of Sully's *Mémoires*.

3. *The poor Captain:* James Mugford of the privateer *Franklin* captured the *Hope* on May 17, 1776. He was killed in another engagement two days later.
4. *the commodore:* Captain Francis Banks, R.N., commanded a British naval force left behind to redirect British ships that had sailed for Boston before the evacuation.
5. *your office:* AA refers to JA's position on the Massachusetts Superior Court.

LETTER 111. JOHN ADAMS

1. *our uncle:* CFA note: "Norton Quincy was solicited to fill responsible stations at the outset of the Revolution, but he preferred to live a recluse all his life, which terminated in 1801 in his paternal mansion at Mount Wollaston."

LETTER 112. ABIGAIL ADAMS

1. *Dr. Lothrop's:* Nathaniel Lothrop (1737–1823) was a physician at Plymouth.
2. *(Harden his name):* Seth Harding (1734–1814) was captain of the Connecticut ship *Defence;* his lieutenant, mentioned in the next sentence, was Samuel Smedley.
3. *Dr. Bulfinch:* Thomas Bulfinch (1728–1802) of Boston inoculated AA and her children in July 1776. See letter 120.
4. *Captain Burk:* William Burke commanded the schooner *Warren.*

LETTER 113. JOHN ADAMS

1. *our disgraces at the Cedars:* On May 20, 1776, an American military outpost at the Cedars, a position forty-three miles above Montreal on the St. Lawrence, surrendered to a British force with little resistance; the commanding officer left as soon as the British arrived, supposedly in order to seek reinforcements.

LETTER 115. JOHN ADAMS

1. *The second day of July, 1776:* Congress approved the resolution in favor of independence on July 2. Debate then followed on the text of

the Declaration proclaiming this, which was approved two days later on the fourth.

LETTER 117. JOHN ADAMS

1. *"The Preceptor"*: JA owned the three-volume fifth edition of Robert Dodsley's *The Preceptor: Containing a General Course of Education* (London, 1769).
2. *Rollin's "Belles Lettres,"*: Charles Rollin's *The Method of Teaching and Studying the Belles Lettres, or an Introduction to Languages, Poetry, Rhetoric, History, Moral Philosophy, Physics &c.* was a popular critical guide of the time; JA eventually acquired the London edition of 1769. His *Antient History* was also highly popular among Whiggish readers, and AA draws upon it for various classical allusions.

LETTER 120. ABIGAIL ADAMS

1. *the small-pox:* CFA used asterisks here to indicate an omission, which has now been restored—from "My uncle and aunt" to "sent by Harry." Here and in succeeding letters he omitted passages that describe the course of the smallpox inoculation of the Adams family, including accounts of specific symptoms that he thought were too personal. They have all been restored in this edition.
2. *Perhaps wise reasons induced it:* JA apparently sent to AA his copy of Jefferson's rough draft of the Declaration, which contained statements about the evils of the slave trade that were later left out from the final version.

LETTER 122. JOHN ADAMS

1. *Lord Howe's letter:* A circular letter to the colonial governors, dated June 20, 1776, announced William Howe's powers to grant pardons to Americans who would renew their allegiance to Britain.

LETTER 123. ABIGAIL ADAMS

1. *Colonel Crafts:* Thomas Crafts, "the Painter," was a leader of the Sons of Liberty in Boston.

2. *the horrid conspiracy . . . to assassinate the General:* New York loyalists had bribed Thomas Hickey, a member of Washington's guard,
to take part in a planned uprising, but rumors of a larger plot to assassinate Washington were unfounded.

LETTER 125. JOHN ADAMS

1. *yours of July 24:* AA's letter of this date survives only as a small frag-
ment.

LETTER 126. JOHN ADAMS

1. *Mr. A.:* Samuel Adams.
2. *Colonel Whipple:* William Whipple (1730–85) was a delegate to
Congress from New Hampshire.

LETTER 128. JOHN ADAMS

1. *a memorable day:* On August 14, 1763, a Boston mob ransacked the
office and house of Andrew Oliver, who was reported to be the agent
for distributing stamps under the Stamp Act.
2. *the two grateful brothers:* General William and Admiral Richard
Howe.
3. *Du Simitiere:* Pierre Eugène Du Simitière (1737–84) was a Swiss-
born artist and engraver, then in Philadelphia.
4. *Hercules, as engraved by Gribelin:* Simon Gribelin engraved this al-
legorical image for inclusion with Treatise VII of Shaftesbury's *Characteristics;* it originally appeared in the 1732 edition.

LETTER 129. ABIGAIL ADAMS

1. *Mr. Smith:* Benjamin Smith (1750–1829) of North Carolina, an aide-
de-camp to Washington.
2. *the Dr.:* Rev. Samuel Cooper, mentioned in letter 19, note 3.
3. *Dr. Chauncy's address:* Rev. Charles Chauncy (1705–87), minister of
Boston's First Church.

LETTER 130. ABIGAIL ADAMS

1. *their professor in philosophy:* I.e., John Winthrop, Hollis Professor of Mathematics and Natural Philosophy at Harvard.
2. *our worthy brother:* I.e., Richard Cranch, AA's brother-in-law.

LETTER 131. JOHN ADAMS

1. *the late Governor Ward, and Mr. Gadsden:* JA refers to Samuel Ward (1725-76) of Rhode Island, who had died of smallpox in March, and Christopher Gadsden (1724-1805), delegate to Congress from South Carolina.

LETTER 132. JOHN ADAMS

1. *Mr. Peale's painter's room:* Charles Willson Peale (1741-1827) was doing portraits in Philadelphia by 1776. After the war he converted his gallery into his famous museum for natural curiosities.

LETTER 133. JOHN ADAMS

1. *Dr. Byles's benediction:* Mather Byles (1707-78) was a Tory minister of the Hollis Street Church and a poet, famous in Boston for his wit.

LETTER 134. ABIGAIL ADAMS

1. *General Lincoln:* Benjamin Lincoln (1733-1810), of Hingham, was appointed a brigadier general of Massachusetts troops in February 1776 and commanded forces in the Boston area. A year later he was promoted to major general in the Continental Army and placed in command of militia forces in Vermont that were opposing the advance of Burgoyne's army.

LETTER 136. JOHN ADAMS

1. *The panic:* On August 27, Washington's army had been defeated at Brooklyn Heights (the battle of Long Island) by a much larger British force commanded by General Howe.

LETTER 137. JOHN ADAMS

1. *Mr. Rutledge:* Edward Rutledge (1749–1800), delegate from South Carolina.

LETTER 138. ABIGAIL ADAMS

1. *a smoking at the lines, . . . purification:* The means of the transmission of smallpox were not well understood at the time, although it was known to be highly contagious. Thus, people who were still infectious with the disease, with active eruptions, walked the streets, but people who left Boston, a center of contagion, were treated with smoke to prevent infecting those in the rural areas, or so it was thought. "Purification" would have involved further sanitary measures, presumably including changing out of smoky clothing.
2. *Zedtwitz's plan:* Herman Zedtwitz, a lieutenant colonel in the Continental Army, was court-martialed for attempting to pass intelligence to royal Governor William Tryon. Some of Zedtwitz's information was fabricated, including a claim that Washington was involved in a plot to poison the water supply on Staten Island.
3. *The herbs:* This is a reference to the canister of tea that was misdirected to Mrs. Samuel Adams. See letter 136.

LETTER 141. ABIGAIL ADAMS

1. *from R. T. P. to his brother-in-law G——fe:* Robert Treat Paine wrote to his brother-in-law Joseph Greenleaf about the delegation sent from the Congress to meet the British commissioners on Staten Island.
2. *Regulus's steward:* Marcus Atilius Regulus (d. c. 250 BCE) was a Roman consul and leader of the Roman fleet against Carthage.

LETTER 142. JOHN ADAMS

1. *Governor Livingston's speech:* The inaugural speech of William Livingston (1723–90) to the New Jersey legislature was delivered on September 11, 1776.

LETTER 143. ABIGAIL ADAMS

1. *The Church:* I.e., the Church of England.

LETTER 145. JOHN ADAMS

1. *faece Romuli non republica Platonis:* "The dregs of Romulus, not the republic of Plato."

LETTER 146. JOHN ADAMS

1. *Dr. Sprague:* Dr. John Sprague (1718–97), a physician in Dedham.

LETTER 147. JOHN ADAMS

1. *Commissary Trumbull:* Joseph Trumbull (1737–78).

LETTER 149. JOHN ADAMS

1. *Colonel Brinkhoff:* Colonel John Brinckerhoff.

LETTER 152. JOHN ADAMS

1. *the Dutch people:* Actually Germans, that is, the Pennsylvania "Dutch."

LETTER 154. JOHN ADAMS

1. *Mr. Chase:* Thomas Chase, father of Samuel Chase, delegate from Maryland.

LETTER 156. JOHN ADAMS

1. *three public institutions:* JA refers to institutions established by the Moravians at Bethlehem.

LETTER 157. ABIGAIL ADAMS

1. *the regulating bill:* An act to fix wages and prices in order to control inflation; passed in January 1777, it needed a supplementary act in May, indicating its ineffectiveness.
2. *the Farmer:* John Dickinson.

LETTER 158. JOHN ADAMS

1. *I have in my mind . . . as well as can be expected:* CFA omitted these lines. JA was concerned for AA's health during her last pregnancy; the child would be stillborn.
2. *Betsey . . . Mr. Shaw:* AA's sister, Elizabeth Smith, married Rev. John Shaw in October 1777 (see letter 218).
3. *a certain mighty office:* I.e., the office of chief justice of Massachusetts.

LETTER 159. ABIGAIL ADAMS

1. *your namesake:* See the letter of January 9, 1777, to JA from Samuel Adams, in *The Works of John Adams* (Boston, 1850–56), 9:448–50.
2. *Colonel Campbell:* Lieutenant Colonel Archibald Campbell, a captured British officer, and the Hessian officers had been put in the common jail in Concord because of British mistreatment of General Charles Lee, who had been captured in December.

LETTER 160. JOHN ADAMS

1. *Colonel Thornton:* Dr. Matthew Thornton (1714–1803), delegate from New Hampshire.

LETTER 162. JOHN ADAMS

1. *R. H. and F.:* I.e., Richard Henry Lee and Francis Lightfoot Lee.

LETTER 163. JOHN ADAMS

1. *his brother's in Westminster Abbey:* George Augustus, third Viscount Howe, the older brother of General William Howe, was killed in the French and Indian War at Lake George in 1758; the monument was erected by order of the Province of Massachusetts.

LETTER 164. JOHN ADAMS

1. *General Wolcott:* Oliver Wolcott (1726–97) was a delegate to Congress.
2. *Ingersoll, . . . Gilbert Tennent:* Jared Ingersoll was a Connecticut loyalist; Roger Sherman was a delegate to Congress also from Connecticut. Rev. Gilbert Tennent (1703–64) was a famous evangelist in the Great Awakening and after.

LETTER 166. JOHN ADAMS

1. *a vessel in at Portsmouth:* The French ship *Mercure* brought military supplies on March 17, 1770.

LETTER 167. ABIGAIL ADAMS

1. *Brydone:* Patrick Brydone, *A Tour through Sicily and Malta; in a Series of Letters to W. Beckford, Esq.* (London, 1773).
2. *'Ah, mon ami,' . . . 'je m'ennuie . . . et je me pend.':* "Oh, my friend, I am bored to death—I, who have never known boredom. But this execrable wind overwhelms me. Two more days, and I hang myself."

3. *The Church doors . . . without breaking his oath:* Church of England required its pastors to pray for the king as the head of the church. The conscientious parson was Edward Winslow.

LETTER 168. JOHN ADAMS

1. *Arnold, . . . Harden:* Captain Arnold was employed by the Massachusetts Committee of War; Captain Harding commanded a ship owned by AA's uncle, Isaac Smith.

LETTER 170. JOHN ADAMS

1. *rather be Sidney than Monk:* Algernon Sidney (1622–83), whose *Discourses Concerning Government* was an important statement of republican political theory, was executed supposedly for treason; George Monk (1608–70) was instrumental in restoring Charles II to the English throne and was named duke of Albermarle in reward.

LETTER 172. JOHN ADAMS

1. *a Mr. Duer:* William Duer (1747–99).
2. *Duane and Jay . . . behave in a manner becoming it:* James Duane (1733–97) and John Jay (1745–1829); JA's comment here reflects the fact that both Duane and Jay were slow to embrace the cause of independence.

LETTER 173. ABIGAIL ADAMS

1. *William Jackson, . . . Joice junior:* "Joice Junior" was the name used by the chair of the prerevolutionary committee on tarring and feathering and who subsequently warned out of town suspected Tories. See articles by Albert Matthews in *Colonial Society of Massachusetts Publications* 8 (1906), 90–104, and 11 (1910), 280–94. The editors of *AFC* note that AA got the names slightly wrong. In addition to William Jackson and Richard Green, James Perkins, Epes Sargent of Gloucester, and Nathaniel Cary were humiliated.
2. *Manly . . . and MacNeal:* Hector McNeill (1728–85) was the captain of the Continental ship *Boston.* Captain John Manley (1733–93) com-

manded the *Hancock*. His exploits had earlier been noted by AA in letter 92.

LETTER 176. JOHN ADAMS

1. *"Evening Post"* ... *the present race of Britons:* The *Pennsylvania Evening Post* of April 24, 1777, gave over its front page to the report by seven members of Congress on British treatment of American prisoners of war and behavior toward civilian noncombatants.

LETTER 179. ABIGAIL ADAMS

1. *General Wooster:* General David Wooster (1711–77) died on May 2 when British forces raided western Connecticut; see Phillis Wheatley's poem "On the Death of General Wooster," *Complete Writings*, ed. Vincent Carretta (New York: Penguin, 2001), 92–93.

LETTER 181. JOHN ADAMS

1. *the famous Mrs. Wright:* Patience Wright (1725–86) was famous for her wax models, and her sister Rachel Wells apparently also sculpted in wax. Born in New Jersey, Wright has been called the first American sculptor.
2. *the figures of Chatham, ... and several others:* These figures represented supposed supporters of American interests. Named here are William Pitt, earl of Chatham (1708–78), Benjamin Franklin, and John Sawbridge (1732–92) and his sister, the historian Catherine Macaulay (1731–91), who both actively supported the patriot cause in the 1770s.
3. *Dr. Chovet's wax-work:* Dr. Abraham Chovet (1704–90) exhibited his anatomical models in Philadelphia as a scientific event.
4. *Mr. Rittenhouse's planetarium, Mr. Arnold's collection:* David Rittenhouse (1732–96), America's most famous astronomer, was also noted for his construction of an orrery, a mechanical model of the solar system. Mr. Arnold's natural history collection was later sold to Tory Governor William Tyron (JA mentions this in letter 263), who took it to England, where JA saw it once again in 1783. See *Diary and Autobiography of John Adams*, 3:151.

LETTER 183. JOHN ADAMS

1. *a petition from Charlestown:* Nathaniel Gorham and Thomas Russell presented a petition from the town of Charlestown for compensation for property losses during the British occupation of Boston.

LETTER 184. ABIGAIL ADAMS

1. *Mr. N——s:* Samuel Niles (1711–1804), a neighbor and political friend of JA's, served as Braintree's representative to the General Court.
2. *Philaleutheros:* The Boston *Independent Chronicle* of March 7, 1777, had printed a proposed state constitution drawn up by "Philaleutherus," who has been otherwise unidentified.
3. *an observation of Bishop Butler's:* Joseph Butler (1692–1752), bishop of Durham, was the author of the *Analogy of Religion Natural and Revealed* (London, 1736).
4. *"By this . . . if ye have love one towards another.":* AA quotes John 13:35 here.
5. *Dr. Tillotson:* John Tillotson (1630–94), archbishop of Canterbury. JA had studied his writings when he taught school in Worcester after graduating from Harvard.

LETTER 185. JOHN ADAMS

1. *"he fought like Julius Caesar.":* In repelling the British raid on Danbury.

LETTER 188. JOHN ADAMS

1. *my friend Parsons:* On June 4, 1777, Philadelphia newspapers printed the account by General Samuel Holden Parsons (1737–89) of Lieutenant Colonel Return Jonathan Meigs's successful encounter with a British detachment at Sag Harbor, New York.

LETTER 191. JOHN ADAMS

1. *Colonel Miles ... General De Heister:* Colonel Samuel Miles, an American officer previously captured by the British; Lieutenant General Leopold Philipp, Freiherr von Heister, commander of the Hessian troops in America before June 1777.

LETTER 192. JOHN ADAMS TO
JOHN Q. ADAMS

1. *The History ... by the Abbé de Vertot:* René Aubert de Vertot d'Aubeuf (1655–1735), a French historian, was the author of individual works on each of these topics.
2. *made for that:* CFA omitted after this the list of twenty-four of the characters portrayed in engravings in Guido Bentivoglio's *History of the Warres in Flanders* (London, 1654). They add nothing to the letter and have also been omitted from this edition.

LETTER 193. ABIGAIL ADAMS

1. *the Northern Storm:* British forces under Burgoyne had begun their advance south from Canada into New York; they took Fort Ticonderoga with its supplies and cannons on July 6.
2. *an eminent, wealthy, stingy merchant:* Thomas Boylston, AA's cousin.
3. *a spanking:* CFA "improved" AA's diction here, substituting "personal chastisement" for "a spanking."

LETTER 194. ABIGAIL ADAMS

1. *"Ye Powers, whom men and birds obey, ...":* Henry Brooke, "The Sparrow and the Dove," lines 79–88.

LETTER 198. JOHN ADAMS

1. *Mr. Laurens:* Henry Laurens (1724–92) had taken his seat as a delegate to Congress from South Carolina on July 22. He would be elected president of Congress in November. In 1779, while en route

to negotiate a treaty with the United Provinces (the Netherlands), he would be captured by the British and imprisoned in the Tower for fifteen months.

2. *The family of Johnson, . . . are pretty well thinned:* Sir William Johnson (1715–74), British superintendent for Indian affairs for the Northern Department, had died just before the Revolution began; William Johnson, his son by a Mohawk woman, Molly Brant, had been reported as dying at the battle of Oriskany (New York). Sir William's nephew Guy Johnson (1740–88) and another son, John Johnson (1741–1836), also worked with the Mohawks and took part in military operations against the patriot side.

LETTER 200. JOHN ADAMS

1. *General Stark:* John Stark (1752–1839) was the victor at the battle of Bennington (Vermont) on August 16, 1777.

LETTER 202. JOHN ADAMS

1. *Governor Johnson, Captain Nicholson:* Thomas Johnson (1732–1819), governor of Maryland; James Nicholson (1737–1804), senior captain of the Continental Navy.

LETTER 203. JOHN ADAMS

1. *Gill and Town:* John Gill, printer of the Boston *Continental Journal*, and Benjamin Town, printer of the *Pennsylvania Evening Post*, each placed on the masthead of his paper a statement about the importance of discipline in the army.

LETTER 204. JOHN ADAMS

1. *General Nash:* Francis Nash (1742–77) had been appointed a brigadier general in the Continental Army on February 5, 1777. He would be wounded in action against Howe's army at Germantown, Pennsylvania, on October 4, 1777, and would die three days later.

LETTER 206. JOHN ADAMS

1. *Mr. Paca:* William Paca (1740–99), delegate to Congress from Maryland.

LETTER 209. JOHN ADAMS

1. *Gansevoort . . . St. Leger:* Colonel Peter Gansevoort (1749–1812) successfullly defended Fort Schuyler on the Mohawk River; Brigadier General Nicholas Herkimer (1728–77) fell in the battle of Oriskany, which effectively ended Colonel Barry St. Leger's attempt to lead a British force from Oswego, New York, to unite with Burgoyne's army near Albany.
2. *Fabian:* After Quintus Fabius Maximus (d. 203 BCE), called Cuncator (Delayer), who avoided confronting the Carthaginians in the Second Punic War and thus allowed Rome time to muster its forces.

LETTER 210. JOHN ADAMS

1. *who call themselves Quakers:* In late August, General John Sullivan had captured papers in New Jersey that seemed to implicate area Quakers in furnishing intelligence to the British. After debate in Congress, Quaker leaders were arrested, interrogated, and required to swear or affirm allegiance. Those who refused were exiled to Winchester, Virginia.

LETTER 211. JOHN ADAMS

1. *Mr. Howe's army is at Chester:* Howe's British troops forced Washington to retreat after the battle of Brandywine in southeastern Pennsylvania on September 11, 1777.

LETTER 213. ABIGAIL ADAMS

1. *a battle at the northward:* The first battle at Bemis Heights, near Saratoga, New York, in which Gates's American troops repelled Burgoyne's forces, had occurred on September 19.

LETTER 214. JOHN ADAMS

1. *Mr. Marchant:* Henry Marchant (1741–96) was elected by Rhode Island as a delegate to Congress from 1777 to 1779.
2. *Major Troup:* Major Robert Troup (1757–1832), aide-de-camp to General Horatio Gates.
3. *General Roberdeau:* Daniel Roberdeau (1717–95), general in the Pennsylvania militia and delegate to Congress, 1777–79.
4. *Biddle in the Continental frigate:* Nicholas Biddle (1750–78), captain of the *Randolph.*

LETTER 215. ABIGAIL ADAMS

1. *a private expedition:* The militias of Connecticut and Massachusetts planned an attack on the British at Newport, Rhode Island; it fell apart in a welter of bad planning and poor support.

LETTER 218. ABIGAIL ADAMS

1. *"Peace o'er this land . . .":* Alexander Pope, "Messiah. A Sacred Eclogue," lines 19–20. AA has substituted "olive branch" for Pope's "olive wand."

LETTER 220. JOHN ADAMS

1. *Commodore Hazelwood . . . Lieutenant-colonel Smith:* John Hazlewood (1726–1800) of the Pennsylvania navy and Colonel Samuel Smith (1752–1839) of Maryland repelled British attempts to open a supply line to Philadelphia in mid-October.

LETTER 221. ABIGAIL ADAMS

1. *"Blockade of Saratoga.":* Burgoyne wrote a satirical play entitled *The Blockade of Boston* when he was in Boston during the siege of 1775–76.
2. *the Old South:* British officers had used the Old South meetinghouse in Boston as a riding school during the occupation.

LETTER 222. JOHN ADAMS

1. *Colonel Greene:* Christopher Greene (1737–81), of Rhode Island.
2. *a certain citizen:* I.e., George Washington.

LETTER 223. JOHN ADAMS

1. *the 25th . . . the 30th:* The first was his wedding day, the second his birthday.

LETTER 224. ABIGAIL ADAMS

1. *"Heaven sure taught letters . . .":* Alexander Pope, "Eloisa to Abelard," lines 51–52.
2. *dreaming Deacons:* One of the commanders of the abortive Newport expedition was the Adamses' friend and neighbor Joseph Palmer, a general in the Massachusetts militia and a deacon in the local church.

LETTER 225. JOHN ADAMS

1. *The cause comes on to-morrow:* JA had been engaged as lawyer for the defense in a case concerning the ownership of a vessel owned by a Cape Cod man and his son-in-law that had been captured by a privateer on the grounds that it was trading with the enemy.

LETTER 226. JOHN ADAMS

1. *Captain Tucker:* Samuel Tucker (1747–1833) commanded the Continental frigate *Boston,* on which JA and the ten-year-old JQA ("Johnny") sailed to France.

LETTER 227. ABIGAIL ADAMS

1. *the bosom of a Franklin:* Rumors had reached America at this time that Benjamin Franklin had been assassinated.

LETTER 229. JOHN ADAMS

1. *Monsieur Chaumont:* Jacques Donatien Leray de Chaumont, Benjamin Franklin's landlord at Passy.

LETTER 230. ABIGAIL ADAMS

1. *"Oh, wouldst thou keep . . .":* Cf. Prodicus of Ceos, *The Choice of Hercules,* as translated by Robert Lowth (1710–87), lines 125–30.
2. *the Duke of Richmond's speech:* Richmond's speech to the House of Lords criticized the ministry's stance toward America; this had been reported on May 14 in the Boston *Independent Chronicle.*
3. *Mr. McCreery:* William McCreery, with whom JA had stayed when he passed through Bordeaux.

LETTER 232. ABIGAIL ADAMS TO JOHN QUINCY ADAMS

1. *"a monster . . .":* Alexander Pope, *An Essay on Man,* Epistle II, lines 17–18.

LETTER 233. JOHN ADAMS

1. *Byron's fleet . . . D'Estaing's:* Admiral John Byron (1723–86) of the British navy; Count Charles Henri Theodat d'Estaing (1729–94), commander of the French fleet ordered to the American theater.
2. *General Clinton's army:* In May 1778, Sir Henry Clinton had succeeded William Howe as commander-in-chief of the British army in North America.

LETTER 234. ABIGAIL ADAMS

1. *Captain Welch, of the* Boston: Hezekiah Welch was actually a lieutenant on the *Boston,* but he had been placed in command of a prize ship that was afterward retaken by the British.
2. *your venerable colleague:* I.e., Franklin.

3. *the letters of Dr. Shebbeare:* John Shebbeare (1709–88) was the author of *Letters on the English Nation* (London, 1755).

LETTER 235. JOHN ADAMS

1. *the wife of Monsieur Grand:* The letter of Madame Grand is missing; the banking house of her husband, Ferdinand Grand (1726–94), handled financial transactions between the U.S. government and France.

LETTER 236. ABIGAIL ADAMS

1. *Monsieur Rivière:* Monsieur de Ribiers was a lieutenant on the *Languedoc* in d'Estaing's fleet, which had reassembled off Boston after being dispersed in a storm near Newport.

LETTER 237. JOHN ADAMS

1. *Captain Niles, . . . Captain Barnes:* Captain Robert Niles of the *Spy;* Captain Corbin Barnes of the schooner *Dispatch.*

LETTER 238. JOHN ADAMS

1. *Madame Dacier:* Anne Dacier (1654–1720) was a French woman of letters, classicist, and author of *Causes of the Corruption of Taste* (Paris, 1714).
2. *Stevens:* JA had engaged Joseph Stevens (or Stephens) as a servant in Paris.

LETTER 239. JOHN ADAMS

1. *M. de Sartine:* Antoine de Sartine, comte d'Alby (1729–1801), was the minister of marine.
2. *Fabricius:* Caius Fabricius Luscinus (early third century BCE), Roman censor in 275 BCE, spoke against luxury and corruption. Jean-Jacques Rousseau, to whom JA refers in the next paragraph, also used the name Fabricius as his mouthpiece in his *Discourse on the Sciences*

and the Arts (1750), in which he condemned modern moral degeneracy.

LETTER 240. JOHN ADAMS

1. *Jersey-men:* British privateers operating out of the island of Jersey preyed on shipping between France and the United States.
2. *discovered a way:* The princess referred to here was the first child of Louix XVI and Marie Antoinette, who had been married in 1770 but had not conceived a child until 1778. Minor surgery had corrected an anatomical problem of the king's that made intercourse painful.
3. *Keppel:* Admiral Augustus Keppel (1725–86) was court-martialed after an indecisive engagement with a French fleet off Ushant, an island off the coast of Brittany.

LETTER 241. ABIGAIL ADAMS

1. *"In one fate, . . .":* Cf. James Thomson, "Spring," lines 1114–15: ". . . in one fate / Their hearts, their fortunes, and their beings blend."
2. *"His very foot has music in't, . . . And shall I hear him speak?":* Anonymous poem, "There's Nae Luck About the House," lines 42–45, attributed to William Julius Mickle (1735–88), but also to Jean Adam (1710–65).

LETTER 242. JOHN ADAMS

1. *Carlisle, Cornwallis, and Eden:* Lord North had appointed Frederick Howard, earl of Carlisle (1748–1825), to head a conciliatory commission that also included William Eden, Baron Auckland (1744–1814), whose *Four Letters to the Earl of Carlisle* (London, 1799) commented on the war and on economic issues. Charles Cornwallis (1738–1805) had been serving as a general under the command of Howe and Clinton.
2. *Byngify:* Admiral John Byng (1704–57) had been court-martialed and executed for dereliction of duty against the French in 1756.
3. *the Duchess d'Enville's:* The husband of Louise-Elizabeth de la Rochefoucauld, duchesse d'Enville, had commanded an expedition to America in 1746.
4. *Mr. Williams:* Jonathan Williams, Franklin's grandnephew.

LETTER 243. JOHN ADAMS

1. *the banner of either party:* JA refers to partisan disagreements between Franklin and Silas Deane on one side and Arthur Lee and Ralph Izard on the other. Later in the paragraph JA refers to Deane's "address," published after he returned to America.
2. *"Bubbles on the sea of matter borne; . . .":* Alexander Pope, *Essay on Man,* Epistle III, lines 19–20.

LETTER 244. JOHN ADAMS

1. *the Marquis:* The Marquis de Lafayette.
2. *Dr. J.:* The editors of *AFC* observe that JA clearly wrote "Dr. J." but surmise that he intended "F" for Franklin; they note Franklin's fondness for Scottish airs. *AFC,* 3:171.

LETTER 245. JOHN ADAMS

1. *the accusation against Mr. Lee:* Arthur Lee had accused Silas Deane of mishandling funds in France, and Deane counterattacked Lee in the *Pennsylvania Packet* of December 5, 1778.

LETTER 249. ABIGAIL ADAMS

1. *Captain Jones:* John Paul Jones (1747–92) had carried out a daring and very successful expedition in the Irish Sea in 1778. His noted fight in the *Bonhomme Richard* against the British warship *Serapis* had taken place in September 1778, but AA had apparently not yet learned of it.

LETTER 251. ABIGAIL ADAMS

1. *"All that a man hath . . . his life.":* Cf. Job 2:4, "And Satan answered the Lord, and said, Skin for skin, yea, all that a man hath will he give for his life."
2. *"Let no weak drop . . .":* James Thomson, "To the Memory of Sir Isaac Newton," lines 176–84. AA has replaced Newton's name with Winthrop's in line 180.

LETTER 252. JOHN ADAMS

1. *Mr. Dana:* Francis Dana accompanied JA as secretary of legation and later became the first U.S. envoy to Russia.

LETTER 254. JOHN ADAMS

1. *Captain Carr:* Captain John Carnes of the Salem privateer *General Lincoln.*
2. *the Constitution:* The Massachusetts state constitution, of which JA had been a draftsman.

LETTER 256. JOHN ADAMS

1. *Sammy Cooper:* Samuel Cooper Johonnot (1768–1806), grandson of JA's Boston pastor, Rev. Samuel Cooper, was sent in JA's care to Paris for schooling.

LETTER 259. JOHN ADAMS

1. *Messrs. Gardoqui and Sons, . . . M. de Tournell and M. Lagoanere:* Joseph Gardoqui and Sons, merchants at Bilbao; M. Detournelle, French consul at La Coruña. Michel Lagoanere acted as an American agent at La Coruña.

LETTER 260. JOHN ADAMS

1. *Captain Babson, . . . Mr. Tracy:* On February 5, 1780, JA shipped a variety of goods to AA on the ship *Phoenix,* commanded by James Babson and owned by Nathaniel Tracy, a Newburyport merchant.
2. *a certain gentleman or his banker:* JA had previously asked Lovell to obtain an order of Congress that would allow him in case of necessity to draw an amount not exceeding his annual salary from Benjamin Franklin or the European banker of the United States. See *AFC* 3:276.

LETTER 262. ABIGAIL ADAMS

1. *Mr. Gellée:* N. M. Gellée had worked for the American commission-ers as a secretary.
2. *Mr. Austin:* Jonathan Loring Austin (1748–1826) had previously acted as JA's secretary in France and was now being sent to borrow money and supplies for Massachusetts. He would be captured by the British at sea.
3. *Penobscot score:* AA refers to a tax assessment to pay for the previ-ous summer's unsuccessful Massachusetts military expedition against the British in Penobscot Bay.

LETTER 263. JOHN ADAMS

1. *Mr. Buffon, . . . whose works you have:* Georges Louis Leclerc, comte de Buffon (1707–88), was the leading French naturalist of his time and director of the Jardin du Roi. JA owned editions of Buffon's *Oeuvres complètes* (Complete works) and of the *Histoire naturelle des oiseaux* (Natural history of the birds).

LETTER 264. JOHN ADAMS

1. *Mr. Edmund Jenings:* Jenings (1731–1819), a friend of JA's, had resided in London for some time. The editors of *AFC* note that in a dispatch of May 6, JA referred to a "Dialogue in the Shades between the Duke of Devonshire, the Earl of Chatham and Mr. Charles York" but they were unable to identify its source. *AFC*, 3:343.

LETTER 265. JOHN ADAMS

1. *London is in the horrors:* JA refers in this paragraph to the anti-Catholic Gordon riots of June 1780. Lord George Gordon (1751–93) led a large mob that marched on the House of Commons in protest of a bill that had relieved Roman Catholics from certain legal dis-abilities. The ensuing rioting lasted for five days.
2. *Governor Bernard, . . . died last fall:* Hutchinson's predecessor as governor of Massachusetts, Francis Bernard, had in fact died in June 1779.

LETTER 266. ABIGAIL ADAMS

1. *Mr. Guild:* Benjamin Guild (1749–92), husband of AA's cousin, Elizabeth Quincy.
2. *The Marchioness, at the Abbé Raynal's:* John Thaxter in a letter dated March 15, 1780, described to AA a breakfast party at the residence of the Abbé Guillaume Thomas François Raynal (1713–96) at which a lady expressed her desire to meet JA, the man she thought had played such a great role in bringing about the Revolution. Raynal was a noted philosophe and friend of America. See *AFC,* 3:303.
3. *"Fame, wealth, or honor,—. . .":* Alexander Pope, "Eloisa to Abelard," line 80.

LETTER 267. ABIGAIL ADAMS

1. *Mr. Warren:* Winslow Warren (1759–91), son of the Adamses' friends James and Mercy Otis Warren.

LETTER 268. JOHN ADAMS

1. *Mr. Searle:* Colonel James Searle (1733–97) had been sent by the State of Pennsylvania to arrange a loan and purchase military supplies.

LETTER 269. ABIGAIL ADAMS

1. *Colonel Fleury:* François Louis Teissèdre de Fleury, a French officer serving as a volunteer in the Continental Army.
2. *M. de Ternay:* Charles Louis d'Arsac, chevalier de Ternay, admiral of the French fleet then off Rhode Island.
3. *an infernal plot:* AA had recently learned of Benedict Arnold's treasonous plan to surrender West Point to the British.
4. *Landais is suspended:* Captain Pierre Landais of the *Alliance* was removed from his command by his lieutenant, who brought the ship into Boston in mid-August 1780. JA had previously observed of Landais, "He seems not to know how to gain or preserve the Affections of his Officers, nor yet how to keep them in Awe. . . . Whether it is his imperfect Knowledge of the Language, or his Absence of

Mind when poring upon his Disappointments, or any defect in his Temper or Judgment, I know not." *Diary and Autobiography of John Adams,* 2:366.

LETTER 270. JOHN ADAMS

1. *stivers and doits:* Dutch coins.

LETTER 271. ABIGAIL ADAMS

1. *Colonel Laurens:* John Laurens (1754–82), son of Henry Laurens of South Carolina, had been sent by Congress as a special envoy to the French court.
2. *the obnoxious tender act:* In 1780 the Massachusetts General Court had ordered an annual tax payable only in specie as the legal tender. Because of the general scarcity of hard money, there was widespread protest and the Court allowed payment in fourteen specific commodities at a fixed rate.
3. *Arnold, with a body of troops:* Benedict Arnold led a British raiding party that arrived in the James River on January 1, 1781.
4. *like Aurelian, . . . to the hands of justice:* Lucius Domitius Aurelianus (c. 215–75), a Roman emperor, conquered the city of Tyana with the aid of a traitor, who was then turned over to its citizens.

LETTER 272. ABIGAIL ADAMS

1. *"Through nature . . .":* AA brings together lines from three different poets here. The first phrase is from Alexander Pope's *Essay on Man,* Epistle IV, line 332. The next two lines, beginning "To feel the present Diety," are from James Thomson, "Spring," lines 902–3, and the quotation from Milton comes from *Paradise Lost,* Book IV, lines 641–56, where Eve responds to Adam.
2. *the parting of Hector and Andromache:* AA is alluding to a passage in JA's diary of May 20, 1778, in which he remarks on his weariness in Paris with "a Profusion of unmeaning Wealth and Magnificence. [A painting of] The Adieu of Hector and Andromache gave me more Pleasure than the Sight of all the Gold of Ophir would." *Diary and Autobiography of John Adams,* 2:314.
3. *the declaration of war:* Britain had declared war on the United Provinces (the Netherlands) in December 1780.

4. *Mr. Storer:* Charles Storer (1761–1829) would replace John Thaxter Jr. as JA's private secretary.

5. *the gentleman, whose memoirs:* AA alludes to Sir William Temple, who in 1688 negotiated in five days an alliance among England, Sweden, and the United Provinces (the Netherlands) against possible French aggression.

LETTER 274. JOHN ADAMS

1. *Major Jackson and Colonel Trumbull:* William Jackson (1759–1828) of South Carolina had come to Europe with John Laurens to seek military aid; John Trumbull (1756–1843) had served in the Continental Army before resigning in 1777 and traveling to England to study painting with Benjamin West.

2. *Captain Hill:* Hugh Hill, captain of the *Cicero*.

3. *Gillon:* Alexander Gillon (1741–94), commodore of the South Carolina navy and also in Europe to seek supplies, had taken Charles Adams with him when he left the Netherlands in August 1781, one step ahead of his creditors. Troubles with his crew, among other problems, prevented an immediate return to America, and Charles returned on the *Cicero* from Bilbao.

4. *The contemptible essays made by you know who:* JA's relationship with Benjamin Franklin had seriously deteriorated by this time. When he received news that Congress had removed his authorization to negotiate a commercial treaty with Britain and had expanded the peace commission to five members, he seems to have suspected Franklin's hand in this and in the criticism of him that had been circulated in Philadelphia.

5. *Mr. Dana and our son are well at Petersburg:* Francis Dana had been sent as the diplomatic representative to the Russian court in St. Petersburg; fourteen-year-old JQA accompanied him as his secretary.

6. *General Greene's last great actions:* Nathanael Greene (1742–86) was the commander of the Southern Department after October 1780; his strategic brilliance helped drive the British armies out of Georgia and the Carolinas into the final trap at Yorktown.

LETTER 275. ABIGAIL ADAMS

1. *Count de Noailles:* Louis Marie, vicomte de Noailles, was Lafayette's brother-in-law.

2. *"An elegant sufficiency, . . ."*: James Thomson, "Spring," lines 1158–61.
3. *Ingraham and Bromfield, . . . De Neufville:* The former were American merchants doing business at Amsterdam; the latter, Dutch merchant bankers who extended credit to JA.

LETTER 276. JOHN ADAMS

1. *Caudine Forks:* In 321 BCE a Roman army attacking the Samnites was trapped and destroyed in an area between two narrow passes called the Caudine Forks after the nearby town of Caudium.

LETTER 278. JOHN ADAMS

1. *my public reception here:* One of JA's diplomatic triumphs was to gain recognition from the United Provinces (the Netherlands) for the United States and for himself as its representative.
2. *the unhappy affair of the county of Hampshire:* JA refers to disturbances in the western counties of Massachusetts earlier in 1782. The "Ely riots," as they were called by some, prefigured the later civil disturbances of Shays's Rebellion.
3. *the Treaty:* The Treaty of Amity and Commerce between the United Provinces (the Netherlands) and the United States was signed on October 8, 1782.

LETTER 279. ABIGAIL ADAMS

1. *an authority:* The Bible; AA quotes Romans 14:7.
2. *Gibraltar:* When Spain allied with France against the British, it stipulated the surrender of Gibraltar as a condition of peace. However, Gibraltar held out against military action, and the Treaty of Paris that ended the Revolution left it out of consideration.

LETTER 280. ABIGAIL ADAMS

1. *"Should at my feet . . .":* Alexander Pope, "Eloisa to Abelard," lines 85–86.

LETTER 282. ABIGAIL ADAMS

1. *Your Daughter . . . :* CFA omitted the lengthy passage here that concludes with "I will inclose it to you" on page 412, in which AA informs JA that Royall Tyler is courting their daughter, Nabby. AA favors the connection, but JA will register strenuous objections in a later response. Tyler (1757–1826) went on to a distinguished career as a man of letters, lawyer, and justice on the Vermont Supreme Court. Nabby's later marriage to Colonel William Smith, approved of by both of her parents, was on the whole not happy.

LETTER 284. JOHN ADAMS

1. *The peace:* CFA note: "The preliminary articles between the three parties, Great Britain, France, and the United States, were signed at Paris on the 28th of January, 1783. Hence this may be considered as the close of the great struggle of the Revolution."

CLICK ON A CLASSIC
www.penguinclassics.com

The world's greatest literature at your fingertips

Constantly updated information on more than a thousand titles,
from Icelandic sagas to ancient Indian epics, Russian drama to
Italian romance, American greats to African masterpieces

•

The latest news on recent additions to the list, updated
editions, and specially commissioned translations

•

Original essays by leading writers

•

A wealth of background material, including biographies
of every classic author from Aristotle to Zamyatin, plot
synopses, readers' and teachers' guides, useful Web links

•

Online desk and examination copy assistance for academics

•

Trivia quizzes, competitions, giveaways, news on
forthcoming screen adaptations